C000007915

04. 9. 01.   189
SALIDA
A
MAHON

DEPARTMENT OF IMMIGRATION
PERMITTED TO ENTER
AUSTRALIA.

24 APR 1996

on

For stay of *12 Months*

SYDNEY AIRPORT 54

IMMIGRATION DIVISION BANGKOK THAILAND
A
72
DEPARTED
- 6 FEB 1998
SIGNED

ETHNIC AFFAIRS
..............Person
30 OCT 1999
DEPARTED
AUSTRALIA
SYDNEY 32

T R A V E L E R ' S
SPAIN
C O M P A N I O N

中华人民共和国
★ 东省公安厅

上陆許可
ADMITTED
15. FEB. 1996
4
Status: 4-1-
Duration: 90 days
NARITA(N)
Immigration Inspector
日本国

ADMITTED
20 OCT. 1998
Status: 4-1-16
Duration   180 days
Port: HANEDA

Signature

№ 011278
THE UNITED STATES
OF AMERICA
NONIMMIGRANT VISA
ISSUED AT   Air Port

U.S. IMMIGRATION
170 HHW 1710
JUL 20 1998

HONG KONG
(1038)
- 7 JUN 1997
IMMIGRATION
OFFICER

The 2002–2003 Traveler's Companions
ARGENTINA • AUSTRALIA • BALI • CALIFORNIA • CANADA • CHINA • COSTA RICA •
CUBA • EASTERN CANADA • ECUADOR • FLORIDA • HAWAII • HONG KONG • INDIA •
INDONESIA • JAPAN • KENYA • MALAYSIA & SINGAPORE • MEDITERRANEAN FRANCE •
MEXICO • NEPAL • NEW ENGLAND • NEW ZEALAND • PERU • PHILIPPINES • PORTUGAL •
RUSSIA • SOUTH AFRICA • SOUTHERN ENGLAND • SPAIN • THAILAND • TURKEY •
VENEZUELA • VIETNAM, LAOS AND CAMBODIA • WESTERN CANADA

Traveler's Spain Companion

First published 1998
Second Edition 2002
The Globe Pequot Press
246 Goose Lane, PO Box 480
Guilford, CT 06437 USA
www.globe-pequot.com

© 2002 by The Globe Pequot Press, Guilford CT, USA

ISBN: 0-7627-1011-X

Distributed in the European Union by
World Leisure Marketing Ltd, Unit 11
Newmarket Court, Newmarket Drive,
Derby, DE24 8NW, United Kingdom
www.map-guides.com

Created, edited and produced by
Allan Amsel Publishing, 53, rue Beaudouin
27700 Les Andelys, France.
E-mail: AAmsel@aol.com
Editor in Chief: Allan Amsel
Editor: Anne Trager
Picture editor and book designer: Roberto Rossi
Original design concept: Hon Bing-wah

Based on an original text by John de St Jorre

Printed by Samwha Printing Co. Ltd., Seoul, South Korea

TRAVELER'S SPAIN COMPANION

By Jack Barker

Photographs by Nik Wheeler

Second Edition

The Globe Pequot Press

GUILFORD
CONNECTICUT

Contents

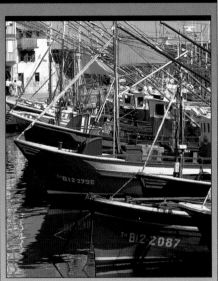

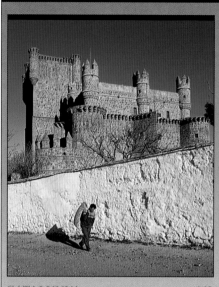

TOP SPOTS

Break for the Beach

The day's sardine catch was being fried over a barbecue, flattened in groups of ten between round paddle grills, drizzled with olive oil and flipped quickly over the glowing coals. Keen young waiters took uncomplicated orders at simple trestle tables set out under sun umbrellas. A basket of bread and a tumbler of local wine came first, while the main meal was prepared.

The bright paint of wooden fishing boats mirrored calmly in the flat, evening glaze of the Atlantic. High above the harbor, a huge cathedral, supported by the delicate fingers of flying buttresses, glowed in the evening sun. To the east, the town beach was emptying fast, with the last few groups packing up, leaving the damp sand of the waterline to chatting pairs of elderly strollers, pacing up and down in a gentle exercise routine. The linking promenade had, at this time of evening, become a highway for baby carriages on high wheels, flounced with lace and topped by jaunty sunshades, smothering cosseted infants in mountains of material. Pushed by grandmothers, aunts, parents and siblings, these newest additions to the Spanish nation took part in the *paseo* (promenade) as if born to it, smiling like cherubs and soaking up praise.

Overwhelmingly, the traffic was one way — heading into the old town, where the narrow streets were thronged with people of all generations, with families cruising from bar to bar, snacking on *tapas* and sipping at drinks. Noisy and populous as seagulls, their animated conversation boomed between the high flat-faced buildings. Night was falling, and Castro-Urdiales was coming alive.

Of all Spain's attractions, most visitors fly in to make the most of the beach. The overwhelming majority, drawn in by the lazy, price-conscious package holiday industry, are safely corralled in tourist ghettos within easy reach of the southern charter airports of Málaga and Alicante, or the Balearic Islands of Mallorca and Ibiza. It is true that you can have a perfectly good holiday experience at one of these resorts, either purpose built on a barren patch of coast or smothering an ancient fishing village, and every year millions of British, German and Scandinavian travelers visit with no complaint. It is, however, possible to combine your beach time with a vivid experience of Spain, by visiting a resort where the Spanish go, rather than one built and run for the European holiday market. Castro-Urdiales is a prime example, within easy taxi distance from Bilbao on Spain's northern, Atlantic, coast. Just up the coast, Donostia-San Sebastián is a larger city, attracting a more sophisticated clientele but with the same, changeable weather.

OPPOSITE: In Asturias a lot of life centers around the beach, right in the heart of town. ABOVE: The Basque coast is dotted with fishing villages that harvest the rich waters of the Atlantic Ocean.

Without the reliable sun of the southern resorts neither of these towns will ever make the grade with the package-tour industry, and they are all the better for it. Even in occasional showers the lively Spanish-filled bars and dignified, well-presented holiday-makers set a tone well above the mass-market resorts such as Benidorm (near Alicante), Torremolinos (near Málaga) or Lloret del Mar (near Barcelona), which have become bywords for the worst excesses of the Spanish tourism industry.

In the south, a slight air of failure is often the best sign of a good place to stop off on the beach. It is the resorts that don't quite make it on the international market that still retain some unspoiled charm, and still attract the domestic visitor. San José near Almería is a good example, an old fishing village marooned in a landscape blanketed in unsightly plastic-sheeting greenhouses. Here yachts haven't taken over the small fishing harbor and fishing boats sail in through the narrow entrance, supplying a line of restaurants with fresh produce. Other good coastal resorts include Cadaqués near Barcelona, sophisticated by its connection with Salvador Dalí, though the beach itself is disappointing, or the atmospheric colonial harbor of Cádiz, with the Playa de la Victoria as its best town beach.

Go for Gaudí

It was a warm evening in 1926 when a number 30 tram, on its regular circuit of Barcelona's crowded streets, hit a tramp who had failed — or refused — to get out of its path. Grumbling, the driver pushed the body to one side: an emaciated figure of a man in his 70s, dressed in a ragged suit held together with safety pins. Four taxi-drivers, worried

about getting their cabs dirty, refused to move the body. Arriving unhurried, stretcher-bearers searched the pockets of the threadbare clothes and found only a battered bible and handfuls of nuts. Shrugging, they dumped the unidentified body in a public ward for disposal. But by the next morning the hospital corridors were lined with state dignitaries and the highest representatives of the Catholic Church; cardinals and councilors paying their respects to one of Spain's most talented geniuses. Antonio Gaudí, Spain's most famous architect and creator of Barcelona's striking *Modernismo* buildings, had died.

Gaudí's death summed up many aspects of his life. He refused to accept that trams should have right of way over pedestrians, and took Christ's doctrine of poverty and humility literally. This principled refusal to compromise was also key to his art.

He wasn't always this way. The son of a coppersmith, he grew up in an era where Catalan nationalism was helping to refocus Barcelona, providing a great opportunity for a working-class youth to flourish as an architect. The industrialist Don Eusebi Güell, who shared Gaudí's Catholicism, nationalism and vision, became the patron of this promising and, at the time, flamboyant young architect. It isn't known what caused the change in Gaudí — a rumored disappointment in love leaving him a lifelong celibate, or youthful experiences transforming him into a virtual hermit whose daily routine was dictated by mass, prayers and confession. What no one now doubts is his powerful influence over the twentieth century.

Perhaps more than anything else, it was Gaudí's fantastical buildings that raised Barcelona from a dull provincial town to a stylish center at the forefront of art. His great buildings were often left unfinished — with God as a patron, he was, as he said, "in no real hurry" — and outraged many critics. Architectural historian Sir Nikolaus Pevsner didn't list him in *Pioneers of Modern Design*, and Dalí, perhaps jealously, called it *"tapas* architecture." But 100 years later, his buildings are recognized for what they are: perhaps the most revolutionary designs of the modern age.

The Casa Milà apartment block has tangled metal balconies that drip down a rippled façade. Bright, strange lizards stand guard in

LEFT: The fanciful turrets of Gaudí's buildings brighten Barcelona's streetscapes. Here, the Casa Battló looks startlingly modernist in the midst of a terrace of traditional period buildings.
RIGHT: Gaudí's unfinished masterpiece is the Sagrada Familia Cathedral. Guided tours end, ideally, with an elevator ride up the east spire for views of the cathedral and the city.

pavilions of contorted stone in the graceful open spaces of the Parc Güell. At the Casa Batlló, railings twist malevolently over glazed eyes. Most ambitious of all was El Templo de la Sagrada Familia, the huge (and unfinished) monumental cathedral in the heart of Barcelona. Under the dreaming spires that absorbed the last burst of his creative genius there's a wealth of detail. In his fevered ornamentation of this, his largest ever commission, he worked from photographs of skeletons, trussed up donkeys as models, and took casts of stillborn babies to try to unlock the secrets of the cosmos. Gaudí's body was finally laid to rest here, at the heart of, perhaps, his greatest work.

Rail across Andalucía

Amid the curving lines of Sevilla's ultra-modern, concrete Santa Justa train station, built to honor the sleek new super-fast trains from the capital, the staid 1930s colors of the Al Andalus Expreso train looked somehow out of place, and I felt rather as though I'd unexpectedly encountered my grandmother in a gym. Opening the clunky train doors I stepped into a beautifully restored art deco carriage, with the original fittings from a graceful age of hope, and settled into my private compartment. There was space to unpack and hang my clothes, a washbasin, a surprisingly comfortable bed, and little belle époque flourishes in the light-shades and fabrics.

Amongst a clatter of bags and cases the other passengers settled in to their compartments in five sleeping carriages, until the train started its leisurely way out of Sevilla. Lulled by the gentle movement of the train the urban sprawl dropped behind and the sophisticated trappings

of modern Spain fell away: watching from my private, temporary home I was transported back to the era of luxury rail travel.

The first thing to note about the Al Andalus Expreso is that it is anything but fast. Under the now out-dated hierarchy of Spanish trains the only thing slower than *expreso* was a *rapido*, which barely moved faster than a horse and cart. And this train's gentle itinerary has anything but speed on its mind. Through the day it trundles from town to restaurant, Parador to palace, and at night, most of the time it just stops, a static home away from home, a brightly lit island of pleasure, happy anywhere its rails might lead.

Nationalities mingled cheerfully in the bar carriage, originally built in France in 1928 as a *wagon-lit* and converted into a bar in 1941. As the light faded over the Spanish countryside and the waiter brought over a new round of drinks it soon became clear I was traveling

with train enthusiasts, and between us we could share experiences of the all the world's great rail routes. The Al Andalus Expreso, we agreed, was less overwhelming than South Africa's Blue Train, not such an adventure as the Trans-Siberian, and much more casual than the Venice–Simplon Orient Express. It is certainly much less expensive than some of its high-profile rivals. What we all agreed — after another glass of *fino* sherry and a quick *calamari* — was that it was probably the most fun, with an eccentric dedication to its overlooked era and a happy, friendly atmosphere.

On this cheerful note I gingerly hopped across the carriage connectors to choose between restaurant cars: the French-built (in 1929) Alhambra car or the British Gibalfaro from the same era. Both offered the best of Spanish cuisine: an ideal way to start six days exploring Andalucía.

Because many guests would like to make the train the centerpiece of their rail safari, the Al Andalus Expreso itineraries are designed to explore the greatest highlights of southern Spain, with meals in the best local restaurants along the way and well-guided expeditions to the most impressive buildings and sights. Its itinerary starts in Sevilla, and travels to Córdoba, Granada, the historic and accessible village of Antequera, Ronda with the oldest bullring in Spain and Carmona, for dinner in its spectacular Parador. A final visit to Jerez gives the chance to see the Real Escuela Andaluza de Arte Ecuestre (Royal Andalusian School of Equestrian Art) and taste a glass or

LEFT: The medieval town of Carmona rises above the sunflowers of the Andalusian landscape.
ABOVE: Lit by the soft light of a winter sunset, Granada's Alhambra Palace is framed by the snow-capped Sierra Nevada.

two of sherry, before returning to Sevilla for a final tour of the city.

Travel on the Al Andalus Expreso is usually packaged as a seven-day, six-night holiday with passengers starting in Madrid spending their first night, appropriately enough, at the Ritz before taking the fast AVE train down to Sevilla for the start of the tour. Costs start at US$2,000 per person, based on two sharing, depending on season. Tickets are best booked through a specialist tour operator or directly through Al Andalus Expreso (915 701621 FAX 915 717482 WEB SITE www.alandalusexpreso.com, Iberrail SA, Calle Capitan Haya 55, 28020 Madrid.

Make a Pilgrimage

Imagine yourself in fields strewn with daisies, buttercups, purple thistles and elderberry flowers. All around are voices, song, laughter. You hear the jingle of a harness, the snort of a horse with too much dust up his nose, and the creak of ancient wagon wheels. A quick glance at the caparisoned carts and the solid silver shrine of the Virgin produces a time warp. There is not a beach, a bikini or a bullfight in sight.

In the southwestern corner of Andalucía, on the edge of the marshland of the Parque Nacional Doñana, is a ghost town called El Rocío. A cluster of modern buildings dominated by a brilliantly whitewashed church with a red-tiled roof, El Rocío sits silent and forlorn for most of the year. But then, as spring turns into summer, it becomes the center of the Andalusian universe as over a million pilgrims converge on it. They come from Madrid, Barcelona, Málaga and the Canary Islands; from Ceuta and Melilla, the Spanish enclaves in Morocco; even from Latin America. They come by air, by train, by car. There are mule-drawn carts, oxen dragging heavy drays, elegant surreys, tractor-towed hay wagons, motorcycles, mopeds, horsemen and hikers.

The pilgrims are a sociologist's dream: a rich slice of Spanish society represented by farmers, factory workers, secretaries, lawyers, government officials and clergy. They come because the mysteries of their religion draw them, or because they feel the call of history and culture, or because it is a great excuse for a marathon binge — for dancing, drinking and showing off. Or — and few people seem to think there is any contradiction — all of the above. It is a thoroughly Spanish festival, as important to the people of southern Spain as the

pilgrimage to Santiago de Compostela is to their northern compatriots.

The focus of the pilgrims' attention is a life-sized figure of the Virgin Mary, holding a diminutive Christ and a golden scepter: Nuestra Señora del Rocío, Our Lady of the Dew. She has a pale porcelain face and hands, which were made in the sixteenth century, and an elaborate gold-embroidered dress and celestial crown. Her story is as rich as her appearance, the stuff of legend. The Rocío cult goes back to Moorish times when Christians hid their relics in trees in the marshlands of this area. In the thirteenth century, King Alfonso X drove the Moors back and Christianity was once again the official religion of this region. As the Moorish forces retreated, the relics were recovered and were said to have miraculous properties, the most renowned being the Virgin of Rocío.

The man who found her in a tree tried to take her back to his home town. He rested for a while on the way and awoke to find she had returned to her original sanctuary in the marshes where the Guadalquivir river winds slowly into the sea. This is the spot, legend has it, where the hamlet of El Rocío stands.

The pilgrimage is organized by lay Catholic brotherhoods called *hermandades.* Each group has a house in Rocío, built with its members' donations, and elects a slate of officials. There is a president, a board of directors and a man in charge of the *simpecado* (literally "without sin"), which is a replica of the statue of the Virgin, drawn on a high-wheeled cart by two oxen. Each brotherhood has one of these heavy, very ornate floats, which lead the slow column of pilgrims along the dusty roads to Rocío. The local priest, although not an official of the brotherhood, usually accompanies it. One I met in Rocío was sitting with his group's governing board during a lull in the pilgrimage's activities. Dressed in a Ralph Lauren polo shirt, he was drinking beer out of a plastic cup and enjoying himself. His role, he said, was to act as the brotherhood's "spiritual counselor."

About one hour's drive from Sevilla, first on the Huelva highway and then on country roads, El Rocío receives hundreds of thousands of casual visitors as the festival moves towards its climax. But the serious way to go is to join a *hermandad* and travel

TOP: Pilgrims on the road to El Rocío with a replica of the Virgin in their *simpecado*, blending religion with a Latin love of theatricality and celebration. BOTTOM: The pageant continues even after the festival. Here, El Rocío pilgrims returning home to Jerez.

with its slow-moving wagons through the flower-strewn countryside, a twenty-first-century Spanish version of Chaucer's pilgrims wending their yarn-spinning way to Canterbury.

At dusk the group will choose a place to stop, often in a small copse or shaded area, place the *simpecado* in the center and circle the wagons, horses, oxen and tractors around it. Then the eating, drinking and dancing begin. There is always music: the rattle of castanets, the urgent thrumming of guitars, the beat of a drum, the hard, rhythmic sound of Spanish clapping. And songs. A fire is made, cooking gets under way, the wine skins circulate. Young bloods, wearing high-waisted Andalusian trousers, short jackets and low crowned hats, parade up and down on their Arab stallions with women side-saddle behind them. Some of the riders are women themselves, with high boots, polka-dotted dresses spread out over the horse's rump and hair swept up, held in place by a large comb and crimped with a carnation or a rose.

The columns slowly converge on El Rocío. At the roadside, two young men offer *copas* of chilled sherry, with the compliments of the maker, to thirsty pilgrims as they trudge by. Two horsemen, reins in one hand and hats in the other, race each other down the road, small puffs of dust spurting from their horses' hooves. Rocío itself, the once-a-year town, has no paved roads; there is a feeling of the American West as the wagons roll down the wide streets.

Stalls sell food, drink, El Rocío medallions and T-shirts, Moroccan knives and Japanese radios. A young woman in a flounced and pleated pink dress and a black flat hat hitches her glossy-flanked steed to a pay telephone and calls home. In the cool of the church, by way of contrast, a large crowd appears mesmerized by the Virgin, calm and peaceful in her tabernacle and cosseted by tall candles and a forest of pink and white gladioli. "*¡Viva la Virgen!*" shouts one devotee. There is a scraping sound on the sandy floor as another pilgrim shuffles slowly forward on his knees towards the altar.

By Sunday evening, Sevilla radio stations report that there are a million and a half people in Rocío and the surrounding area. The midnight mass is televised nationally and most of the leading Madrid newspapers run special reports on the event. The moment to bring the Virgin out of the church and take her around the 80 or so *hermandades* in El Rocío has arrived. The honor of carrying her under the silver-roofed canopy goes to the men of Almonte, the oldest brotherhood. The crowd surges forward as the shrine appears at

the door of the church and begins its slow perambulation around the town. To touch the Lady of the Dew is to be specially blessed and there are apparently no rules governing how contact is made.

As the seething mass of bodies and the swaying but serene Virgin go by, bells clang, groups of people break into songs of praise, individuals cry out and cross themselves and rose petals shower down from the rooftops. A man on the edge of the crowd laughs and displays a tooth in his upper jaw that has the Virgin engraved on it. A woman climbs on somebody's shoulders and works her

way to the shrine over a sea of backs, heads and necks. She manages to touch one of the silver poles supporting the canopy before being wrenched away. "*Viva! Viva! Viva!*" roars the crowd.

The special power of the Rocío pilgrimage over its devotees seems to derive from its blend of religion, nationalism and rural simplicity. The 700th anniversary of the cult was celebrated in 1984, and the pilgrimage is confidently expected to roll on for another seven centuries. Meanwhile, Nuestra Señora del Rocío returns to her marshland sanctuary, her residence a ghost town once more.

The Romería del Rocío takes place at Pentecost. To join in with the festivities the best place to get information is Sevilla's Tourist

Information Office (95 4221404 FAX 95 4229753, Avenida de la Constitución 21, Sevilla. During the festival this is also probably the best place to stay, as rooms in the tiny village of Rocío book out several years in advance, and at several times their normal rate.

Tour Toledo

Spain, rich in architectural heritage and solidly seated among modern European nations, offers visitors a dense past preserved alongside a vibrant present. And this is building some of Spain's finest churches, mosques and synagogues. In 1085 BC King Alfonso VI, helped by El Cid, conquered the town in the name of Christianity, but Toledo's history of cultural tolerance continued, and some of the country's greatest buildings, including the awesome cathedral that is still home to the primate of Spain, were constructed in a remarkable collaboration between Christian and Arab architects and craftsmen.

When, in the sixteenth century, the Spanish capital was moved to Madrid, Toledo quietened into relative obscurity, only recently being accorded Unesco World Heritage status. Now

perhaps best demonstrated in one, approachably small, city: Toledo.

Encircled on three sides by the Tajo river, Toledo was, for many years, the courtly capital of Castilla, and contains many of the country's finest buildings from the earlier part of the last millennium. Its present reduced status makes it pleasantly compact and, once the tourist buses have departed, calm and uncrowded.

Toledo's superb defensive position, perversely, made it a magnet for invaders, starting with the Romans who took the small town of Toletum in 193 BC. Just over 500 years later the Moors arrived to find a prosperous trading post, and over the following years Moors, Jews and Mozárabes (Christians living under Moorish rule) lived in harmony, its wonders, tightly compacted in the city walls and easy to explore in just a few days, present a great opportunity for an imaginative journey through the centuries.

Start, perhaps, with the cathedral, whose 250-plus years of construction spanned the eras of Gothic Renaissance and baroque art. The cool nave, divided into four aisles by 88 mighty pillars, vaults above rays of light that shine through exquisite stained-glass windows dating back to the fifteenth century. At the heart of the cathedral is the *coro*, or choir, a masterpiece of carving in stone and wood that tells the tale of

Protected on three sides by the Tajo River, Toledo's ancient buildings are packed into a small medieval center, with spectacular views at every turn.

the conquest of Granada through actual scenes of individual villages. Facing it is the exuberant artwork of the Capilla Major, with the entire New Testament portrayed in pictural form. Around the periphery are 20 smaller chapels, some with beautiful tombs, others housing priceless art works. It would be easy to spend a day in this magnificent building without exhausting its appeal.

Press on instead, as Toledo has so much else to see. There's the Alcázar, formidably sited overlooking the gorge and scarred by the bullets of the Spanish Civil War, a second church almost as large as the cathedral, two ancient synagogues, several mosques and countless convents, stately homes and palaces.

Weighed down by such architectural gems, modern Spain squeezes itself into small chinks in the masonry, filling the side walls of narrow alleys and spilling out onto the cobbled streets. There are shops selling local hams and cheeses, and others offering swords and knives, cast from the famous Toledo steel and with handles inlaid with gold and silver filigree. *Tapas* bars that through the day feed undiscriminating day-tripping hordes come alive at night for the local market, piling high specialist *tapas* and serving local wine by the glass. As the light fades from the sky, yellow streetlights take over, casting deep shadows into the lined façades of ancient buildings and glittering on the time-worn sheen of historic flagstones, smoothed by countless generations of leather-shod feet. In this atmospheric setting sounds filter through the air. The beat of *discobares* where the young dance and preen, quieter jazz clubs for an older crowd and, just occasionally, the glorious sound of voices raised in unison as a full orchestra and choir fill the ancient nave of the huge cathedral with the music it was built to hear. As a microcosm of urban Spain, redolent with history but very much of the modern age, it's hard to beat Toledo.

Tread like a Toreador

Is it a "sport," an "art," or a "slaughter?" Casual fans and many foreign visitors regard a bullfight as they might any other form of outdoor entertainment, albeit one with a peculiarly Spanish character. (Bullfights are also popular in southern France, Portugal and in many Latin American countries.) To the aficionado and to Spanish newspaper editors, there is no doubt about it. It is the "art of tauromachy," and reporting and commentary is naturally handled in the newspapers' arts and culture sections. For the anti-blood-sports fraternity, including Spain's own active league,

bullfighting is a bloodthirsty, anachronistic outrage that should be banned forthwith. Clearly, its objective is to prove man's skill and superiority at killing a live animal using weapons. And no amount of preening, glorious clothing will disguise this basic principle.

However, leaving aside the debate for a moment, most visitors to Spain will probably see at least one bullfight, even if only on a restaurant's wide-screen television. Apart from anything else, the *corrida* is a quintessential Spanish spectacle. The ring itself, with its circle of sand, its wooden barriers, high terraces, lively crowd and moving line of sun and shade is worth seeing. The band strikes up with the traditional paso doble, three teams of toreros in their "suits of lights" enter, and the officials, dressed in doublets, capes, buckled shoes and broad-brimmed hats, ride in on horseback.

The ritual of the fight rarely changes. The band stops playing, a trumpet sounds and the bull enters the ring. The animal invariably appears huge, menacing, invincible. Bulls more often weigh in excess of 500 kg (1,100 lb), but they move fast and, if they are good, with the sure-footedness of a dancer. The bull will race around the ring, head held high, and sometimes crash its heavy, angled horns against the barrier in a vain attempt to reach the human prey on the other side.

The fight proceeds in three phases or *tercios*. Members of the *cuadrilla* (team), led by the matador, play the bull with their flowing pink and gold capes to size him up. Then the picadors enter, two large men on horseback wearing low-crowned hats and sequined suits and carrying lances. Their job is to stab the bull in the thick pad of muscle on its neck to weaken it. The bull will charge one of the horsemen, jab its horns into the pads wrapped around the horse's belly and flanks and try to toss both horse and rider.

Until the 1920s, the horses were not padded. They were often horribly injured and not infrequently killed by the bulls. Today, they are well padded and blindfolded, but they smell the bull and the fear remains. The picadors, who usually make sure the bull bleeds profusely, are never popular figures with the crowd and are booed noisily if they spend too much time in the ring.

During the second act, *banderilleros* (assistants to the matador), or sometimes the matador himself, approach the bull at an angle and, running fast, plant *banderillas*, or wooden-shafted darts with streamers attached, into the back of the bull's neck. This requires great fleetness of foot, split-second timing and daring. The bull is supposed to be on the move, which makes the feat more difficult and

spectacular. The purpose is to reveal the spirit of the animal and goad it into action.

The third and last act is when the matador faces the bull alone, the *faena*. This is where artistry comes into play. By now the bull's head should be lower than it was to begin with, but he should have a lot of fight left in him. The matador begins by putting the animal through a series of moves with the *muleta*, a short crimson cape draped over a sword. There are a variety of recognized passes, but in recent years many matadors have introduced gimmicks to please the crowd, such as kneeling in front of the bull and tapping it on the nose with the sword. El Cordobés, who carried daring to almost suicidal lengths, was one of the early practitioners. But he was not judged to be a great bullfighter by the experts, who frown on such innovations.

The finale is the *suerte suprema,* the moment of truth, the kill. It is not easy, no matter how weak the bull has become. The target area is a five-centimeter-wide (three-inch) space between the bull's shoulder blades. The matador has to keep the bull's head down and still by manipulating the cape, and then launch himself over the horns and thrust the sword home in exactly the right spot. If he misses, the sword will buckle and bounce off the bull's bony back. Most matadors miss, often several

times. When this happens the matador uses a heavier sword with a cross-piece and jab into the bull's brain, a more effective way of dispatching him but missing all the artistry and drama of the approved way.

The origins of bullfighting go back to the Greeks and Romans, perhaps even further. It has been an important feature of Spanish life since the Middle Ages though fighting from horseback was more popular than on foot for many centuries. El Cid is believed to have fought bulls to celebrate some of his victories, and no coronation of a monarch is complete without bullfighting forming part of the festivities. Breeding bulls, a critical aspect of the business, was traditionally a pursuit of the aristocracy and was socially on a par with horse breeding and hunting.

In the eighteenth century, under the Bourbons, bullfighting became a popular spectacle. The process of codifying and regulating it began in Andalucía, where posters advertising forthcoming *corridas,* started to appear. The most famous bullfighter in this period was Pedro Romero, from Ronda, who killed nearly 6,000 bulls in his 28-year career without injury.

The third and last act of the bullfight, when the matador faces the bull alone.

Bullfighting's greatest era is generally considered to have been in the early part of the twentieth century, when José Gomez ("Josélito") of Sevilla and Juan Belmonte were fighting, and in the 1940s and 1950s, when "Manolete" from Córdoba, Antonio Bienvenida, Luis Dominguin and Antonio Ordoñez (Hemingway's favorite) were the stars. Josélito and Manolete were both killed in the ring, adding to their personal aura and enhancing the drama of the epoch.

Soccer has overtaken bullfighting as Spain's most popular sport, but the *corrida* retains its grip on Spaniards with 40 million spectators — the size of the Spanish population — passing through the turnstiles every year. It's big business. Tickets are divided into *sol* and *ombre,* with the shady seats costing more — though the recent trend to perform later in the day has made the sunny seats less hot. Most of the action still happens in the shade, as top *matadors* don't want to look sweaty whatever their emotions. The Bullfighting season runs from March through October, and although most southern villages are likely to stage their own atmospheric if amateurish *corridas*, the best are to be found in Madrid or Sevilla, later to be replayed endlessly on television bars nationwide. Further information can be found on the Internet, at www.mundo-taurino.org.

Taste a Sherry

Long before you reach Jerez by road you see the vineyards. Approaching the town you smell the sherry, a deep, rich vinous aroma from the juice that turns into pale straw-colored *finos* (dry, light sherries), golden *amontillados* (also dry but older and with more body and a nuttier flavor than the *finos*), and the teak, mahogany and walnut-colored *olorosos* (medium-to-sweet, aromatic sherries; pure *olorosos* are dry on the palate but they are usually blended with sweet wines to produce medium-sweet, cream and brown sherries).

The sherry *bodegas* are a fascinating blend of the traditional and the modern. Sherry "cellars" are above ground, and are light airy structures, often very beautiful and many over 100 years old. Most of them have large patios shaded by oak, acacia and cypress trees and edged with shrubs and banks of flowers. But in the same complex you will find modern bottling plants, warehouses and computer-driven offices. Many of the proprietors' names have become household words: Gonzalez Byass (Tio Pepe), Pedro Domecq, Harvey & Sons, Sandeman, Osborne, and so on. While

sherry is the lifeblood of the business, a great quantity of brandy is also produced in Jerez. The *bodegas* are used to visitors and, whether or not you are a sherry-drinker, a tour of a *bodega* is an aesthetically pleasing and educative experience that usually ends up with a glass or two of their local production.

At Williams and Humboldt, the makers of Dry Sack sherry, Thomas Spencer, a former London taxi driver who married a woman from Jerez, serves as our guide. He is something of a poet on the subject of sherry. He takes us into the oldest cellar, which was built in 1863. Columns made out of simple limestone blocks support the high wooden ceiling. There are no artificial lights, no wiring, nothing except row upon row of casks, or butts, made by hand on the premises. Each butt contains 500 liters (108 gallons) of the precious fluid and weighs half a ton. The floor is clay and is watered in

summer to maintain the correct degree of humidity. Sunlight filters in, at a discreet angle, through small windows set high in the walls. "Sherry in the cask," says Spencer, "is a living thing. At night in here, it's very quiet, very peaceful, like a cathedral."

Sherry is not a vintage wine. It is neither bottled, nor sold, by the year in which was made. It is aged in wooden butts by the *solera* system to ensure a consistent quality. When sherry is drawn off the most mature batch (the *solera*), it is replaced by younger wine, which in turn is replenished from butts containing still younger wine, and so on. The new wine "refreshes" the old, and the old "fortifies" the new. The normal cycle lasts five or six years. During that time, unlike other wines, sherry matures with the stopper removed from the cask so that it can "breathe." White American oak is the best material for the butts because

the resin in the wood helps the yeast to bloom and the wine to breathe. The resulting evaporation means a loss of three to four percent, but it helps the wine to consume the yeast in it, leaving it clear and dry. The evaporation is known among sherry-makers as "the angels' share," but as Thomas Spencer says in a less poetic afterthought, it simply sticks on the ceiling.

Carlos Williams, the son of one of the co-founders of the firm, created Dry Sack in 1906 as a medium sherry, blended from *amontillados* and *olorosos*, for the British taste. Falstaff's term for his favorite tipple, "sack,"

Since time immemorial, Jerez has been the sherry capital of the world. Redolent with the sweet scent of this ultimately civilized drink, this traditional sherry cellar is racked with ancient wooden barrels, many signed by royalty and Hollywood stars who have visited over the years.

has three possible origins, according to Spencer. The first is that it came from the Spanish verb *sacar*, to draw out, describing the action of taking the sherry from the cask. The second version is that the word derived from the sacks that covered the casks. The third derivation (the most exciting, though least likely) is that the term came from the "sacking" of sherry-laden Spanish ships by British predators. Whatever your choice, there seems little doubt that Falstaff, no slouch when it came to drink, had sherry in mind.

Outrun Pamplona's Bulls

A brass band brayed under my window, marking the start of the last *encierro* of the six-day fiesta of San Fermín, the famous running of the bulls in Pamplona. There are already large crowds moving down to the twisting corridor of cobbled streets where the bulls will run. The July air is fresh and cool, the sky still gray. Spectators are positioning themselves on top of the heavy wooden posts and planks that cordon off the route.

Catching sight of a young redheaded Englishman I had talked to the day before, I climb over the fence and join him and the other runners. Many of them are standing around in small groups reading accounts of the previous day's *encierro* in the local newspapers. There are vivid photographs of youths fleeing in all directions, of hurtling bulls and fallen bodies. Those newspapers will be rolled up and thrown as a last resort to deflect a bull's attention should the need arise. The runners are mostly Spaniards, dressed in traditional white slacks and shirts with red sashes around their waists and red scarves around their necks.

The young Englishman, who is on an extended cycling tour of Europe, has run every day of the fiesta. "It's a drug," he says, "there's no way I would have missed any of it."

There are a few other foreigners, but the big contingents, especially the Australians who come en masse every year, have already left Pamplona, burned out after several days and nights of continuous drinking. As zero hour approaches, people converge on a small figurine of San Fermín in a niche in a church wall, near the corral where the bulls are waiting. The bishop Fermín has a shepherd's crook on his arm and a red bandanna around his neck and is surrounded by candles. Starlings wheel and scream in the gray sky overhead. The crowd sings a hymn to the martyred bishop; there is a strong emotional undercurrent in the gathering. Red scarves

flutter in a fitful breeze as the sun's rays begin to warm the slate roofs of the old town.

The ceremony comes to an end and the spectators clamber back over the railings where Red Cross workers prepare their stretchers for action. The runners, now alert and tensile, dance on the balls of their feet and stare down the hill.

The redhead turns to me. "It looks like you're going to run" he says. We are about halfway along the course, well clear of the two most dangerous spots. The first is at the beginning of the run. Freshly released, six bulls and six accompanying heifers pound up a narrow street lined with the solid stone surfaces of churches and remnants of the city's walls. There are virtually no doorways to duck into and nothing to leap over. The second danger zone is the narrow passageway that leads into the bullring: congestion and panic there can have serious consequences. Thirteen people have been killed during the run in the last 50 years, and scores injured.

The street is now jammed with runners, many of them jumping up and down and trying to see what is happening further back. The wooden fencing that seals off the side streets is festooned with spectators; more onlookers are on balconies or hanging out of windows. Conflicting emotions — anticipation, fear, excitement — pulse through the runners. There is a whoosh and a crack as the first rocket goes off and a loud cheer from the onlookers. I am suddenly aware of some very youthful runners, including a few young women. My friend is leaping up and down like a leprechaun. Some runners have already taken off although the bulls are nowhere in sight. "You're not supposed to start running until you can see the tips of their horns," he says reprovingly.

A second rocket explodes, indicating that all the bulls are out of the pen. There is the beginning of a mass movement. The real danger, I begin to think, is not being tossed by a bull but flattened and pounded to death by the other runners. I let my friend do the jumping. "There they are," he yells. There is an incredible stampede, feet, legs, arms and elbows flailing in all directions. I keep directly behind the young veteran and away from the center of the street. Fear truly lends wings. I turn for a fleeting second and at that moment six huge black bulls, weighing half a ton each, their horns held high,

Pamplona's running of the bulls" first made famous by Hemingway, continues to draw visitors from all over the world. The fit and the brave run through the streets followed by the bulls. For most visitors the heady mixture of adrenalin and alcohol is a perfect formula for a week-long party.

career past at about 20 miles an hour and are gone, scattering runners like raindrops. One person is down but apparently not badly hurt. A rocket is fired to announce that all the bulls have reached the ring. The running of the bulls, which lasted approximately two minutes and thirty seconds from start to finish — but felt much longer from my panting perspective — was over until next year.

Pamplona offers more than bullfights in this heady week. You go to sleep with the sound of music in your ears and it is still there when you awake. There seem to be scores of different bands, and along with the singing and dancing are street processions with costumed performers on foot and on horseback. Lavishly dressed dummies move in procession from the town hall down to the church of San Fermín. Some are "giants" — nine-meter-tall (12-ft) figures depicting the Catholic Monarchs (Ferdinand and Isabella), Moorish princes and other historical characters — others are "fat-heads," life-sized comical caricatures. The giants move in as stately a fashion as their great weight allows, spinning around slowly to the applause of the crowd; the fat-heads also pirouette and dart from side to side, bringing screams of delight from the children.

The whole festival unfolds in a spirit of enthusiasm and friendliness. Local inhabitants clearly enjoy their own show and not only tolerate the vast invasion of outsiders, they give them a genuinely friendly welcome.

Flash at Flamenco

Flamenco, Spain's special contribution to the world of music, is rare in Spain. As you scan through the airwaves in your rental-car radio it's rock, pop and pap you hear. However, you only need to catch it for a few seconds to feel its power, its depth (true flamenco is called *cante jondo*, "deep song"), its emotion, and its strangeness. Despite flamenco's absence from daily life, it is still Spain's unmistakable musical signature, whether it is heard in a tourist nightclub, at a concert or, occasionally, on the radio or television. The best place to see it is during one of Spain's endless festivals, performed live on the streets, but the best way to understand flamenco is to learn how to dance it.

To make this easier, there is a new simplified version, probably not a true flamenco at all, but with enough skirt-twirling, flourishing arm movements and imperious foot-stamping to keep Carmen happy. You need the gear to do it: women wear long-skirted traditional dress (to hide the mistakes your feet are making), embroidered shawls for lavish gestures, fans for preening and light, tapping dance shoes; men dress in tight *bolero* jackets, hugging pants and, often, high heels.

You also need a teacher. These can be arranged through the local tourist office — if, in trainers and jeans, you can muster the courage to ask about breaking into a Spanish cultural tradition — or there is a British company, Dance Holidays ℂ (01206) 577000 WEB SITE www.danceholidays.com, which runs dance-lesson tours of Spain.

The word flamenco, which first became identified with the music and the dance in the mid-eighteenth century, poses a mystery. Some people believe it comes from the Spanish word meaning "Flemish," which was used derogatorily of Carlos V's rapacious Flemish courtiers whom he brought with him when he ascended the Spanish throne in the early sixteenth century. Others think it derives from the Arabic for a "fleeing peasant" *(felah mengu)* and referred to the gypsies who, then as now, lived on the edge of society.

Flamenco's origins are as obscure as its name. What is certain is that it is the music of Andalucía, where it developed from a mingling of Moorish, gypsy and Jewish influences. In the eighteenth century, flamenco became closely identified with the Andalusian gypsies, and waxed and waned as a popular art form during the nineteenth and twentieth centuries. But it traveled well, both to other parts of Spain and through its influence on different musical forms, ranging from classical (Georges Bizet and Joaquín Rodrigo), to jazz (Miles Davis and Gil Evans) and to pop (The Gipsy Kings).

The heart of the music is a passionate, at times almost agonizing, attempt to express the misfortunes of love and life in the ever-present shadow of death. When this happens as perfectly as it can, when the performers lose all sense of self, this is what is known as *duende*, flamenco's moment of truth.

The fiery, swirling, stamping dance associated with flamenco is as much part of the music as the guitar, the voice and the percussive hand clapping. Flamenco also embraces a collection of styles, songs and rhythms that include the *saeta*, sacred songs that originated with Spain's Jewish community and are sung during Easter's Holy Week in Andalucía, and popular dances like the *fandango* and the *sevillana*.

Spontaneous flamenco performances in a gypsy cave, an atmospheric bar or on the street in a festival are hard to find. The easiest way to hear and see the real thing is on stage in

YOUR CHOICE

The Great Outdoors

It is hard to ignore the open countryside in Spain — there is so much of it. Whether flying, driving or traveling by train, you are constantly reminded that, despite its sophistication, Spain possesses some of the largest, wildest and least spoiled land in Europe. It has everything a nature-lover could want: towering snow-covered mountain ranges, green hills and valleys, tranquil and gushing rivers, wetlands and wildlife, golden beaches, rocky, secretive coves, expansive bays. The landscapes of Spain are astonishingly diverse. Parts of Galicia could be mistaken for Ireland, while the desert landscapes of Almería often stand in for Arizona in cowboy movies.

This diversity is a bonus to any visitor interested in nature in all its shapes and forms. Although competition between the forces of change and those of conservation continues as

the country develops its economic infrastructure, Spain has a pretty good record of preserving its natural inheritance. Of the national parks, the greatest perhaps is in the northern mountains: the **Parque Nacional de los Picos de Europa** straddles the borders of Asturias, Cantabria and Castilla-León. Amongst its beech, oak and birch forest chamois are the most distinctive resident. In the Pyrenees of Aragón the **Parque Nacional de Ordesa** includes hanging glaciers and deep karst gorges. In the Catalonian Pyrenees the **Parque Nacional d'Aigüestortes i Estany de Sant Maurici** protects a less dramatic, but more representative, region of the continental Pyrenees, with its winding streams, lakes and fir-fringed crags.

Waterways are not the first natural feature that comes to mind when you think of Spain, but they exist and lend themselves to leisure activities. You can rent a boat and cruise on the **Río Ebro** in Tarragona province or float around the **Albufera wetlands**, just south of Valencia, which doubles as a bird sanctuary and the birthplace of Spain's national dish, *paella*.

There are also a number of lakeland parks, especially in the region of La Mancha. The **Parque Nacional de las Tablas de Daimiel** is known for its waterfowl and waders, a hugely important nesting site and migratory haven. Another La Mancha park is the **Parque Natural de Cabañeros,** which is the biggest and best example of Iberian Mediterranean

OPPOSITE: Calella de Palafrugell, on the Costa Brava, retains its fishing village charm despite a new wave of holiday apartment developments. ABOVE: The Sierra de la Grazalema, Andalucía, is ideal hiking country, with traditional white washed villages smouldering under the warm Spanish sun. OVERLEAF: La Calobra and the Torrent de Pareis are washed by the warm waters of the Mediterranean Sea.

woodland, with Paleozoic hill country, wide plains and areas of dense thicket.

Further south, the **Parque Nacional de Doñana**, recognized as a Unesco Biosphere Reserve, is perhaps the most outstanding of all Spain's national parks, encompassing a complex seepage system of rivulets, underground streams and marshlands leading into the Guadalquivir estuary in Andalucía, with more wildlife in the coastal strip of beaches, shifting dunes and hill scrub. The Doñana is the largest nature reserve in the country and is home to deer, mongoose, lynx, badger and a huge range of migratory birds that includes, if you a lucky, occasional appearances of the rare imperial eagle, Spain's national emblem.

The arid beauty seen in countless cowboy films is protected in the **Parque Nacional Sierra Nevada** in the provinces of Granada and Almería, and combines high mountain and Mediterranean habitats: you'll find high-altitude deserts, sub-alpine steppe and forests of conifer. And finally, the Balearics have a park of their own: the **Parque Nacional Marítimo-Terrestre de Cabrera** protects a tiny archipelago of limestone islands, clothed in stunted Mediterranean vegetation, an important refuge for shearwaters, cormorants and raptors.

In addition to the fully protected national parks there are around 60 reserves where controlled activities, including hunting, are allowed. Further information can be obtained from the government organization responsible for conservation, **ICONA** (Instituto Nacional para la Conservación de la Naturaleza) (912 668200 WEB SITE www.mma.es, Gran Vía 35, 28005 Madrid.

One activity continually growing in popularity — amongst Spaniards and foreigners alike — is **hiking**. The most popular trails are found in the north, among the snowy Picos de Europa with their almost Alpine atmosphere and the Pyrenees; the Sierra de Gredos and Valle del Jerte in the center; Sierra de Cazorla, Sierra de Aracena and the Alpujarras in Andalucía, and parts of the Balearic Islands, especially in the unspoiled mountainous northwestern side of Mallorca. The best way to enjoy them is to contact a travel group specializing in hiking before you travel. There are many in Europe and North America. Two good ones in Britain are: **Ramblers Holidays** ((01707) 331133, Box 43, Welwyn Garden City, AL8 6PQ, and **Exodus** ((020) 8675 5550, 9 Weir Road, London SW12 0LT. In the United States, try **Adventure Center** ((510) 654-1879 TOLL-FREE (800) 227-8747 WEB SITE www.acventurecenter.com, 1311 63rd Street, Suite 200, Emeryville, California 94608, or **Mountain Travel/Sobek** ((888) 687-6235 WEB SITE www.mtsobek.com, 6420 Fairmount Avenue, El Cerrito, California 94530.

Bird-watching enthusiasts can head for Albufera if they are in the east; almost anywhere in Extremadura, where the black storks come from Africa and build their nests in the cork trees, if they are in western Spain;

Mallorca's bird sanctuary (another wetland called S'Albufera), if they are in the Balearics; and in the south head for the Parque Nacional de Doñana, which is Spain's most extensive area for concentrated bird life, being the habitat of six world-protected species including the imperial eagle, and the winter retreat of thousands of migratory aquatic birds.

For many visitors to Spain there is one type of outdoors: it's sunny, it's sandy, and is on the beach. Spain is blessed with countless **beaches** all along its Mediterranean coast, where steady sun, small waves and negligible tides spell paradise for families. Tourist ghettos within easy reach of the southern charter airports of Málaga and Alicante or the Balearic Islands of Mallorca and Ibiza draw in millions of visitors every year and send them back tanned and happy. The European-orientated mass-market resorts such as Benidorm (near Alicante), Torremolinos (near Málaga), or Lloret del Mar (near Barcelona), may have become associated with the worst high-rise concrete over-developments of the Spanish tourist industry, but the visitors here never seem to mind and the nightlife is, it has to be admitted, very lively.

In the south of the country, failing fishing villages spent most of the 1970s and 1980s trying to match the spectacular growth of the mass-market boom, and plenty that didn't succeed are pleasantly populated by a more local clientele. San José near to Almería is a good example, an old fishing village where yachts haven't taken over the small harbor and fresh produce is brought in by local fishing boats to supply a string of restaurants waiting on the waterfront. Other small coastal resorts with something special to offer include Cadaqués near Barcelona, with its poor gravel beach balanced by it's cultural connection with

Salvador Dalí, or the atmospheric southern city Cádiz, where good beaches add family appeal to a city that once hosted the cream of the Spanish navies. Spain's Atlantic coast also has some wonderful beaches, whose occasional clouds and rain keep mass tourism at bay. Castro-Urdiales is a prime example, within easy taxi distance from Bilbao, on Spain's northern Atlantic coast, with nearby Donostia-San Sebastián a larger and more sophisticated city.

Sporting Spree

The sporting scene in Spain is as varied as its landscape, both for the active participant and the spectator. The development of sporting facilities has followed Spain's explosive economic growth in tourism and, encouraged by significant successes on the international scene, sporting facilities are as good if not better than in any other European country. Golf is a growth industry, attracting plenty of enthusiasts from the United Kingdom, and tennis and sailing schools are becoming increasingly popular in the pleasant sunshine of the southern regions.

SKIING
"Sunny Spain" is not a country you usually associate with skiing and most travel agents do not bother to list it in connection with the sport. This is fine with two million Spanish skiers who like to keep the slopes to themselves.

Spain is the most mountainous country in Europe after Switzerland and has 27 ski resorts, in the **Pyrenees**, **Andorra**, **Cantabria**, **central Spain** (60 km/37 miles from Madrid) and the **Sierra Nevada**. More foreigners are already in the know, especially as a result of the 1996 World Alpine Skiing Championships on the slopes of the Sierra Nevada.

The Spanish ski resorts are still relatively uncrowded, but you have to keep an eye on weather reports to make sure snow conditions are good, especially in the Sierra Nevada. The great bonus in that southern resort is that you can literally ski in the morning and then, just over two hours later, play golf, tennis or swim along the Costa del Sol. (The only other place you can do that in the Mediterranean is in

OPPOSITE: Boats are still a common means of transport in the Parque Nacional Doñana when the seasonal rains bring floods. LEFT: Horses were Spain's decisive weapon in their conquest of South America. With its rugged terrain, horses are still an ideal way to explore a Spain beyond the reach of roads. Here, a young boy rides in the Sierra Nevada.

Lebanon.) You can even combine skiing and golf in a holiday that provides instruction in both sports. This is organized by the **Sierra Nevada Club** (952 474858, Estación de Ski Sierra Nevada, 18196 Monachíl, Granada. For more information contact the **Federación Española de Deportes de Invierno** (913 440944, Calle Infanta María Teresa 14, 28016 Madrid, or the Spanish Tourist Office.

TENNIS

The growth of tennis courts, training camps and stadiums for competitions has been remarkable in the last few years. Municipal tennis courts are available in most holiday resorts and in hotels designed for the tourist trade. Again, the **Costa del Sol** is the best endowed, but you will find tennis facilities all over Spain. There are many places where you can stay in comfort and study the game. A good one, founded by the late former Wimbledon champion, Lew Hoad, is the **Campo de Tenis de Lew Hoad** (952 474858 FAX 952 474908, on Carretera Mijas km3.5, Apartado 111, Fuengirola, on the coast of the Costa del Sol. For general information on tennis, the **Real Federación Española de Tenis** (932 005355 WEB SITE www.fedetenis.es, Avinguda Diagonal 618, 08028 Barcelona, will be able to provide further details.

GOLF

Spain's sunshine and the abundance of water have produced perfect conditions for the pursuit of the small white ball over the fairway. There are now over 260 golf courses in the country and golfing holidays have become a regular feature for foreigners and Spaniards alike. The game has been greatly popularized by Spanish prowess in international competitions, with Severiano Ballesteros leading the way.

Madrid has 11 courses, of which Golf La Moraleja and the Real Club Puerta de Hierro (created by the British in the nineteenth century) are probably the finest. Barcelona's top club is the Real Club de Golf El Prat, there is also the Club de Golf de Pais in Girona province and another seven courses in Catalunya. Further south, in the Levante, there is a fine course next to the Parador (state-run hotel chain) just outside Valencia (El Saler) and the Torrevieja course in Alicante. In northwest Spain, Santander has the classy club, Real Golf de Pedrena, and there is the pretty La Toja course, on an island of that name close to Pontevedra in Galicia. The Balearic Islands, a favorite spot for golfers, have eight courses, with the top three in Mallorca (Son Vida, Magalluf and Santa Ponsa).

The mecca for golfers, however, is the Costa del Sol or, as some people now call it, the "**Golf Coast**." There are 15 well-designed courses along the coast, dovetailed with all the other classic resort facilities: hotels, restaurants, health spas, nightclubs and marinas. The greatest advantage is the weather, virtually a 100-percent predictable sunshine throughout most of the year. Marbella, as the swankiest spot on the coast, has five courses with the Golf Río Real and the San Roque Club at the head of the list. There are other courses at Estepona, Benalmadena and Torremolinos, all in the province of Málaga; in El Ejido to the north in Almería province; and in Sotogrande further south in Cádiz province.

An excellent source of information on golf, in English, is the monthly magazine, *SunGolf*, which is published in Mijas on the Costa del Sol. Useful, too, is the national federation: **Real Federación Española de Golf** (914 552682, Calle Capitán Haya 9, Madrid. Spain's national tourist offices, travel agents and specialist travel organizations can also provide detailed information. Golfing holidays which include green fees and pre-booked tee-off times are readily available.

HUNTING, SHOOTING AND FISHING

Spaniards are passionate hunters and fishermen. Hunting is strictly controlled and licenses are required, but the ethos of hunting is deeply embedded in the Spanish psyche and there is plenty of opportunity. Game includes wild boar, deer, chamois and red-legged partridge. Hunting holidays are quite popular and are arranged by specialist agencies. One such is **Hunting Spain** (923 380001, Pedro-Llen, La Veguillas, 37454 Salamanca. The **Federación Española de Caza** (913 111411, Calle Francos Rodríguez 70, 28039 Madrid, is the best source of general information. Similarly, the **Spanish Fishing and Casting Federation** (912 328352, Calle Navas de Tolosa 3, Madrid, can supply details on fishing.

MOUNTAIN BIKING AND CLIMBING

For regular cycling and mountain-biking, the **Federación Española de Ciclismo** (915 420421 FAX 915 420341 E-MAIL info@rfec.com, Calle Ferraz 16, 28008 Madrid, is the central organization. And if you are contemplating mountain climbing or trekking through mountainous areas, contact the **Federación**

In Spain, golf is a sport enjoyed seriously by visitors and locals alike. At Real Club de Golf El Prat, Barcelona, it isn't worth making jokes about the club's name. They have heard them all before.

Española de Montañismo (914 451382, Calle Alberto Aguilera 3, 28015 Madrid, for information on mountain refuges and other places to stay overnight.

WHITEWATER RAFTING AND CANYONING

Spain's development was hampered by a lack of navigable rivers, but there are plenty of unnavigable waterways that are perfect for canyoning and whitewater rafting. The best tend to be in the north, where sheer mountain gorges are filled with regular downpours of rain. The local tourist offices of Castro-Urdiales and Donostia-San Sebastián have leaflets about local operators. **Aventur** (942864726, Apartado de Correos 213, Castro-Urdiales, is a good place to start; they run expeditions throughout the Cantabria region. When gorges are in short supply, try

potholing: the **Potholing** (*espeliologia*) **Federation** (933 107062 FAX 933 151624 E-MAIL fed-es-esp@mx2.redestb.es, Avinguda de Francesc Cambo 14, 08003 Barcelona, will tell you where to make like a mole.

WATER SPORTS

Virtually any kind of sporting activity associated with water — fresh or saline — can be pursued in Spain. Facilities for **sailing, windsurfing, scuba diving** and **canoeing** are available in most resorts along the coast and in the Balearic Islands. Windsurfing can be done off almost any beach in Spain and most resorts rent boards. The best general area with constant yet not too boisterous winds are the southern Atlantic beaches between Gibraltar and the Portuguese frontier, with Tarifa generally regarded as the best beach of them all.

To facilitate the expansion of water sports, three "Nautical Sports Resorts" have been established, with seven more planned. At present, the three are the **Estación Náutica Mar Menor** (968 574994 FAX 968 171901 E-MAIL con-marmenor@forodigital.es, Fuster 63, 30710 Los Alázares, Murcia; the **Estación Náutica de L'Estartit** (/FAX 972 750699 E-MAIL estanaut@intercom.es, L'Estartit-Illes Medes, Eglesia 86, 17258 L'Estartit, Gerona; and the **Estación Náutica de Tarifa** (956 684360 FAX 956 685307 E-MAIL melaria@telelin.es, Amador de los Ríos 22, 11380 Tarifa, Cádiz. Backed by the Spanish Tourist authorities, these have been established in the country's top water sports resorts, and are fully set up to help book specialized water sports and also appropriate accommodation for enthusiasts.

Scuba diving has also become a popular sport in Spain, especially in the warmer waters of the southern Mediterranean coastline and the Balearic Islands. If you are taking part in an organized dive, permission will probably be obtained on your behalf, but otherwise you need a permit. The national organization, based in Barcelona, **Federación Española de Actividades Subacuaticas** (932 006769, Carrer Santalo 15, Barcelona, can tell you more.

For **sailing** enthusiasts, new yacht marinas have been built in many areas and boats can be rented — or bought and sold — in most yachting centers. Some of them, notably on the Costa del Sol and in parts of the Balearics, cater to the stratospheric reaches of the international yachting crowd (for example, Puerto Banus on the Costa del Sol and Palma's Club de Mar), but many others are designed for the ordinary sailor and are both well equipped and affordable. For detailed information on sailing contact: the **Federación Española de Vela** (912 335305, Calle Juan Vigon 23, Madrid.

Canoeing is possible in dams and small rivers across the country. To find out more contact the **Canoeing (*Piraguismo*) Federation** (915 064300 FAX 915 064304 E-MAIL correo.fep @ibm.NET, Antracita 7-3º, 28045 Madrid.

SPECTATOR SPORTS

Soccer (*futbol*) is Spain's universal sporting passion, outranking bullfighting and everything else by a long way. Top league and international games are heavily televised and there's no way you'll avoid seeing them in bars, restaurants and offices as you go about the country. To catch the true flavor, there is no substitute to going to a game. Hotel concierges and travel agents can arrange tickets and give you details of how and when to get to the stadium.

Bullfights are also televised — they are Spain's summer equivalent of baseball or cricket — and **basketball** is becoming increasingly popular both in the flesh and on television.

The Open Road

Spain is a large country, only slightly smaller than France. And because it is such a varied country — from the lush, green hills of Galicia in the northwest, through the great open tableland of the center, to the deserts of Almería and the subtropical coastal plain of Murcia in the southeast — it invites a close inspection by road. You can bike it, hike it, even ride a horse over it, but most people will be content to jump into their rental cars and drive into the great open spaces.

However, you simply cannot do it all in one fell swoop unless you are a transcontinental rally driver. You have to be selective; a helpful way to plan is to think of regions or themes. But before some suggestions, a word of warning. Spanish roads have improved dramatically in recent years and there now is a useful network of highways (*autopistas* or *autovías*), designated with an "A" or an "E" in front of the number. Nevertheless, in many cases you will have no alternative but to take the old *carreteras nacionales* (national roads), marked with an "N." These roads usually have only two, or sometimes three, lanes and tend to be congested with heavy traffic, especially long-distance trucks. Where you have a choice, I would recommend using the *autopistas* (many of the trucks deliberately avoid them to save on the tolls), or look for the smaller — and less frequented — roads in the "C" and "D" categories.

There are many possible itineraries and there is no right or wrong way of doing things — wherever you travel in Spain you will come across varied scenery and interesting places. But I will suggest two regional rides and a thematic one which provide a good sampling of the Spanish experience.

AROUND MADRID

A handy way of starting, assuming that you have "done" Madrid, is to take a leisurely tour of the cities and sights that lie in a rough circle around the capital. Begin by driving to **Toledo** on the N-401, a dismal but mercifully short run of about an hour. It is best to spend the night in Toledo and move on the following day to Ávila. The most scenic way to go is to take the N-403 in a northwesterly direction. This passes through the **Sierra de Gredos**,

A ski lift in the Sierra Nevada, Granada, the southernmost and sunniest ski resort in Europe.

a beautiful, unspoiled range of mountains with panoramic views over the *meseta*, where you can lunch in a village restaurant or picnic in the hills.

Ávila, Spain's most perfectly preserved medieval walled city, comes next. You then turn eastwards on the N-110, cut across the Madrid–Valladolid highway (A-6) on to **Segovia**, justly famous for its Roman aqueduct, its magnificent Alcázar, Gothic cathedral and good eating, especially suckling pig and game. After Segovia, you swing south and drive up on the N-603 into the snowy **Sierra de Guadarrama**. From there you can return to Madrid via **El Escorial**, the extraordinary palace-monastery-mausoleum of Felipe II, and the **Valle de los Caídos** (Valley of the Fallen), Franco's bizarre monument to the Civil War dead and to himself, thus completing the circuit of major attractions while breaking it up with plenty of country air and mountain scenery.

ANDALUCÍA

Another attractive regional circuit takes you through the jeweled cities of Andalucía. Leave Madrid on the *autopista* (E-25) that links the capital with the south. If you fancy a more comfortable and quicker method of reaching Córdoba or Sevilla, jump on the high speed AVE train at the revamped Atocha station in Madrid and rent your car in either of those cities. (The train journey from Madrid to Sevilla is only two hours.) Either way, begin with **Córdoba**: relatively small and manageable, this is a good way to get the feel of Moorish Spain. Head straight for the Mezquita, Córdoba's strange and wonderful mosque-church, then wander around the narrow cobbled streets of the old Jewish quarter (Judería). From Córdoba to Sevilla, you can either take the highway or, more interestingly, follow the C-431, which runs along the north bank of the **Río Guadalquivir**

and passes through a number of picturesque whitewashed Andalusian villages. **Peñaflor**, about halfway, is a good place to stop for lunch.

Sevilla deserves at least a couple of days, then head south towards **Jerez** on the A-4. An elegant town, Jerez offers the performing horses at the Real Escuela Andaluza de Arte Ecuestre (Royal Andalusian School of Equestrian Art) and a dozen or so *bodegas* (cellers) for sherry sampling. After that you should turn east on the N-382 and head towards Granada. The place to spend the night is in the mountain-top Parador in **Arcos de la Frontera**, a marvelous little town that dominates the surrounding countryside and gives you a feeling of what the frontier between Christian and Moorish Spain must have been like.

Ronda is your next destination, which you reach by continuing eastwards along the N-382, turning south at **Algodonales** and driving along a twisting mountain road.

Perched over its famous gorge, Ronda should not be missed. After Ronda, go down to the **Costa del Sol** on the same road and, if you enjoy contrast, sample the sophistication and glitter of **Marbella** with a stroll around the Puerto Banus marina, which caters to the seriously rich yachting crowd, and with a drink or a meal in the Marbella Club.

I would not advise lingering on the Costa del Sol, which has been mortally wounded by mass tourism. It has the advantage, however, of positioning you for the **Alpujarra** mountains and **Granada**, with a stop at **Málaga**, if you wish. You drive along the coastal road until **Motril** and then head inland to Granada. The Alpujarra mountains with their charming villages, made famous by the long residence of Gerald Brenan, the British writer and hispanophile, are on the right; an optional diversion, but worth it if you have time. Finally, you reach the outskirts of Granada. Stop for a moment at a place romantically called El Suspiro del Moro (you can't miss it because there is a totally unromantic gas station that carries the name). From here, a breathtaking view of the city is laid out before you. Legend has it that this is the place where the vanquished king of Granada turned for the last time to look back at his beloved city, and wept. Give yourself plenty of time in Granada to absorb the Alhambra; that it is what you are meant to do — entrance tickets remain valid for two days.

If you are returning to Madrid by car you can finish your Andalusian journey by heading north on the N-323 through countryside, where the olive tree reigns supreme, to **Jaén**, which boasts a spectacular hilltop castle with a Parador alongside it, to rejoin the Sevilla-Madrid highway. If you have taken the train to Córdoba, then drive back to that city along the N-432, drop your car off, and stretch your legs in the spacious AVE train as it whisks you back to Madrid at 200 km/h (120 mph).

PILGRIM'S WAY

If you fancy a thematic tour that takes you to a totally different part of Spain, then follow the ancient pilgrims' way from the French border in the Pyrenees to Santiago de Compostela in Galicia. There were two traditional routes. The "Asturian" began at the western end of the Pyrenees and ran along the Asturian coast before turning south. The other, known as the Camino Francés (French Road), began at the

Even the most remote and mountainous regions of Spain are latticed by a good network of roads. The Sierra de Alhma is just one of many outstanding areas that can be explored with a self-drive car.

Roncesvalles Pass, high up in the Pyrenees where the Frankish hero, Roland, fell in battle in 778.

Unless you are actually driving from France to Spain, the best place to begin is **Pamplona**, the capital of Navarra, and worth a visit in its own right whether or not the bulls are running. You can then drive up to Roncesvalles on the twisting C-135 — an hour's run. From Pamplona you take the N-111 to **Logroño** on the Río Ebro, a relatively rapid transition that takes you from the hills and valleys of Navarra to the vineyards of **Rioja**, and the opportunity to drink Spain's most famous wine at its source. A good place to spend a night is the Parador in **Santo Domingo de Calzada**, an authentic medieval stopping place for pilgrims which now offers all the comforts of the twenty-first century. This puts you close to **Burgos** (continuing on the N-120) which, with its magnificent Gothic cathedral, river frontage and Castilian elegance, merits a morning or afternoon of sightseeing.

You should now head due west to León, Old Castilla's other famous city, although you may consider taking a detour to the south to the Benedictine monastery of **Santo Domingo de Silos**, which has the world's best preserved Romanesque cloister, a ravishingly beautiful architectural masterpiece on two levels. A second reason to visit the monastery is the Gregorian chant for which the Silos monks have become famous. To everyone's surprise, including their own, one of their old recordings,

Canto Gregoriano, became a chart-busting hit in the 1980s, selling over six million copies worldwide. The monks perform the chant eight times a day in the monastery church.

From Burgos, resume your pilgrimage on the N-120 across the vast, open expanse of the *meseta* through the small towns of Osorno, Villada and Sahagúa, until you reach the Valladolid-León main road (N-601). Turn north and within half an hour you will be in **León**, a major pilgrim resting spot. And here you too should rest, preferably in the twelfth-century Monasterío de San Marcos, which was built expressly for the pilgrims and is now a Parador. It is a truly marvelous place to spend a night and perfectly in tune with the nature of your journey.

The last lap to Santiago is at hand. Take the most direct route to Lugo (N-120, again, to Astorga, then the N-VI). You are now in green **Galicia**, whose patchwork, stone-walled fields look more Irish than Spanish. **Lugo**, a beautiful old town, is slightly off the pilgrims' path but worth a detour, if only to see the well-preserved third-century Roman walls that still encircle the town, complete with defensive towers and gateways. The final stretch is best on country roads. Leave Lugo going south until you reach the C-547, which continues west to Santiago where, if your pocket will stand it, you should lodge in another authentic pilgrims' hospice, the magnificent **Hotel dos Reies Católicos**, built by Ferdinand and Isabella at the end of the fifteenth century.

Backpacking

When Laurie Lee stepped out one midsummer's morning in the 1930s and began his walk across Spain, he did it on a few pesetas a day, supplementing his meager budget by playing his fiddle on street corners. Spain, however, is no longer the backpacker's dream at bargain prices. But neither is it prohibitive, and there are still buskers plying their trade, quite lucratively, in the major tourist centers and along the Rambla of Barcelona. Inexpensive food, lodging and transportation are all widely available and

ABOVE: Hikers from Granada cross the bridge over the Barranco de Tesorio. Walking is the ideal way to experience the beauty of the region. OPPOSITE TOP: The perfectly preserved town of Ávila is within easy reach of Spain's capital, Madrid. Through the day it can be crowded, but it is at its best in the evening when the day-trippers have left. OPPOSITE BOTTOM: La Mezquita, Córdoba, is a prime example of the grace and elegance achieved by Spain's Moorish architects.

are likely to remain so for the simple reason that the Spaniards themselves are traveling more than ever within their own country, and in every destination we do specify at least one good, inexpensive place to stay.

The backpacker capital of Spain is probably Barcelona, famous party capital for any size of wallet, with the quiet beaches of the Costa Brava perfect hideaways. But wherever you go, the key is to prepare yourself with specialist information before you arrive, plug yourself into the network of cheap hostels, pensions, restaurants and trains and buses (you will find many others doing the same thing), and keep your eyes and ears open to the bargains of the moment. First stop, inside Spain, should always be the local tourist offices: unlike some other countries, they don't sneer at those whose funds are limited, and the officials here, who invariably have a good command of English, will provide vital information on accommodation, buses, trains, and on specialist clubs, associations and companies that deal with different activities and methods of travel. Not only will you cover your basic travel needs but you will also find out about some interesting diversions that may be special to the area you are in, such as mountain biking, horse trekking, canoeing, mountaineering, skiing, caving and such esoterica as hang-gliding, paragliding and bungee-jumping.

Don't be shy about asking for deals. Off-season, you will find them everywhere. If you are a student, be sure to take appropriate identification. There are regular special student travel rates on long distance buses and trains and admission to museums. If you are traveling through rural Spain, inquire about "agro-tourism" at the local tourist offices. Farmers receive government help to open up their farms to visitors for food and lodging at extremely modest cost. Further details about individual properties, searchable by region, can be found on www.toprural.com. It's a great way to plan a hike.

How much will the basics cost? Bed and breakfast in hostels (*hostales*, designated H), guesthouses (*casas de huespedes* — CH), or pensions (*pensiones* — P) will generally cost €16 and up, with the most remote places invariably the least expensive. You can have a sustaining, often surprisingly good lunch or dinner by choosing the fixed-price daily special (*menú del día*), which is always three, and sometimes four, courses and includes bread and wine — for as little as €6. Add on transportation costs, picnic lunches, snacks and other incidentals and you can get by on between €44 and €55 a day, perhaps less if you are very frugal.

Camp sites are generally inexpensive, and there are more than 350 camp and caravan sites all over Spain. For more detailed information, contact the **Federación Española de Empresarios de Camping** (242-3168, Gran Vía 88, 28013 Madrid, but it has to be said that most are geared more to camper vans and caravans, and few make many concessions to

To pick up casual work in Spain, its best to go where the foreigners are — there are already plenty of unemployed Spanish nationals, but where there are plenty of tourists and foreign companies being foreign can be an advantage; it can be much easier to pick up bar work and construction jobs, or freelance work for tour operators, so good places to start are in the booming costas of the Mediterranean coast. Torremelinos on the Costa del Sol, Benidorm on the Costa Blanca and Palma in the Balearic Islands are all good places to find casual employment.

Living it Up

It tends to be the expats and tourists, rather than the Spanish, who spend huge amounts of money on living it up. The Spanish character doesn't, generally, need to spend a lot to justify a perfectly healthy self-esteem. As a consequence of this the high life here doesn't usually cost a huge amount. But if you want to really splash out, the cities are the best place to start.

In **Madrid**, a large choice of luxury hotels greets you. The Ritz is still pre-eminent in terms of location, style, elegance and service, but the Palace, from the same belle époque era and immaculately renovated, is an excellent alternative at a more affordable price. If you want to try one of Spain's top restaurants, dine at Zalacaín, where reservations are essential. If you have a craving for anything that comes out of the sea, La Trainera is a good choice. Madrid's *movida* embraces everything from flamenco to ballroom dancing to sevillanas to jazz and to heavy metal. While you are making up your mind, go and have an expertly made, old-fashioned cocktail in a tall glass in Bar Chicote.

Barcelona rivals Madrid in its elegant hotels and the variety and quality of its restaurants. The Ritz, again, is a classic but if you prefer something ultra-modern, overlooking the sea and city but away from the traffic, try the lofty Hotel Arts in the Olympic port. And if dining with Barcelona's fashionable set appeals to you, reserve a table at Via Veneto, in the charming Sarrià district; it serves excellent Catalan and French food. For fish go to Botafumeiro, a Galician establishment, which has a busy and cheerful oyster bar.

impecunious backpackers with tents. Most backpackers will be more interested in the fact that, for groups of fewer than 10 people, camping outside campsites is legal except in restricted areas.

Youth hostels (*albergues juveniles*) are rarely open year-round, are not usually usefully located for urban areas and are subject to a barrage of petty regulations including stringent curfews. As an occasional backpacker myself I'd rather club together to share a room in a cheap hotel, but for those who do want further details the best place to start is with their home hostel associations. From the United States, contact **Hostelling International** ((202) 783-6161 WEB SITE www.hiayh.org, Suite 840, 733 Fifteenth Street NW 840, Box 37613, Washington DC 20005. In the United Kingdom try the **Youth Hostels Association** ((01727) 855215 WEB SITE www.yha.org.uk, Trevelyan House, 8 St. Stephen's Hill, St. Albans, Herts AL1 2DY, who can put you on to separate splinter groups covering Scotland and Ireland. In Australia, contact the **Australian Youth Hostel Association** ((02) 9261 1111 WEB SITE www.yha.com.au, 422 Kent Street, Sydney, and in New Zealand try the **Youth Hostals Association of New Zealand** ((03) 379 9970 WEB SITE www.yha.com.nz. From anywhere, reservations up to six months in advance can, for a small fee, be made with Hostelling International's **International Booking Network** (IBN) at www.iyhf.org.

OPPOSITE: The fashionable resort of Marbella, on the Costa del Sol, continues to attract celebrities throughout the season, with the yachts of the rich and famous jostling for moorings in the summer months. ABOVE: Once a palace, the Casa de Carmona, in the whitewashed town of Carmona, Andalucía, has now been restored into one of the country's most impressive Paradors.

A good place to begin an evening out is in one of the city's *cava* (local champagne) bars such as La Cava del Palau, at Carrer Verdaguer i Callis 10, in the Barri Gòtic.

In **Sevilla**, the grandest hotel is the Alfonso XIII, which opened its doors in 1929 to the monarch whose name it carries. A smaller but elegant alternative is the conveniently sited Doña María Hotel, which is opposite the Giralda. Sevilla is not as distinguished gastronomically as Marid and Barcelona, but if you want to enjoy the ambience of an ancient and beautiful Sevilla mansion and eat some really good pasta, San Marco is the ticket. For *tapas* bars and after dinner drinks head for the narrow streets, small squares and flower-bedecked balconies of the Santa Cruz district, the old Jewish quarter.

In the south, the Mediterranean may beckon. While most of the Costa del Sol should be avoided, **Marbella** is an exception, offering comfort, style and fun. Swanky places to stay are the Don Carlos or Los Monteros; if you prefer a ranch-style hotel with a fine tropical garden, try the Marbella Club. For the ultimate in luxury in a country setting, stay among the arabesques, pools and gardens of the Byblos Andaluz near Mijas. This hotel has the added attraction of its own golf course. For eating, drinking and nightclubbing, head for nearby Puerto Banus, Spain's ritziest yachting marina. The San Roque Club in Sotogrande, not far from Gibraltar, attracts royalty and world leaders, who you're most likely to bump into on the hotel's private 18-hole championship golf course, which seems to be de rigueur for luxury hotels around this part of the world. Don't worry, the sea is close at hand as well. For a graceful taste of sixteenth-century indulgence in inland Andalucía, you can't do much better than the Casa de Carmona, near

Sevilla, a lavishly restored palace in a small and atmospheric walled Andalusian town.

When in northern Spain, don't miss **Donostia-San Sebastián**, the classy seaside resort whose history is inextricably linked with royalty, the wealthy and the famous. Here you can combine a great hotel (the María Cristina) with gourmet eating (try Arzak, Spain's best restaurant, according to some experts), an animated nightlife (in La Parte Vieja, the picturesque old quarter) with the bonus of marvellous beaches.

Finally, for those who find it difficult to burn through money quickly enough in Spain, there are also **casinos** in Villajoyosa (Alicante), Ibiza and Calviá (Balearics), San Pedro de Ribes (Barcelona), El Puerto de Santa María (Cádiz), Santander, Ceuta, Corunna, Prerelada and Lloret del Mar (Girona), San Sebastián, Torrelodones (Madrid), Puerto Banus and Benalmádena Costa (Málaga), La Manga del Mar Menor and Murcia (Murcia), Puzol (Valencia), Bilbao and Alfajárin (Zaragoza).

Family Fun

Spaniards love children. A truism perhaps, but noticeable wherever you go. Never hesitate to take your children into a hotel, restaurant or bar. They will not only be welcomed but, very likely, pampered. Spanish kids stay up late, like their parents, so your children will be in good company if your family is eating out late.

"*Vamos a la playa*" ("Let's go to the beach") is a popular children's summer song in Spain, and the sea is clearly the best place to head for if you are traveling with your children. Apart from swimming, building sandcastles and chasing each other over piles of moribund, oil-drenched roasting flesh, children now have many other diversions down at the beach. Most resorts have pedal boats, windsurfing boards and small sailboats for rent. Spains beach resorts also offer **coastal excursions** in cruise boats — some with glass bottoms — and quite often have aquatic theme parks with exciting water slides and shoots.

Museums, art galleries and churches always pose a problem for the traveling family. While a certain amount of force-fed cultural sightseeing is no doubt good for the children, you can sweeten the pill by looking for things that might interest them more. Madrid and Barcelona both have new and fascinating **aquariums** housing a huge number of species, ranging from angel fish to rays and sharks. Madrid's aquarium is in a futuristic pyramid-shaped building in the **Casa de Campo Zoo**

and Barcelona's is down in the old renovated **Port Vell**. Look out too for performing dolphins and seals. The Madrid Zoo has regular dolphin shows, and if you happen to be in Mallorca in the Balearic Islands, there is a place called **Marineland**, just outside Palma, that puts on daily dolphin, seal and parrot shows throughout the summer.

In your cultural sightseeing, castles, moats, drawbridges and dungeons usually appeal to children. So does armor. When in Madrid, bear in mind the **Armería Real** (Royal Armory) in the **Palacio Real**, where there are enough mounted knights, lances, swords and crossbows to stage a small battle. There are even models of children — royal princes — clad in armor, not to mention one monarch's favorite dog similarly attired.

In Barcelona, try the **Museu Marítim** (Martime Museum), just across from Columbus's column near the port. Apart from artifacts demonstrating a wide range of shipbuilding techniques through the centuries, there is a virtual reality show that puts you on a galley during the Battle of Lepanto, tosses you through a Caribbean storm in a Spanish sailing ship, and plunges you down under the sea in a submarine.

PORT AVENTURA

France may have Disneyland Europe, but Spain has Port Aventura. Opened in 1995, this US$500 million theme park at Salou on the Costa Daurada, 10 km (six miles) south of Tarragona, managed to pull in 2.7 million visitors during its first season. With none of the fanfare that greeted Disney — and far fewer problems — Spain's answer to Donald Duck and Mickey Mouse has been a huge success.

About the same size as Disneyland Paris, Port Aventura, whose principal shareholder and manager is the British Tussauds Group, is a mixture of worlds and rides. There are five different lands, all with a special theme: Mediterranea, where you set off by boat, steam train or by foot for the other lands; China, with its recreation of the imperial city; Polynesia, a series of islands linked by bridges and covered with dense vegetation and an active volcano; The Wild West, a recreated cow-punchers' town called Penitence; and Mexico, featuring elements of Mayan and colonial Mexico. Each area has restaurants, bars, shops and craft centers selling food, drinks and artifacts of the country. Shows, including dancers from the Polynesian islands, Chinese acrobats and a Western stunt show, are presented in air-conditioned theaters at regular intervals throughout the day.

OPPOSITE: La Almoraima Hotel, set in the midst of an extensive plantation of cork trees and cattle ranchland, where the experience of living in one of Spain's largest agricultural estates is an added element to a night of luxury accommodation. ABOVE: Barcelona's aquarium fascinates visitors of all ages. Here vivid displays showcase the beauties and wonders of ocean life in one of Spain's most sophisticated cities.

The main attractions, however, are the rides. The most popular is also the most terrifying. This is the Dragon Khan roller coaster, Europe's largest and scariest, which takes its riders up to a height of 45 m (147 ft) and then, at speeds reaching 110 km/h (66 mph), hurls them up and down over a distance of one and a quarter kilometers (just over three quarters of a mile), turning them completely upside down no fewer than eight times. There are also water rides where you get very wet, and gentler affairs for young children; such as canoeing, mechanical ponies on a special track, log-riding on a small river, carousels and bumper cars.

Port Aventura is open from the end of March to the end of October. There is parking for 6,000 cars and 250 buses and a special area for motorbikes and disabled drivers. The theme park is just off the A-7 coastal highway, which connects it with Barcelona and France to the north and Valencia to the south. Entry for the day is €28.85 for adults, with reductions for children and pensioners; for more information, contact Port Aventura TOLL-FREE 0800 966540 WEB SITE www.portaventura.es.

Cultural Kicks

One of the great gifts of Spain is that its cultural riches remain highly visible and accessible. Prehistoric artifacts can be seen from the roadside; architectural masterpieces from half a dozen eras look little different from the day they were built; the visitor is overwhelmed with the works of Spanish painters in Madrid's Museo del Prado, or made to feel part of the painter's entourage in Salvador Dalí's extraordinary gallery-mausoleum in Figueres; the routine pageantry of the bullfight plunges you into the eighteenth century; the anguished sound of flamenco's *cante jondo* and the click of the castanets have hardly changed over the centuries; most of Spain's best novelists, poets and playwrights have been widely translated; domestic architecture, especially in the south, has altered little, preserving the Moors' love for patios, balconies, flowers, and fountains; and the makers of pottery and ceramics continue to follow ancient Moorish and Christian designs.

Spain is a country of great buildings. There are more **Roman architectural remains** in Spain than in any other country in the world apart from Italy. There are aqueducts in Segovia, Tarragona and Mérida; bridges in Salamanca, Córdoba and Alcantará (Cáceres); magnificent city walls in Lugo (Galicia); and theaters in Sagunto (Valencia), Mérida, Tarragona and Itálica (Sevilla).

THE MOORISH MASTERPIECES

The architectural achievements of the Moors in the south ran parallel with those of the Christian kingdoms in the north. The Moorish contribution came in three phases. During the eighth and eleventh centuries, the caliphate of Córdoba produced the unique **Mezquita** (mosque), the **Alcázar** (a fortress-palace) and other buildings in a classic Moorish style with double horseshoe-shaped arches, rectangular patios and rich geometric and calligraphic ornamentation.

The second period of Moorish architecture began with the arrival of the Almoravids and Almohads in the eleventh and early twelfth century. After an initial period of mayhem they settled down and over the next two centuries built mosques and other structures in a more austere style, using brick and glazed tiles *(azulejos)*, favoring pointed arches over the traditional horseshoe kind and carved wooden coffered ceilings. Sevilla, notably the **Giralda** and the **Alcázar**, has good examples of this legacy.

The third and greatest expression of Moorish creativity came with the Nasrid dynasty in Granada between the fourteenth and fifteenth centuries. Granada was the last of the Moorish kingdoms to survive as the *Reconquista* swept south. But the Nasrids did not seem to be too worried about their gradual encirclement because the **Alhambra** was clearly built with comfort, elegance and leisurely pursuits in mind. Or perhaps it was because it was built behind huge stone ramparts that they felt they could leave aside the matter of security. The result is an architectural marvel, miraculously intact, that combines the use of space, light and shade, wood, brick, plaster and tiles, and trees, shrubs and flowers in an unmatched way.

CHURCHES OF NORTHERN SPAIN

The Romanesque style flourished in northern Christian Spain between the eleventh and thirteenth centuries, producing somber stone churches and monasteries with rounded arches, tall square towers and sparse ornamentation. **Catalunya** and the **Pyrenean valleys** have many examples of the earlier Romanesque churches, which tended to be small, while **Segovia** and **Zamora** have larger churches from the later period. The grandest of all, disguised by a much later, baroque, façade, is the **cathedral in Santiago de Compostela**. Ávila's famous city walls also date from this time.

The Arab and European influences produced a unique Spanish style of building and design known as "Mudéjar," which was developed by Moorish architects, craftsmen and builders working under Christian rule

after the Reconquest. Using brick and tile and preserving geometric patterns and designs, Mudéjar work can be seen all over Spain. But it is particularly striking in the **Alcázar in Sevilla**, in the two surviving **synagogues in Toledo**, and in the towers of the older of the two **cathedrals in Zaragoza**.

During the thirteenth century, Spain discovered the joy of Gothic architecture, introduced from France. Taller naves, flying buttresses, pointed or ogival arches instead of round ones, more elaborate carving and ornament, larger and larger stained glass windows and a growing sense of confidence — even exuberance — characterized the new style. The cathedrals of **Burgos** and **León**, followed by **Toledo**, are the best examples. In Catalunya and Mallorca, a variation developed with a single, towering nave and wooden vaulting. The cathedrals in **Barcelona**, **Girona** and **Palma** are good examples.

The Gothic style became more ornate and unrestrained in the sixteenth century, as Spain entered its "Golden Age," although the structural elements of Gothic buildings remained relatively unchanged, becoming, if anything, more austere under Felipe II. His palace-monastery-mausoleum, **El Escorial**, reflected this tendency. But when it came to the surfaces of the buildings it was a different matter. Virtually every nook and cranny, every available flat surface, became a designer's drawing-board, a craftsman's workbench, an artist's palate. The heavily carved stone surfaces in the interior and on the façades of so many Spanish churches, which you will see as you travel around the country, derive from this period. The style came to be known as "plateresque" because the carving resembled work done by silversmiths *(plateros)*.

In the seventeenth and eighteenth centuries, baroque arrived and soon took a peculiarly Spanish twist as the Churriguera brothers (Alberto and Joaquín) introduced an even more lavish style of carving and decoration that became known as "Churrigueresque." This was the great era of new and fanciful façades being put on old churches and cathedrals, and of the building of some of Spain's finest squares and city halls. Good examples are the Obradoiro façade on the cathedral in **Santiago de Compostela**, the façade of **Granada**'s cathedral, and the lovely Plaza Mayor in **Salamanca**.

As one of Barcelona's most accomplished avant-garde artists, Joan Miró has left his trace throughout the city. His pavement mosaics decorate La Rambla and a ceramic mural dominates the airport. Shown here is one of his greatest works, *Woman and Bird*, a landmark sculpture in the Parc Joan Miró.

While the early Bourbons indulged themselves in the baroque, Carlos III, the monarch who nudged Spain into the Age of Enlightenment in the latter part of the eighteenth century, turned to classical Greece and Rome for inspiration. His Neoclassical legacy can be seen best in Madrid in buildings such as the **Museo del Prado**, the **Alcalá arch**, and the **Cibeles fountain**. This, in turn, led to another revival with the Neomudéjar architecture of the nineteenth century, which is reflected in many of the country's brick-built churches, railway stations and bullrings.

The end of the nineteenth century brought Modernism and the genius of Antonio Gaudí, whose flowing lines, plant motifs, and organic use of stone and wrought iron left an indelible mark on the urban landscape. **Barcelona** provides a rich panorama of the work of Gaudí and his disciples, from the houses in the center of the city to the Parc Güell, to the Temple of the Holy Family (**El Templo de la Sagrada Familia**), his unfinished masterpiece. In the modern era, it tends to be concrete and reinforced steel that captures Spanish architects' imagination as they tumble over each to construct new highways, dams, tunnels and high-rise office and apartment blocks, with notable new structures including the Guggenheim in Bilbao.

THE VISUAL ARTS

It is said that the quality of the light in Spain made it inevitable that the country would produce remarkable painters, probably even helping to inspire the Paleolithic painters of the Altamira Caves in Cantabria.

The necessary skills were nurtured by the all-important religion of the day, with painters and sculptors working hand-in-hand with the church or the mosque during the medieval period. A careful look around any major church or monastery in Spain usually reveals carvings and paintings, barely credited or recognized, but often of sublime beauty. In the cathedral in Santiago de Compostela, the work of **Mateo**, the master carver, is a special feature; **Juan Guas**'s imprint is on the church of San Juan de los Reyes in Toledo; **Gil de Siloé** was responsible for much of the fine carving in Burgos cathedral and **Alonso Cano** produced the façade of Granada cathedral.

From the sixteenth century onwards each century was dominated by a master painter. Domenikos Theotokopoulos — El Greco — who spent much of his life in Toledo, was the first, followed by **Diego Velázquez** in the seventeenth century, **Francisco de Goya** in the nineteenth and **Pablo Picasso** in the twentieth. The Prado is full of works by the first three and another museum in Madrid displays Picasso's *Guernica*, his terrifying depiction of the aerial bombardment of the Basque town of that name in the Civil War.

There are several other painters whose work is worth keeping in mind when traveling in Spain. **Zubarán**, **Murillo** and **Valdes Leal**

Shop till You Drop

After the isolation of the Franco years, Spain's growing integration into Europe rapidly expanded its shopping horizons. **Shopping malls** arrived and are now found in all the major cities; they tend to include major design outlets as well as the ubiquitous chain stores. Madrid, for example, has an extremely elegant one called the **Serrano ABC**, in an old building in the Salamanca district (it has entrances on Calle Serrano and the Castellano), where all the main Spanish and international stores are located. Spain's largest department store, **El Corte Inglés**, has swallowed up its main rival, Galerias Preciados, and expanded its operations accordingly. It has also become more sophisticated; customers can wait in a *tapas* bar in the men's clothing section if they become bored. Most of the branches are huge and comprehensive, selling everything from toothbrushes to motorcycles, with a cool, upmarket atmosphere: great for a serious browse.

Zara, a phenomenally successful Spanish **clothing** chain (for men and women), is reasonably priced with a fast turnover of the latest fashions. Sybilla purveys expensive and stylish women's clothes, and Sebastién Bachiller is a good place to buy **shoes**, **handbags** and **luggage**. The Loewe group, all over Spain, specializes in high quality **leather goods** in the luxury range.

If you are looking for indigenous Spanish **arts and crafts**, a good place to start is at the Artespaña shops, which are located in the major centers and stock a broad selection of furniture, fabrics, pottery, ceramics, glass and rugs — all reflecting traditional Spanish designs and manufacture. These government-sponsored cooperatives are designed to preserve traditional craft skills and sell the products. In Barcelona, the Artespana is at Rambla Catalunya 75; in Bilbao it is on Colón de Larreatgui; in Cáceres on San Antoni 17; in Granada, Corral de Carbon; in Marbella Ricardo Soriano 54; in Sevilla Rodríguez Jurado 4; and Madrid has four outlets: Gran Vía 32, Ramón de la Cruz 33, Hermosilla 14, Plaza de las Cortés 3.

from the Sevilla school in the seventeenth century produced a number of religious and other paintings of merit. Jumping to the last century, there is a **Joan Miró** museum in Barcelona and a **Salvador Dalí** museum in Figueres, both worth a detour.

As a result, for those interested in art, Spain is a treasure-trove. There's El Greco's House in Toledo, the Dalí Museum in Figueres, and, of course, the artistic heart of the country in Madrid: with the triangle of the Prado Museum, packed with old masters, the Palacio Villahermosa with the world's largest private art collection, and the contemporary art of the Reina Sofía. The new kid on the block is Bilbao's Guggenheim Museum, an unparalleled collection set in a building that is, itself, half the attraction.

MUSIC AND DANCE

Music in Spain extends well beyond the headline attraction of flamenco. Unfortunately, the enthusiastic adoption of folk traditions by the Franco regime did much to undermine the credibility of regional music traditions, and only in the last few years have regional sounds undergone a dramatic revival. The *muiñera* in Galicia, the *zorziko* in the Basque regions and the *sardana* in Catalunya are all dances particular to each area that resonate, respectively, with the styles of bagpipes, accordions and salsa rhythms. Specialist late-night music venues can be hard to find, and the best way of enjoying each region's particular sound is at the exuberant festivals laid on by towns and communities. There will always be plenty of musicians around and it is just a matter of listening for that distinctive sound that cuts through the ubiquitous electronic sounds of more common dance music.

OPPOSITE: Picasso's famous painting, *Guernica*, brought the horrors of the Spanish Civil War to his own generation and still resonates today.
ABOVE: Barcelona has a lively interest in the arts both current and past. Here a busy antique market seethes with activity.

The best place for traditional artifacts, however, is at the spot where they are made. There is an enormous amount of junky tourist stuff for sale in places like Toledo (swords, armor, daggers, etc.) and in coastal resorts (silly straw hats, phony bullfight posters where you can have your name inscribed alongside Paco Romero and El Cordobés, and cheap castanets). But there are also good things, traditional and modern, if you are patient and prepared to look. **Leather goods** are well known, if no longer the bargain they once were, and there is a huge selection of fine leather products at the upscale Loewe stores and other more modestly priced shops.

Fine (and famous) **glass and crystal** are sold at source in La Granja, near Segovia; good hunting, hiking and riding **boots** in Salamanca, Sevilla and Córdoba (home of the famous flat, black Spanish hat); handmade **furniture fabric** in Almería and Mallorca; jet jewelry and brightly colored traditional **bedspreads and rugs** (*tenederías*) in Galicia; and Spain's best **tiles** in Valencia, which has a fascinating museum devoted to the craft. Mallorca specializes in **cultured pearls** and Navarra in **wineskins**.

Shops generally open at 10 AM, close for lunch at 1:30 PM or 2 PM, and reopen from 4 PM or 5 PM until about 8 PM or later in tourist areas. (Banks run a tighter ship, with opening hours from 9 AM to 1:30 PM and 3 to 5 PM.)

Short Breaks

The ready welcome of Spain's sociable culture and good internal communications are ideal conditions for a short break: almost any of the towns featured in the touring chapters would reward a stay even of a single night.

To stretch the experience further, it is possible, even over a few days, to link two rather different Spanish experiences that can be sampled within a brief period of time — a day or two. **Madrid** is the city best served by international scheduled flights, and its vibrant café culture can make the most out of a short break. A rental car and an hour on the road, or even a short journey by rail or bus, will get you out to **Toledo**, **Segovia** or **Ávila**, which have the advantage of being smaller towns and easy to explore in a limited time. This means a short break can include the famous art galleries of Madrid, followed by a sleepless night exploring the city's infamous nightlife, which can in turn be followed by a quieter immersion amongst the time-honored cathedrals and museums of these provincial highlights.

Relaxing in Mallorca.

Sevilla is the natural hub of Andalucía and is a good base for a short break in Spain. The city doesn't see too many foreign visitors and is all the more welcoming for it. One of the first cities to be colonized by the Moors, this retains a strongly Moorish feel and many of the buildings are classic examples of Almohad architecture at its best. Once there, an excellent excursion is to take the E-25 highway or the train to **Córdoba** (about an hour and a half travel time), pace the Córdoba sightseeing with a leisurely lunch, and return to Sevilla in the evening. Another pleasant trip is to go south on the A-4, or again by train (less than an hour), to Jerez and from there, if you have a car, drive north to **Sanlúcar de Barrameda**, a delightful place to have a fresh fish lunch in a beach restaurant, accompanied by the local Manzanilla, a delicate sherry-style wine that can be drunk throughout the meal.

Barcelona is perhaps Spain's most popular destination for a short break. There are galleries and bars aplenty, a thriving street culture and one of the most atmospheric and rewarding city centers in Europe. Strolling down La Rambla and the narrow alleys of the old town is enough for many short-break visitors, though Gaudí's great cathedral and modernist constructions are irresistible, lighthearted cultural sights. Two forays from the city are particularly appealing. The first is to the famous mountaintop monastery of **Montserrat**. In a spectacular setting it is the home of the Black Virgin, Catalunya's miracle-working national icon. The second is to go south along the coast to the elegant, slightly faded town of **Sitges**, the ideal spot for a day's outing when you are a bit faded yourself. Sitges is distinguished by a fine palm-fringed esplanade, civilized beaches and rather grand turn-of-the-twentieth-century houses. Both Montserrat and Sitges can be reached within an hour of Barcelona.

Bilbao is also well served by scheduled flights, opening up the possibility of spending a day immersed in the Guggenheim Museum before driving out to spend some time on the beach before a night out in the carnival atmosphere of a Spanish beach resort. Head west, and **Castro-Urdiales** is a great place for a *tapas* tour of the old town, or east and **Donostia-San Sebastián** is an elegant coastal resort. If you want to fit in some tanning time here, check the weather forecast, as the hills of this region don't stay green without rain.

If the beach is your priority, it is safest to head south. There are plenty of resorts within an hour or less of the airports of **Alicante**, **Almería** and **Málaga** as well as the Balearic Islands, of which the three main islands are **Mallorca**,

Menorca and **Ibiza**. All attractive and different, these beach-focused destinations are ideal for families. Here a dash of Spanish culture comes as a bonus to some time spent tanning and swimming in the sea. They do richly reward even a short visit, with a rental car helping to explore quickly and conveniently.

Festive Flings

Festivals never really stop in Spain. There are literally thousands of them and the calendar is full throughout the year. Most of them celebrate religious events and saints, although often building on pagan antecedents. Many semi-religious processions visibly celebrate battles against the Moors and other invaders. Others are sparked by wine and other harvests and always involve a hearty consumption of everything found behind the bar, and a significant proportion mark the culmination of lengthy pilgrimages: always best if you participate in the journey as well as the — often riotous — conclusion.

A few of the most famous festival are: Sevilla's Semana Santa and Feria de Abril (April Fair); Pamplona's San Fermín running of the bulls bash, which celebrates the city's bishop-saint who was killed by one of the animals; and the pilgrimage to Santiago, which ends in a celebratory mass at the saint's shrine in Santiago's cavernous cathedral. Other major fiestas include: the fiery Fallas in Valencia; Madrid's San Isidro; the grape harvest festival in Jerez de la Frontera in September; and the Rocío pilgrimage in Huelva, near Sevilla.

Spanish festivals, large or small, famous or obscure, have two things in common. First, they are authentic Spanish entertainments, mounted neither for the tourist trade nor for commercial gain. Second, everyone is welcome; most of them take place in the streets with processions, bands and floats but they rapidly become participatory events for the general public.

Here is a sampling of fiestas, which is not exhaustive but will give you a good idea of what is on offer. Spanish tourist offices will be able to give you a comprehensive list, with exact dates for the current year, as well as more background information.

WINTER
If you happen to be in Spain over the Christmas holidays look out for three events. **Christmas Eve (La Noche Buena)** is a time for family

In Pamplona, the Parade of the Giants is a dramatic and theatrical procession that blends religion and celebration.

reunions, with midnight mass in the cathedral or local church and a large dinner afterwards. Spaniards celebrate **New Year's Eve (La Noche Vieja)** with gusto, and pop a grape in their mouths on every stroke of the midnight chimes. Epiphany (January 6) is the feast of the **Three Kings (Los Tres Magos)**, which is celebrated on the night of January 5. Three people are decked up as the kings who brought gold, frankincense and myrrh to the manger in Bethlehem. The kings usually ride on horses or donkeys and have an impressive entourage. In some places, like the Balearic Islands, they arrive by boat. This is a great favorite with children, who are given presents by the "kings" in a church or town hall.

In January come the festivals of **San Antonio** (16th) and **San Sebastián** (20th), occasions for processions, bonfires, folk music and dancing.

In February there are mock battles between Moors and Christians — a common feature of many Spanish festivals — at **Bocairente**, near Valencia.

It is **carnival** time in many towns and villages just before Lent. Cádiz has the oldest and probably the best carnival in the country, but many other towns have a last fling before the Lenten shutdown. One of the most curious carnivals occurs in Villanueva de la Vera (Cáceres province) in Extremadura. A gigantic wooden figure in a dark suit and black hat is carried through the streets and then beaten, beheaded and buried as part of some ancient, almost certainly pagan, ritual. At the other end of the spectrum is urbane **Sitges**, the fashionable and heavily gay seaside resort south of Barcelona. Sitges celebrates its carnival with an antique car rally.

Valencia's famous **Fallas** begin on March 12 and reach their incandescent climax a week later on the night of **San José**. That is when the elaborate floats, which have been circulating through the streets all week, are burnt in a series of vast bonfires. Firework displays add to the din as night becomes day, bands strike up and virtually the entire population pours out into the streets.

SPRING

Semana Santa (Holy Week) in Sevilla opens the festive season and is replicated in many towns, on a lesser but still fervent scale, around the country. While the basic format of processions, penitents, Christs and Virgins swaying above the crowds, accompanied by chanting, hymn singing and the thud of

A colorful parade past the chapel of the Virgin during the El Rocío pilgrimage.

drums, does not greatly vary, each town or province imparts its own flavor. Málaga's Holy Week is also impressive but, as a rule, the celebrations become more austere and religious as you move northwards, the most stark being in the towns of Old Castilla, notably Valladolid and Zamora.

What they all have in common is that many of the penitents — accountants, lawyers, clerks and bus-drivers in real life — submit themselves to flagellation and other mortifications of the flesh. For the onlooker this is probably the fastest way of understanding what life must have been like back in the Middle Ages.

After the agony, the joy. Sevilla's **Feria de Abril (April Fair)** is the grand catharsis. Jerez's **Feria del Caballo (Horse Fair)** in early May is a wonderful spectacle, especially if you like fine horses. There are many festivals around the country at this time as Spaniards celebrate the rites of spring that have little to do with Christianity.

Whitsun, or Pentecost (60 days after Easter), brings the unique **Rocío Pilgrimage** (its full name is Romería de Nuestra Señora del Rocío, or "Pilgrimage of Our Lady of the Dew"): the slow progress of pilgrims from all over Spain, and beyond, through the lovely countryside of the Parque Nacional de Doñana, west of Sevilla in Huelva Province. The pilgrimage draws Spaniards from all walks of life and can take as long as two weeks, depending on which method of transportation the pilgrim chooses. The slow,

serious way to go is by horse or mule-drawn covered wagon with plenty of stops in shady copses to eat, drink, sing, dance and get to know your fellow pilgrims.

Madrid celebrates its patron saint, San Isidro, in the second week of May, also a good time, climatically, to visit the Spanish capital. Drama, music, sporting events and the best bullfights of the season take place during the **Feria de San Isidro**. The feast of **Corpus Christi**, which usually falls at the end of May, is next and is celebrated all over Spain with religious processions which move solemnly through streets over carpets of freshly-cut hay, straw or flowers, with the host carried in the center by a senior member of the clergy, and groups of robed monks, nuns and choirboys singing traditional hymns. Sevilla, again, adds the grace note. Young choirboys, called *seises*, dressed in sixteenth-century costume, sing and dance in front of the host on the high altar in the cathedral.

SUMMER

In June come two important saints' days: **San Juan** on the 24th and **San Pedro** and **San Pablo** on the 29th. Many towns hold local fiestas to celebrate their adopted saint, for example Ciutadella, to celebrate San Juan, offers brilliantly accoutered horses that dance to music and resist the attempts of the youth of the town to unseat their riders.

In July, Pamplona, in Navarra, celebrates its martyred bishop, **San Fermín**, with the

running of the bulls during the second week of the month. On Saint James Day (July 25), Santiago de Compostela, in Galicia, greets the tens of thousands who have made the long pilgrimage.

FALL

This is the time of the **wine festivals** *(vendimias)* in Jerez (Andalucía), Valdepeñas (La Mancha), Penedés (Catalunya), Rioja (Old Castilla) and other wine-producing regions. Zaragoza, the capital of Aragón, celebrates its local Virgin with the **Fiesta de Virgen del Pilar** (Virgin of the Pillar) on October 12, a deeply religious event where locals wear traditional dress and elaborate floral displays are followed by lively dancing of the *jota*, Aragón's best-known folk dance; this is also a national holiday.

Galloping Gourmet

There was a time when Spanish food and drink was associated in the foreign mind with *paella* and plonk, and not much else. No longer. The variety of Spanish cuisine, especially its regional diversity, and the renown of Spanish wines have spread far and wide. You may still eat poorly in Spain — that happens everywhere, including France — but you will not be bored and, if you keep your eyes and mind open, you are in for a gastronomic treat.

Before starting a quick regional tour, a few general points. Spaniards eat late, very late.

Hotels usually serve breakfast from 8 AM to 10:30 AM (a generous self-service, buffet-style spread is becoming more and more common, following the lead of the Paradors); lunch runs from 1:30 PM to 4 PM; and dinner starts at 9 PM and goes on until 11:30 PM (later in many restaurants).

Most restaurants serve excellent hors d'oeuvres (*entremeses*), fresh salads and tasty, sustaining sandwiches. **Tapas**, a Spanish gastronomic invention, can be taken as pre-prandial snacks, or serve as a complete meal. And when it comes to tasting, the Spanish tradition of *tapas* makes sampling a huge range of flavors in a short time easy and convenient. The origin of the word *tapas*, meaning a cover, dates from the time when innkeepers would place a slice of ham, pie, or omelet on top of the traveler's drink when it was served. They double as tasty snacks to accompany your dry sherry (*fino*), glass of wine (*vaso de vino tinto*, *rosado* or *blanco*), or draught beer (*un caña*) beer, or serve as a convenient and unusual meal.

For many Spaniards, the local bar is an institution where business is done, friends are met, and the barman becomes a confidant-confessor. And *tapas* are an integral part of that institution. There is in an infinite variety of dishes but some of the more common offerings include: *albondigas* (meat balls in a rich sauce); *boquerones* (fresh anchovies); *croquetas* (meat, fish, potatoes, dipped in bread crumbs and fried); *calamares* (squid); *riñones* (kidneys);

OPPOSITE: Córdoba's May fiesta brings all ages together in an affirmation of the regional culture. ABOVE: Street musicians and dancers come together to celebrate a local saint's festival in the Sevilla region, bringing a swirling cascade of color to the sunbaked summer streets. BELOW: *Zarzuela de marisco* is a traditional delicacy.

tortilla española (Spanish omelet — eggs and potatoes — no onions or pimento in the authentic version); *higado* (small pieces of liver cooked in sherry); *jamón serrano* (cured ham); and *empanadillas* (small pies filled with meat, fish or vegetables).

You can order by the dish (*una ración*) or, if you would like to sample a selection, ask for *un plato combinado*. Bar hopping for *tapas* is a pleasant and relatively economical way of spending an evening in somewhere like Madrid, Barcelona, Sevilla or, indeed, in any large city. Just cruise from bar to bar, sampling the *tapas* and the atmosphere. There is nothing forced, phony or exorbitant about these places and you will find yourself in good company — Spanish company.

In restaurants, remember to check out the fixed-price special (*menú del día*). (All restaurants, modest or grand, are required by law to provide one.) They consist of three or four courses, with wine and bread included, and are invariably excellent value, especially for travelers on a tight budget.

In **Andalucía**, don't miss *gazpacho*, that refreshing cold soup of tomato, cucumber, onion, garlic and olive oil; *pescado frito*, mixed fish lightly fried; and *ajoblanco*, another cold soup of crushed almonds and garlic served with muscatel grapes. Spain's best *jamón serrano* (Parma-style country cured ham), comes from Jabugo in Huelva province, and Andalucía offers a wide variety of pastries and confectionery, derived from its Moorish past.

The Spanish heartland — **Old and New Castilla** — is the home of rich soups (*sopas*) and stews (*estafados*), of roast suckling pig (*cochonillo*), lamb (*cordero*) and other meat, of game and of meat and vegetable pies (*empanadas or empanadillas*). If you like pulses, this is the place: chickpeas (*garbanzos*), lentils (*lentejas*), white beans (*alubias*). They are usually cooked in a meat broth with slices of spicy sausage (*chorizo*). Castilla is also the land of bread — Spanish bread rivals French bread for the title of best in the world.

Northwest Spain — Asturias, the Basque country and Galicia — is noted for its fish, especially tuna (*bonito*), squid (*chipirones*), baby eels (*angulas*) and salt cod (*bacalao*). **Asturias** is well known for a flavorful fish stew called *caldereta* and for an interesting way of cooking hake with apple cider (*merluza a la sidra*). Away from the coast, *fabada*, a tasty stew made from white beans cooked slowly with pork and piquant sausage, is the Asturian equivalent of the French *cassoulet*.

Galician and **Basque** cuisine are generally thought to be the best in Spain. Galicia spells fish in all its myriad forms from oysters,

scallops and mussels to sole, turbot and salmon. The region is also famous for its ham hocks and turnip greens (*lacón con grelos*), large savory pies (*empanadas*) and, in the dessert department, its pancakes (*filloas*) and ground almond tart (*tarta de Santiago*).

The Basques are also great cooks and are renowned for their imaginative skills with that plain Jane of the sea — cod, specifically salt cod (*bacalao*) — extremely tasty cooked in olive oil with sweet peppers and garlic. Try *bacalao a la vizcaina*, a cod casserole with

sweet peppers, cured ham and egg yolk or, if you prefer a spicier version, *bacalao a la bilbaina*. Another tasty fish dish is *marmitako*, a stew of tuna, tomatoes and potatoes. A typical Basque dessert is *canutillos de crema*, puff pastry filled with custard and dusted with icing sugar and cinnamon.

Catalunya is also gastronomically rich. A specialty is combining fruit with fowl and game, such as baby goose with pears (*oca con peras*), duck with apples and figs (*pato con manzanas e higos*), and hare with chestnuts (*liebre con castañas*). If you fancy a seafood mixed grill try *zarzuela de mariscos* and for something heartier, *escudella de pagés* (a bean, rice and noodle stew with spicy sausage and vegetables).

Finally, to the **Levante** (Valencia and Murcia), where home-grown rice, fish, chicken, rabbit, peppers, olive oil and saffron all come together in the large open pan that has given its name to Spain's national dish — *paella*. There are many versions of *paella* (seafood, meat and game, eels, etc) and some interesting spin-offs. *Arroz marinera*, for example, is a delicious and filling fish soup with rice that can be a meal in itself. *Paella* should be cooked

rosé and white wines, as well as all sorts of sherries, brandies and local liqueurs.

There are 31 official wine-making areas in the government-controlled system of *"Denominación de Origen"*; each bottle of wine has its place of origin marked on it. You will also be able to check the vintage by the harvest date ("*Cosecha* 1992", for example) and the aging process. "*Vino de Crianza*" means that the wine has been in the barrel and bottle for at least two years, usually a year in each; "*Reserva*" means three years of maturing; and

while you wait (between 20 and 40 minutes); beware of promises of anything faster, it won't be the real thing. It is worth waiting for (try to not eat anything before it comes) — a dish of culinary beauty in its broad, blackened pan, and a joy to eat.

Mention **wine** in Spain and most people will think of sherry and Rioja. But Spanish wines are much more varied than that. From the green hills of Galicia to the sun-drenched vineyards of Andalucía, and from the rolling plains of Extremadura to the stony fields of Mallorca, grapes are grown and wine is produced. Look in any supermarket in Spain and you will find a huge range of Spanish red,

"*Gran Reserva*" indicates at least two years in the barrel and three in the bottle before consumption. Less matured wines will be marked "*Vino de Mesa*" (table wine) but normally their region will be also marked with the phrase, "*Guarantia de Origen*."

While Andalucía is famous for traditional sherry, its other sherry-related wines should not be overlooked. Manzanilla from Sanlúcar

The Spanish tradition of *tapas*, small saucers of culinary delicacies are served alongside local drinks, is an essential part of an evening out. Here the Bar Juanito in Jerez de la Frontera serves a sizzling selection.

de Barrameda and Montilla-Moriles from Córdoba are lighter than Jerez's wines and have the advantage of being drinkable throughout a meal, especially with fish.

La Mancha is Europe's largest wine-growing region. Its best known wine is the light red Clarete of Valdepeñas, which is drunk all over Spain; a finer red, with a stronger bouquet and flavor, comes from Almansa in the east of the region.

Catalunya has several important wine-producing areas. Alella, a pleasant light white wine in a tall, slender Hock-style bottle, comes from north of Barcelona; Penedés, to the south, produces the Cavas (sparkling white wine) and some strong, fruity reds of which Torres's Sangre de Toro is the best known; and Priorato, in the Tarragona area, also turns out some fine red wine, almost purple in color.

Moving west, Rioja is familiar to most people, especially the reds. But don't neglect the whites; Marqués de Cáceres, in the more expensive price range, is excellent, and lower down, El Coto resembles a French Loire wine — light, fruity and with a wonderful bouquet. Just south of Rioja, along the Duero river, is a relatively new wine area that produces some of Spain's finest vintages, of which the Vega de Sicilia reds are the most famous.

Aragón is a developing area with its strong reds (Cariñena) and Beaujolais-style lighter reds (Campo de Borja); Navarra is also a wine-producer, similar to Rioja but not as sophisticated; the Basque Country makes a light, slightly bubbly "green" wine called Txacolis, and Galicia is the home of two fresh white wines (Albariños and Ribeiros) which are also slightly fizzy.

Spanish **beer** is also good, especially the draft beer. The best brand is a matter of taste, but my preferences are Estrella Dorada in central and northern Spain and the rich, creamy Cruzcampo of Andalucía. And when it comes to **spirits**, watch out: measures are often huge, with barmen pouring as if they're waiting for you to say "enough."

There are plenty of cooling soft drinks in Spain, but good fruit juice is surprisingly rare.

Special Interests

Religious pilgrimages, historic routes, language courses, cookery classes, hunting holidays, mountain trekking, art and literary tours, music festivals and bird-watching trips are amongst those special interests catered to in Spain.

To contact the specialist operators in these fields, your nearest Spanish tourist office will be your best first source. But here are a few suggestions. Salamanca, Spain's oldest university town, holds regular residential courses in the **Spanish language and literature** and Granada is another center for language teaching.

Cultural theme tours are becoming more and more popular. "Roman and Medieval

Iberia," "Prehistoric Cave Art and Ancient Cultures," and "Arab, Jewish and Gothic Art" are some of the cultural offerings in recent years. Two specialist travel agents in the United States are: **Hartours** ((617) 482-0076, 20 Park Plaza, Boston, Massachusetts 02116; **Spanish Heritage Tours** ((718) 520-1300, 116 Queens Boulevard, Forest Hills, New York 11375. In Britain, **Swan Hellenic Art Treasures Tours** ((020) 7247 0401, 47 Canberra House, London E1 7AA, organizes cultural trips to Spain, as well as to Greece.

Hiking and other more vigorous holiday activities have been covered in THE GREAT OUTDOORS and SPORTING SPREE sections, above, but **nature lovers** such as bird, butterfly and garden enthusiasts will be able to find organized tours to suit them. **Ornitholidays** ((01243) 821230, 1–3 Victoria Drive, Bognor Regis, West Sussex PO21 2PW, in Britain, for example, is one of several travel agencies that caters to bird-watchers. For the active, the **Adventure Center** TOLL-FREE (800) 227-8747 WEB SITE www.adventure-center.com, 1311 63rd Street, Suite 200, Emeryville, California 94608, specializing in the Picos, Andalucía and the Sierra Nevada.

If you like **cooking** and want to spend time in Andalucía, **Janet Mendel** (956 248 6210 puts on cooking courses in a country house. An American who has lived in Spain for many years, she has written several books on Spanish cooking and writes a culinary column in the English-language monthly magazine, *Lookout*. Her address is Apartado de Correos 150, 29650 Mijas, Málaga. If you're interested in wine, **Winetrails** ((01306) 712111, Greenways, Vann Lake, Ockley, Dorking EH5 5NT, offers 10-day tours of Navarra, Andalucía and La Rioja.

Spain's monasteries and *conventos* offer an interesting travel variation if you want to absorb at close quarters the country's ecclesiastical architecture and history, if you feel like a religious retreat, or if you simply want to spend time in a relaxed and peaceful environment. Many monasteries have accommodation for guests; some are for men only but a growing number cater to men and women and even children. Accommodation is surprisingly comfortable — central heating, private bathrooms, even elevators — and the food always wholesome and plentiful. To book, call the monastery and ask for the *hospedería* (hostel). The monasteries most accustomed to accepting foreign tourists are on the Camino de Santiago, the pilgrim's route that traverses northern Spain, but there are also spectacular monasteries in Catalunya and Mallorca.

For religious tours, **Pilgrim Adventure** ((0117) 957 3997, 120 Bromley Heath Road, Downend, Bristol BS16 6JJ, are the people to help. There are further specialists for individual interests, including **EC Tours** TOLL-FREE (800) 388-0877 WEB SITE www.ectours .com, 12500 Riverside Drive, Suite 210, Valley Village, California 91607-3423, which runs pilgrimages as well as tours of historic cities and famous wine areas.

Taking a Tour

In a relatively mature travel market such as Spain, taking a tour can not only simplify your travels — it can also save you a great deal of money. This is especially true on the very simplest sort of travel package: the beach break. If you want to stay in a resort hotel, with all the facilities that entails, on a sandy beach then there are plenty of mass-market specialists catering to the British market who will have negotiated discounts you can't hope to meet yourselves. One specialist is **Spain at Heart** ((01373) 814222 FAX (01373) 813444

OPPOSITE: A selection of *tapas* from Asturias, photographed in the Hotel los Lagos in Cangas de Onis. Clockwise from right: a Cabrales cheese; *lacon* from a shoulder of pork; *paté de cabracho*, made from scorpion fish; and *pulpos a la gallega*, octopus Galician style. ABOVE: Sherry is more than a drink in Jerez: it's a passion. The Williams and Humboldt *bodega* brings a sense of drama to Andalucía's most famous export.

WEB SITE www.spainatheart.co.uk, The Barns, Woodlands End, Mells, Frome BA11 3QD, who are also able to organize villas, city center apartments and package travel throughout Andalucía, often at very reasonable prices. For city breaks, try the **Spanish Travel Services** ((020) 7387 5337, 138 Eversholt Street, London NW1; **Time Off** ((0345) 336622, 1 Elmfield Park, Bromley, Kent BR1 1LU; or **Travellers Way** ((01527) 836791 WEB SITE www.travellers way.co.uk, The Barns, Hewell Lane, Tardebigge, Bromsgrove, Worcestershire B60 1LP.

From the United States, the market is perhaps less competitive, but there are still operators who can help without loading the price too much. **Central Holidays** TOLL-FREE (800) 227-5858 WEB SITE www.centralh.com, 120 Sullivan Avenue, Englewood Cliffs, New Jersey 07632, is the United States representative of Iberia's tour department, and can help arrange group and independent travelers. For simple city breaks with car rental facilities, **Delta Vacations** TOLL-FREE (800) 872-7786 WEB SITE www.delta vacations.com, Box 1525, Fort Lauderdale, Florida 33302, will be able to help. For pre-arranged group tours, **Petrabax Tours** TOLL-FREE (800) 634-1188 WEB SITE www.petrabax .com, 9745 Queens Boulevard, Rego Park, New York 11374, does coach tours and set packages.

Traveling to Spain from Australia and New Zealand, specialist operators include **Adventure Specialists** ((02) 9261 2927, 69 Liverpool Street, Sydney, which offers overland, walking and camping trips across Spain, while for city stays **CIT** ((02) 9267 1255, 2/263 Clarence Street, Sydney, is a good bet, with further offices in Melbourne, Brisbane, Adelaide and Perth. A sound operator with a good range of tours and accommodation around Spain, including monasteries and palaces as well as more conventional hotels, is the **European Travel Office** (ETO), with branches across Australasia: contact details include ETO Melbourne ((03) 9329 8844, 122 Rosslyn Street, West Melbourne; ETO Sydney ((02) 9267 7714, Suite 410/368 Sussex Street, Sydney, and ETO Auckland ((09) 525 3074, 407 Great South Road, Auckland.

For guided and independent walking and cycling journeys in Spain, try **Peregrine** ((03) 9662 2700 WEB SITE www.peregrine.net.au, 258 Lonsdale Street, Melbourne, with offices in Sydney, Brisbane, Adelaide and Perth, who are also represented in New Zealand by the **Adventure Travel Company** ((03) 379 9755, 164 Parnell Road, Parnell, Auckland.

The legacy of Spain's Moorish occupation is everywhere. Here the restored castle of Almodovar del Rio overlooks the Guadalquivir River.

Welcome
to Spain

The Moors originally thought that Spain was an island, and in a sense it was. Cut off from the rest of Europe by the Pyrenees and separated from Africa by the sea, Spain grew into a distinct and individual entity, absorbing waves of invaders to become one of the world's great empires, united by religious fervor and fanatical self-belief.

But Spain is too large, and far too diverse, to resemble an island. In size and complexity it has more in common with a continent. It encompasses glaciers, mountain ranges, desert regions and forest zones. More importantly, its rugged landscape, often compared to a crinkled hide spread out to dry under the hot Spanish sun, is home to 40 million loud, proud individual people, four distinct languages and seven major dialects. Around Barcelona, they speak Catalan, influenced more by the French regions of Languedoc than the accents of Andalucía. The Galician language has more in common with Portuguese. Near Bilbao, the Basques speak a language with roots in the Stone Age, untouched by three millennia of European linguistic groups and dialects. Arrive from South America, for instance — once a Spanish colony — thinking you'll have a handle on the language, and you'll quickly discover your mastery is of the language of Castilla only: you might call it Spanish, but only a minority of the people who live in Spain will call it theirs.

The architecture reflects years of invasion — by Romans, Visigoths, Moors and others. Fortified towns grow in huddles on hilltops ringed by high stone defensive walls. Massively built and lavishly decorated cathedrals inspired awe in a population living under constant threat in an unforgiving landscape of crumpled hills and a climate that can be best described as reliably unreliable. The rain in Spain may fall upon the plain, but it can do so fast, in almost biblical torrents; the winters are harsh and the summers baking hot.

In this environment, the Spanish character was formed. A strong, self-reliant people whose isolated world has never had neighbors to call on in times of need. From this "island," Spanish navigators read the stars and stretched the knowledge of the Western world. From this land where rivers are few and rarely navigable and the mountains huge and immovable, they deciphered astronomy, mapped the world's oceans, raised armies and built armadas to mount perhaps the greatest military conquest of recorded history.

Later, their world closed in. Plundered gold may have paid their soldiers wages, but it didn't contribute to lasting progress at home. Clashing ideologies led to a sapping civil war, and Spain entered the post-industrial age blanketed into international isolation by the stifling Franco regime. While Europe moved on, Spain stayed still.

But when Spain changes, it is said, it changes incredibly fast. And the Spain of today is a distant cry from the Spain of yesteryear. On the street, a visibly taller and more confident younger generation carry cell phones and drive new cars, while an older, smaller generation continue a lifestyle now lost in a social time warp. Old men, 60 cm (two feet) shorter than their children, use sticks to walk to their local bar. Elderly village women move through their world in mourning black, while their daughters and granddaughters are smartly turned out, sophisticated and assured.

Yet in Spain, where families stick together across the generations, almost everyone shares, in some way, in the changes that are sweeping the country in the newly liberal environment. This country's recently narrow horizons have suddenly hugely expanded, and an agrarian lifestyle co-exists with a sophisticated awareness of the outside world.

Even the most casual observer rapidly notes among the country's diversity some shared character traits. The Spanish don't seem to sleep in the way other nations do. Nightlife goes on late but days start, after a fashion, on time. The work ethic holds little charm in Spain, not due to laziness, but to a strong sense of self-worth — surely there are more important things in life than the daily grind. It's estimated that fully half the population have some sort of claim to a title: there's a word for it, *hidalgo*, "son of someone," a term of respect for anyone with ancestral significance. Not that most Spanish need a title to feel more than the match for any visiting foreigner. It's easy to see why the concierge at your hotel doesn't rush to pick up your bags.

But the irrepressible sense of self-worth directly benefits visitors. While the Spanish treatment of clients is often off-hand, this cannot be said of their treatment of guests, and it is not at all uncommon for the Spanish to slip over from their understandable resentment at finding themselves working in a service industry into a totally instinctive, natural hospitality. After suffering a few outbreaks of the *mañana* (tomorrow) approach to travel arrangements, when things are done the next day, if at all, foreign visitors are often stunned by unexpected acts of kindness, small and affecting gestures that make all the difference. Strangers may buy you drinks, guide you to your destination, or even give you small gifts. People who don't speak your language will labor to maintain a cordial conversation even if you don't speak theirs.

Spain, with its mix of different languages, cultures and regions, has individuals as varied and distinct as the landscapes they call home. And beyond this, there are few cultures as receptive to — and as fast to adopt — change. Every visit to Spain is a different experience; every area is new. For those who've never visited, this is a good time to go, as those who return, year after year, know only too well.

TOP: Spain's northern Costa Verde ("green coast") near Gijon, Asturias. BOTTOM: The spectacularly situated town of Arcos de la Frontera in Andalucía.

Welcome to Spain

The Country and its People

A SUN-TANNED HIDE

The modern traveler flying over Spain may well agree with the ancient description of it looking like a cowhide, pegged out and drying in the sun. The central part of the animal is the *meseta*, an upland area that ranges in height from 600 m (1,968 ft) to 1,000 m (3,280 ft) and gives Spain its physical and spiritual character. This vast, tawny, undulating plateau with its brilliant skies and limitless horizons is where the Spanish people and the state developed during the centuries of solitude. It is also where the Spanish imagination derived sustenance, where the epic poets looked

Atlantic are the two largest; but they have never been great waterways in the style of the Rhine in Germany or the Rhône in France. The other main rivers, the Duero (Duoro), the Tajo (Tagus) and the Guadiana all flow westwards and reach the Atlantic through Portugal. By contrast, Spain's long coastline and good harbors have given it access — and made it vulnerable — to northern Europe and the Atlantic, Africa and the Mediterranean.

Geography and climate have shaped such diversity that it is hard to believe the moist green countryside of Galicia with its stone walls, cows and Swiss-looking chalets has anything in common with the sun-drenched olive groves and whitewashed houses of Andalucía. But that is Spain.

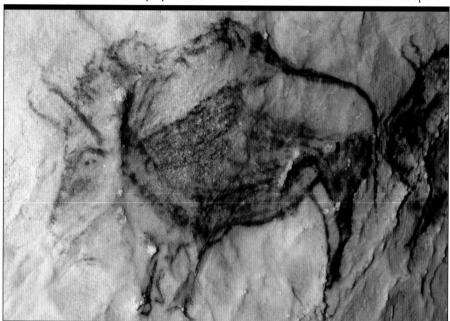

for material to glorify El Cid, where Goya went for his scenes of everyday life and where Cervantes found Don Quixote philosophizing and tilting at windmills.

But the *meseta* is also deceptive because it suggests uniformity, whereas Spain is one of the most diverse countries in the world. Many mountain ranges top the plateau, from the Sierra Nevada — with the highest peak in the country (3,478 m or 11,408 ft) — in the south, through the Sierra Morena to the Sierra de Gredos and the Sierra de Guadarrama in the center, on up to the Cordillera Cantábrica in the northwest and the Pyrenean wall (Pirineos) in the north.

Somewhat surprisingly for a land with so many mountains and a good deal of rain and snow, Spain has few important rivers. The Ebro in the north that runs into the Mediterranean and the Guadalquivir in the south that flows into the

SPAINS FIRST SETTLERS

While traces of man date back hundreds of thousands of years to the Neanderthal era, the most significant evidence of early man's presence in Spain was unearthed at the Altamira caves in the north. Here, some time around 14,000 or 15,000 BC, Stone Age hunters pursued stags, wild boars, horses, bison and other game, later rendering them in exquisite paintings on the walls and ceilings of their caves. There are Neolithic cave paintings in eastern Spain (5000 BC to 2000 BC) and Megalithic tombs along with other artifacts in the Balearic Islands (2000 BC).

The first waves of intruders entered Spain in the Megalithic period, with the Ligurians coming from Italy and settling in the northeast, and the Iberians crossing the narrow straits from Africa and establishing themselves in the south. Celts, sailing in from Britain and France, settled in north-western Spain a thousand years before the birth of Christ. These people did not mingle much, and the Iberians seemed to have done rather better in the warm, mineral-rich south than the Ligurians and Celts in the north. They are believed to have been the creators of the fabled kingdom of Tartessos in Andalucía ("Tarshish" in the Bible), although no trace of the city has yet been found.

Stories of Iberian workmanship in copper, silver and gold attracted the Phoenicians, who arrived around 1100 BC, built towns at Gadir (Cádiz) and Malaka (Málaga), and bequeathed the skills of writing and a standardized monetary system. The Phoenicians were followed by their maritime rivals, the Greeks, who established colonies in the seventh and sixth centuries BC at Ampurias (Girona), Dianion (Dénia) and Mainake, east of Málaga. The famous stone bust of the Dama de Elche, with her stern gaze, elaborately braided hair and rows of amulets, is a spectacular example of Ibero-Grecian artistic fusion. Strabo, the Greek geographer, reported on some of the contradictions that later became clichés. The peninsula's inhabitants were, he noted, haughty yet hospitable, xenophobic yet intrigued by foreigners.

The Greeks introduced the vine and olive to Spain, and made a serious attempt at colonization in the attractive coastal lands of the Mediterranean. They also incorporated their new possession into their mythology. One of the labors of Hercules — the golden apples of the Hesperides — was located in Spain, not far from Cádiz, then an important and cosmopolitan city.

Carthaginians were to follow, as Hamilcar Barca led the way up the Mediterranean coast on a circuitous attack of Rome. He gave his name to Barcelona, and the Carthaginians also founded Cartagena. Hamilcar's son, Hannibal, and son-in-law, Hasdrubal, spent much of their lives in Spain, strengthening Carthage's position in the peninsula. The Punic Wars, however, ended Carthage's control when it was forced to surrender its Spanish possessions to Rome in 201 BC.

THE ROMANS AND THEIR LEGACY

It took the Romans almost two centuries to subdue the fiercely independent Celto-Iberians. Rome's best soldiers — Cato, Pompey, Julius Caesar and Augustus — all served in Spain. The province became a wealthy and important part of the Roman empire and produced the emperors Trajan, Hadrian, Marcus Aurelius and Theodosius, as well as some of the most prominent writers of Rome's "Silver Age" of letters, including the two Senecas, Lucan, Martial and Quintilian.

Five centuries of Roman rule oversaw a period of prosperity in Spain, whose lasting monuments can be seen all over the country in Roman amphitheaters, aqueducts, bridges and mosaics. The Romans founded a number of cities, such as Hispalis (Sevilla), Corduba (Córdoba), Tarraco (Tarragona), Augusta Emerita (Mérida), and Caesar Augusta (Zaragoza); they also gave Spain things it had never had before: unity, a common language (Latin of course), and law.

The Romans' also left Spain a Christian country, though that was not their original intention. Spain began its Christian life with a number of martyrs put to death with typical Roman gusto in the centuries before Christianity became the official religion of the Roman Empire. The Romans added another element to Spain's human diversity during the Jewish Diaspora, when it became official

policy to settle Jews in odd corners of the Roman Empire, an act that later had a significant impact on Spain's economic and cultural development.

When, in the fifth century, the Roman Empire crumbled, Spain became one of the first victims. Vandals, living up to the later meaning of their name, swept down from the north, burning, pillaging, raping and killing as they went. Their momentum took them into Africa, leaving nothing but a wasteland and a name ("Vandalusia" which later lost its "V" to become Andalucía) behind them. Other Germanic tribes, such as the

OPPOSITE: Prehistoric cave paintings provide evidence of Spain's first inhabitants. This painting from Sanitmamine, near Guernica, evokes a time when bison roamed the plains of Spain. ABOVE: The Romans, during a 500-year occupation, made a lasting impact on Spain. A statue in the Roman town of Réalion, just outside Sevilla, where the Roman emperors Hadrian and Trajan were born.

Suebi and Alans, paid plundering visits of varying duration in the north, and the Byzantine Empire, under Justinian, seized part of the south. Relative order was not restored until the Visigoths ("West Goths"), who came from Gaul, established themselves during the sixth century.

THE VISIGOTHS

A Teutonic although semi-Romanized tribe, the Visigoths were ruled by a military elite who elected their kings. They were never numerous in Spain and for a long time did not intermarry with the local population. Used to Roman ways, they left much of their predecessors' system intact. The Visigoths established Toledo as the capital of the country and, under King Leovigild in the second half of the sixth century, managed to unite the country by expelling the Byzantines from the south and the Suebi from Galicia, while bringing the incorrigibly separatist-minded Basques to heel.

The Visigoths ruled Spain for three turbulent centuries, their empire suffering from structural flaws. Built around the cult of the warrior caste, with no clear hereditary path of succession, every royal death caused damaging in-fighting and times of uncertainty. The Visigoths also brought with them the schismatic Arian branch of Christianity, which was not well received by the orthodox Hispano-Roman population, causing more friction. However, by end of the sixth century, King Recared, Leovigild's son, converted to his subjects' faith, setting a pattern for state and church unity that became a driving, and at times fanatical force during much of Spain's subsequent history. The Visigoths also set another trend: they persecuted the Jewish population.

In addition to re-establishing the unity of the country and welding church and state, the Visigoths left the occasional — often simple, sometimes surprisingly beautiful — reminder of their sojourn in Spain. A few Visigothic churches remain in the north, along with plenty of stone carvings on church walls and friezes, and some fine jewelry and royal artifacts that shimmer and gleam before the twentieth-century viewer's eyes, casting a new light on Western Europe's "Dark Ages."

THE MOORS

Spain's last great invasion came from Africa. In the early eighth century, the Moors established a foothold in the south and within three years had conquered most of the country. (General Franco, coming from the same direction 1,200 years later, took about the same amount of time to accomplish the same task.) The next 800 years were the story of the Moorish dominion and the long, century-by-century Christian struggle to drive them out of the peninsula.

The great flowering of the Moors' civilization encompassed agriculture, architecture, medicine, literature, music, design, and the art of making war. Signs of the Moorish era can still be seen, heard and sensed wherever you go in modern Spain. Its grand monuments such as the Alhambra in Granada and the Mezquita (mosque) in Córdoba need neither introduction nor praise. Yet it is the name of an obscure village, a church tower that began life serving another religion, a quavering half-tone overheard as you pass a crowded bar, that suddenly remind you how deep the Moorish imprint was.

The time of the Moors was also a period of the greatest tolerance and intermingling of Spain's many different peoples. Although those eight centuries were also a time of constant if sporadic war, Muslim, Christian and Jew often lived side by side in peace. Moreover, the different peoples of the northern part of the country — notably the Catalans, Basques, Asturians and Galicians — managed to establish a considerable degree of autonomy and preserve their ancient laws and customs.

The period, especially the earlier part, was remarkable for its lack of fanaticism and the productive interaction of the newcomers with the indigenous inhabitants. Alliances cut across religious lines (El Cid, for example, served Christian and Muslim masters at different times); intermarriage was common even at the princely level; many Christian kings could speak Arabic as well as they could Spanish; Jews were valued members of the community as scientists, teachers, businessmen and royal ambassadors and advisers.

The influx of more fanatical Moorish factions from North Africa and the launching of the Crusades in the latter part of the Moorish occupation did much to poison the good relations between races and religions. Jews were persecuted again and Christian and Moor fought more bitterly for territorial control. But the picture was never wholly dark. The Moors, reduced to Granada, produced another great outburst of administrative, commercial and artistic energy, resulting in the building of the Alhambra. Christians and Moors lived successfully enough under each other's sway to develop distinctive blends of architecture and design that are known to this day as Mozarabic (Christian workmanship under Moorish control) and Mudéjar (Moors, or Moriscos as they were known, developing a distinctive style of craftsmanship under Christian rule).

The Moorish advance in Spain had been halted in an obscure Asturian valley in 718 at a place called Covadonga, and it is here that the Christian *Reconquista* ("Reconquest") began. It wasn't

A painting by El Greco, commissioned by King Felipe II for display in the El Escorial, where it still can be seen. El Greco was born in Crete, studied in Italy and spent the greater part of his life in Toledo.

to end until almost eight centuries later with the fall of Granada in 1492.

The story of the Reconquest concerns two parallel developments: the gradual expulsion of the Moors from the peninsula, and the growing unity of the Christian kingdoms. The Christian drive began in the northwest with the kingdoms of Asturias, León, Navarra and Castilla, whose military alliances eventually merged under the banner of Castilla. In the northeast Aragón and Catalunya drew together and began a reconquest of their own in the eastern part of the mainland and the Balearic Islands in the Mediterranean. The final catalyst, however, was the union of these powers in 1474, when King Ferdinand of Aragón married Queen Isabella of Castilla.

THE CATHOLIC MONARCHS

The Catholic Monarchs *(Los Reyes Católicos)*, as they were called, changed Spain in a number of ways, setting it on a new course. Firstly, they weakened the existing feudal order and established an absolute monarchy. Secondly, they increased the power and the militancy of the Church by obtaining permission from the Pope to set up the Inquisition. Thirdly, they completed the task of the Reconquest with the capture of Granada in 1492. Fourthly, in that same dramatic year, Christopher Columbus made his first landing in the New World under their patronage.

With hindsight, Ferdinand and Isabella have much to answer for. The power of the monarchy, with a few lapses, lasted well into the nineteenth century, impairing the growth of a modern state. The Inquisition exerted a terrible arbitrary authority over the lives of Spaniards for several centuries. The end of the Moorish occupation meant greater unity, but human, economic and cultural impoverishment. The discovery of the New World brought fabulous wealth to Spain but left in its wake overweening ambition, political decay and economic disaster.

An early casualty was Spain's industrious and cultured Jewish population. Shortly after the fall of Granada in 1492, on the advice of Tomás de Torquemada, the first head of the Inquisition and himself the son of a converted Jew, Ferdinand and Isabella expelled all those who would not convert to Christianity. One hundred and fifty thousand Sephardic Jews moved out of Spain to North Africa, Greece and Turkey.

During the following two centuries (1516 to 1700) Spain belonged to the Habsburgs, a foreign dynasty that climbed onto the Spanish throne by way of the marriage bed. Chauvinistic Spaniards call it the "Golden Age"; dissenters prefer the "Age of Greed" or something equally pejorative. The first of the line was Carlos I, a gentleman who spoke no Spanish, had a passion for war, and who

acquired the title of Holy Roman Emperor by locking up his mother, the rightful queen of Spain, in a cell for 40 years.

Carlos, known in Spain as Emperor Carlos V, inherited a large European empire consisting of Austria, the Netherlands and half of Italy. Then he added an even larger prize: the Americas. Hernán Cortés defeated the Aztecs in Mexico and Francisco Pizarro conquered the Incas in Peru under the banner of their king-emperor. Huge amounts of treasure flowed into Sevilla and other southern ports, and most of it was spent on waging interminable wars.

This and other abuses resulted in a peasant rebellion in Castilla (the Communero revolt, which took place in 1520 to 1521). The rebellion shook the establishment but was bloodily crushed as the monarchy tightened its hold on power another notch. While fighting virtually every country in Europe, as well as the Ottoman Turks, Carlos

launched the Counter-Reformation at home in response to the Protestant surge further north. The Society of Jesus, or Jesuits, was founded by Ignatius of Loyola during Carlos's reign. Yet after 40 years of effort, Carlos had nothing to show for the money spent, the blood spilled, the opportunities missed. So he did an uncharacteristic thing: he handed the Spanish throne over to his son, packed his bag and retired in a certain comfort to the monastery of Yuste in Extremadura.

Felipe II, Carlos' son, was very different — studious, introverted and pious. He inherited a bankrupt state that was saved only by the gold and silver of Spain's New World possessions. His foreign ventures fared no better than his father's with the one exception of a great naval victory over the Turks at Lepanto in 1571. Felipe's brother, John of Austria, led the Spaniards and their allies into the battle, and on one of his ships a Spaniard, who was later to achieve another kind of fame, fought

hard and was wounded three times, ending the battle with a permanently maimed left hand. His name was Miguel de Cervantes Saavedra, the author of *Don Quixote*.

Felipe lost Spain's Netherlands colonies and saw his great Armada, which went to conquer heretical England, repulsed by an unlucky storm. At home he focused his attention on stamping out anything that remotely resembled heresy. The Inquisition redoubled its efforts.

For the sizeable populations of remaining Jews and Moors, life under Felipe and the Inquisition exceeded their worst fears. In an atmosphere that had a lot in common with Nazi Germany four centuries later, Felipe and the Inquisition's network of interrogators, spies, informers and thugs

A fresco depicting the battle of Higueruela in 1431 where King Juan II defeated the Moors of Granada. This immense tapestry covers one wall of a cloister known as the "Hall of Battles" in El Escorial.

relentlessly pursued anyone suspected of being "tainted" by Jewish or Moorish blood. A rich and talented mixture of races was brutally unraveled and countless skilled, productive people were lost. While all this was happening, Felipe was building that huge and unique mausoleum, El Escorial, which reflects his strange cold-eyed, hard-driven personality.

DECLINE OF THE MONARCHY

The story of the last three Habsburg kings is a sad tale of incest and decline. The imbecilic Felipe III was followed by the well-meaning but weak Felipe IV, and then another infirm monarch,

French rulers brought French ways and sensibilities, and built palaces on a grand scale. The age of baroque and rococo had begun. The eighteenth century was distinguished by the rule of one Bourbon king, Carlos III, who reigned from 1759–1788. He believed in the absolute power of the monarchy as much as any of his Spanish predecessors and his European contemporaries did, but Carlos III and his progressive ministers also believed in reform. The power of the Inquisition was curbed, the Jesuits were expelled, and the economy was revived. Spain thus shared in the Age of Enlightenment.

Unfortunately, it was not to last. Carlos IV, whose uncle, King Louis XVI of France, died on

Carlos II. Half a million productive Moors were expelled, and vibrant and prosperous Castilian towns (Toledo, Segovia, Ávila, León, Burgos and others) became frozen in time. The childless Carlos II left Spain and its diminished possessions to the Bourbon Philip of Anjou, grandson of Louis XIV. But the Habsburg Archduke Carlos from Austria, backed by the Catalans, disputed the succession. Most Spanish stood back while the European powers fought the "War of Spanish Succession." The English, supporting Carlos, won some memorable battles under Marlborough and seized Gibraltar and Menorca but, in the end, it was the French candidate who was installed as Felipe V. Thus began over two centuries of Bourbon rule and a new period of experiment, foreign invasion and revolution, setting up the conditions that would lead to the ultimate cataclysm of the Spanish Civil War.

the scaffold in 1793, declared war on Revolutionary France and lost. French rule followed under Napoleon's brother, Joseph, until 1808, when a popular uprising launched Spain's "War of Independence" and the British army came in to help. Six years later the French retreated, burning and plundering what they could.

Yet although liberal visionaries had gathered in Cádiz and drawn up a democratic, parliamentary constitution which abolished the power of the monarchy and the Church, Spain instead ended up under the next Habsburg in line, Ferdinand VII, who reigned from 1808 to 1833. He reasserted the absolute power of the monarchy and the influence of the Church, and brought back the Inquisition. Through his short reign Spain lost most of its Latin American colonies, and he died leaving a bankrupt state and a disputed succession, with his female heir, the liberal Isabella, being challenged by his brother, Don Carlos. Three baffling and inconclusive Carlist Wars were to follow, over which the Inquisition collapsed, a spasm of anticlericism resulted in the expropriation of the monasteries, and a republican movement was born — in the military.

The second half of the nineteenth century was not much better. An extraordinary succession of dictators, revolts and finally a royalist restoration followed, making Spain look as fragile and immature as any modern banana republic. In a final spasm, Spain lost a war with America in 1898, losing control of Cuba and Puerto Rico and ending its dreams of empire.

Underneath the political turmoil, important things were happening. The country was at last industrializing, a great cultural renaissance was under way in Catalunya and modern ideas and ideology were penetrating the Pyrenean defenses and bringing with them notions such as socialism, communism and anarchism. A collection of Spanish writers and thinkers, known as the "Generation of '98," began to reassess Spain's position in the modern world.

Spain wisely opted out of World War I and managed to pull itself together. The 1920s brought prosperity and a military dictator, General Miguel Primo de Rivera, who governed with the approval of King Alfonso XIII until being ousted in 1930. The following year, the left-wing parties won elections and forced the king to abdicate and go into exile, ushering in Spain's Second Republic. Political rivalries, heightened by Europe's widening ideological differences as fascism gained in Italy and Germany, became more acute. The Depression, which hit Spain as hard as anywhere, made matters worse. Peasant revolts, industrial strikes, an attempted coup, unilateral declarations of regional autonomy and the seesawing fortunes of the right and the left at elections scarred the first five years of the republic.

In 1936, the Popular Front, a coalition of left-wing parties, won the elections and took power. By this stage Spain looked like a chemistry laboratory for politics. On the left were the socialists, communists, Trotskyites, anarcho-syndicalists and others, some supporting the government, others opposing it in different ways and to different degrees, and still others largely ignoring it. On the right there were the monarchists (orthodox supporters of the Bourbons and unorthodox Carlists), conservatives of many hues, ambitious generals and the newly formed Falange movement, Spain's fascist party. The situation became more anarchic, with political violence becoming commonplace, as the new government struggled unavailingly to maintain control.

On July 18, 1936, the army rebelled and, calling themselves "Nationalists," launched Spain's Civil War.

CIVIL WAR

The story of the Spanish Civil War, which ended three years later, in 1939, leaving more than 500,000 dead, has been chronicled and mulled over in many volumes.

A story of its time, the Spanish Civil War became the first battlefield in which the ideologies of communism and fascism confronted each other. It quickly attracted outside attention: Italy and Germany supported the Nationalists; the Soviet Union backed the Republicans. Foreigners rushed in to fight on one side or the other, or simply to observe and record for posterity. New techniques

of modern warfare were tested in Spain for the first time, the most dramatic being the aerial bombardment of civilians.

But, when all is said and done, the war was the *Spanish* Civil War. The great divide between the trinity of king, Church and army, backed by a conservative-minded, traditionally Catholic bourgeoisie on one hand and the coalition of landless peasants, factory workers and ardent regionalists led by anti-clerical intellectuals on the other, split Spain down the middle.

The Republican side, outgunned and weakened by divisions in its ranks, eventually succumbed to

OPPOSITE: While El Escorial was, in intent, primarily religious, private royal apartments were lavishly decorated to provide regal comforts for generations of Spanish rulers. ABOVE: The royal mausoleum beneath the church in El Escorial, where the bodies of Spain's monarchs lie in marble sarcophagi.

General Francisco Franco's better-equipped forces, which received considerably more support from Italy and Germany than the Soviet Union provided for the Republicans.

In March 1939, Franco's forces marched into a battered and hungry Madrid and the war was over.

THE FRANCO YEARS

During the next 36 years Franco put his stamp on Spain in a way that differed little from that of a Habsburg or Bourbon monarch. Calling himself "El Caudillo" (the leader), he was merciless, repressive, authoritarian, pious, narrow and unimaginative. The government shot, imprisoned or hounded its Republican opponents in the early post-war years. Spain became a police state. Censorship smothered ideas, as well as political opinions. Authority was rigidly centralized in an attempt to squeeze the life out of Spain's regional diversity. An iron hand crushed any sign of opposition. As a result, Spain, pummeled at home and ostracized abroad, turned in on itself once more, hungry, suffering and forgotten.

But Franco differed in some important respects from most of his absolutist predecessors. He was not an ideologue; he never embraced fascism, for example, and kept the Falange movement at a distance. He also knew the limits of Spain's strength. He avoided joining his old friends, Italy and Germany, when they went to war. When World War II was over, Franco cashed in on the tensions aroused by the Cold War by making an astute deal with the United States that involved renting out military bases in Spain for much-needed dollars. Later, in the 1960s, he allowed a new generation of technocrats their heads in restructuring the Spanish economy.

This new class knew little of the violent past and cared less about the passions that had brought it about. Instead, they concentrated on building factories, improving agriculture, modernizing the infrastructure of roads, railroads, ports and airlines, and encouraging mass tourism. They were helped by the steady flow of foreign currency sent home by over a half a million Spaniards working abroad.

INTO TODAY'S WORLD

When Franco died in 1975, Spain had at last entered the modern world as far as the economy was concerned. But it lagged behind socially and politically. It was still a pariah in Europe, banned from the European Community and parliament, and from the NATO alliance. It is one of the great ironies of Spanish history that it was, finally, the monarchy that completed Spain's modern transformation. The man who did it was the present king, Juan Carlos, the grandson of King Alfonso XIII and Franco's appointed heir.

Juan Carlos has guided Spain through the shoals of a difficult transition, transforming it from a repressive military dictatorship into a freewheeling but relatively disciplined parliamentary democracy with himself presiding as constitutional monarch. It wasn't easy; a critical test came in 1981 when a Civil Guard colonel and his followers tried to launch a coup by seizing the Cortés (parliament) while its members were in session. Some of the army generals were behind the attempt, but after the king stepped in and made it clear that he supported the new order, the plot fizzled out.

Since then Spain has broadened its democracy and granted its regions a large degree of autonomy and the right to use their own languages. A socialist government has been in power for more than half a decade, extreme right-wing and extreme left-wing parties are legal, if not flourishing, and as you can see from any newspaper kiosk

or bookshop, the country is wide open to the world of ideas. Theater, filmmaking, painting — indeed the arts in general are enjoying a renaissance in the vibrant post-Franco era.

These days Spain is a fully integrated member of the European Community and of the North Atlantic Treaty Organization (NATO). 1992 marked a turning point, with Expo 92 in Sevilla and the Olympic Games in Barcelona well-organized, stylish, and peaceful events that brought hundreds of thousands of visitors and universal praise. This proof of national maturity and international acceptability occurred during the quincentenary of the fall of Granada and the discovery of the Americas. And since then, Spain has continued to grow: revitalizing the port of Bilbao, protecting their heritage in Unesco-recognized World Heritage Sites and national parks, and continuing to set its unmistakable mark in the world of arts and ideas.

At the same time, there continue to be problems in Spain as regional identities struggle to assert their independence from a land generally unified only by force. Both the Basque Separatist Group (ETA) and the Catalan independence movement have, in the past, been responsible for kidnapping and bombing outrages, with the high-profile tourist areas prime targets. The hope shared by most of Spain's present-day population of 40 million citizens is that regional cultures will be able to peacefully flower under the new umbrella of the European Union.

In a city already known for being progressive and unconventional, the building of the Olympic Village in 1992 gave the capital of Catalunya the chance to showcase local talent. While the games themselves drew in a new generation of visitors to Barcelona, the Olympic Village continues to provide a focus for national and international sports.

Madrid and Central Spain

When King Felipe II pointed his regal finger at the spot where he wanted Spain's new capital to be built in the mid-sixteenth century, it made administrative sense; but it upset many of his courtiers who had no desire to leave the cosmopolitan delights of the previous capital, Toledo, 71 km (44 miles) to the southwest. Nor did they appreciate the climate of his choice, as Madrid was then, and is now, an inferno in the summer and freezing in winter. It is, at least, usually sunny, with a claimed 2,824 hours of sunlight a year, and despite its detractors remained the administrative center for 450 years through to the present day. Madrid is at the heart of the country's communications, government and social life. This is where you'll find, most notably, the country's best nightlife, but also the easiest communications — at the heart of the network of buses and trains that reach to every corner of the country — and by far the finest collection of art. As the landing point for most intercontinental flights, most visitors will spend some time here, and it is within day-trip distance of the spectacular — and rather less frantic — historic towns of Aranjuez, Toledo and Ávila, the monastery of El Escorial and the ancient city of Segovia.

A broader sweep from the capital encompasses three quintessentially Spanish regions that most travelers will want to sample however fleetingly. These are the lower part of Old Castilla, northwest of Madrid, with the cities of Valladolid and Salamanca; the remote and little-visited region of Extremadura to the southwest, with its atmospheric cities of Mérida, Badajoz and Cáceres; and La Mancha and the city of Cuenca to the southeast.

MADRID

Once placid and leisurely paced, Madrid has become bustling, congested and polluted. What hasn't changed is the climate — it can still be hotter than Hades in summer and bitterly cold in winter. Madrid does not have the visual impact of some other European capitals. There is still a frumpish, rather tired look about its predominantly nineteenth-century architecture, and the ancient city core is ringed by the dense but charmless apartment developments characteristic of the Franco era. There is no easily recognized symbol, no equivalent of the Eiffel Tower in Paris, the Houses of Parliament in London, or the Acropolis in Athens. Curiously, the city has no classic cathedral, an omission that Spain's other major towns redress in no uncertain fashion. But Madrid has lovely fountains almost wherever you turn; beautifully lit, they are particularly spectacular and romantic at night. Madrid also offers the best eating in Spain, followed closely by Barcelona.

Madrid's merits far outweigh its disadvantages and make it worthwhile spending a few days there before heading off in other directions. Most important is the human factor. Capital of a booming, modern and democratic Spain, Madrid is a brighter, more fashionable and more exciting place than it used to be. *madrileños*, who never had any doubts that they lived in the center of the universe, have few rivals in knowing how to have a good time. They do this publicly — in the streets, the countless *tascas* (taverns) and bars, restaurants, cinemas, theaters, discos, nightclubs and so on. And they do it late into the night, every day of the week. *La movida* — animation — is the name of the game in Madrid and it transforms the "plain

Jane" appearance of the place into something quite different. As capital for 450 years, Madrid is a most vibrant city for those who love nightlife and being at the heart of things. It is certainly a world center for fine art of all kinds, and this is one of the main reasons that many visitors allot several days to Madrid. The Museo del Prado houses one of the world's greatest collections of paintings, and there are other interesting museums dotted around the city.

When you've put these considerations together, the congestion, the noise and even the climate do not seem so bad. There are ways of circumventing the first, you grow used to the din (especially with a glass in your hand), and Madrid's climate has the advantage of being *dry*, regardless of how hot or cold it becomes. High above sea level (600 m or 2,000 ft), there are many lovely sparkling days with golden sunrises and crimson sunsets, days on which Madrid recalls its origins as a fresh-faced village on Castilla's broad plateau.

GENERAL INFORMATION

There are four main Tourist Information Offices. Arriving by plane at Aeropuerto de Barajas, your first port of call should be the **Tourist Information Estación de Atocha**, Madrid's central station.

Office (913 058656, International Arrivals, Terminal 1, Hall 1, open Monday to Friday 8 AM to 8 PM, Saturday 9 AM to 3 PM. In the city itself there are several other year-round offices, of which the most useful are at the railway station, **Estación de Charmartin** (913 159976, Concourse Gate 14, open Monday to Friday 8 AM to 8 PM, Saturday 9 AM to 1 PM, and the **Duque de Medinaceli** 2 (914 294951 FAX 914 290909, open Monday to Friday 9 AM to 7 PM, Saturday 9 AM to 3 PM. In the summer other tourist information kiosks open in popular areas, and all year there is also a public English-language information service in Madrid: just call 010 to be connected to an operator.

For **medical emergencies** dial (112, which will also connect to the police, or 915 884500 or 915 222222 for an ambulance, with the most central hospitals including **El Clinic** (913 303747, Plaza de Cristo Rey, and the **Ciudad Sanitaria La Paz** (913 582831, Paseo de la Castellana 261. For **Internet access**, there are a growing number of Internet cafés, but here, more than anywhere, they come and go very quickly. A good bet is **La Casa de Internet**, Calle Luchana 20.

ORIENTATION

The capital, despite its recent growth, is still a relatively compact city. To get your bearings, focus on the **Paseo de la Castellana**, a broad boulevard that sweeps down through the city, bisecting it from north to south, and the **Calle de Alcalá**, which cuts across it, west to east. Some rough compass points are **Estación de Atocha** (Atocha Railroad Station) in the south, the **Palacio Real** (Royal Palace) in the west, **Estadio Bernabéu** (Real Madrid's soccer stadium) in the north, and the **Plaza de Toros** (bullring) in the east.

The northern end of town is where modern, expanding Madrid is happening and where **Aeropuerto de Barajas** lies. Lower down on the west side is **Old Madrid** (built predominantly in the seventeenth and eighteenth centuries) with its winding streets and teeming humanity. On the east, there is **Parque del Buen Retiro**, laid out in the seventeenth century, and the orderly boulevards and the solid houses built for the nineteenth-century bourgeoisie. A useful point of reference is the **Plaza de la Cibeles** where the Calle de Alcalá crosses Paseo de Recoletos, an extension of Castellana. The traffic swirls around a lovely fountain here and past Madrid's main *Correos* (post office), a confectioner's dream of a building that is unmistakable and, as such, an ideal meeting place if you don't know the town.

There are plenty of hotels in this lower segment, on or off the Castellana, so this makes a good base. From here you can reach all the sightseeing landmarks in less than half an hour. Madrid has the virtue of a good all-round public transportation

system. Taxis are plentiful, inexpensive and driven by rational and usually polite people who are not under the illusion that they should have been grand prix drivers.

GETTING AROUND

The **Metro** (915 525909, or subway system, is excellent: clean, safe, easily understood (lots of maps and clear directions), with frequent trains. You can buy tickets singly (€0.75) or in batches of ten (€4.25) at automatic vending machines in the stations; these tickets also permit travel on buses. Trains run from 6 AM until 1:30 AM every day of the week, including public holidays, and close an

hour later on Fridays and Saturdays. The Metro covers the center of Madrid thoroughly and the rolling stock has been modernized, providing a comfortable and swift ride beneath the busy streets of the capital.

Buses (914 011409 are also available but have more complicated route patterns and are subject to the same delays as all surface transportation.

There are plenty of red-striped **taxis** cruising the streets, with green lights above the cap when available. Local taxi companies include **Madrid Radio-Taxi** (914 475180 and **Tele Taxi** (914 459008. Wheelchair users should call **Eurotaxis** (915 478200, while long-distance specialists include **Independent Radio-Taxis** (914 051213.

A car is not necessary, but if you have one for trips further afield, you will find there are few formal parking restrictions but often, quite surprisingly in a country where no one seems to pay much attention to parking regulations, it is your vehicle that is towed away. *Madrileños* park anywhere and everywhere, but you will probably be better off leaving the beast at the hotel or parking in one of the well-signposted underground parking lots as car-crime is rife. In any case, one of the major attractions of Madrid is the theater of the streets. And the best way to enjoy that is on foot.

FESTIVALS AND CELEBRATIONS

Despite its status as the capital city, Madrid still takes its festivals very seriously. The parades and costume parties of the **Fiestas de Carnaval** culminate in, on Ash Wednesday, the traditional burial of the sardine, which celebrates the run-up to Lent. The **Fiestas del 2 de Mayo** incorporate a variety of concerts, dances and bullfights. May 15 is the start of a month-long **Fiesta de San Isidro**, ushering in the **Feria Taurina**, or bullfighting fair, which lasts until the middle of June. In August the celebrations move into the suburbs, with fiestas celebrating **San Lorenzo**, **San Cayetano** and the **Virgen de la Paloma**.

WHAT TO SEE AND DO

Madrid has three major art museums. While the Museo del Prado is in a class of its own, the doors have opened at two new art museums, each spectacular in its own way. These are the Centro de Arte Reina Sofía and the Museo Thyssen-Bornemisza. All three are within walking distance of each other in what is known as the "Paseo del Arte" or, more geometrically, the "Art Triangle." Tickets to enter the museums can be bought individually, although if you plan to visit all three the Bonoarte, at €6, is worth buying.

Museo del Prado
The city's star turn is without doubt the Prado (913 302900 WEB SITE http://museoprado.mcu.es, on the east side of the Paseo del Prado, open Tuesday to Saturday 9 AM to 7 PM, Sundays and holidays 9 AM to 2 PM, €3. Like most museums, palaces and other public buildings, the Prado is closed on Mondays when everyone makes at least a token effort to recover from the weekend. To avoid the crowds, it is best to time your visit here in the early morning or during the Spanish lunchtime between 2 PM and 4 PM. The entrance is at the north end, close to the Ritz Hotel and the Fuente de Neptuno (Neptune's Fountain). Opened in 1819, the museum's vast collection of paintings began as an exhibition of the royal collection but has been steadily augmented by purchases ever since.

Here you will not only see the masterpieces of Spain's three greatest painters (El Greco, Velázquez and Goya), but also works from the Flemish school (Breughel, Rubens, Hieronymus Bosch — "El Bosco")

to Spaniards — and Memling) and Italian masters (Raphael, Boticelli, Tintoretto and Titian). This embarrassment of riches is a little overwhelming; if you have to be selective, concentrate on the Spaniards who, between them cover three centuries and provide a visual panorama of Spain's eventful history, along with a not always flattering vision of their royal patrons. Velázquez is wonderful, but for sheer power, Goya probably leads with his often idealized view of daily life in Madrid in the late eighteenth century, his dramatic depiction of rebellion against the French invader in the early nineteenth century, and his tormented "black" paintings that have a room of their own. The museum catalog is well worth buying.

Centro de Arte Reina Sofía
The Reina Sofía (914 675062 WEB SITE http://museoreinasofie.mcu.es, Calle de Santa Isabel 52, open Monday to Saturday 10 AM to 9 PM, Sundays and holidays 9 AM to 2 PM, €3, at Paseo del Prado and Calle de Santa Isabel, is Madrid's showcase of modern art. Its notable works are by Picasso, Miró and Dalí, but it also encourages contemporary talent with a program of exhibitions. Picasso's famous "Guernica," depicting the destruction wrought on the Basque town of that name by aerial bombardment during the Spanish Civil War, is now here, having moved from the Casón del Buen Retiro annex of the Prado. The picture, finally divested of its bulletproof glass protective screen, is superbly displayed with a fascinating collection of the artist's preliminary sketches and

OPPOSITE: The metro, Gran Vía. ABOVE: Museo del Prado

a videotape documentary explaining the background to the event that inspired the painting.

Museo Thyssen-Bornemisza and Around

Spain won a fierce international contest to become the permanent home of Baron Hans Heinrich Thyssen Bornemisza's remarkable collection of over 700 paintings. Appropriately, they are hung in a former palace — Palacio de Villahermosa — now **Museo Thyssen-Bornemisza** (913 690151 WEB SITE www.museothyssen.org, Paseo del Prado 8, open Tuesday to Sunday 10 AM to 7 PM, €3, next to the Palace Hotel. It also has a gift shop and cafeteria. The paintings cover the history of European art from the thirteenth century to the

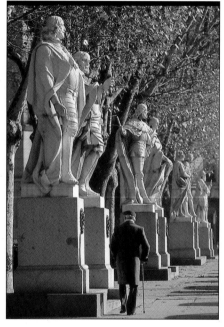

present and are helpfully arranged in chronological order with plenty of space and perfect light. Italian and German Renaissance, seventeenth-century Dutch masters, nineteenth-century North American works, Impressionism, Cubism and even Pop Art are strongly featured in this marvelous collection. If you want to spend a manageable and enjoyably instructive morning or afternoon looking at pictures in Madrid, do so at the Thyssen collection.

This area of Madrid has other, if lesser attractions, that include the **Museo Nacional de Artes Decorativas** (915 326499, Calle de Montalbán 12, open Tuesday to Friday 9:30 AM to 3 PM, a showcase of Spanish interior design from the fifteenth to the twentieth centuries. If you like Spanish tiles, don't miss the eighteenth-century tiled Valencian kitchen on the top floor. The **Museo Arqueológico Nacional** (915 777917, Paseo de Recoletos 18, open

Tuesday to Saturday, 9:30 AM to 8:30 PM, Sundays and holidays 9:30 AM to 2:30 PM, is on the right-hand side going north up towards Castellana (entrance on the Calle de Serrano), and contains Spain's most complete collection of archaeological remains, including the famous fifth-century BC bust of **La Dama de Elche**, and a re-creation of the **Altamira caves** and their prehistoric murals. Spain's long history of military prowess isn't forgotten either, in the **Museo del Ejército** (915 228977, Calle Méndez Núñez 1, open Tuesday to Sunday 10 am to 2:30 PM, €0.6, free on Saturdays, which has El Cid's sword on display. The **Museo Naval** (913 795299, Paseo del Prado 5, open Tuesday to Sunday 10:30 AM to 1:30 PM, no charge, displays the first map of the New World and a beautiful collection of model early sailing ships.

Parque del Buen Retiro

A stroll in the Retiro Park, conveniently at hand, might well be in order at this stage. Sunday is the best day to catch Madrid at ease, but the park is well worth a visit on any day, and in any season. There are many physical attractions: a lake where you can rent rowboats, a glass and delicate wrought-iron palace for art and other cultural exhibitions, botanical and Japanese gardens, a rich variety of trees and flowering shrubs, and plenty of open air cafés. (There are public toilets but they often seem to be closed.)

Empty, the park would be simply beautiful; full of *madrileños*, it is also fun. Palm and tarot readers, sitting on stools in front of little cloth-covered tables, line the walkway near the lake; small sticks of licorice root ("the best cure for catarrh") are on sale; puppeteers put on shows for children dressed in their Sunday-best; and down a shady avenue, you might see a clutch of jugglers practicing. A particularly pretty spot to rest is behind the **Palacio de Cristal** (Crystal Palace) where there is a pond with a fountain, the home of black and white swans, geese and ducks. All around are stately firs, cedars and graceful willows. Or, if you prefer to watch the slow moving stream of *madrileños*, enjoying their Sunday *paseo*, there is no better way than to sit at a café by the lake, with a refreshing drink or a coffee.

Old Madrid

Old Madrid is on the west side of the Castellana, and the best way to approach it is by walking up the Calle de Alcalá, which leads you into the **Puerta del Sol**, the traditional center of the city and of Spain. All distances are measured from the "Gateway of the Sun" which is, in fact, a bustling arc-shaped plaza where several roads meet. Not far away is the **Plaza Mayor**, a superbly proportioned

ABOVE: Plaza de Oriente. RIGHT: The Palacio de Cristal in the Retiro Park.

cobbled square built in the early seventeenth century and sensibly closed to modern traffic. Its faded ochre walls are best seen in the setting sun, and on the eastern façade there are portraits of Spain's literary luminaries — Cervantes, Lope de Vega and Calderón, among others. You will find similar, though often less lovely, enclosed squares in the center of towns throughout Spain. The Plaza Mayor in Madrid is a place where people meet, eat, drink and rest before making their next move in the old town.

A jumble of streets, squares, churches, markets, department stores, little shops, restaurants, cafés and bars, Old Madrid is eminently walkable. Its rough boundaries are the Palacio Real (Royal Palace) in the west, the Plaza de España to the north, a few streets beyond the Puerta del Sol in the east, and the Puerta de Toledo to the south. If the area is more than a little shabby. The smarter folk and their habitat are elsewhere. This area is most fun after the sun goes down. While you can eat well in plenty of atmospheric restaurants, the main attraction lies in the *tascas* and *cervecerias* (beer-halls), where you stand at the bar to drink and munch on *tapas*, the delightful and infinitely varied snacks that are a Spanish specialty. In the old days, there used to be a lot of spontaneous flamenco singing, hand-clapping and even dancing. This can still happen, but a more likely sight is a troupe of students in medieval doublet and hose, with mandolins and guitars, singing folk songs and peddling cassettes of their own music.

Palacio Real

Back on the sightseeing trail, the Palacio Real (915 420059, Calle de Bailén, open Monday to Saturday 9 AM to 6 PM, Sundays and holidays 9 AM to 3 PM, is worth a visit. The most pleasant approach is down Calle de Arenal from the Puerta del Sol, past the Opera, and into the Plaza de Oriente, a graceful, leafy square guarded by statues of Spanish kings with worn stone faces. While the relatively austere Habsburgs were responsible for the Plaza Mayor, it took their grandiose successors, the Bourbons, to conceive and construct this vast palace in the eighteenth century. Felipe V seemed to have had Versailles in mind when the old palace burned down and he had to replace it. Overlooking the park of the Campo del Moro, the palace has 2,800 rooms (!) and a gray limestone courtyard the size of a football field. Accordingly, a sampling, rather than the complete tour, is advisable. There is plenty to see and it is all incredibly lush: tapestries, lavishly decorated ceilings, silk brocaded curtains, priceless furniture, silverware, massive chandeliers and a whole roomful of gold clocks. The last king to live in the palace

RIGHT: A panoramic view of Madrid. OVERLEAF: A lake in Retiro Park.

was Alfonso XIII, who went into exile in 1931. The present monarch, King Juan Carlos, resides in a much more modest palace in Madrid's suburbs, although the Royal Palace is sometimes used for state functions.

At the far end of the courtyard is the **Armería Real** (Royal Armory). Essentially one cavernous room, it is full of suits of armor with huge lances and heavy swords. So many of them are on horseback that you feel you have suddenly burst into a medieval encampment where the king's men are about to tilt at a Moorish army advancing across the plain. Pistols, muskets, swords, shields, lances abound, along with a fascinating selection of crossbows. There are diminutive princes'

under their seats in an attempted coup; the **Casa de Lope de Vega**, on Calle de Cervantes 11, the restored sixteenth-century house of the playwright and poet; and the **Convento de las Descalzas Reales**, on Plaza de las Descalzas, a richly decorated seventeenth-century convent that is now brimming with tapestries, paintings, furniture and religious artifacts. The **Plaza de España**, at the north end of the **Gran Vía**, is disappointing apart from its bronze statues of Don Quixote and his stout squire, Sancho Panza. But it is worth going to because the municipal tourist office is in the ground floor of the nearby **Torre de Madrid**, an ugly modern tower that is the tallest building in the city.

armor — for mere children — and even a suit for a dog. All the artifacts, including the cloth banners and the embroidered and tasseled quilts that cover the horses, are authentic and remarkably well-preserved. Everything is on a large scale — horses, lances, swords, bows, etc. — except the knights themselves, who seem strangely frail by modern standards.

Other Westside Sights

Other places of interest on this side of the main north–south avenue include: the **Ayuntamiento (City Hall)** in the Plaza de la Villa, built in the mid-seventeenth century; the **Mercado de San Miguel**, a busy and aromatic fresh produce market, just west of the Plaza Mayor; the **El Congreso de Los Diputados**, or Spanish parliament, Plaza de Cortéz, where as recently as 1981 a group of disaffected Civil Guards had the deputies diving

SHOPPING

The swanky section of Madrid, where you find the best shops, many of the foreign embassies and consulates and some of the most popular restaurants, is back across the Castellana, north of the Parque del Retiro. This is the **Salamanca** district. Laid out in a grid pattern in the nineteenth century, it has broad tree-lined avenues, solid townhouses and apartment buildings and the comfortable, confident air of the bourgeoisie who have always lived here. In appearance and atmosphere it has much in common with the parts of Paris designed by Baron Haussmann during the same era.

The most exclusive shops are along the **Calle de Serrano**, which runs north from the **Puerta de Alcalá** and is Madrid's equivalent of London's Bond Street or New York's Fifth Avenue. The large department stores are found around the Puerta del Sol, and on the streets of Princesa, Goya and the city's most modern section, Castellana, where the major banks, offices, international hotels, and newest residential buildings are located. Some of the architecture is interesting, and there is sleekness about this part of Madrid that contrasts with the older parts of the city and reflects Spain's new prosperity, entrepreneurial spirit and glitter.

On Saturdays and Sundays the **Rastro** is the most famous of Madrid's flea markets, taking up the area between the Plaza de Cascorro, La Latina and the street of Embajadores. There are huge crowds and an awful lot of junk, but it's fun to let yourself flow with the crowd — often you have

while the smartest hotels are found around the Paseo del Prado, Salamanca and Recoletos. For nightlife, the Malasaña area — centered round the Plaza Dos de Mayo — or the lively Chueca area north of Gran Vía (Madrid's "Gay Zone") are best. With several hundred hotels in Madrid, this is a mere selection. At the lower end of the price-band, would-be revelers planning to make the most of Madrid's nightlife should make sure their chosen hotel has an all-night porter to let guests in after one of this city's famously late evenings.

Very Expensive and Above

The most palatial and elegant of Madrid's older hotels, perfectly situated near the Prado, is the

no alternative — and soak up the scene. You can buy everything from a pince-nez to a pig-skin wallet, from a doorknob to a German World War II helmet; you can also stop and play a game of bingo if the mood takes you. Watch your purse, pockets and camera, and be wary of taking photographs. For reasons best known to themselves but not hard to guess, many of the denizens of the Rastro do not welcome the recording of their likeness.

WHERE TO STAY

There is no shortage of centrally located hotel accommodation in Madrid, though curiously nothing spectacular at the top end of the market. The most important factor here is location. If you want to be at the heart of the old city, choose the areas around Plaza Santa Ana or Plaza Mayor,

Ritz (915 212857 FAX 917 016789 WEB SITE WWW .ritz.es, Plaza de la Lealtad 5 (extremely expensive). An elegant garden is perfect for summer dining, and the Old World style extends to obligatory jackets and ties for even the most casual male visitors. **Villa Magna Park Hyatt** (915 871234 FAX 914 312286 WEB SITE http://Madrid.hyatt .com/magna, at the New Paseo de Castellana 22 (very expensive), is a super-luxury choice. The **Palace** (913 608000 FAX 913 608100, Plaza de las Cortés 7 (very expensive), like the Ritz, is a grand hotel, built in the belle époque but more reasonably priced. It has recently been renovated and

OPPOSITE LEFT: The **Museo Arqueológico Nacional**. OPPOSITE RIGHT: Knights in armor at the Armería Real which shares a courtyard with the Palacio Real. ABOVE: Puerta de Alcalá — Madrid's equivalent of London's Bond Street or New York's Fifth Avenue.

has fine public rooms, ultra-modern bedrooms and sophisticated business facilities. Perhaps the smartest of Madrid's hotels is however the **Gran Hotel Reina Victoria** (915 314500 FAX 915 220307, Plaza de Santa Ana 13 (extremely expensive), with beautiful rooms in a historic setting.

Gran Hotel Velázquez (915 752800 FAX 915 752809, at Calle de Velázquez 62 (very expensive), is a good functional hotel in the heart of the Salamanca district, though at the price you might expect a bit more. A good international hotel in the newer part of the city off the Castellana is the **Miguel Angel Occidental Hoteles** (914 420022 FAX 914 425320 E-MAIL hma@occidental-hoteles .com, Calle Miguel Angel 31 (very expensive).

Smartly located in the Salamanca district, **N.H. Balboa** (915 630324 FAX 915 626980, Calle Núñez de Balboa 112 (very expensive), is very new, comfortable and offers excellent service.

Moderate and Expensive

For old-fashioned good value try the centrally located **Tryp Gran Vía** (915 221121 FAX 915 212424, Gran Vía 25 (expensive). In a good position near the Palacio Real, with fine views, the **Principe Pío** (915 478000 FAX 915 411117 WEB SITE www.principepio.com, Cuesta de San Vicente 16 (moderate), offers good value for money. In the center of Old Madrid the **Hotel Santo Domingo** (915 479800 FAX 915 475995 E-MAIL sdomingo @stnet.es WEB SITE www.stnet.es, Plaza Santo Domingo 13 (moderate), is an excellent base, with valet parking for motorists.

Inexpensive

There are a number of inexpensive hotels in Madrid, but once more your choice will probably be dictated by area. A good choice around the late-night center of the Plaza de Santa Ana is the **Hostal Carreras** (915 220036, Calle de Principe 18, which is worth a try, especially as two other hostels, the **Regional** (915 223373 and **Villar** (915 316600, are found in the same building. Around the Plaza

Mayor the **Hostal Europa** (915 212900 FAX 915 214696, Calle Carmen 4, has been recently refurbished, and in the quieter region around the Paseo del Prado the **Hostal Mora** (914 201569 FAX 914 200564, Paseo del Prado 32, is well located to visit the city's great museums. On a real budget, one of the better choices, and rather a find in the capital city, is the **Hostal Los Perales** (915 227191, Calle Palma 61 (extremely inexpensive), in the lively Malasaña district, with a choice of other hostels in the same building.

WHERE TO EAT

Together with Barcelona, Madrid is where Spanish cuisine reaches its peak. There is some debate about whether the city has a distinctive cuisine of its own, but its sophisticated blend of the influences of Andalucía, Galicia and Asturias certainly translates into some superb gastronomic experiences, and this is a good place to splash out on a genuine Spanish feast. Most famous of all is the *cocido madrileño*, a stew where the principal ingredient is chickpeas, combined with carrots, celery, cabbage, turnips and potatoes, as well as various types of meat. Despite its distance from the sea, fish dishes are widely available, with *bacalao* (cod) amongst the most popular. Be warned that the Spanish eat their evening meals late, at a time when many tourists expect to be back in their hotel rooms thinking about sleep. In this fast-moving, moveable society *tapas* are especially convenient; delicious saucer-sized meals to snack on before moving on to the next venue. These can be a meal in themselves, especially for those too hungry to wait for the city to be ready to eat — or serve — the evening meal.

Among the best restaurants in the city, where you're likely to spend more than €50 per head, is the hugely popular Basque restaurant **El Amparo** (914 316456, Callejón Puigcerdá 8, where you'll have to book well in advance. Rather less notice is needed for **El Bodegón** (915 628844, Calle del Pinar 15, which also serves new-wave Basque food; try the special menu that provides small portions of many creative dishes. The **Jockey** (913 191003, Calle Amador de los Ríos 6, is one of Madrid's best-known and consistently good restaurants, with an excellent wine list. It is on the formal side — tie needed. **La Dorada** (915 702004, Calle de Orense 64, serves Andalusian cuisine, concentrating on fish. It has a pretty decor and is very fashionable and always crowded; the owner has two more restaurants of the same name, one in Sevilla and the other in Barcelona. The **Zalacaín** (915 614840, Calle Alvarez Baena 4, is widely believed to be Spain's top restaurant, with creative haute cuisine, elegant surroundings and impeccable service. Pricey, but worth a splash or an expense account dinner. **Botín** (913 664217, Calle

Cuchilleros 17, is, according to the *Guinness Book of Records*, the oldest restaurant in the world (opened in 1725). Once a favorite of Hemingway's, now it is popular with American tourists for its good Castilian food, especially roasts and game, and efficient service.

Step down to restaurants costing less than €50 per head and **Alkalde** (915 763359, Calle Jorge Juan 10, is a rustic-looking Basque restaurant in the Salamanca district with homely tasty cooking. **Cabo Mayor** (913 508776, Calle Juan Ramón Jiménez 37, is an elegant predominantly fish restaurant in the modern part of city; its bread and desserts are homemade. **Café Gijón** (915 310548, at Paseo de Recoletos, has wood-paneled walls

It is not essential to spend so much on eating in Madrid, and an enormous range of inexpensive restaurants, cafés and *tapas* bars offer delicious snacks and meals costing less than €20. Even the most expensive restaurants usually offer perfectly affordable *tapas* at the bar. Usually, the best way to find inexpensive restaurants is to just follow your nose: delicious smells, animated crowds and the colorful arrays of *tapas* at the bar are clues to look for. **Carmencita** (915 316612, Calle de la Libertad 16, is an atmospheric wood-paneled, brass-fitted restaurant charging less than it should for great Basque cuisine. **Momo** (915 327162, Calle Augusto Figueroa 41, has very inexpensive meals, especially the *menú del día*. **Museo de Jamón** is a

and Art Nouveau lamps and manages to preserve the turn-of-the-twentieth-century atmosphere of this famous literary café-restaurant. It's a bit passé as an intellectual watering hole, but is cozy in winter and has tables outside on the Castellana in summer. **La Fuencisla** (915 216186, Calle San Mateo 4, is a gourmet's favorite: thoughtful cooking and wide choice of wines. **La Trainera** (915 768035, Calle de Lagasca 60, is a great fish restaurant in an unassuming setting. Try the fish soup and then the lightly steamed then fried *merluza* (hake), accompanied by a Fontousal, a light dry white wine from León. **Viuda de Vacas** (913 665847, Calle Cava Alta 23, is a family-run restaurant near the Rastro (flea-market). It is a great place for weekend lunches, favored by artists, writers and film stars. It does not take reservations, so come on time — at 2 PM when they start serving lunch.

well-run and stylish chain, dispensing Spanish "fast-food." They are instantly recognizable from the scores of hams hanging from the ceilings. This is a great place for a sandwich or a plate of ham or cheese, with pungent fresh bread, helped down with a glass of wine or draught beer. Each Museo has a well-stocked delicatessen counter for take-out purchases.

NIGHTLIFE

Madrid's nightlife is famous. This is a city where you can get traffic jams at 3 AM. Experienced ravers come here, party for a few days and then trickle away, exhausted and defeated. Even with

OPPOSITE: Madrid's great Rastro (flea market) on a Sunday morning. ABOVE LEFT: Museo de Jamón. ABOVE RIGHT: The salon of the Palace Hotel, one of the city's refurbished belle époque hotels.

a midday *siesta*, no one quite knows how the *madrileños* keep up this grueling pace.

Several places put on flamenco, but two of the best are: **La Peña Flamenca La Carcelera**, Calle de Monteleón 10, and **Café de Chinitas** (915 485135, at Calle Torija 7.

If you want a classic cocktail to fuel — or refuel — the evening, drop into **Bar Chicote** (914 623875, Gran Vía 12, which has art deco architecture and is another echo of Hemingway. Live jazz can be heard — very inexpensively — nearly every night at the **Café Central** (913 694143, Plaza Angel 10. For classical chamber music, again at low cost, go to the elegant **Salon del Prado** (914 293361, Calle del Prado 4.

There is a special word in Madrid for the hours between midnight and dawn: *la madrugada*. Given no one ever seems to go to bed here, this is a time that is, according to *madrileños*, best spent partying. *Discobares* are an excellent Spanish tradition, where loudish music allows conversation but is perfectly danceable for those in the mood. The popular venues, spilling onto the street, are easy to assess as you stroll past, but **Cliché**, on Calle Barquillo, in the Chueca area, is in the middle of a line of *discobares* and is a good starting point.

A step up from *discobares* are *discotetecas*, which have more lights, often a strict dress code, and usually charge for admission. There are over 250 discotheques in the city and their popularity changes quickly. Many open and close in a single season: check the magazine *Metrópoli*, a free supplement with Friday's *El Mundo* newspaper, for recent listings. Few will even open until well after midnight. A selection of the more established are **Archy** at Calle Marqués de Riscal (corner of Calle de Fortuny), a lively place with a restaurant as well; for techno music **Pachá**, Calle de Barceló 10; or, slightly expensively, **Joy**, Calle de Arenal, frequented by those who can afford to dress well enough to get in. Don't be too discouraged if it's quiet when you get there. It doesn't liven up until about 3 AM.

HOW TO GET THERE

Madrid is at the heart of Spain's transportation systems. Many travelers will arrive in Madrid on international flights, in which case they'll land at the **Aeropuerto de Barajas** (913 058343, 13 km (eight miles) east of the city center. The best way to get into town is by the subway, which takes about 30 minutes, while there's a **shuttle bus** (914 316192 (€2.25) to the Plaza de Colón every fifteen minutes between 7 AM and 11 PM and less frequently outside these hours; the ride takes between 20 minutes and an hour to reach the center, depending on traffic. At the airport there are several car rental companies, a 24-hour currency bureau and a RENFE office for train tickets.

Madrid has two main train stations: the **Estación de Chamartin**, in the north of the city, is for trains to northern Spain and France, and also serves Cádiz, Córdoba, Málaga and Alicante. The more central **Estación de Atocha** serves the regions of Andalucía and Extremadura as well as Portugal, with a separate terminal for Toledo and local destinations. This is also the terminus for the high-speed trains (AVE), which reach Sevilla, for example, in two and a half hours. AVE trains need booking; call RENFE (913 289020. Both stations are on the subway system.

International buses stop at the **Estación Sur de Autobuses** (914 684200, one and a half kilometers (just over a mile) south of Atocha train station. There are also a number of independent bus and coach companies; for more information check with the tourist offices or on the **bus information line** (914 352266.

Most of Spain's main roads hurtle towards Madrid, to be tamed by the speed cameras now installed around the ring road that circles the city. There's a free information service for motorists, the **Highway Assistance** (ADA) (902 232423.

AROUND MADRID

Around Madrid, all within easy reach by road, are several places no one visiting Spain should miss. These include Spain's former capital, Toledo. In an hour or so from central Madrid, you can reach the Sierra de Guadarrama, a range of granitic, pine-covered mountains to the northwest of the city. If Madrid is the heart of Spain, the Sierra de Guadarrama are its lungs. In the hills, skiing (at **Navacerrada** and **Cotos**), hiking, fishing, hunting and crystalline mountain air draw *madrileños* and countless others. There are also four major sightseeing attractions, worth a daytrip at least, in or around this area: El Escorial, Valle de los Caídos (Valley of the Fallen), Ávila and Segovia. All these can — and often are — visited in day-trips, but each is worth a longer stay.

TOLEDO

Originally a Roman town, Toledo later became the capital of the Visigoths. The Moors captured it in the eighth century and turned it into their northern capital. Under Moorish rule, Toledo established itself as a center of learning and a crossroads of cultures. The city became renowned in the Mediterranean world for its school of translators and its philosophers, alchemists and mathematicians, and its population grew to 200,000, more than three times what it is today. Moorish rule came to an end when King Alfonso VI of Castilla and El Cid conquered the city in 1085.

Toledo became the capital of Christian Spain but continued to show tolerance to the country's largest Jewish population and its Moorish residents. During the next three centuries, the city continued to flower, a wonderfully cosmopolitan center where Christian, Jew and Muslim lived in harmony, and where politicians, soldiers, painters, writers, poets, priests and savants gathered. It was perhaps not just concidence that Alfonso the Wise, Spain's most erudite monarch, was born in Toledo. All that ended, though, over four centuries ago, with the expulsion of the Jews and the Moors, the introduction of the Inquisition, and Felipe II's decision to make Madrid the new capital of his dominions. Toledo retained some religious importance as the seat of the Spanish primate, but its only short-lived political reappearance was during the Civil War, when the Alcázar underwent an epic siege. The town's famous silk and steel industries disappeared to be replaced much later by marzipan and mass tourism. Toledo became a museum city long before museums were invented.

Today, it lives on, and for tourism. This carries with it obvious drawbacks: the rows of shops purveying almost identical goods, the phalanx of tourist buses outside the city gates, the endless stream of visitors, and so on. But the physical unity of the town and its great wealth of individual attractions make it all worthwhile. Toledo is a splendidly preserved microcosm of the Spanish experience, and the whole town is a national monument. Try and stay overnight. Most people arrive with the crowds and leave with them before nightfall, thus only seeing the place awash with humanity. The town takes on a much more natural, relaxed feeling after sunset.

General Information

It's not a bad idea to begin by inspecting it at a distance by driving around the ring road on the outer bank of the Tagus. There is a particularly good view from the **Parador Conde de Orgaz**, set on a bluff high above the river. This is also a good place to stay. To really get a feel of the city, you'll then need to drive into the city and, if in your own car, find somewhere to park. The only 24-hour parking lot is on the Paseo del Miradero, below the Plaza de Zocódover, with ad-hoc parking always running the risk of getting towed.

The **Tourist Information Office** (925 220843 FAX 925 252648 WEB SITE www.jccm.es, Puerta Nueva de Bisagra, open Monday to Friday 9 AM to 6 PM, Saturday 9 AM to 7 PM, Sunday 9 AM to 3 PM, is just outside the city walls, while there is a smaller bureau just outside the cathedral in Plaza del Ayuntamiento, open Monday to Friday 9 AM to 2 PM. Local taxis can be called through **Radio-Taxi** (925 255050 and 925 227070. For the local **hospital** call (925 269200, but a rather easier number to remember

— and more useful in an emergency — is that of the **ambulance** service (925 222222.

Finally, a word of warning. All photography, not just with a flash, is banned inside public buildings in Toledo, because of the damage constant flash-lighting can cause to delicate paintings and murals.

Festivals and Celebrations

There are three festivals of note every year: **Corpus Christi**, a week of processions, bullfights and concerts during which the streets are strewn with flowers and herbs; **Holy Week**, with more somber religious processions; and a week-long **musical festival** in October.

What to See and Do

The present **Alcázar** (925 223038, Cuesta del Alcázar (from "castle" in Arabic), was rebuilt after the pounding it received in the Civil War. It is open Tuesday to Sunday 9:30 AM to 2:30 PM, €1.25, free to European Union citizens on Wednesdays, closed Mondays and holidays. The site of a fortress

OPPOSITE: Student minstrels singing for their supper in a tavern in old Madrid. ABOVE: The synagogue of Santa María le Plenea, Toledo. OVERLEAF: A view of Toledo's Alcázar and the city from the terrace of the Parador.

since Roman times, it was destroyed and rebuilt on several occasions through the centuries. There is not a lot to see inside: a courtyard, a cloister, some military memorabilia. But for Civil War buffs, the high point will probably be the bullet and shrapnel-riddled headquarters of Colonel José Moscardó, a 58-year-old infantry officer who commanded the anti-Republican forces in the early chaotic and bloody stages of the war.

When General Franco and other officers launched their rebellion in Spanish Morocco in July 1936, Colonel Moscardó gathered about 12,000 soldiers and civil guards, plus 500 or so civilians including many women and children, into the Alcázar. The siege lasted 10 weeks, during which the Alcázar

was almost completely demolished by Republican artillery, mines and aerial bombing. The defenders, their numbers reduced by disease, death in battle, and starvation, hung on grimly until a column of Franco's Army of Africa relieved them in September. The assault troops, ironically, were Moors, reconquering the city that their ancestors had lost over nine centuries earlier. The most famous incident, according to the winning side's chroniclers, occurred in the first week of the siege when an officer of the attacking forces called Moscardó on the telephone. The ensuing conversation is now displayed in several languages on the walls of Moscardó's office. In short, the Republicans said that if Moscardó did not surrender the Alcázar immediately, they would shoot his 16-year-old son. The boy was put on the telephone and spoke to his father.

"What's happening, son?" Moscardó asked.

"They say they're going to shoot me if you don't surrender."

"Then commend your soul to God, shout 'Viva España, Viva Cristo Rey' (God the King), and die like a hero," his father replied. The siege continued and the boy was shot, according to the legend. Anti-Franco accounts, however, say the boy was not killed, although an older brother did die in another war zone; and the incident if not actually

apocryphal was over-dramatized and of little significance in the story of the siege. True or untrue, Moscardó went on to lead a heroic resistance and became famous for his laconic reports during that long hot summer as the Alcázar crashed into ruins around him and his dwindling band of followers. *"Sin novedad en el Alcázar,"* ("All quiet in the Alcázar") the aging colonel would report regardless of what was happening.

Toledo is a city of legends but it is the artifacts that people come to see and there are so many of those that it is hard to be selective. Fortunately, everything is within walking distance, and the narrow, winding streets are a delight to stroll in, some of which are so narrow it is possible to stand in the middle and touch the buildings on either side simultaneously.

The **cathedral** (closed 1 PM to 3:30 PM) is the focal point and is much more impressive inside than out. Begun in thirteenth century it was finished in the late fifteenth. Essentially Gothic, it has Mudéjar, Mozarabic, baroque and rococo flourishes, and the second longest nave in Spain (after the cathedral in Sevilla.) Under soaring arches and illuminated through the stained glass of over 800 windows, there is a rich assortment of wrought-iron grilles, paintings, sculpture, carved wood and carved stone. For Jan Morris, in her travel book on Spain, the cathedral was "a great hall of triumph, a victory paean for the Christian culture … nothing in Christendom, I suspect, better expresses the militancy of the Church than the *retablo* or reredos of Toledo, which rises in serried magnificence from the high altar to the roof." There are several chapels inside, which can be visited only by purchasing a ticket (€3), but there is plenty to see on a simple stroll around the atmospheric interior.

Another ecclesiastical treat is the church of **San Juan de los Reyes** (925 223802, Calle San Juan de los Reyes, open 10 AM to 1:45 PM and 3:30 PM to 5:45 PM daily, €1.25, and its lovely cloister, built in the fifteenth century by Juan Guas who was also the principal architect for the cathedral. The church was originally intended to be the last resting place of Ferdinand and Isabella, the Catholic Monarchs, but after the conquest of Granada they decided to be buried in that city. The outside of the church is draped with the chains of freed Christian prisoners.

Not far from the church is the **Judería**, Toledo's Jewish quarter. Only two of the city's original dozen synagogues survive, and these are **Santa María la Blanca** (925 227257, Calle de los Reyes Católicos 2, open daily 10 AM to 2 PM, 3:30 PM to 6 PM, €1.25, and **El Tránsito**, with its **Sephardic museum** (925 223665, Calle Samuel Levi, 10 AM to 2 PM and 4 PM 6 PM, closed Sunday evening and Mondays, €3, both beautiful and poignant reminders of Spain's Jewish heritage. Also close by is the

Casa del Greco (925 224046, Calle Samuel Levi 3, 10 AM to 2 PM and 4 PM to 6 PM, closed Sunday afternoon and Monday, €3, set in a restored sixteenth-century house. The painter never actually lived here, although he lived in the neighborhood, but the idea was to recreate the kind of dwelling he inhabited during his decades in the city. The house, carefully restored, has a number of El Greco's paintings, including a room devoted to portraits of the Apostles, although they are occasionally removed for exhibition elsewhere, and you're left looking at a scrap of paper saying where it's gone. The picture that many think is his greatest, *The Burial of the Count of Orgaz*, is, in any case, in the church of **Santo Tomé**.

Toledo's Moorish past is exquisitely evoked by the church of **Cristo de la Luz**, which was really a mosque and was built in the late tenth century on the site of a Visigothic church. It is very small but has classical horseshoe-shaped arches and airy vaulting, and is one of Spain's oldest and best-preserved Moorish structures. There is a legend that when King Alfonso VI and El Cid entered Toledo at the head of their victorious troops, the king's horse stopped dead in its tracks in front of this mosque and refused to move. The king ordered the mosque to be searched and, hidden in the walls, they found a crucifix and an oil lamp dating from the time when the building had been a Visigothic church. The lamp, the story goes, was still burning.

Toledo's two oldest bridges, the thirteenth-century **Alcantará** bridge and the fourteenth-century **San Martín** bridge, are worth walking across. They both provide good views and a sense of the physical power of the city in medieval times. There are an abundance of other churches, convents, museums and architectural riches.

Where to Stay and Eat

In the summer and on weekends it is a good idea to book your accommodation here ahead. Although the hotels are relatively good value, there aren't that many of them and they do fill up. Worse, they're spread around town in odd little corners so a last-minute search for a room is no fun at all. The smartest place to stay is just outside Toledo, in the **Parador Conde de Orgaz** (925 221850 FAX 925 225166 E-MAIL Toledo@parador.es, Cerro del Emperador (expensive), with an unparalleled view; rooms with views are surcharged. It's worth a visit for an evening drink, if only to see the illuminated Toledo cityscape, but personally I'd prefer to stay in town, with the chance to wander round the narrow lanes, soaking up the atmosphere, a drink and a *tapas* or two.

If you prefer to reside inside the town, there are several hotels that put you comfortably within walking distance of the city's treasures. These include the **Pintor El Greco** (925 214250 FAX 925 215819, Alamillos del Tránsito 13 (expensive), in a restored seventeenth-century townhouse, atmospheric and simply furnished. The **Alfonso VI** (925 222600 FAX 925 214458, Calle General Moscardó 2 (expensive), is well located, facing the Alcázar — make sure your room has a view of it.

Rather less expensive options do exist. The **Pensión Descalzos** (/FAX 925 222888 E-MAIL descazo @hostaldescalzos.com, Calle Descalzos 30 (inexpensive), is small but comfortable, though without a restaurant so you'll have to walk for breakfast, and parking depends on striking lucky. With its own parking the **Hotel Santa Isabel** (925 253120 FAX 925 253136, Calle Santa Isabel 24 (inexpensive), is centrally located. Travelers on a real budget should try instead for the **Fonda La Belviseña** (925 220067, Cuesta del Can 5 (inexpensive), or the out-of-town **Castillo San Servando** (925 224554, in a converted fourteenth-century castle (very inexpensive), signposted from the railway station.

Thanks, perhaps, to the day-tripping crowds there is a good selection of restaurants here, which are at their best in the, quieter, evenings. Some of the best are in the hotels, notably in the **Parador** (expensive).

Others are found in and around the narrow alleyways of the town center. The **Restaurant Adolfo** (925 227321, Calle La Granada 6 (expensive), is located in a medieval Jewish house, and **Cason de los López Toledo** (925 544774, Silleria 3 (moderate), which specializes in La Mancha cuisine. Toledo is well known for its partridge (excellent) and marzipan (not so good). For *tapas*, search out the **Café Sierpe** (925 225367, Calle Sierpe (inexpensive). Otherwise, as for all *tapas*, just follow your nose: in the pedestrianized town center there is plenty of choice. Nightlife here is a far cry from the late-night hysteria of Madrid, but is pleasant enough and the steep narrow alleys of the town center are especially atmospheric lit by streetlights.

How to Get There

Toledo is 70 km (44 miles) from Madrid, along the N-401, a rather dreary and congested road that passes through a series of small industrial towns. As you near the town, however, you round a curve and see roughly what El Greco gazed at when he painted this unique town nearly 400 years ago, making the drive worthwhile. Once there, your car will not be much of an asset. Trains from Madrid take 75 minutes, leaving hourly throughout the day, with information available at (925 223099. Direct buses are quicker, taking an hour; they leave on the hour in the morning and evening, and at odd hours through the day. For bus information call (925 223641.

Calle de los Reyes Católicos, Toledo.

EL ESCORIAL

The Monasterio de San Lorenzo de El Escorial — it's full title — was Felipe II's monument to God, to Spain, to his family and to himself. It is part palace, part monastery, part pantheon, part museum; and wholly astonishing. Why Felipe dedicated such an undertaking to Saint Lawrence (San Lorenzo), a relatively obscure religious figure, is not clear. One theory is that it was to celebrate a Spanish victory in France that fell on the saint's feast day. Another is that Felipe wanted to give Saint Lawrence his due for allegedly bringing the Holy Grail to Spain. There is also a belief that the

rectangular plan of the buildings and courtyards depicts the gridiron upon which the Romans roasted the saint alive.

The derivation of the rest of the name is much more mundane. There was, apparently, a mine in the area, and an *escorial* is a mine-tailing. In any case, once Felipe's orders were issued, his architects and builders did not lose any time. Juan Bautista of Toledo, the first architect, began work in 1563 but died four years later. Construction continued under the direction of his assistant, Juan de Herrera, and was completed in 1584.

Approaching the monastery from Madrid (55 km or 34 miles distant on the 505 road), you see it from a long way off in the foothills of the Sierra de Guadarrama, gray, somber and majestic. It completely dominates the small town of San Lorenzo de El Escorial, which has grown up in its shadow. Another good view, looking back down

on its immense proportions, is from a branch off the road that goes on to Ávila. This is where Felipe is said to have watched his dream take shape and is known as **La Silla del Rey** (The King's Chair.) El Escorial's impact, like its origins, evokes a variety of conflicting interpretations. This writer finds it cold, gloomy and forbidding, depicting the Spanish taste for combining the grandiose and the austere in its most extreme form, though it justifies its status as a must-see excursion, thanks to the serenity of its setting·and some lovely surprises inside those fortress-like walls.

General Information

El Escorial is open Tuesday to Sunday from 10 AM to 6 PM April through September and 10 AM to 5 PM from October through March, €5.50. It is closed on Mondays and public holidays. On Wednesday the site is free for European Union citizens, but this means it becomes impossibly crowded. There is a **Tourist Information Office (** 918 901554, Calle Floridablanca 10, open Monday to Saturday 11 AM to 6 PM and Sunday 10 AM to 3 PM, just north of the visitor entrance to the monastery.

What to See and Do

You enter on the north side and start with the area Felipe considered the least important, the palace quarters. When the House of Bourbon succeeded the Habsburgs on the Spanish throne at the beginning of the eighteenth century, they were appalled at the bleakness of the place, and spent much time and treasure brightening up the interior. The result was room after room of gorgeous tapestries, marble floors, crystal chandeliers, painted ceilings, gilded window frames and shutters, gold clocks, huge gilt-encrusted mirrors, and sumptuous furniture. The tapestries are not only in excellent condition despite their age, but they also provide a vivid panorama of eighteenth-century life. There are old men playing *boules* or cards, young boys practicing with the matador's cape and a pair of horns on a wicker frame, and bucolic binges in which a reveler, who has had more than he can handle, gets rid of it — all exquisitely woven in rich colors.

The contrast with the Habsburg apartments where Felipe lived and finally died in ulcerous agony is striking, and says a lot about the tastes and state of mind of this Spanish pharaoh. The tapestries cede to plain, white painted walls, in the place of marble floors are wooden parquet or gray flagstones, and the animated scenes are replaced by stern religious paintings. Felipe's study and cell-like bedroom, with its four-poster bed, are here, with tiny fireplaces that barely took the chill out of the air during the cold, dank winter

The Monasterio de San Lorenzo de El Escorial, built by King Felipe II in the sixteenth century.

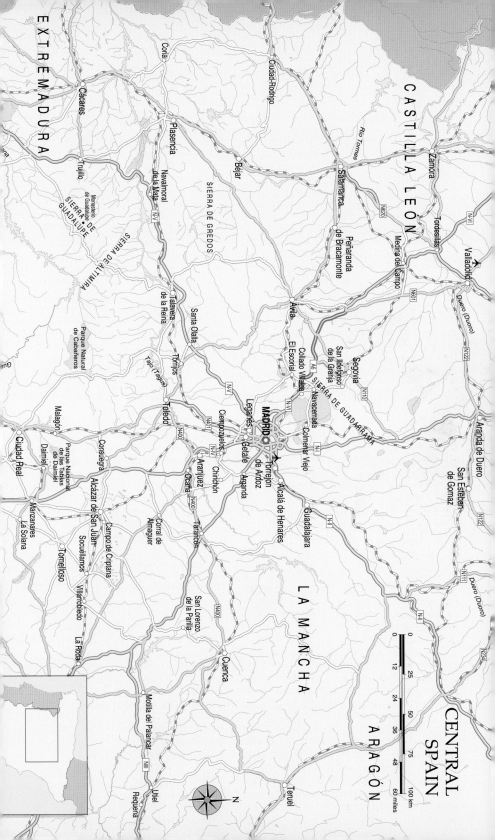

months. This is where the creator and the lord of the Escorial died in 1598, at the age of 71.

Across the **Patio de los Reyes**, the monastery's largest courtyard, a row of Old Testament kings, carved in stone, glower down. This is the **church**. Juan Bautista, the architect, was a pupil of Michelangelo, and the size and the proportions of the Escorial's church genuflect to St. Peter's in Rome. Inside, the centerpiece is the *retablo*, a soaring and richly decorated panoply that is flanked by sculpted figures of the Emperor Carlos V (Felipe II's father) and Felipe himself, accompanied by three of his four wives. (Mary Tudor, the English one, is absent.)

Beneath the church is the royal mausoleum. You descend a spiral staircase and enter a circular chamber. The walls are made of black and pink marble, there is a lot of gilt around, and light is provided by a centrally hung chandelier. Stacked on shelves around the walls are marble sarcophagi. In all but three lie the remains of nearly every Spanish king who has reigned since the Escorial was built. Queens, princes and princesses are also accommodated, but there is a traditional waiting period before a royal corpse is interred in the main chamber.

On the way to the library and museum, you will pass through the cloister that is also known as the **Hall of the Battles**. Along one wall there is a vast fresco depicting the battle of Higueruela in 1431 where King Juan II defeated the Moors of Granada. The **Library** is a lovely, spacious, well-lit room with colorful frescoes on the ceiling illustrating the liberal arts and sciences as they were recognized in the sixteenth century. Felipe was a book-worm and bibliophile. There are over 40,000 volumes in his collection and many of the most beautiful illustrated manuscripts are on display. Felipe is also still there, in one of his best portraits, gazing down at his books and wearing that familiar black stove-pipe hat.

The **Museum** is really an art gallery and contains paintings by El Greco, Velázquez, Ribera and Zubarán, Titian and Tintoretto, and a whole room of stunning canvases by Hieronymus Bosch, including his famous *Creation*. (His *Garden of Earthly Delights* is in Felipe's bedroom.)

There is one Bosch painting, showing Christ surrounded by a crowd with crafty and knowing expressions on their faces, that effortlessly spans the five centuries since it was painted, and recalls the satirical film, *The Life of Brian*.

There is more to see, but this should whet the appetite of most travelers. You can take photographs wherever you wish, without a flash. Beware Mondays and public holidays when the Escorial is closed; and plan to spend at least half a day here, although there is nowhere especially enticing to stay — or even eat. It is, however, well worth the detour.

Where to Stay and Eat

Accommodation here does book out in summer, so reserve well ahead. The best options are the **Hotel Botánico** (918 907879 FAX 918908158, Calle Timoteo Padrós 16 (expensive), set in the grounds of a former palace, or the **Hotel Florida** (918 901721 FAX 918 901715 E-MAIL hotelflorida@teleline.es (moderate), right next to the monastery itself. On a budget, try the **Hotel Tres Arcos** (918 906897 FAX 918 907997, Calle Juan de Toledo 42 (inexpensive). The best meals tend to be had away from the monastery: try the **La Cueva**, Calle San Antón (expensive).

How to Get There

There are 31 trains a day from Madrid's Atocha Station, with a local shuttle bus heading up to the center of town. By car, the monastery is 55 km (34 miles) northwest of Madrid on the 505.

VALLE DE LOS CAÍDOS

Not far from the Escorial, on the road to Guadarrama, there is another monument built by a more modern Spanish leader with similar religious, political and personal motives in mind. This is the Valle de los Caídos (Valley of the Fallen), open Tuesday to Sunday 9:30 AM to 7 PM from April through September, and from 10 AM to 6 PM from October through March,€4.25. The brainchild of — and grandiose mausoleum for — General Francisco Franco, it was built by prisoners from the defeated Republican side in the 1936–1939 Civil War. Although the monument is ostensibly for all those who fell in that bitter struggle, most Spaniards tend to think of it as Franco's paean to the fascist cause. The dictator is buried here, and whatever you think of the symbolism, it is a spectacular if bizarre edifice in a pretty mountain setting.

To reach it, you go up a long fir tree-lined drive to a monastery (with a hostel for guests), a gigantic granite cross — 125 m (410 ft) high, and a basilica buried deep in the rocky hillside. The nave-like tunnel that leads into the basilica is 260 m (830 ft) long. Lamps high up on the walls, thrust out at an angle, illuminate the tunnel and its avenging angels with long swords, large billowing tapestries, and shadowy side chapels. The overall impression is a scene from the *Lord of the Rings*.

The basilica is less mythic and pretentious. Under flagstones close to the altar lie the bodies of Franco and José Antonio Primo de Rivera, the founder of the Falange Party, who was murdered by the Republicans early in the war.

The king's frescoed library in El Escorial. Felipe II was quite a bookworm, with over 40,000 volumes in his collection.

ÁVILA

There are few better ways to see how most Spanish towns looked in the Middle Ages than to visit Ávila, a city totally encircled by crenellated walls and towers of gray granite, and one of Spain's Unesco World Heritage Sites. All the modern buildings and factories are outside this stone perimeter. Even today, it's not hard to imagine heavily armored Castilian knights riding out of the gates with a flourish of trumpets.

The best view, from a distance, is approaching Ávila from Salamanca; a good spot to pause and gaze is at the stone cross, opposite a gas station,

What to See and Do

There is no mistaking the military nature of the city; even the apse of the cathedral is part of the city walls, with the dual function of a place of prayer and a defensive tower. But for many visitors it is Santa Teresa de Ávila and her mystic appeal that is the city's most important attraction. Santa Teresa — Saint Theresa to the English-speaking — was a reformist Carmelite nun and a mystic who was born in Ávila in the early sixteenth century. She came from a wealthy family of Jewish converts but spent much of her life traveling around Spain urging religious orders to return to their vows of poverty and service. She died in 1582, leaving behind her a body of religious writing that

just before you reach your destination. From there you can get a sense of the frontier fortress town that Ávila was from Roman times. The medieval walls were built on Roman foundations in the eleventh century, after Alfonso VI of Castilla captured the city from the Moors. There are 88 turrets and nine gates in the walls that stretch for 2.4 km (1.5 miles) around the city. Historically, Ávila is famous for militarism and mysticism: the first associated with its strategic position and its fighting men, and the second with Saint Theresa of Ávila.

General Information

The **Tourist Office** (920 211387, Plaza de la Catedral, is open July to September 9 AM to 2 PM and 5 PM to 7 PM, October to June 10 AM to 2 PM and 4 PM to 7 PM, daily, while a smaller office opens for the same hours through the summer season at the **Basílica de San Vicente**. For a local **taxi** call (920 250800.

earned her the papal title of "Doctor of the Church" and became a best-selling book for centuries. Even now, she is still held up as an example to schoolgirls, who arrive in the city by the busload, where they get to buy a rather unpleasant confectionery made out of candied egg-yolks (*Yemas de Santa Teresa*), made by the local nuns.

Santa Teresa has the most interesting monuments in the city. The first stop might be her birthplace, at the **Convento de Santa Theresa**, Paseo del Rastro, open 8:30 AM to 2 PM and 3:30 PM to 8 PM, admittance free, with a small museum (daily 10 AM to 1 PM, 3:30 PM to 8 PM, €1.75) that contains a few relics, including one of her fingers, of interest mainly to her fans. The **Convento de la Encarnación**, open daily 9:30 AM to 1 PM, 4 PM to 7 PM, winter closing at 6 PM, €1, is a veritable homage to Santa Teresa, with rooms devoted to her slightest word. The first convent she founded, the **Convento de**

San José, open daily 10 AM to 1:30 PM, 4 PM to 7 PM, closing at 6 PM in winter, €1, has even more relics and collectibles, but by this time I'd gone into Teresa overload.

A good way to orientate yourself in Ávila is by walking around the perimeter of the old city walls or, better still, by strolling along the top. Unfortunately now there is a charge for this, and like so much else in Spain, they are closed on Monday. From Tuesday to Sunday between 10 AM to 8 PM it is possible to walk along the walls from Puerta del Alcázar to Puerta del Rastro for €1.25.

There are a number of significant churches in the city. The **Catedral** (open daily from 10 AM to 7 PM in the summer, in the winter it closes at 5 PM

and is shut for lunch, €1.50) is part fortress, part church. The **Basílica de San Vincente** (open daily from 10 AM to 1:30 PM and 4 PM to 6:30 PM, €1.25) has twelfth-century doorways overlaid by a medley of later styles, and the **Monasterío de Santo Tomás** (daily 10 AM to 1 PM, 4 PM to 8 PM, museum €1.25) has perhaps the most interesting exhibits in the town, including a weird sample of artifacts gathered during missionary activities in the Far East, and contains, in its sacristy, the infamous inquisitor, Torquemada.

Where to Stay and Eat
Ávila has several upmarket hotels. Perhaps the best is the **Palacio de Valderrábanos (** 920 211023 FAX 920 251691, Plaza de la Catedral 9 (expensive), atmospherically sited in a former Bishop's Palace. The **Parador Raimundo de Borgoña (** 920 211340 FAX 920 226166 E-MAIL avila@paradores.es, Calle

Marqués de Canales y Chozas 2 (expensive), is a step down, being in a converted mansion. The most expensive option is the **Palacio de los Velada (** 920 255100 FAX 920 254691, Plaza de la Catedral 10 (expensive), which is very smooth. On a budget, a good option is the **Hostal El Rastro (** 920 211218 FAX 920 251626, Plaza del Rastro 1 (inexpensive), set against the city walls. The most renowned restaurant is attached to this hotel, the **Mesón del Rastro (** 21-12-18, at the Plaza del Rastro 1, which serves local specialties such as beans with sausage, game and other fortifying Castilian dishes at moderate cost.

How to Get There
There are 24 trains a day to Ávila from Madrid, and eight buses a day on weekdays. By car, it is 115 km (72 miles), which takes a little over an hour on the N-505 from Madrid: find the walls (*muralles*) and you should be able to find somewhere to park.

SEGOVIA

Moving in a northeasterly direction in the circle of easily accessible places from Madrid, Segovia is more mellow and interesting than Ávila, less formal and self-conscious than Toledo. Catch its tawny profile in the evening light as the sun sets over the Castilian *meseta*, and it will take your breath — and perhaps your heart — away. Three features distinguish it: the Roman aqueduct, the cathedral and the Alcázar; but the whole city, secure and serene on its lofty hilltop and clothed in a warm limestone, has a physical and human quality that sets it apart, with grand squares and Renaissance mansions, small little-visited churches and graceful forgotten corners. It is a favorite spot for lovers and for Madrid's literary and film crowd, and it is not hard to see why.

General Information
The **Tourist Information Office (** 921 460334, Plaza Mayor 10, open daily 9 AM to 2 PM and 5 PM to 8 PM, has a full list of accommodation, which should probably be your first priority if this hasn't already been arranged. More people want to visit Segovia than there are hotel beds. There is a second office in the Plaza de Azoguejo, open from 10 AM to 8 PM.

For a **taxi** call **(** 921 445000. You'll probably need one from the train or bus stations, which are otherwise connected to the old city center by bus number 3.

The major **festivals** here are San Juan and San Pedro, between June 23 and 29, with major processions, and San Frutos, on the October 25, when

OPPOSITE: The medieval walls and battlements of Ávila. ABOVE: Segovia's heavily-turreted Alcázar.

big-headed figures roam the streets. In the last week of August the town holds its own running of the bulls, and the province as a whole, especially the town of Zamarramala, just north of Segovia, celebrates the Fiestas de Santa Águeda, when the men are driven (in jest) out of the towns, which are taken over by the married women.

What to See and Do

The Roman emperor Trajan ordered the building of the **aqueduct** in the second century AD just outside the eastern city walls. For nearly 2,000 years, this monumental piece of plumbing brought water into the city from the Río Frío about 18 km (11 miles) away. Its ancient granite columns and arches, laid without mortar, soar over the outskirts of the old city, and the lead-lined water duct that they support is in remarkably good shape; only recently has traffic vibration caused the authorities to make alternative arrangements for getting water into the town. For those who like figures, it has 167 arches, is 813 m (2,667 ft) long, and at a height of 28.1 m (100.53 ft) is the tallest surviving Roman aqueduct.

The Gothic **cathedral** (open 9:30 AM to 6 PM in winter, to 7 PM in summer) is the last of its kind to be built in Spain; construction began in 1525 and continued for the next 200 years, as flying buttresses and pinnacles were added on feverishly. There is a cloister attached, which belonged to the original cathedral and is now a museum (€2).

The **Alcázar** (10 AM to 6 PM in winter, to 7 PM in summer, €2.50) rears upward from a rocky promontory on the western edge of the city where two small rivers meet and act as a natural moat. Built as a fortress it was later a royal palace for the monarchs of Castilla: it fell out of history — much like Segovia itself — until 1862 when a group of discontented military cadets burned it down, apparently as a way of making their point that it was time to be transferred to Madrid. It was rebuilt and festooned with lots of turrets so that it looks more Bavarian than Spanish, and served as a model for the Disneyland castle in California. However, it is full of the delightful, if predictable, artifacts of Castilla's golden age: armor, heavy oak furniture, swords, muskets and cannons, tapestries and heraldic banners. There is a dizzying view from the topmost tower, a hard spiraling climb but worth the effort.

Facing the Alcázar is the ancient church of **Vera Cruz** (open 10:30 AM to 1:30 PM and 3:30 PM to 6 PM, to 7 PM in summer, closed Mondays and November, €1.25), a 12-sided masterpiece built by the Knights Templar in the thirteenth century, when it housed what was claimed to be a part of the relic of the True Cross.

The Gothic cathedral in Segovia with the Sierra Guadarrama in the background.

Where to Stay and Eat

Segovia, like Toledo, has a Parador, the **Parador de Segovia** (921 443737 FAX 921 437362 E-MAIL segovia @parador.es, Carretera de Valladolid (expensive), but disappointingly here it is a modern building outside the city's walls. Although it has great views of the city, especially when illuminated at night, you'll need a car to get back into the center, which seems a shame in such an atmospheric place.

Better, perhaps, to stay in town, where a good, moderately priced option is **Los Linajes** (921 460475 FAX 921 460479, Calle Doctor Velasco 9, which has the prettiest location, built into the city's northern wall with views over the valley, and a very useful underground parking lot. Some of the rooms have terraces and the restaurant here has a good reputation. A good moderately priced hotel, but without a restaurant, is the very central **Hotel Infanta Isabel** (921 461300 FAX 921 462217, Calle Isabel La Católica 1, an elegant nineteenth-century townhouse furnished with antiques and collectibles; take a room overlooking the square. They do have a small breakfast room.

Budget travelers will have to put up with the small rooms in the centrally located, inexpensive **Pensión Aragón** (921 460914, Plaza Mayor 4.

Segovia is famous for its cuisine, particularly in winter when the roast suckling pig (*cochinillo*), lamb, beef and game are at their best — you won't have to walk far before being tempted in to a restaurant. The most famous is **Mesón de Cándido** (921 428103, Plaza Azoguejo 5, a picturesque spot that has been attracting the famous — and not so famous — for over half a century (moderate). Other good places to eat include **Mesón José María** (921 461111, Calle Cronista Lecea 11, for new-wave Castilian cuisine (expensive); the **Mesón Duque** (921 462487, Calle Cervantes 12 (moderate); and **Casa Amado** (921 432077, Calle Fernandez Ladreda 9, which serves traditional dishes, mainly to locals (moderate).

How to Get There

Segovia is well-connected to Madrid by public transportation, with nine trains a day from Atocha Station and 30 buses a day. The distance from Madrid is 87 km (55 miles).

With your own car there are two ways back to Madrid, and each offers an attraction. Twenty minutes out of Segovia on the N-601 brings you to the village of **San Ildefonso**, where Felipe V, the first Bourbon to ascend the Spanish throne, built a royal palace called **La Granja** (the Farm). The name was deceptive. Felipe and his successors had an eighteenth-century sense of scale and style that they indulged freely. Their French ancestors, especially Louis XIV, the "Sun King," seemed to provide their principal inspiration. The gardens, on the slopes of the Sierra de Guadarrama, are particularly lavish and noted for their fountains.

The other route, along the N-603, takes you close to the **Palacio Riofrío** (Royal Hunting Lodge), built by Felipe V's widow, Isabella de Farnese. This is an Italianate baroque palace with a hunting museum full of stuffed trophies; a hunter's — and a taxidermist's — delight. For gentler nature lovers, there is an elegant park populated by living deer, which do not fear ending up on the hunting lodge's walls.

OTHER EXCURSIONS FROM MADRID

Continuing the circuit around Madrid, there are some other places of interest. To the east, along the N-11, there is **Alcalá de Henares**, which was the site of Spain's leading university in the sixteenth century, and was the birthplace of Miguel de Cervantes, author of *Don Quixote*. Then there is **Chinchón**, to the southeast off the N-III, a picturesque country town with a pretty main square (the Plaza Mayor), and a popular bolt hole for *madrileños* on weekends and on holidays.

Due south, on the N-IV, lies **Aranjuez**, a spacious and leisurely paced town on the banks of the Río Tajo, which was chosen by Felipe V to be his Versailles. The palace does not make it, but the interiors are remarkably decorated and the well-maintained gardens are superbly laid out. With its broad plane-tree-lined avenues, Aranjuez has a French feel to it. That impression, however, vanishes if you should ever hear the haunting strains of Joaquín Rodrigo's Concierto de Aranjuez — nothing could be more Spanish.

NORTHWEST FROM MADRID: OLD CASTILLA

Moving out beyond Ávila and Segovia, the traveler penetrates the historic core of Spain, where the Spanish language, which is still known as Castellano, has its roots, and where the kings of Castilla began their drive for conquest and unity in the peninsula. There are several interesting towns that give life and character to the Castilian *meseta*, that great interior plateau whose monotony is atoned for by its fecundity and pastoral beauty. The most notable in this outer arc around Madrid are Valladolid and Salamanca, but there are smaller ones, like Zamora, that have appeal (see CAMINO DE SANTIAGO for the more distant cities of BURGOS, page 211, and LEÓN, page 214).

VALLADOLID

Twice the capital of Spain in the heyday of empire, Valladolid is where Ferdinand of Aragón and Isabella of Castilla — collectively known as the Catholic Monarchs — were married, where an impoverished Columbus died and where Felipe II was born, and where Cervantes wrote the first part of *Don Quixote*. Today, Valladolid, never a city that could be termed elegant, swims in a smaller pond. It is the capital of the autonomous region of Castilla-León, and is an important industrial center.

Felipe II's architect, Juan de Herrera, who designed the Escorial, also started building Valladolid's cathedral, but he died before it was completed. In fact, the building was never finished, although it later received the attentions of Alberto Churriguera in the early eighteenth century, thus combining the work of a master of austere grandeur with one of baroque fantasy. Churriguera's stone filigree façades are ranked amongst the greatest of Spain's architectural achievements.

General Information

The **Tourist Information Office** (983 354731, Calle Santiago 19, open daily 9 AM to 2 PM and 5 PM to 7 PM, is in the heart of the city, with the central State-run office at (983 351801, Plaza de Zorillo 3. To get around, call **Radio-Taxi de Valladolid** (983 291411. To keep in touch, there is Internet access at **Bocattanet** (983 378804, María de Molina 16, open 10 AM to 10 PM.

What to See and Do

Amid the new developments that have largely robbed Valladolid of much of its architectural heritage, one art form that has survived, with exuberance, is sculpture. There was something about Valladolid that appeared to uncap the imagination and fantasies of stone-carvers and sculptors, evinced in the stunning façades in the Plaza San Pablo — with the church of **San Pablo** and the **Colegio de San Gregorio** — and the **Museo Nacional de Escultura** (983 250375, Cadenas de San Gregorio 1, open Tuesday to Saturday 10 AM to 2 PM and 4 PM to 6 PM, Sunday 10 AM to 2 PM, €2.40, free on Saturday afternoon and Sunday. The museum houses the largest and finest collection of sixteenth-century sculpture in Spain. While in the city, another worthwhile museum is the **Museo Oriental** (983 306800, Paseo de Los Filipinos 7, open weekdays 4 PM to 7 PM, Sundays and holidays 10 AM to 2 PM, €2.40, which has a superb collection of gleanings picked up by sticky-fingered Catholic missionaries in China and the Philippines.

Most famous of all Valladolid's residents was Cervantes, and his work here is commemorated in the **Casa de Cervantes** (983 308810, Calle del Rastro, open Tuesday to Saturday 9:30 AM to 3:30 PM, Sunday 9:30 AM to 3 PM, €2.40, which was his home from 1603 to 1606, and was where he wrote part of *Don Quixote*. The museum recreates a nobleman's house of the era; guided tours last 30 minutes.

Where to Stay and Eat

Valladolid's best hotels are the **Olid Meliá** (983 357200, Plaza San Miguel 10 (expensive), and the

Felipe IV (983 307000, Calle Gamazo 16 (expensive). Set in a graceful Renaissance mansion by the Plaza Mayor is the **Imperial** (983 330300 FAX 983 330813, Calle Peso 4 (moderate), which provides excellent value, a central location and a good atmosphere.

Stepping down in cost is the **Hotel el Nogal** (983 340333 FAX 983 354965, Calle Conde Ansurez 10 (inexpensive), which is well located and has its own bar and restaurant. Travelers on a budget should head for the **Pensión Dani** (983 300249, Calle Perú (very inexpensive), south of the city center.

There are a number of good middle-price-range restaurants here, the most popular being **La Goya** (983 231259, Calle Puente Colgante 79, and **La Fragua** (983 337102, Paseo Zorrilla 10. The best-known restaurant in the city remains the **Mesón Panero** (983 301673, Calle Marina Escobar 1 (expensive), closed Sunday. If you are finding that long and varied menus have become daunting, try **La Pedriza**, Calle Colmenares 10 (moderate), where there is no menu and the only dish on offer is roast lamb — at its best. Closed Mondays. Many of the city's smartest restaurants are found on the Calle Correos, to the west of the Plaza Mayor, so this is a good street for a hungry evening stroll.

How to Get There

Situated 182 km (109 miles) north of Madrid, Valladolid is linked to the capital by the N-VI freeway and the connecting N-620 road. The towns of León and Burgos are 122 km (76 miles) northwest and 134 km (84 miles) northeast respectively. The train station, with regular connections to Madrid, is in the center of town at the Paseo de Campo Grende, while the bus station is to the west at Calle Puente Lodgante 2. The city also has an **airport** (983 415400 to the west, with internal services mainly aimed at the business traveler.

SALAMANCA

Salamanca, the ancient university town, is distinguished by its golden sandstone architecture and broad, timeless squares. It is one of Spain's World Heritage-listed cities, and one of its most graceful and well preserved.

To fully appreciate its beauty, it is best to approach, slowly, overland; preferably in the morning with the early sun warming Salamanca's domes and spires. The banks of the Tormes, a broad but shallow river, are lined with poplars, larches and silver birches, and the countryside intrudes with flocks of sheep browsing in the lush grass along the water's edge. Later in the day, at the hour of the *paseo*, you may find lovers strolling along the bridge or gypsies encamped beneath it. To complete the cycle, the best night view of Salamanca is from the same side but at a higher elevation, with the twin cathedrals atmospherically lit.

Salamanca's university was founded in the early thirteenth century. By the middle of that century, the university had progressed far enough to rank with Oxford, Bologna and Paris. At its height, in the mid-sixteenth century, it had over 7,000 students, 60 professors and 24 constituent colleges. Its greatest teacher, Fray Luis de León, a theologian and poet, was active at this time, but the scourge of the Counter-Reformation undermined its institutions and its liberal spirit, and one of Europe's finest seats of learning went into an irreversible decline.

By the early nineteenth century, its student body had dropped to little more than 300. A brief resurgence took place in the first decades of the

and 4:30 PM to 6 PM, Sunday 10 AM to 2 PM and 4:30 PM to 6:30 PM, as well as the **Provincial Tourist Office** (923 268571, Rua Mayor, open Monday to Friday 9 AM to 2 PM and 5 PM to 7 PM, Saturday and Sunday 10 AM to 2 PM and 4 PM to 7 PM. Both can be relied upon for good details about local hotels as well as a monthly guide, *Lugares*, with details of local events.

For transportation call **Radio-Taxi** (923 271111 or **Radio-Tele-Taxi** (923 250000, and in case of medical emergency call the Red Cross — the **Cruz Roja** (923 222222. To collect e-mail, there is an Internet café just to the north of the Plaza Mayor: **Internet Bar**, Calle Zamoro 7, open Monday to Friday 9 AM to 2 AM, weekends 11 AM to 2 AM.

twentieth century when the Basque philosopher and novelist, Miguel de Unamuno, taught here. However, another intellectual blight, in the shape of Franco's narrow-minded outlook on matters of the mind and soul, seriously damaged its recovery. Today, it ranks about seventh in the country's university ratings, although it has become well known abroad for its excellent courses for foreign students of Spanish history, language and culture. And in a way, the lack of interest in the city over the first half of the twentieth century was its salvation. It was spared Franco's brutal building programs and remains a small, welcoming and undeniably graceful city.

General Information

At the heart of the old city is the Plaza Mayor, where you'll find the main city **Tourist Office** (923 218342, open Monday to Saturday 9:30 AM to 2 PM

What to See and Do

Some of the greatest sights in Salamanca can be found just by walking around. There are so many churches, small and large, so many ancient palaces, mansions, convents and colleges, interspersed with gently paved squares that days, if not weeks can pass here. There are, however, some highlights that should on no account be missed.

A unique feature of this ancient city is the phenomenon of the **twin cathedrals**, built almost on top of each other. The one that imperiously dominates the city is the **Catedral Nueva**, open daily 9 AM to 2 PM, 4 PM to 6 PM in winter, to 8 PM in summer, free admission, which was erected in the sixteenth century. Late Gothic, it is impressive, but is upstaged by the smaller, older Romanesque cathedral, the **Catedral Viejo**, open daily 10 AM to 1:30 PM and 4 PM to 5:30 PM in winter, to 7:30 PM in summer, €2, which is entered from the right side of the nave of the new cathedral. With simple columns, fan vaults and no central *coro* (choir) to block the view, it has a special charm. There is a cloister, backlit tombs in an aisle off the nave, and side chapels where you can sit and rest in the company of the sarcophagus of a medieval bishop.

Salamanca's ultimate marvel is the **Plaza Mayor**, built in the early eighteenth century, and by general acclaim Spain's greatest public square. Made of a rich, loamy sandstone that has turned into a burnished gold through exposure and age, the square is like a gigantic, superbly proportioned carving. It is completely enclosed by houses four stories high that are further bonded by long stretches of wrought-iron balconies and underpinned by a colonnaded arcade. After wandering around this golden city's jumbled streets and squares that are rarely square, there is no better place to sit with a *copa* or *café con leche* at your side and watch the Spanish world go by.

The ultimate expression of plateresque architecture, a technique of fine relief decoration ideally suited to Salamanca's soft, versatile sandstone, is found at the **Salamanca University**, Calle de los Libreros, which is open Monday to Friday 9:30 AM to 1:30 PM and 4 PM to 6:30 PM, weekends 9:30 AM to 1:30 PM and 4 PM to 7 PM, €3. The façade, lavishly decorated with floral designs, heraldic emblems and medallions, is said to contain a small, hidden frog: anyone who finds this (unassisted) is apparently assured of good luck and marriage within the year. For a good feeling of what Salamanca University represented, walk around the courtyard of the **Patio de las Escuelas**, into the lecture hall — where Fray Luis de León uttered his famous "As we were saying yesterday ..." greeting to his students after five years in the Inquisition's dungeons — and on into the university library with old books and ancient globes. There are plenty of students to add atmosphere and life to this venerable center of learning

Where to Stay and Eat

As a university town where many foreign students come to study Spanish history, culture and language, Salamanca has a large inventory of accommodation, restaurants and bars. Its top hotels are the **Gran Hotel** (923 213500, Plaza Poeta Iglesias 5 (expensive), the **Monterey** (923 214400, Calle Azafranal 21 (expensive), and the stunning **Palacio de Castellanos** (923 261818 FAX 923 261819, Calle San Pablo 58-64 (very expensive), which is set in a fifteenth-century palace. The **Parador de Salamanca** (923 228700 FAX 923 192087 E-MAIL Salamanca@parador.es, Teso de la Feria 2 (expensive), is undistinguished architecturally, and it's position, over the Roman bridge that leads to the city's walls, is not ideal while the bridge is closed for renovation, as is currently the situation. The views, however, are good.

For those on a more limited budget, the outstanding option here is the **Hotel Rector** (923 218482 FAX 923 214008, Rector Esperabé 10 (moderate), a lavishly furnished boutique hotel in a *palacete*, or town mansion, which has its own parking. Less expensive again is the **Hotel Emperatriz** (923 219200, Calle Comañia 44 (inexpensive), quietly set in a car-free zone.

The **Residencia-Albergue Juvenil Salamanca** (923 269141 or 923 213193 FAX 923 214227, Calle Escoto 13–15 (very inexpensive), is the only youth hostel in the city center.

As a student city, the nightlife is lively, and there is a rich selection of *tapas* bars and modestly priced restaurants in the back streets around Plaza Mayor. To dine with a little more style try **El Candil Nuevo** (923 219027, Plaza de la Reina 2, which has good snails and delicious grilled kidneys (moderate), and **Chez Victor** (923 219027, Calle Espoz y Mina 26, which specializes in French dishes (expensive) and is closed on Sunday nights, Mondays and through August. When it comes to music, there are plenty of *discobares* and nightclubs in the southeastern part of the old city, off the Gran Vía, full and busy until late at night.

How to Get There

By road, Salamanca is 212 km (132 miles) west of Madrid and 97 km (60 miles) from Ávila along the N-501. This brings you in on Salamanca's best side, where the countryside edges in close to the town, and the Río Tormes, crossed by the Puente Romano. Salamanca is 197 km (123 miles) south of León and 115 km (72 miles) southwest of Valladolid. The **bus station** (923 236217 and the **train station** (923 120202 are fifteen minutes walk east and west respectively of the city center. The **airport** (923 329600 is to the city's east.

ZAMORA

The countryside to the north of Salamanca is an atmospheric throwback to a rural life, fast disappearing from Europe. At harvesting time, hamlets and villages from another era — with crumbling churches, wooden carts, clumps of olive trees, the smell of dung, and the entire population getting ready to thresh newly harvested grain — imprint themselves on even the most transient visitor's memory. At the heart of this area of rural Castila is the small town of Zamora.

Zamora is not a large or particularly notable town but it is a pleasant place to stop for lunch, a drink or even overnight. Rising up above the Río Duero (the Douro when it crosses into Portugal), it has the quality of an oasis: cool, dimly lit buildings, shady squares and niches protected by cypresses, firs and pine trees, and the soothing sound

The Plaza Mayor in Salamanca, Spain's ancient university town.

of running water. The Romanesque cathedral dates from the twelfth century and has an unusual Byzantine dome and finely carved sixteenth-century choir stalls that contrast oddly with the plain, untreated pinewood floors. Zamora was in the frontline of both the Christian-Moorish wars and the conflicts between the Christian potentates themselves. Appropriately, El Cid was knighted in a church here.

General Information

The Old Quarter of Zamora is set on a ridge over the Río Duero. The **Tourist Information Office** (980 531845, Calle Santa Clara 20, is open Monday to Friday, 9 AM to 2 PM and 5 PM to 7 PM, and

on weekends from 10 AM to 2 PM and 5 PM to 8 PM. To collect e-mail check in to **Ciberc@fe** on Plaza Viriato, open daily from 11 AM to 3 AM, and for transportation call **Tele-Taxi** (980 534444.

What to See and Do

Most of the city's attractions date back to the twelfth century, including 12 **Romanesque churches**, topped with the bulky nests of storks. These are generally open between 10 AM and 1 PM and 5 PM to 6:30 PM in winter, to 8 PM in the summer, and entrance is free of charge. The rather more recent **cathedral** shares the same hours, and is notable mainly for its museum, which is open Tuesday to Saturday 11 AM to 2 PM and 4 PM to 6 PM in winter, 5 PM to 8 PM in summer, Sunday 10 AM to 2 PM, €2; it has a notable collection of incredibly detailed Flemish tapestries dating back to the fifteenth century.

Where to Stay and Eat

Zamora's Parador, previously — and sometimes still — known as the Fernando II de León, is the **Parador de Benavente** (980 514497 FAX 980 530063 E-MAIL zamora@parador.es, Plaza de Viriato 5 (expensive), a good enough reason in itself to visit the town and stay a while. Set in a palace built on the site of a Roman fortress, this is a wonderfully atmospheric hotel of rugs and armor, wooden galleries and coats of arms. This is also, arguably, the best place to eat in town, for an expensive meal. There's another excellent hotel, the **Hostería Real de Zamora** (980 534545 FAX 980 534522 E-MAIL hostzamora@wanadoo.es, Cuesta Pizarro 7 (moderate), set in the 400-year-old Palacio de Inquisidores. Less expensive, the **Hostal La Reina** (980 533939, Calle La Reina 1 (inexpensive), is a central and good alternative.

The best place to find restaurants is in and around the Plaza Mayor, which has plenty of *tapas* on offer.

How to Get There

The bus and train stations are one and a half kilometers (just over a mile) to the north of the town center. Zamora is 62 km (39 miles) north of Salamanca and 96 km (60 miles) west of Valladolid.

SOUTHWEST OF MADRID: EXTREMADURA

Extremadura, which means neither "over-ripe" nor "extremely hard" but "beyond the Duero River," is one of the least-visited parts of Spain, and perhaps all the better for it. This is a wild and beautiful if impoverished land, a changing landscape of wheat fields, evergreen oaks, eucalyptus and cork trees, framed by hazy mountain ranges. It is also a land of bull-breeding, of whitewashed villages, of storks untidily nesting on the top of castle turrets and church steeples, and of ancient unspoiled towns.

Extremadura has a long history, but its highpoints are separated by clusters of centuries rather than a smaller measure of time. The Romans were strongly attracted by the region's strategic position, its rivers, notably the Tajo (Tagus) and the Guadiana, and by its silver deposits. Their mark can be seen in bridges, temples, amphitheaters and other artifacts. The Muslim conquest left fewer traces, but the Christian knights who drove the Moors southward in the Reconquest scattered castles and fortified towns throughout the province.

Another long period elapsed before Extremadura came into historical view again, this time with the exploits of the conquistadors in the New World. Hernán Cortés, the conqueror of Mexico, Francisco Pizarro, vanquisher of the Incas in Peru, Francisco Orellana, explorer of the Amazon, conquistador Vasco Núñez de Balboa and many others came from Extremadura. Most of the conquistadors who survived brought their plunder home and the results can be seen in the towns, palaces and monasteries, upon which they lavished their ill-gotten gains.

With the passing of the era of the conquistadors, the region disappeared again only to be re-awakened during the Napoleonic Wars when some epic battles took place between Wellington's army, supported by its Spanish allies, and the French. Today, Extremadura slumbers on.

There is no escaping the fact that the province is somewhat out of the way. Its main towns and attractions are too far from Madrid, or even Andalucía, to be handled by daily sorties. This would be conceivably on the way to neighboring Portugal. However Extremadura is best treated as a destination in its own right: heading west from Madrid, you'll first pass the monastery at Guadalupe, continue to the conquistador town of Trujillo and proceed to Cáceres, remote and atmospheric in the Extremadura heartlands. Further south, Mérida still possesses more Roman ruins than any other part of Spain, dating back to its glory years as the capital of the Roman province.

MONASTERÍO DE GUADALUPE

The Monasterío de Guadalupe was, through the fifteenth and sixteenth centuries, one of Spain's most important pilgrimage centers. It was built on the site of a wooden sculpture of the Virgin, thought to be carved by Saint Luke, which had been found by a local shepherd. The Virgin of Guadalupe was used as a key symbol by the conquistadors of the New World: Columbus used the name for the Caribbean Island of Guadeloupe, and much of the monastery's wealth came from looted gold and the spoils of war from the Americas.

The monastery church (open daily 9 AM to 8:30 PM, free) is on the Plaza Mayor, and to wander around its Gothic interior is to step back in time. The monastery itself (open daily 9:30 AM to 1 PM and 3:30 PM to 6 PM, €1.80) can only be explored by guided tour, ending with an audience with the Virgin herself, blackened by the soot of several hundred years exposure to votive candles. You can take a Virgin home here, as there are plenty of plastic replicas on sale outside.

A good place to stay here is in the **Parador** (927 367075 FAX 927 367076 E-MAIL guadalupe @parador.es, Calle Marquéz de la Romana 12 (expensive), set in the fifteenth-century Hospital of Saint John the Baptist. Rather less expensive is the **Hospedaría del Real Monasterío** (927 367000 FAX 927 367177, Plaza Juan Carlos 1 (inexpensive), a hotel for Spanish pilgrims set in the wing of the monastery. Book ahead, especially for the Easter period or the Virgin's festival on September 8.

Guadalupe is a two-hour drive west from Madrid, along the N-V, turning south onto the N-502 at Talavera de la Reina and, after 48 km (30 miles) bearing right onto the CM411, a slow but spectacular road. It is 80 km (50 miles) east of Trujillo. There is no train station, and although there are direct bus services from Madrid, it is often easier to change in Talavera de la Reina.

TRUJILLO

Of all the conquistadors who subjugated the South American continent, perhaps the greatest — and certainly the best rewarded — was Francisco Pizarro, conqueror of Peru. The town of his birth, Trujillo, is littered with palaces and grand houses built by the conqueror himself, by his relatives and by his comrades in arms. The concentration of period mansions, in this remote and untouched Extremadura town, makes Trujillo well worth a visit, with an excellent Parador justifying an overnight stay.

Start at the Plaza Mayor, where churches, palaces and café/restaurants, topped by the bulky nests of storks, are set around a bronze statue of Trujillo's greatest son. This is where you'll find the **Tourist Information Office** (927 322677 E-MAIL www.ayto-trujillo.com, Plaza Mayor, which is open daily 10 AM to 2 PM and 4 PM to 7 PM. A walking tour can take in the **Palacio del Marqués de la Conquista**, the **Palacio de los Duques de San Carlos** and the **Torre del Alfiler**. The Moorish walls of the pre-conquest city have been restored and the battlements make an ideal viewpoint of the confident, if not grandiloquent wealth that followed the conquest of the Americas.

The prime accommodation here is in the converted monastery of Santa Clara, the **Parador** (927 321350 FAX 927 321366 E-MAIL trujillo@parador.es, Calle Santa Beatriz de Silva 1 (expensive). A less atmospheric alternative is **Hotel Victoria** (927 321819 FAX 927 323084, Plaza de Camillo 22 (moderate), or the very inexpensive **Pensión Boni** (927 321604, in a central location at Calle Domingo de Ramos 11. The best place to eat in town is the Parador, with its tomato and cumin soup and *cochinillo de montanera* (moderate), but there are plenty of restaurants in the Plaza Mayor, including **Pizarro**, which charge less.

There is no train station at Trujillo, but buses serve it from Madrid: a reasonable distance of 249 km (156 miles) along a fast motorway. Cáceres is 48 km (30 miles) to the west.

CÁCERES

Cáceres is the pivot of Extremadura, and ranks as one of Spain's most exquisite medieval towns. The old city, with elements dating back to Roman times and an architecture laid down in the days of Moorish

The façade of Salamanca's Gothic cathedral.

occupation, is also glorified by the mansions and palaces dating from the sixteenth century when the tide of money from the Americas reached full flood. It is surrounded by defensive Moorish walls and has been declared a national monument as well as a World Heritage Site. Magnificent, if a little stage-like, Cáceres has often been chosen for the filming of historical dramas, and is no bad place for the contemporary setting of a vacation.

General Information

The **Regional Tourist Office** (927 246347 E-MAIL www.turismoextramadura.com, Plaza Mayor 1, is open from 9:30 AM to 2 PM daily, and also 4 PM to 7:30 PM on weekdays; they run hourly tours of the city's major sights, lasting an hour and a half and costing €3. This contains entry fees for the various museums, so is something of a bargain. For Internet access, try **Cibercity**, Plaza de Buselas

(10 AM to 10 PM), while for medical attention the **Cruz Roja** is at (927 222222.

What to See and Do

This historic walled city is basically Moorish in design, though parts date back to the time of the Roman occupation. The Plaza Mayor is outside the ancient walled city: head south to get into the **Parte Vieja**. The severe houses here are adorned only with countless coats of arms: signs of warrior nobles, accustomed to conquering wars yielding more glory than gold.

The **Plaza de Santa María** is at the heart of the old town, containing the restored **Palacio Mayoralgo**, the **Palacio Episcopal** and the **Iglesia de Santa María**. Much of the pleasure is in strolling around the narrow alleys and streets, but for a vivid insight into the influence of the conquest of South America, visit the **Casa de los Toledo-Moctezuma**,

option set just outside the city walls in a sixteenth-century palace. A more reasonably priced option is the **Hotel Iberia (** 927 247634 FAX 927 248200, Calle Pintores 2 (moderate), in a restored mansion off the Plaza Mayor. Travelers on a budget should try the **Pensión Marquez (** 927 244960, Calle Gabriel y Galán 2 (inexpensive).

How to Get There

By road, Cáceres is 297 km (186 miles) east of Madrid, 210 km (131 miles) south of Salamanca and 264 km (165 miles) north of Sevilla. The better-connected city of Mérida is 68 km (42 miles) to the south by road, and the town of Trujillo is 48 km (30 miles) to the east. Both the **railway station (** 927 235061 and the **bus station (** 927 239550 are three kilometers (about two miles) from the old town.

MÉRIDA

Once the capital of the Roman province of Lusitania that extended into modern Portugal, Mérida is still a showplace for Roman architecture. There is a particularly fine bridge over the Guadiana, a theater (still used), the remains of a Roman house, mosaics, and the best-preserved amphitheater in the world. Add to this a beautifully designed museum that brings the era to life, and you start to understand why Mérida claims to be the best place to experience Roman Spain in all its aspects. The Roman theater here comes to life in July and August, with atmospheric performances of Roman and Greek plays, as well as classical concerts.

General Information

The esplanade in front of the Roman theater is the best place to park and launch your tour, and it's also where you'll find the **Tourist Information Office (** 924 315353, open Monday to Friday 9 AM to 1:45 PM, 5 PM to 6:30 PM in winter, to 7:15 PM in summer, Saturday and Sunday 9 AM to 1:45 PM, which has a good collection of maps and guides.

For a taxi, contact **Radio-Taxi (** 927 371111 or **Tele Taxi (** 927 315756. The **Insalid Hospital (** 927 381000 has a 24-hour emergency facility, and for an **ambulance** call **(** 927 381018.

What to See and Do

The Tourist Information Office is at the center of the major sights: the **amphitheater**, the **Teatro Romano** and the **Casa Romana del Amfiteatro** are all accessed with a combined ticket costing €3.65. Summer hours are 9 AM to 1:45 PM and 5 PM to 7:15 PM, and in the winter 9 AM to 1:15 PM and 4 PM to 6:15 PM.

Facing the tourist office is the fascinating **Museo Nacional de Arte Romano (** 924 311690,

built with the dowry of the daughter of the Aztec emperor. The ethnological and archaeological departments of the provincial museum are housed in the **Casa de las Veletas**, Plaza de las Veletas (open Tuesday to Saturday 9:30 AM to 2:30 PM, Sunday 10:15 AM to 2:30 PM, €1.80), where the building itself is an even greater attraction than the exhibits on display.

Where to Stay

The most atmospheric place to stay here is the **Parador (** 927 211759 FAX 927 211729 E-MAIL caceres @pardor.es, Calle Ancha 6 (expensive), the only hotel within the city walls (and with the only access for cars), sited in a restored fourteenth-century palace. It is not the most expensive accommodation here, as this honor is taken by the **Hotel Meliá Cáceres (** 927 215800 FAX 927 214070, Plaza de San Juan 11 (very expensive), which is a super-luxury

Don Quixote country. The windmills at Consuegra in La Mancha.

open Tuesday to Sunday 10 AM to 2 PM, and 4 PM to 6 PM in winter, 5 PM to 7 PM summer, €2.40, designed by one of Spain's leading architects, Rafael Moneo. It showcases some of Mérida's greatest treasures in a light and accessible setting. If this whets your appetite, there are plenty more Roman sites scattered around the town.

Where to Stay and Eat
The best place to stay here is at the **Parador (** 924 313800 FAX 924 319208 E-MAIL merida@parador.es, Plaza Constitución 3 (expensive), sumptuously set in an eighteenth-century convent. If this is full, **Hotel Emperatriz (** 924 313111 FAX 924 313305, Plaza de España 19 (moderate), is well located on

the main square and has a rooftop patio garden. On a budget, the **Hotel Vettonia (** 924 311462, Calle Calderón de la Barca 26 (inexpensive), is small, friendly and comfortable.

Mérida has a very competitive restaurant scene, with fliers being handed out in an endless search for custom. Probably the best place to eat is at the Parador (expensive), where truffles (*criadillas de la tierra*) are just one of the regional specialties on offer.

How to Get There
Mérida is 350 km (219 miles) southwest of Madrid along the main N-V road, 60 km (37 miles) from Badajoz to the west and 70 km (44 miles) south of Cáceres. The train station is near the center of town, with connections to Madrid, while the bus station is a fair walk across the Río Guadiana: best take a taxi to get there.

SOUTHEAST OF MADRID: LA MANCHA

Heading southeasterly from Madrid brings you to La Mancha, a vast dry plain with boundless horizons that is impossible to separate from the figures of Cervantes' imagination: the hallucinatory Don Quixote, his long-suffering nag, Rocinante, and the loyal Sancho Panza. However, as you move deeper into La Mancha, keeping an eye open for those castles and windmills that watch over the fertile plain, another trinity emerges.

This is the land of wheat, olives and vineyards, which have provided the essentials of life in the Mediterranean world — bread, oil and wine — from time immemorial.

The wind always seems to be blowing in La Mancha, an impression heightened by the almost total absence of trees. It sweeps in great gusts across the wheat fields and along the bare streets of the whitewashed villages. If you want to *feel* La Mancha, go to **Consuegra**, a typical farming town about an hour and a half's drive from Madrid. Drive or walk up the hill above the town, sit in the company of nine windmills and a ruined castle, and watch the sun go down or the moon come up over this ancient land. The colors of the surrounding plain and the distant hills are gentle on the eye: light shades of green, tawny yellows, a splash of ochre, and rolling fields the color of a lion's hide.

The wind that tugs at the tattered sails of the windmills brings the lowing of cows, the growl of a tractor, cries of children playing and a cock crowing. Narrow your vision in order to shut out the electricity pylons and the farm silos, and it is not hard to see the profile of the demented knight, his lance pointing toward the heavens, riding slowly across the treeless plain.

While it seems clear that Cervantes spent little time in the area he wrote so vividly about, and that the word *"mancha"* in Spanish means a "blot" or a "stain," this landscape has a magnetic quality that is hard to resist.

But when it comes to towns or monuments, there is not much to see. The two largest towns, Ciudad Real in the south and Albacete to the east, have little to divert the traveler. **Valdepeñas**, the center of Spain's most prolific wine-growing region, is worth dropping by if you feel like sampling some of the light dry red wine that is typical of this area. La Mancha is also the home of one of Spain's best known cheeses, the firm, tangy *manchego*. Then there is **El Toboso**, the home of Don Quixote's beloved Dulcinea, which has a modest Quixote museum. An exception is the World Heritage town of Cuenca.

CUENCA

Cuenca, in the northern part of La Mancha, close to the Aragón border, is an old town built on top of cliffs overlooking deep gorges. Its famous "hanging houses" *(casas colgantes)* cling to, rather than hang over, their rocky foundations, but that they have done so for centuries is truly remarkable. Look a little closer and this remarkable town begins to reveal less obvious attractions. There is a delightful modern art museum, established by artists in the 1960s in a couple of converted, cantilevered fifteenth-century hanging houses, and the town still has a strong tradition of the visual arts. The town also has a number of large houses built by the nobility in the fourteenth and fifteenth centuries, a few of which have been turned into cozy inns, an impressive (inside, at least) cathedral and an atmospheric lattice of old city squares.

General Information

The main **Tourist Information Office** (969 232119 WEB SITE www.citelan.es/cuenca/, Plaza Mayor 1, open Monday to Thursday 10 AM to 2 PM and 5 PM to 8 PM, Friday and Saturday 10 AM to 8 PM, Sunday 10 AM to 2 PM, is helpful. There's a second Tourist Information Office at the Plaza de Hispanidad, which is also the place to find **taxis** (969 213636 and **Radio-Taxis** (969 213343.

For Internet access try **CiteLAN** (969 233677, Centro de Impresas, Camino de Terminillo 2 km.

For medical treatment there is a **clinic** (969 228562 at San Ignacio de Loyola 13, while the **Sanitorio San Julián** (969 212224, Calle Dr Ferrán 1, offers full facilities.

The town's patron saint, San Julian, is celebrated in the last two weeks of August, but this has been overtaken in sheer exuberance by the festival of San Mateo, where bulls are released into the streets and everything goes wild. The starting date of the festivities varies from year to year, from September 17 to 19, but the festival ends on September 21.

What to See and Do

The unmissable sight is the hanging houses. Photographers take note: they get the sun in the morning and lose the light in the afternoon. The best vantage point is on a footbridge suspended over the Río Huecar. Anyone with the slightest interest in modern art should visit the **Museo de Arte Abstracto** (969 212983, Calle Casas Colgadas, open Tuesday to Saturday 11 AM to 2 PM and 4 PM to 6 PM, Sunday 11 AM to 2 PM, €1.2, which has an excellent core collection and hosts some of the best traveling exhibitions you'll see in Spain. Three other museums, sharing the same hours and prices, are the **Museo Catedralicio** (969 212463, Plaza Mayor, which has a collection of gold and silver; the **Museo Diocesano** (969 212011, Palacio Episcopal, which includes two works by El Greco; and the **Museo Arqueológico** (969 213069, Calle Obispo Valero 12, which is mainly devoted to Roman finds in the region.

Where to Stay and Eat

The best hotel in town is the **Hotel Leonor de Aquitania** (969 231000, Calle San Pedro 58-60 (expensive), which has superb views and luxurious rooms. The **Parador** (969 232320 FAX 969 232534 E-MAIL cuenca@parador.es, Hoz de Huécar (expensive), is housed within a former convent in a dramatic gorge on the outskirts of the city; some rooms have views of the hanging houses. On a budget, try the **Pensión Tabanqueta** (969 211290, Calle Trabuco 13 (inexpensive), which has great views and a good restaurant, let down only by no ensuite rooms.

The best restaurant in town is the **Figón de Pedro** (969 226821, Calle Cervantes 15 (moderate), for Castilian specialties, while a good restaurant in a restored hanging house is the **Mesón Casas Colgada** (969 223509, Calle Canóginos 3 (expensive). Otherwise, there are plenty of bars centered around the Plaza Mayor.

How to Get There

The town is 163 km (98 miles) from Madrid; take the N-III towards Valencia and branch off on the N-400 at Tarancón. It is linked by rail to Madrid, with the **train station** (969 220720 on Paseo de la Estación, and also by bus, with the **bus station** (969 227087 on Calle Fermin Caballero.

The "hanging houses" *(casas colgantes)* of Cuenca.

Andalucía

In the popular imagination, Spain has long been synonymous with Andalucía. The image evoked is a multidimensional kaleidoscope of colors, sounds, smells and sensuality. There is the swirl of the gypsy dancer's polka-dotted skirt; the spine-tingling wail of the *cante jondo*, the "deep song" that conjures up Andalucía's Moorish past; straight-backed riders with swarthy, arrogant faces under flat black hats; provocative eyes behind restless fans; the strains of the paso doble fading as the matador raises his sword for the kill; sunlight on a whitewashed wall and a cascade of red geraniums spilling over a balcony; the intoxicating scent of jasmine, and the smell of aging sherry the color of polished teak.

Beneath the romantic flourishes there is a nub of truth. Andalucía has enough of its Moorish heritage left in spirit and stone to make it distinctively different from the rest of Spain. Flamenco, bullfighting and sherry all originated in this region. The people have a lightness, sparkle, and fatalism not found elsewhere in the country. When Benjamin Disraeli, writer and future prime minister of Britain, visited Andalucía in 1830, he observed: "There is a calm voluptuousness about life here that wonderfully accords with my disposition."

The other side of the image was either not seen or ignored by the romantics. This was the huge gap between the wealthy landowners and the impoverished peasantry, the lack of industry and infrastructure, an unresponsive Church and an oppressive government. Modern Andalucía is a different place. Poverty and inequality, though still a visible feature of the Andalusian landscape, have been reduced by the impact of dramatic and relatively recent economic changes. Romance, by the same token, has also taken a knock. The land of the Alhambra, Don Juan, Carmen and spontaneous flamenco dancing has become the land of mass tourism, the family car and the business lunch.

Today, Andalucía sees itself on the crest of a new wave of development and Spanish-style perestroika. Its leaders are fond of saying that it is on the way to becoming Europe's California. Its detractors, while acknowledging the reality of the economic upsurge, say a down-market Florida is more like it.

Andalucía has a special place in Spanish history. Accessible and attractive, it has invited foreign curiosity from the time of the Phoenicians. The Greeks came later and the Romans settled it heavily. But it was the Arab conquest and long sojourn — they came in the eighth century and were finally driven back into Africa at the end of the fifteenth century — that gave Andalucía its unique imprint. The Moors were the great civilizers of the Middle Ages, turning their beloved Al-Andalus into an earthly paradise with its mosques, palaces, gardens, its irrigated agriculture, and its centers of arts, crafts and learning. The rest of

Europe, including Christian Spain, appeared rough-hewn and philistine by comparison.

Andalucía anchors Spain. As large as Portugal, it straddles the Atlantic Ocean and the Mediterranean Sea and faces Africa. It has one-fifth of the country's population, its highest mountains (the Sierra Nevada), one of its longest rivers (the Guadalquivir), its warmest climate (gentle winters and broiling summers), its largest national park (Coto de Doñana) and its most developed coastline (Costa del Sol). It is a surprisingly lush and fertile part of Spain, a relief after the interminable and virtually treeless *meseta* of the interior; and it is the cradle of unusually picturesque cities, towns and villages.

SEVILLA

Sevilla is Andalucía's capital and the country's fourth largest city, so let us start there. The Andalusian character distills itself in its most pure form in Sevilla. It is a city of beauty, grace and spirit. *Sevillanos* are renowned for their wit and spontaneity, for their sense of style and for their easy-going nature. It has been described as Spain's most Mediterranean city, although it is not actually on the coast. Its allure attracted writers (Tirso de Molina, Lope de Vega and Cervantes — who spent some time in Sevilla's jail, where he got a lot work done), and painters (Velázquez, Murillo

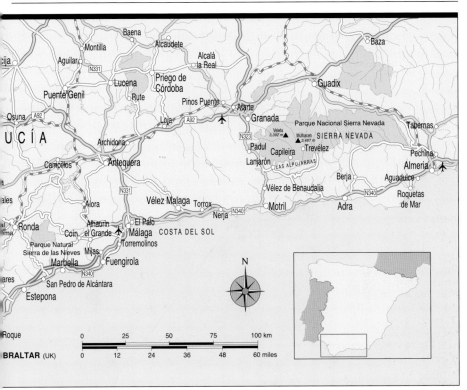

and Zubarán); it also produced memorable fictional characters such as Carmen, Don Juan and Rossini's famous barber. It is unclear how all this came to pass, but there is little doubt that a long and continuous history and a seductive climate had a lot to do with it.

Hercules himself, according to legend, founded Sevilla on the banks of the Guadalquivir within navigable reach of the sea. Its ancient name was Hispalis, and it was the site of Phoenician, Greek and Carthaginian settlements before the Romans made it the capital of Baetica, which roughly corresponds to modern Andalucía. Vandals and Visigoths followed, and then in the eighth century the Moors captured the city. Although never the capital of Muslim Spain (Córdoba had that privilege), Sevilla, or Isbiliya as it was known, flowered under its Moorish rulers.

Its conquest by Ferdinand III (the "Saint") returned it to Christendom in 1248, and it became the southern capital of the Castilian monarchs. Sevilla reached its zenith in the sixteenth century when it profited from the wealth of the New World on whose trade it had a monopoly. (The first man to sight land from Columbus's ship, the story goes, was Rodrigo de Triana, a sailor from Sevilla.) After those heady decades, the city steadily declined.

The decay continued until the last century, when Sevilla began to prosper again. It hosted the Ibero-American Exposition in 1929 and played the same role for the Universal Exposition in 1992, the quincentenary of Columbus's discovery of America. Expo 92 had a huge physical impact on Sevilla. The exhibition site on the Isla de la Cartuja, a largely unused marshy island in the Guadalquivir river, was transformed and linked to the city by several new bridges. New construction included the expansion of Sevilla's airport, a new railway station built for the high-speed AVE train that links Sevilla to Madrid, and a ring road around the city. The Cartuja site is not fully utilized now but retains some of its pavilions, the cable-car and monorail train, and facilities for shows, concerts and exhibitions.

GENERAL INFORMATION

Sevilla has a number of spectacular sights, but it is infinitely more than the sum of its parts. Its broad avenues, parks and gardens, labyrinthine old quarter, cobbled streets, cool flower-filled patios and riverine boulevards combine to make it one of Europe's most dazzling cities. The **Tourist Information Office** (954 221404 FAX 954 229753, Avenida de la Constitución 21, is open Monday to Saturday 9:30 AM to 2 PM and 4 PM to 7 PM, Sunday 10 AM to 2 PM. There is another bureau (954 234465, at Paseo de las Delicias 9, and a desk at the international airport (954 255046 FAX 954 449129, Autopista de San Pablo. There are

taxi ranks, or **Radio-Taxi** (954 417118 will collect you if called. There are various places to pick up your e-mail, including **Alfalfa 10** (954 213841, Plaza de Alfalfa 10, daily noon to 1 AM, and **Ciber-Café Undernet** (954 991419, Calle O'Donnell 19, 10 AM to 10 PM.

The **Hospital Universitario Virgen Macarena** (954 557400, is on Calle Dr. Marañon. In a **medical emergency**, dial (061. You may need to contact the **police**, in this city where unemployment runs at 40 percent and bag-snatching sometimes seems to be, after bullfighting, the city's favorite sport: in an emergency call (092, or go direct to the Plaza de la Gavidia Police Station (954 289300, near the Plaza de la Victoria.

FESTIVALS AND CELEBRATIONS

It is impossible to separate Sevilla from the great rites of spring: the **Holy Week** penitence and pageantry in the week before Easter and the joyous, extrovert **April Feria** that follows it. The *Semana Santa*, or Holy Week, celebrations date from the sixteenth century when *cofradías* — charitable brotherhoods or guilds connected to local churches — took to the streets to re-enact the passion and crucifixion of Christ. The ceremonies begin on Palm Sunday with processions of penitents in their white robes and sinister pointed hoods (the Ku Klux Klan in the United States borrowed the design for their own unchristian purposes) and floats bearing images of Christ and the Virgin. The processions, a slow moving river of shuffling sinners and swaying canopies and religious statuary illuminated by candlelight, converge on the cathedral. There are moments of great fervor; such as when the Virgin of La Macarena, the lady whose tears are frozen in glass on her cheeks, leaves her church at midnight on the eve of Good Friday, and when the figure of Christ departs from San Lorenzo church in the early hours of that day. Imperial Rome is represented by carefully-put-together legionnaires, and there is no shortage of material for the crowd scenes as the *sevillanos* pour into the streets. The festival ends on Easter Sunday with more processions and floats, but this time on a joyous note with singing, hand-clapping and the sway and swirl of Sevilla's own graceful dance (the *Sevillana*) engulfing the city.

The April Fair, or **Feria de Abril**, is both younger and older than the rituals of Holy Week. It began as a cattle market and fair in the mid-nineteenth century, but its celebration of the coming of spring goes back to pagan times. It used to take place in the center of Sevilla, but is now held in fairgrounds of **Los Remedios**, a modern suburb across the Guadalquivir river. It officially lasts five days, beginning on the Tuesday 10 days after Easter Sunday — but since people hardly seem to go to bed during that time it really adds up to 10 days'

worth of fiesta. "The most tiring and exhilarating public celebration on the Iberian Peninsula," in the view of one veteran travel writer.

As with Holy Week, the April Fair in Sevilla is a vivid, constantly shifting and unashamedly public theater. During the mornings, people stroll around the fairgrounds admiring the immaculately turned-out horsemen, their bright-eyed *señoritas* and the no-less-gorgeous display of horseflesh and accouterments that parades before them. If Spaniards can ever be said to "strut their stuff," this is the time and the place. There is constant movement as people drop into one *caseta* — the gaily decorated stalls that cover the grounds — after another, for a gossip, a drink, a laugh.

A long lunch may be followed by a trip back across the river to **La Maestranza bull-ring**, where Spain's leading matadors strut *their* stuff; some of the best *corridas* of the season take place during the April Fair. As the sun goes down the revelers return to the fairgrounds for a night of strolling, drinking, eating, dancing, singing and enjoying themselves.

There is no statutory hour for the night's revelry to end. Sevilla's great Feria, while it is in motion, knows no tomorrow. James Michener, an aficionado of Holy Week and the April Feria, reckoned there was nothing in the world to surpass these festivals, not Mardi Gras in New Orleans, the Palio in Sienna, Bastille Day in Haiti, not even Carnival in Rio de Janeiro. "At any time of year Sevilla is a distinguished city," he wrote in *Iberia*, his massive

Parque de María Luisa, Sevilla OPPOSITE, and one of its famous white pigeons ABOVE.

travel book about Spain, "but during Holy Week and the days that follow, it is without peer."

Michener advised setting aside several weeks to cover the spring festivals in and around Sevilla. Most travelers will not have the luxury of so much time, but if you should miss the Easter period, there is another event on the religious calendar that is rather different yet equally passionate and moving. This is the **Romería del Rocío** (Pilgrimage of Rocío) that takes place at Pentecost, 60 days after Easter: which means it usually falls in mid-May. Rocío is as rural as Holy Week and the April Feria are urban, and it unfolds in some of the most beautiful countryside in Spain, in the Parque Nacional de Doñana, which lies about 80 km (48 miles) southwest of Sevilla. The best access is from the Sevilla to Huelva highway (E1/A49), heading south from exit 10 along the A-483.

WHAT TO SEE AND DO

For first-time visitors in vehicles, the first problem in Sevilla is to find the old city, where most of the tourist attractions are found. This is on the eastern bank of the Río Guadalquivir, and is surmounted by Sevilla's greatest buildings: the Giralda Tower, the cathedral and the Alcázar. A good way to get your bearings is to hop on the open-topped double-decker bus, **Sevilla Tour** (954 502099 E-MAIL sevillatours@arrakis.es, which tours the city. But while touring the monuments on dry land, don't forget that this is a port city on a warm sea: good people to call to blow off any dusty cobwebs are **Fun & Quads** (965 787228 WEB SITE www.funquads.com, who rent out kayaks, snorkels and windsurfers at sea, and quad bikes, scooters and bicycles on land.

The Giralda

Sevilla's emblem, evoking its Moorish past, is the ancient Giralda (954 563321, open Monday to Saturday 10:30 AM to 6 PM, Sunday 10 AM to 1:30 PM and 2 PM to 5 PM, €1.80. This lofty tower was built as a minaret 800 years ago and was preserved by the Christians as they erected a new cathedral beside it. Embedded in Sevilla's ancient core, the Giralda is what you see when you approach the city, and it is named after the weather vane that sits on top of it. It provides a magnificent bird's-eye view of the Andalusian capital and is well worth the long climb up sloping ramps that take you to where the Moorish muezzins once called the faithful to prayer.

From the summit you can get a sense of the shape of the city and a panorama of the countryside beyond. The first impression, as you look around from a height of 92 m (300 ft), is a colorful jumble of ochre, rust and umber rooftops, whitewashed walls, gray spires and purple jacaranda trees. If it is the dead part of the afternoon,

you may see a line of horse-drawn carriages drawn up under the orange trees at the foot of the Giralda, horses and drivers alike obeying the imperative of the siesta.

On the northern side of the Giralda is the Patio de los Naranjos, which was the mosque's courtyard and is now an orangery, as the name suggests. Beyond is the Alcázar and the old Jewish quarter of Santa Cruz. Moving around the compass to the northeast, there is the massive density of the university (the second largest building in Spain after El Escorial), which was built in the mid-eighteenth century as the site of the Royal Tobacco Factory, where Carmen and the other *cigarreras* rolled — and quite often smoked — their cigars. Beyond lie the Parque María Luisa (Sevilla's equivalent of the Parque del Buen Retiro in Madrid), and the Plaza de España.

To the southeast is the Torre del Oro (Tower of Gold), built by the Moors and now a maritime museum, and the Guadalquivir (the "big river" in Arabic), which still provides a navigable link to the Atlantic Ocean some 45 km (30 miles) away. Due south is La Maestranza, Sevilla's exquisite eighteenth-century bullring with its Moorish arches and whitewashed exterior.

The Cathedral

The cathedral (954 563321, open Monday to Saturday 10:30 AM to 6 PM, Sundays 2 PM to 5 PM, €3.80, next to the Giralda, was built in the fifteenth century on the site of the city's largest mosque. A gigantic Gothic construction, it is the third largest cathedral in the world after Saint Peter's in Rome and Saint Paul's in London. Its founders are reputed to have said: "Let us raise up so great a church that those who contemplate it should take us for madmen."

They succeeded in a way. The place is a cavernous rectangle, at once impressive and oppressive. However, the high altar is superbly offset between a golden screen and an intricately carved *retablo* that is the largest in Spain. At the feast of Corpus Christi, in June, a minuet is danced in front of this altar by a group of young boys dressed up as Renaissance choirboys and called *seises*. The cathedral also has two richly decorated sacristies (the Sacristy of the Chalices and the Main Sacristy) in which religious paintings by Zubarán, Murillo, Van Dyck and Luis de Vargas, as well as silverware and vestments, are on display. The cathedral contains the tombs of Ferdinand III, the conqueror of Sevilla, as well as those of Alfonso the Wise, Pedro the Cruel, and Christopher Columbus.

Columbus has his own pantheon, and his bier is supported by four regal figures representing the kingdoms of Castilla, León, Navarra and Aragón. After his death, his remains were destined to make two more journeys across the Atlantic, first from Valladolid to Hispaniola (modern

Haiti and the Dominican Republic), then to Cuba and finally back Spain, this time to rest in Sevilla. Legend has it that some of his remains were left behind in Havana, so that, in death as well as life, he straddles two worlds.

The Alcázar

Built to accommodate the needs of man rather than to deify the almighty, the Alcázar (954 502323, open Tuesday to Friday 9:30 AM to 6 PM and Sundays 9:30 AM to 2 PM, €3.8, is an almost necessary antidote to the cold grandeur of the cathedral. The site of royal palaces since the Muslim conquest, most of the buildings are the work of Christian kings, notably Pedro the Cruel, who admired the Islamic style and used Moorish workmen to build much of the present complex in the mid-fourteenth century. (He also murdered a number of people in it, including his half-brother, thus earning his sobriquet.) Subsequent monarchs and noblemen added pieces to the mosaic, and the whole adds up to one of the most intriguing examples in all of Spain of the Christian-Moorish Mudéjar architectural marriage.

There are a number of salons, halls and state rooms to see, but the centerpiece is the **Salon de Embajadores**, which has hardly changed since the finishing touches were put to it over 600 years ago. It has triple horseshoe arches along three sides, a beautiful carved wooden cupola, and doors that were probably the work of Toledo craftsmen. Phrases from the Koran in flowing Arabic script adorn the walls. Pedro was no paragon, but his failings did not include religious bigotry or cultural philistinism. There is a tendency to think more kindly of him as you wander past dreamy arabesques, across marble-floored courtyards where a small fountain may spill water into a moss-covered basin, through gardens dense with hibiscus, jacaranda, palms, cypresses and orange trees, where birds sing and the sun's rays are cooled and softened.

Barrio de Santa Cruz

From Alcázar, a pleasant walk, a drink, dinner or a flamenco show can be had in the Barrio de Santa Cruz, the old Jewish quarter of Sevilla, and the best (but also the most expensive) place to stay. A good way to enter is from the **Patio de Banderas**, an attractive square close to the Alcázar, and then to follow the narrow streets up to the **Plaza Alfaro**, which is close to the **Jardines de Murillo**. The route is a succession of ancient whitewashed houses and flower-bedecked balconies and squares, with restaurants, bars and cafés on every corner. Gentrification has laid its homogenizing hand on the quarter but there is still plenty of music, laughter and spontaneity in the streets and bars.

RIGHT: Sevilla's emblem, La Giralda. OVERLEAF: The lovely renaissance Parque de María Luisa in Sevilla.

Other Sights

There are many other places worth visiting in the city. There is the **Parque de María Luisa**, a lovely park laid out during Sevilla's renaissance in the 1920s, and the **Plaza de España**, a less-than-lovely arc of neo-baroque towers, bridges, terraces and staircases, which was the site of the Ibero-American Exposition in 1929. A sense of the domestic architecture of Sevilla and Andalucía is superbly conveyed in the **Casa de Pilatos** (Pilate's House), so named because it was apparently a copy of Pontius Pilate's palace in Jerusalem. A blend of Mudéjar, Gothic and Renaissance styles, it was built in the early sixteenth century and contains Roman antiquities, paintings, furniture and some of the best tile-work in the city.

Museums

Sevilla is also rich in museums. There is a fine art museum, the **Museo de Bellas Artes** (954 221829, open Tuesday 3 PM to 8 PM, Wednesday to Sunday 9 AM to 3 PM, €1.5, second only to the Prado in Madrid. It has a splendid collection of paintings by Bartolomé Esteban Murillo (a native son of Sevilla) and the Extremaduran painter Francisco de Zubarán, who lived in the city for many years. There is also an archaeological museum, the **Museo Arqueológico** (954 232401, Plaza de Americas, open Tuesday to Sunday 9 AM to 8 PM, €1.5, and an archive of the Americas, **Archivo de Indías** (954 229644 (visits by arrangements on weekday mornings only), which documents the discovery of the New World and Spain's trading relations with it when Sevilla was at its commercial peak.

Wandering

Sevilla is a lovely city to wander in. It is relatively compact and one of the few places in the world where to take a horse-drawn carriage is neither an affectation nor a rip-off. The superbly maintained carriages drawn by well-fed and well-groomed horses are centrally located, provide a perfect slow-paced, open view of the surroundings and cost little more than a taxi. The downside is the growing level of street crime. Sevilla has one of the highest unemployment rates in the country and, like many Spanish cities, has acquired a serious drug problem. Cameras, handbags, purses and wallets should be carefully guarded, and late-night strolling is best confined to populous areas.

WHERE TO STAY

In the festival season, hotels in Sevilla can book out. At other times there is usually plenty of space, though prices are often slightly higher than in other parts of Spain.

La Giralda. Sevilla's distinctive landmark was built as a minaret in the thirteenth century.

The grandest hotel in town is the **Alfonso XIII** (954 222850, Calle San Fernando 2 (extremely expensive), built in 1929 and opened by the king whose name it adopted. His grandson, the present monarch, reopened it after extensive renovation work. The heavy, ornate Sevillian style is a bit gloomy and overpowering, but it is unique and undeniably luxurious, if a bit self-important. A friend of mine once strolled, appropriately dressed, into the lobby and then out, asking the concierge if his car was safe left outside. Assuming he was a guest, the concierge said definitely not, called a valet to move it to the (free) hotel parking lot, and gave him a map of the city for his stress-free day of sightseeing.

The **Doña María** (954 224990, on Calle Don Remondo 19 (expensive), is a pretty place perfectly sited opposite the cathedral. It has great views of the Giralda from the roof where there is a swimming pool. The **Macarena Sol** (954 375700, Calle San Juan de Rivera 2 (moderate), opposite the basilica of the Macarena, is a bit noisy but has a good traditional atmosphere and a fine interior patio. The **Inglaterra** (954 224970, Plaza Nueva 7 (moderate), is a nicely situated hotel with gracious public rooms and patio. The **Fernando III** (954 217307, Calle San José 21 (moderate), is conveniently located close to the colorful Santa Cruz district. The centrally located **Hotel Simón** (954 226660 FAX 954 564421 E-MAIL hotel-simon@tet.es, Calle García de Vinuesa 19 (moderate), is the best of the bunch, with a cool interior patio in a pedestrianized part of town; ask the police to let your car through. The **Monte Carmel** (954 279000,

Calle Turia 7 (moderate), is across the river in Remedios, close to where the April Fair takes place, although otherwise it's not ideally situated.

On a tight budget, try the **Hostal Gravina** (954 216414, Calle Gravina 46 (very inexpensive).

WHERE TO EAT AND NIGHTLIFE

The city that inspired the character Don Juan has no problem providing entertaining bars and restaurants. For dining, the Barrio Santa Cruz area has the most atmospheric choices, but also the most expensive. If you drift across the river corresponding restaurants drop a category in price.

One of the best restaurants in Sevilla is thought to be the **Taberna del Alabardero** (954 560637, Zaragoza 10 (moderate), which is where Sevilla's school of hotel management try out their skills, and it provides very good value. Making no concessions to cost, the restaurant at the **Hotel Alfonso XIII** (954 222850, Calle San Fernando 2 (expensive), makes the most of its setting. The **Enrique Becera** (954 213049, Calle Gamazo 2 (expensive), is near the Plaza Nueva and city center and has good selection of Andalusian dishes. For a change in atmosphere, the **San Marco** (954 212440, Calle Cuña 6 (expensive), is a lovely old rambling Sevilla house and serves haute and nouvelle cuisines. It is more international than Spanish, but everything is in exquisite taste. Another former mansion is home to **La Albahaca** (954 220714, Plaza Santa Cruz 12 (expensive), well-respected for its fish.

There are plenty of restaurants with less of a sting in the bill. In the moderate price range you'll find **Don Raimondo** (954 223355, Calle Argote de Molina 26, in a cul-de-sac close to the cathedral. It specializes in Andalusian dishes with a Moorish influence and has an enclosed patio, a large fireplace and much culinary decoration. The **Oriza** (954 279585, Calle San Fernando, is a modern bar and restaurant, popular with the literary set, and a good place for a light snack or a full-blown meal. The **Río Grande** (427-8371, Calle Betis (moderate), is in the Triana district on the river. It is famous for good fish, especially the assorted fried fish (*pescaditos*), and it has great views over the river to the Torre del Oro and the Giralda. For a really inexpensive meal, try **La Judería** (954 214338, Calle Cano y Cuesto 13, near the Jardines de Murillo. Simple, honest food is served with the best kind of Spanish service: courteous, efficient and accomplished with a smile.

Sevilla is full of interesting *tavernas* and *tapas* bars, many lavishly decorated with local tiles, and quite a few serve local wine and sherry directly from the barrel.

ABOVE: Horse-drawn carriages under orange trees in front of Sevilla's cathedral. OPPOSITE: The center of Sevilla.

Sevilla is also a good place to see flamenco. This dance invariably takes place in a formal setting these days, and it is best to book the show in advance through your hotel, or to buy tickets directly from the restaurant or theater where the performance takes place. One of the more consistent places, though not the cheapest nor the most spontaneous, is **Los Gallos** (954 216981, Plaza de Santa Cruz 11, in the picturesque Barrio de Santa Cruz, which charges €21 per person including a drink. It can be worth crossing the plaza late at night to another music bar, **El Tamoril**, in case singers or dancers have dropped in and started to perform; this will be much cheaper and more relaxed.

The **Tablao de Curro Velez** (954 216492, on the Calle Rodo 7, is another place where the people at the next table are likely to be locals. The liveliest spot, with the most Sevillian dancers, is most often **La Trocha** (954 355028, Ronda de Capuchinos 23.

HOW TO GET THERE

Sevilla is a hefty 538 km (334 miles) from Madrid, and 138 km (86 miles) from Córdoba. As such, many visitors choose to fly into **Aeropuerto San Pablo** (954 510677, to the east of Sevilla. A shuttle bus links the airport with the city center for €4.50, though as a taxi for the same ride will only cost about €15, only solo travelers save much through this effort. It is well connected by rail (**railway station** (954 231918, Calle Zaragoza 29) and by bus, with two **bus stations**; at the Plaza de Armas (954 907737 and the El Prado San Bernado (954 417111, with myriad connections to the rest of Andalucía, Extremadura and Madrid.

EXCURSIONS FROM SEVILLA

Near the village of Santiponce is the Roman town **Ruinas de Itálica**, open Tuesday to Saturday from 8:30 AM to 8:30 PM, Sunday 9 AM to 3 PM (€1.50, but free to European Union citizens), an open-air museum of the ancient world. On your way there you can see the **Isla de la Cartuja** to the left as you cross the Guadalquivir River, where the Universal Exposition was held in 1992.

Italica was the birthplace of the emperors Trajan and Hadrian, and the remains of an amphitheater, a forum, baths and several villas can be distinguished. There is a rumpled feeling to the site, as if an earthquake had given it a good shaking, and some of the best mosaics are in Sevilla's archaeological museum. But the profusion of flowers — oleander, hibiscus, geraniums and poppies — and the cypress, acacia and fig trees in the formal gardens among the ruins go a long way to redeeming the place. Itálica is eight kilometers (five miles) north of Sevilla, and is easily reached by taxi, car, or a bus from the Plaza de Armas.

Thirty kilometers (18 miles) east of Sevilla, the walled village of **Carmona** is one of the best-preserved in the area, perhaps most satisfactorily visited by staying at the exclusive Parador at its heart: the **Casa de Carmona** (954 4141010 FAX 954 141712 E-MAIL carmona@parador.es, Alcázar, Carmona, near Sevilla (very expensive).

THE FRONTIER TOWNS

Heading south from Sevilla brings the traveler to the "frontier" towns of Arcos de la Frontera and Jerez de la Frontera. In an area that was once renowned as a largely lawless wilderness — a region of brigands and bandits — these picturesque towns were outposts of law and order. While those days are long gone, a touch of the frontier remains in the towns' fortified walls and defensive architecture.

ARCOS DE LA FRONTERA

Off the main Sevilla to Cádiz road lies the hilltop town of Arcos de la Frontera, one of the many beautiful fortress towns that defined the boundary between the Christian south and the Moorish kingdom of Granada.

Arcos de la Frontera lies on what is today commonly known as the **Ruta de los Pueblos Blancos** (Route of the White Towns). Arcos is one of the most picturesque of these white towns, which are spread, in the words of one guidebook "like icing on the top of a craggy limestone outcrop." There are marvelous views of Arcos from a distance from this road. The excellent Parador Casa del Corregidor hotel, a restored palace at the top of the town with mod cons and great views, shares a pretty square with the sixteenth-century church. Further attractions include a ruined castle and plenty of steeply graded, torturous, cobbled streets that have resisted the assault of the twentieth century both physically and in ambience.

General Information

There **Tourist Information Office** (956 702264, Plaza de Cabildo, open Monday to Friday 10 AM to 2 PM and 5:30 PM to 7:30 PM, Saturday 10 AM to 2 PM, Sunday 10:30 AM to 12:30 PM, which offers guided tours of the old town.

Where to Stay and Eat

One good reason to stay here is the range of good places to sleep. Top of the pile is the **Parador Casa del Corregidor** (956 700500 FAX 956 701116 E-MAIL arcos@parador.es, Plaza del Cabildo (expensive), which has perhaps the best views of all. **El Convento** (956 702333 FAX 956 704128, Calle

The hilltop Parador at Arcos de la Frontera.

Maldonado 2 (moderate), is a delightful hotel filled with works by local artists; the owners also run one of the best restaurants in Arcos, just up the road in a colonnaded patio of a sixteenth-century palace (moderate). Alternatively the **Hotel Los Olivos del Convento** (956 700811 FAX 956 702018, Paseo de Boliches 30 (inexpensive), is a pleasant and well-appointed Andalusian townhouse near the old quarter.

How to Get There

Arcos de la Frontera is 70 km (43 miles) from Cádiz and 90 km (56 miles) from Ronda. It sometimes seems that most people arrive here by bicycle, though a vehicle is a better bet.

Jerez de la Frontera

Jerez de la Frontera, the birthplace, production plant and museum of sherry, is an elegant city that is also known for its equestrian activities and as the place where flamenco had its origins. Two great annual festivals celebrate these attractions: the **Feria del Caballo** (the Jerez Horse Fair), which follows Sevilla's April Feria in early May, and the **Fiesta de la Vendimia**, the wine harvest festival, which takes place in September.

The wealth that has derived from Jerez's international wine business over the centuries is evident in the fine aristocratic mansions, in the sherry *bodegas* (cellars) — many of which are virtual palaces — and in the leisurely feel of the clean streets lined with orange trees. The *bodega* owners have a reputation for being close-knit and over-impressed with their own importance, but the local

people are friendly and can be exceptionally obliging. A thoroughly unbureaucratic official at the Post Office, for instance, opened up his window and sold me stamps when I turned up shortly after closing time.

Jerez is a very old town, its roots going back to the Phoenicians. It had already become well-known for its wine under the Romans, and is mentioned by Pliny, the Roman historian. The Moors also left their imprint with the **Alcázar**, built in the eleventh century, the remains of the city's walls, and some baths, all now restored and embellished by gardens and fountains. Although Islam forbids the drinking of alcohol, the art of making sherry survived the Moorish period.

The British connection with Jerez goes back to the Middle Ages and one of the sherry *bodegas* advertises the fact with a quote from Shakespeare prominently displayed among the slowly maturing casks of the heady stuff. "If I had a thousand sons," says Falstaff in *Henry IV*, "the first human principle I would teach them should be to forswear thin potions and to addict themselves to sack." In a word, sherry. Less well-known, but a good deal more useful, is the specialized skill, perfected in Jerez, of making brandy.

General Information

The **Tourist Information Office** (956 331150, Calle Larga 39, Monday to Friday 8 AM to 2 PM and 5 PM to 8 PM, Saturday 10 AM to 2 PM, is set on the pedestrian-only main street. They can arrange tours of the vineyards as well as handing out maps and hotel information.

What to See and Do

It's worth postponing the tours of the sherry and brandy *bodegas* for a while, as there are some attractions here that reward a clear head. The **cathedral** and The **Alcázar** are, of course, prime attractions, but more unusual is the **Real Escuela Andaluza de Arte Ecuestre** (Royal Andalusian School of Equestrian Art) (956 319635 or 956 311111, Avenida Duque de Abrantes, which does fantastic displays of dressage to music — at noon on Thursdays year-round, and on Tuesdays in the summer. Entry, depending on season, costs €9-14.

The main sherry and brandy tours are run by **González Byass** (956 357016, €5.40 and **Pedro Domeque** (956 151500, €3.6, and usually take about an hour. Smaller *bodegas* can be contacted through the tourist office for more personal tours. With an alcohol spin, it is perhaps time to explore the town's other specialty: flamenco. A good place to start is in the **Centro Andaluz de Flamenco** (956 349265 FAX 956 321127, Plaza de San Juan 1, Monday 9 AM to 2 PM, open Tuesday to Friday 9 AM to 2 PM and 5 PM to 7 PM, entry free, where you'll get details of performances and venues. It is in the heart of the gypsy quarter.

Where to Stay and Eat

The luxury hotel is the **Jerez** (956 300600, Avenida Alvaro Domecq 35 (expensive), which has a nice garden and swimming pool. In the moderate range are the **Ávila** (956 334808, Calle Ávila 3, and the **Mica** (956 340700, Higueras 7. Good, medium-priced restaurants include **Gaitán** (956 345859, Gaitán 3, and **Tendido 6** (956 344835, Circo 10, a lively spot close to the bullring.

How to Get There

Jerez is linked to nearby Cádiz and more distant Sevilla by train and bus, with both stations close together on the east of town. By car, it is on the main Sevilla–Cádiz road, which is currently being

It does reward a visit, however. At the broad mouth of the Río Guadalquivir lies Sanlúcar de Barrameda.

Meanwhile the decaying charm of the historic Atlantic Ocean port of Cádiz never fails to charm, and the countless bars of the British island of Gibraltar offer a vivid contrast with mainland Spain.

SANLÚCAR DE BARRAMEDA

While in this area, Sanlúcar de Barrameda, an unspoiled fishing and wine-making town at the mouth of the Guadalquivir, is well worth a detour. Its moment in history came in the late fifteenth century when the explorers Ferdinand

upgraded to *autopista* standard. The **Aeropuerto Internacional de Jerez** (956 150010 or 956 150011, is just to the north of town, with its new cut-price service to the United Kingdom making it a useful access point into this part of Spain.

COSTA DE LA LUZ

Spain's southwest coast, washed by the clear waters of the Atlantic Ocean, is known as the "Costa de la Luz," thanks to the clarity of the light in this sunny latitude. Wilder and windier than Spain's Mediterranean shores, the Costa de la Luz has always looked outwards, to the riches of the New World, and was gateway for conquistadors and explorers throughout Spain's colonial days. In modern Spain it is quieter, somehow overlooked, and has been slower to cash in on the tourist book.

Magellan and Christopher Columbus left from the port on their great voyages of discovery. But Sanlúcar is also famous for its **Manzanilla** dry sherry, a delicate creation that is normally served — and enjoyably drunk — throughout a meal. Sanlúcar's large townhouses and elegant public buildings reflect the prosperity that the wine trade brought, but it is the natural beauty of its beachfront that is the town's main attraction.

This consists of a fine sandy beach on the estuary of the Guadalquivir, facing the Parque Nacional de Doñana. Along the beach, a garland of colorful painted fishing boats bob at anchor, with others beached on the strand: the picture is framed by a row of seafood restaurants and *tapas*

OPPOSITE: Autographed sherry casks in the Humbert and Williams sherry *bodega*, Jerez. ABOVE: Horsemen performing in the Real Escuela Andaluza de Arte Ecuestre, Jerez.

bars. Pilgrims going to and from El Rocío cross the Guadalquivir on primitive ferries that look like small military landing-craft. The coastal bars are atmospheric, with their amphorae, fish nets and skeletons and their delicious seafood snacks. The restaurants are unpretentious and inexpensive, the fish as fresh as the sea itself, and the view, especially at sunset, sublime. Sanlúcar's beach — slightly shabby, uncommercial and wholesome — typifies Andalucía's Atlantic coast and contrasts favorably with the modern madness of its Mediterranean shoreline.

The best time to visit here is in the last two weeks of August, when horseraces pound up the coarse sand of the beach. The well-informed staff

Sanlúcar de Barrameda is almost 17 kilometers (10 miles) west of Jerez on the C-480. There are rural buses, but your own vehicle is the best way of getting there.

CÁDIZ

Cádiz is a port city built on a rocky promontory that juts out into the Atlantic. The town is not on the normal tourist itinerary, but it has both history and atmosphere. The origins of Cádiz reach back into mythology with the claim that this is where Hercules raised his pillars as he gouged open the Mediterranean Sea so that it could flow into the Atlantic.

at the **Tourist Information Office** (956 366110, Calzada de Ejército, open Monday to Friday 9 AM to 2 PM and 6 PM to 9 PM, weekends 10 AM to 1 PM, can help with maps and advice.

The **Bodega Antonio Barbadillo** (956 360394, open 12:30 PM Wednesday and Thursday only, runs tours of Sanlúcar de Barrameda's *bodegas* for €1.80 if booked ahead. This area saw Magellan and Columbus sailing from its beach, and is also superbly placed for the Parque Nacional de Doñana, with four-hour boat cruises through the marshes offered by the **Real Fernando** (956 563813, summer 9:30 AM and 5 PM, winter 10 AM only, €13.20; booking is essential.

Accommodation is limited. By far the best place to stay is the **Posada de Palacio** (956 364840 FAX 956 365060, Calle Caballeros 11 (inexpensive), set in an eighteenth-century mansion, with rooms individually decorated with taste and style.

Less fancifully, there is documented evidence to show that the Phoenicians established a city here called Gadir in 1100 BC. Carthaginian, Roman, Moorish and, finally, Christian occupation followed. Cádiz was one of the launching points for the discovery of the New World and the object of Sir Francis Drake's attentions, notably when he sacked it in 1587, boasting he had thereby "singed" King Felipe II's beard. In the eighteenth century it was given the trade monopoly of Spain's New World empire — displacing Sevilla — and the city prospered. The Franco-Spanish fleet sailed from Cádiz to its doom at Cape Trafalgar in the Napoleonic Wars, and it was here that Spain's first democratic constitution was drafted.

The old town is cocooned in an unpleasant chrysalis of modern suburbs and industrial zones which have to be suffered before the real Cádiz can be seen. No individual building, including the fusty baroque cathedral, amounts to much on its own, but the tightly woven streets, the salt-bleached colors on stone, brick and paint and the intensely Spanish feel of the place make it an interesting place to stop for an hour or so. The **Tourist Information Office** (956 211313 FAX 956 228471, Calle de Calderón de la Barca 1, Plaza de Mina, Monday 9 AM to 2 PM, open Tuesday to Friday 9 AM to 7 PM, Saturday 10 AM to 2 PM, gives out maps and advice. There is a further kiosk at the Plaza de San Juan de Dios that opens on weekends and holidays. There are city beaches but they tend to be dirty: best to join the locals on the ferry that leaves regularly from the Estación Marítima over to the **Puerto de Santa María**, across the bay.

Where to Stay and Eat

Cádiz is not renowned for its hotels and many people find a day-trip is enough to get a salty flavor of the city, perhaps staying just outside town. One hotel, midway between Cádiz and Jerez, is the **Hotel Monasterío San Miguel** (956 540440 FAX 956 540525 E-MAIL monasterio@jale.com, Calle Larga 27, Puerto de Santa María (expensive), a converted monastery with a golf-course attached.

But Cádiz itself does reward a longer stay. The modern **Parador Hotel Atlántico** (956 226905 FAX 956 214582 E-MAIL Cádiz@parador.es, Avenida Duque de Nájera 9 (expensive), is beautifully sited at the very tip of the peninsula by the Castillo de Santa Catalina, with views over the sea, its own swimming pool, and a program for children. Less expensive is the **Hostal Fantoni** (956 282704, Calle Flamenco 5 (inexpensive), in a cool, renovated townhouse. On a real budget, the **Quo Quádis Youth Hostel** (956 221939, Calle Diego Arias 1 (very inexpensive), also offers bicycle rental, courses in flamenco and city tours, tempting many guests to extend their visit far longer than planned.

Gastronomy, especially fish, is the town's strong suite, and it makes sense to time one's visit to include lunch or dinner. **El Faro** (956 211068, San Felix 15, and the **Mesón del Duque** (956 281087, Paseo Marítimo 12, are both good and moderately priced. To the dismay of the British, Cádiz makes a convincing claim to have invented fish and chips as a takeaway snack; you can buy some in a twist of paper from *frieduras*, scattered about the town.

How to Get There

Cádiz is most easily reached by the highway from Jerez de la Frontera, where you'll also find the nearest airport. By road, it is rather out of the way: Sevilla is 125 km (78 miles) away, Granada 355 km (222 miles), and Madrid 663 km (414 miles). The **train station** (956 254301 is on the northern edge of the old town, with the bus station a few blocks north again. The new service from the United Kingdom bringing low-priced flights into Jerez airport makes Cádiz far more accessible too.

TARIFA

From Cádiz the N-340 heads southeast towards the Costa del Sol, arriving first at Tarifa, the southernmost point of Spain, whose "Hurricane Beach" is probably the best place for windsurfing in the entire country. Before windsurfing caught on, it was better known for the highest suicide rate in the country — winds that appeal to windsurfers can be very wearing on the rest of us — but over recent years it has exploded into a busy, and very young, resort.

The **Tourist Information Office** (956 680993, Paseo Alameda, Monday to Friday 10 AM to 2 PM, is generally swamped by backpacking windsurfers in search of a room; in the summer, somewhat frantically. Call ahead, perhaps to the rather unusual **100% Fun** (956 680013 FAX 956 680013 E-MAIL 100x100@tnet, Carretera de Málaga a Cádiz km76 (inexpensive), which brings a touch of Mexico to the Costa and a good surf shop. The **Hurricane Hotel** (956 684919 FAX 956 684508, Carretera de Málaga a Cádiz km78 (moderate), is more Californian, with a gym, horses and a windsurfing school.

Tarifa is easily approached from either Cádiz or Algeciras: buses stop by the supermarket. It also offers quick and easy access to Morocco, with a daily ferry to Tangier from May to September: tickets from Tourafrica (956 684751 or from travel agents are €36 each way. Algeciras, however, has cheaper ferries that run year-round.

GIBRALTAR

While Cádiz is Spain's guardian of the Mediterranean, Gibraltar, "The Rock," controlling the rather tighter entrance to this sea, is Britain's. Africa is so near that the low bulk of Morocco is almost always visible to sea, but the atmosphere on Gibraltar is pure England. Captured from Spain in the Spanish War of Succession in 1704, Gibraltar has remained a disputed British colony ever since. Its minute yet heterogeneous population prefers British colonialism to Spanish immersion, and there the matter rests. Gibraltar offers some splendid views of the Straits and not-so-distant Africa, duty-free goods, a colony of Barbary apes whose presence, according to legend, will ensure the Rock remains British, and retains the flavor of a somewhat seedy, out-of-date England from the pages of Graham Greene.

However, if you are British or an Anglophile and want to absorb a little nostalgia of the old country during your Spanish tour, go to Gibraltar. The frontier doubles as an airport runway. A valid passport and car insurance will get you across,

Don Alvaro Domecq Romero tasting the bravery of a brooding cow on the Los Alburejos Ranch near Jerez.

but lines for vehicles can be long and slow. Once there, you can marvel at the British bobbies wearing blue serge and the traditional domed helmets, the red letter-boxes and telephone kiosks, the Union Jack fluttering over a Moorish castle, and enjoy — if you can — a pub lunch consisting of a paralyzed pork pie (or a stale cheese and tomato sandwich), washed down with a glass of tepid McEwan's ale, the whole rounded off with a cup of tea and a Walls choc-ice.

If you do want to wallow in a sense of Englishness, a good place to stay is the **Bristol Hotel** ((+350) 76800 FAX (+350) 77613 E-MAIL brislhtl @gibnet.gi, 8/10 Cathedral Square (very expensive). Of the 365 public houses (bars) perhaps the

Nerja, Motril and on to Adra, where the tired and dangerous N-340 cuts inland to Almería. The most densely built-up areas, however, are in the stretch between Estepona and Málaga, and it is here that the explosion of the Spanish leisure industry has earned Andalucía unwelcome comparisons with Florida. With that has come adverse criticism and jokes: "Costa Geriatrica," "Costa Mierda," "Costa Fortune" and so on.

The good news is that although this coastline has been largely wrecked by property speculators, it was never one of nature's marvels in the first place. Forty years ago, it was a rather featureless stretch of gray sandy beaches, punctuated by small rocky promontories and bays and

best is down at the marina, where a constant stream of working yachts stop before or after long transatlantic hauls. Meanwhile, a few kilometers inland, a more sophisticated clientele stop off at the **San Roque Club** (956 613030 FAX 956 613012 WEB SITE www.sanroqueclub.com, Carretera Nacional 340 km127, Sotogrande, where the super-rich put down their roots on one of the world's most luxurious golf courses, helped occasionally by partner Seve Ballestaros.

COSTA DEL SOL

The Costa del Sol, playground of five million tourists every year, as well as being an expatriate home for thousands, runs from Gibraltar up the coast through Málaga to beyond Motril, a distance of some 300 km (186 miles). It changes its name, but not its character, to the Costa Tropical through

inhabited by desperately poor fishermen. It was the combination of cheap land, great weather and a low cost of living that made it perfect for northern Europe's sun-starved holidaymakers at a time when air travel became affordable. Today, the Costa del Sol is still a rather featureless stretch of gray sandy beaches, punctuated by small rocky promontories and bays — when you can catch a glimpse of them through the concrete jungle of hotels, apartment buildings, restaurants, cafés and shops. But the Spanish population of the "Sunshine Coast" is a bustling, relatively affluent segment of the Andalusian workforce, whose knowledge of fishing rarely goes beyond a menu. In this, they are close to the millions of foreigners whom they welcome, and it takes only one look at the local teenage disco scene in a place like Marbella to see Spaniard and foreigner are not far apart socially either.

All along the Costa del Sol there is a mushroom-like fecundity of "urbanizations," to use the Spanish term. These range from unimaginative concrete slabs of hotels, shops, restaurants and so on, to contoured clusters of villas, apartments and sport facilities, to ambitious attempts to recreate the physical appearance and intimate ambience of the traditional Andalusian *pueblo*, albeit equipped with modern conveniences. There is no need to search for the first category as, it is visible wherever you turn. The more sophisticated developments, often with a specialist purpose in mind, are rarer and vary in quality, but they are usually visually pleasant and comfortable to stay in.

The only way to see the Costa del Sol properly is to drive along it on the main coastal road, the N-340. But beware of the many driving hazards. The road is still a *carretera nacional* (national route), not an *autopista* (freeway), which means it is narrow, often winding, and always congested. There is the additional risk of semi-naked pedestrians, weighed down with beach impedimenta, dawdling across it, since many of the hotels are on one side of the road and the sea is on the other. If they're British, they'll often be drunk and looking the wrong way for oncoming cars. More than a hundred people die on the N-340 every year. You'll travel more quickly, but miss the fun, on the new *autopista*, the A7/E15, known as the Autopista del Sol, which zooms inland, though expensive tolls mean it has done little to relieve the coastal traffic situation.

The coast caters to all tastes. It is perfect for the package tourist on a 10-day spree where the idea is to spend the day on the beach developing a tan that will knock them dead at the office in Manchester, Mannheim or Malmo, and where the nights can be fruitfully passed eating, drinking, dancing and — assuming the excesses of sun, alcohol, food, and fancy footwork permit — making out. It is also a good place for those who have healthier though equally sybaritic thoughts in mind. There are plenty of opportunities for golf, tennis, riding, sailing, windsurfing and other sports. There are also amusement parks and adventure playgrounds for children and for the child in the adult. And there are quieter, more luxurious playgrounds in a few elite watering holes for an international coterie of the extremely rich.

Along the length of the C340 coast road, the Costa del Sol passes through a number of different moods, as each town and resort asserts its individual character. At its southwestern extent, the town of Estepona has long been a favorite for beach-lovers, overlaying the original fishing village with a concrete glamour of tanned bodies and water-skis. Marbella is the swankiest spot and has a large selection of luxury hotels at luxury prices. Fuengirola is a slightly frumpy family resort, while Torremolinos is a bizarre, kitsch and brash high-rise metropolis, packed with expatriate criminals, families on holidays with teenage children, and endless discos and bars. Málaga is the business capital and the main airport of the coast, but not the place to stay or linger in if you are sightseeing, interested in sport, or pursuing the sybariti pleasures of beach, bar and nightclub. Conveniently, most-out-of-town hotels on the main C340 road use the distance in kilometers (from Cádiz) as a clear and effective address.

ESTEPONA

Estepona, once a picturesque fishing village, is now a thoroughly modern town, but, perhaps

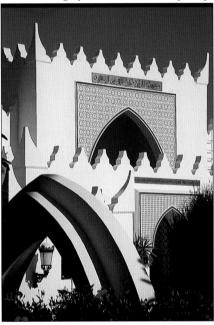

because most of the tourists are Spanish, is not quite as overwhelmed as other places further along the coast. A large number of foreign residents live in and around Estepona, and it has an all-year nudist colony in an Andalusian-style village close to the beach just outside the town. The immediate hinterland is always worth keeping an eye on for touches of an older and calmer Spain. Only twenty minutes' drive into the hills from Estepona, for instance, brings you to the dazzling whitewashed mountain village of **Casares**, surmounted by a ruined castle.

General Information
The **Tourist Information Office** (952 800913 or 952 802020, Avenida San Lorenzo 1, Monday to

OPPOSITE: A seafront resort on the Costa del Sol.
ABOVE: A new mosque, built with Arab money, outside Marbella on the Costa del Sol.

Friday 9:30 AM to 9 PM, weekends 9:30 AM to 1:30 PM, is near the seafront. **Radio-Taxi Estepona** (952 802900 is a local taxi company. Sights include the ruins of the city walls and archaeological sites from the Roman era. The town's principal festival is on July 16, the day of the Virgen del Carmen, when the fishing boats are decked out for a watery procession.

Where to Stay

In the luxury category of hotels, Estepona offers the **Stakis Paraíso** (952 883000, on Carretera N-340 km168.5, which is just outside the town (extremely expensive), and **Atalaya Park** (952 884801 FAX 952 889002 E-MAIL hotel@atalaya-park.es, Carretera N-340 km167 (also in the extremely expensive category), both of which have golf courses, tennis courts, swimming pools and gardens. A new, but characterful and more reasonably priced, hotel is **Albero Lodge** (952 880700 FAX 952 885238 WEB SITE www.alberolodge.com, Carretera N-340 km164.5 (moderate), near the beach and with access to horseback riding, diving and other holiday activities. Slightly inland, but far more interesting, is the six-bedroom **Casa Tanga Tanga** (952 886590 FAX 952 886590, Apurtado 349 (moderate), run by a professional tennis coach who used to run a safari camp in East Africa. Tennis, is, of course, a feature here, but there is also a swimming pool. On a budget, head for the **Hostelleria Padron** (952 113308, Carretera N-340 km159 (inexpensive).

How to Get There

Estepona is 165 km (103 miles) east of Cádiz, and about 30 km (19 miles) west of Marbella, the nearest hub for public transportation, linked by a fast new freeway, the A7/E15, and the old N-340.

MARBELLA

Continuing along the coast road there are signs of the new Arab conquest in the shape of an elegant and classically styled mosque on the outskirts of Marbella. This time, it is the power of the checkbook, not the sword, that has returned small parcels of Spain to the Moors. Marbella is the star resort of the Costa del Sol, the place where, as one guide book has it, "the very beautiful and very talented try to rub shoulders with the very the rich."

Marbella has 28 km (17 miles) of beaches, acres of luxury hotels, exclusive country-clubs, marinas stuffed with nautical marvels, and plenty of fancy restaurants, bars and discotheques. There is a so-called "Golden Mile" of vast mansions on the seafront, many of them belonging to oil-rich Arab princes and their families. **Puerto Banus**, six kilometers (four miles) west along the coast, has the best marina for watching the rich at play — the floating palaces in the water are complimented

by the Rolls Royces, Ferraris and Mercedes ashore — a drink at the **Marbella Club**, a comfortable sprawl of buildings set in a tropical garden, will allow you to experience the voyeur's satisfaction of watching without having to become more than marginally involved.

There is a **Tourist Information Office** (952 823550, Plaza de los Naranjos, Monday to Friday 9 AM to 9 PM, Saturday 10 AM to 2 PM, though most of Marbella's residents wouldn't deign to enter. A local taxi company is **Taxi Sol** (952 774488.

The best hotels include the **Don Carlos** (952 831140, Carretera de Cádiz km192 (very expensive); the **Marbella Club** (952 822211 FAX 952 829984 E-MAIL reserves@marbellaclub.com, Bulevar Principe Alfonso von Hohenlohe (extremely expensive); and the slightly cheaper **Los Monteros** (952 771700 FAX 952 825846 WEB SITE www.monteros.com, Carretera de Cádiz km187 (very expensive). Those looking for full-on luxury can try the **Hotel Puente Romano** (952 820900 FAX 952 775766 E-MAIL hotel@ puenteromano.com, Carretera de Cádiz km177 (extremely expensive), a member of the Leading Hotels of the World.

For excellent golf and tennis facilities, head west for the **Golf Hotel Guadalmina** in San Pedro de Alcántara (952 882211 FAX 882291 WEB SITE www.hotel-guadalmina.com, Guadalmina Baja km170 (very expensive).

In town, the **Princesa Playa** (952 820944 FAX 952 821190 E-MAIL hprincesa@spa.es, Paseo Marítimo, Avenida Duque de Ahumada (expensive) is perfectly placed between the old town and the beach, with a selection of apartments and suites and a good spa. Less luxurious, the **San Cristóbal** (952 771250 FAX 952 862044, Avenida Ramon y Cajal 3, Marbella Downtown (moderate), is a good mid-range choice, or alternatively try the **Baviera** (952 772950 FAX 952 772958, Camino de Calvario 2, Marbella Downtown (inexpensive). On a budget you're probably not in the best place, but the **Hostal Juan** (952 779475, Calle Luna 18 (inexpensive), will probably be able to help.

Marbella is 170 km (106 miles) from Cádiz and 64 km (40 miles) from Málaga, and a major regional hub. The **bus station** (952 764400 is at Avenida de Trapiche, while the **train station** (952 771743 is at Avenida Ricardo Soriano 14.

FUENGIROLA

Next comes Fuengirola, a fairly typical Costa town which has made a specialty of catering for family-style holidays. There is a small zoo and a *parque acuatico* ("aquapark"), both popular with children, and the beach has been carved up into a sort of holiday hell by restaurant concessions that also rent out pedaloes and lounge chairs. In the hills behind the town, the pretty village of **Mijas** sits in the sunshine, once a true Andalusian pueblo but now heavily commercialized by mass tourism. However, the curving, hilly streets retain their charm, and there are splendid views of the Mediterranean and the rolling countryside.

For travelers without their own transportation, **Radio-Taxi Fuengirola ℂ** 952 471000 should be able to help.

There are plenty of hotels here. One, near Mijas, provides the ultimate in luxury in a sprawling country setting, with pools, gardens and its own golf course: the **Byblos Andaluz ℂ** 952 473050 FAX 952 476327 WEB SITE www.byblos-andaluz.com, 138 Fuengirola (extremely expensive). A huge hotel overlooking the marina and 200 m (219 yds) from the beach is the **Hotel Las Palmeras ℂ** 952 472700

TORREMOLINOS

If Marbella is the Costa del Sol at its most sophisticated, Torremolinos, further along the coastal road just before Málaga, is it at its most brash. A peaceful though impoverished fishing village not so long ago, it is now the Mecca of the package tourist, especially the rowdy Brits, a place of relentless drinking and carousing where all thoughts of tomorrow, including monumental hangovers, are shelved until the homeward aircraft starts its engines. Torremolinos is where the hoary yarns of hotels still being built as the guests poured into the floors that were finished, actually

FAX 952 472908, Paseo Marítimo (expensive), with a full range of international facilities. Mid-range, try **Las Rampas ℂ** 952 470735 FAX 952 470912, Complejo Las Rampas (moderate). In an emergency — and on a budget — the central **Sarasol ℂ** 952 470344, Avenida de los Boliches 89 (inexpensive), is a possible standby.

Lew Hoad's **Campo de Tenis ℂ** 952 474858 FAX 952 474908 is set in the hills just off the Fuengirola to Mijas road. Hoad, who won the Wimbledon singles title in 1955 and 1956, died in 1994. The tennis camp, which he founded and ran until his death, is an appealing option for tennis aficionados, providing both tennis coaching and competitions, but the large villa and sporting complex here also provides residents, whether villa owners or renters, with full club facilities: including an excellent, if somewhat expensive, restaurant and a bar and swimming pool.

came true. (I passed a noisy night in one in the early 1970s and almost did not live to tell the tale through taking a wrong turn along an unfinished corridor on the seventh floor.)

The main **Tourist Information Office ℂ** 952 379512 on Plaza Pablo Picasso (open Monday to Friday 9:30 AM to 1:30 PM) and it's beach-front offshoot (open daily 10 AM to 2 PM and 5 PM to 8 PM) will help with accommodation, and amongst the desperately competitive bars and restaurants prices are usually very keen. The eastern end of Torremolinos is marginally smarter, and the restaurants tend to be better.

Hotels here are much less costly when booked as part of a package (which can make for a very affordable beach break), but walk-in rates are relatively expensive. If you do need to stay here, the best hotel is the **Meliá Costa de Sol ℂ** 952 386677

Hotel Byblos Andaluz, a luxury hotel near Marbella.

FAX 952 386417, Bajondillo-Paseo Marítimo (extremely expensive). The **Hotel Isabel** (952 381744 FAX 952 381198 E-MAIL hotelisable@arrakis.es, Paseo Marítimo 97 (moderate), is smaller and rather less impersonal. There are some less expensive *hostales* squeezed in between the concrete monoliths, including the **Pensión Beatriz** (952 385110, Calle Peligro 4 (inexpensive).

Torremolinos is 10 km (seven miles) west of Málaga, easily reached by the C340 by vehicle or bus, or by an electric train that hums along past a line of beach developments.

MÁLAGA

Málaga — port, capital of a province and the second largest city in Andalucía — has waxed fat as the service center of the Costa del Sol. Although it is hardly a lovely city, despite its mellifluous name, it is not without interest, as you'll find out if you visit the **Tourist Information Office** (952 604410 FAX 952 214120, Avenida de Cervantes 1, Paseo del Parque, which has three branches citywide: at Plaza de la Merced, on the Avenida de Andalucía, and at the Estación de Autobús. There is also an **Andalucía Tourism Office** (952 213445, Passaje de Chinitas 4.

There is an Internet café next to the Corte Inglés department store: **Ciber Málaga**, Avenida Andalucía 11. For a **taxi** dial (952 327950.

Two striking remains of the city's Moorish past as the Kingdom of Granada's Mediterranean port are the largely ruined **Alcazaba** (fortress) (952 216005, open Wednesday to Monday 8:30 AM to 7 PM, built in the eleventh century and surrounded by terraced gardens, and the **Gibralfaro Castle**, constructed 300 years later on the site of a Phoenician fortress. Back in the city, there is a rather ugly sixteenth-century cathedral that looks lopsided because it has only one tower — the second was planned but never finished. It is known as **La Manquita**, the "One-Handed One." The city was the birthplace of Picasso and there is a new **Picasso Museum** (952 215005, Calle San Agustín, open Monday to Saturday 10 AM to 2 PM and 6 PM to 8 PM, Sunday 10 AM to 2 PM, free entrance. Head down to the beach and you'll find the former fishing villages of El Palo and Pedregalego lined with some of the Costa's best seafood restaurants.

The best place to stay in Málaga is the **Parador Málaga Gibralfaro** (952 221902 FAX 952 221904 E-MAIL gibralfaro@parador.es, Castillo de Gibralfaro (expensive), stunningly set with views over the city, especially from the rooftop swimming pool. Less characterful and 12 km (eight miles) out of town towards Torremolinos is a second Parador, the **Parador de Málaga Golf** (952 381255 FAX 952 388963, Apartade de Correso 324 (expensive), which is a lot better for golfers and offers good access to the beach.

Back in town a good mid-range hotel is the **Hotel Bahia Málaga** (952 224305 FAX 952 229268 E-MAIL hbahia@activanet.es, Calle Somera 8 (moderate). Slightly less expensive is the **Hotel Las Vegas** (952 212712 FAX 952 224889, Paseo de Sancha 22 (moderate), which is near to the beach and has its own pool. The **Hotel Sur** (952 224803 FAX 952212416, Calle Trinidad Grund 13 (inexpensive), is central and, impressively for the price, has its own garage. This is important in a city where car-crime is the local sport.

For dining, matadors usually patronize the **Antonio Martin** (952 227289, Paseo Marítimo (moderate), where you'll get excellent seafood overlooking the sea, but expect a chill breeze wafting from the waiters as well unless you're a national hero. The centrally located **Gorki** (952 221466, Calle Strachan (inexpensive), is an outstanding *tapas* bar. For nightlife, the best idea is to go to bed, getting up again around midnight, when Málaga really gets going.

The **Aeropuerto de Málaga** (952 048484 is one of the busiest in Europe, and is linked to the town center by a half-hourly electric train (€0.85). It is a hub for bus connections and for the train. Be warned, the main **RENFE railway station** (952 360202 is not the nearest stop to the town center: the "Centro-Alameda" station is the one you need. There is also a **ferry terminal** for ferries connecting with (Spanish) Mellila in Morocco, though the crossing is not as fast or as cheap as the regular ferry service between Algeciras and Tangier; call **Trasmediterranea** (952 224391 WEB SITE www.trasmediterranea.es for details.

INLAND ANDALUCÍA

Heading inland from the Costa del Sol is a refreshing experience for the jaded traveler. First, there is cultivation — orchards, market gardens, wheat and olives — then the countryside begins to undulate and climb to the Las Alpujarras, and later to the Sierra Nevada.

And finally, there are Andalucía's great cities: atmospheric Ronda, and the larger centers of Granada and Córdoba, completing the trinity of which Sevilla is the cornerstone.

RONDA

The best way to plunge into the hinterland of Andalucía as quickly as you can is to head north, through a fertile, aromatic countryside where you can occasionally glimpse a wooden plough being pulled by a team of mules, past whitewashed villages perched on hilltops, and end up in Ronda. Set in its own small range of mountains, Ronda is a spectacular piece of urban sculpture that both attracted and defied the region's successive conquerors. Built on a towering crag that is virtually sheer on three sides, the old Arab town and its more modern companion are separated by a 92-m (300-ft) chasm. It was these natural defenses and the wild surrounding terrain that made Ronda a refuge throughout history for those who were not of a submissive disposition. Iberian warlords held out against the Romans, Christians against Moors, Moors against Christians (Ronda remained Moorish almost to the end of Arab occupation of Andalucía) and Spaniards against the French. When the tides of invasion and conquest had receded, the bandits and highwaymen took over providing both genuine hazard and exciting copy for the resolute travelers of the nineteenth century.

iron casement grilles and balconies and a sense of intimacy, peace and introspection that manages to ignore the steady tramp of the tourist hordes, Ronda's latest conqueror.

The town has a reputation for attracting a variety of artists and personalities. It has a flamenco connection through Vicente Espinel, born in Ronda, who famously added the fifth string to the flamenco guitar. Rainer Maria Rilke, the Austro-German poet, spent some time in the Hotel Reina Victoria, the grand old British-built hotel that has spectacular views of the town and countryside.

Ronda is also renowned for its contribution to the art of tauromachy or, more simply, bullfighting. Its pretty **bullring** was built in 1784 and is

General Information

The **Tourist Information Office** (952 871272, Plaza de España 1, Monday to Friday 9 AM to 7 PM, weekends 10 AM to 2 PM, is a good place to get hold of a map and information about forthcoming events. The best way to see Ronda is to approach the old town by walking across the **Puente Nuevo** (the New Bridge). This impressive construction was built in the eighteenth century; the other smaller and much older bridges, the Roman and the Arab, can be seen down the gorge on the left as you cross over. Unfortunately, the assault on the nostrils is not as pleasant as the impact on the eye. The river, at the bottom of the ravine, stinks. (There are plans, one is told, to clean it up). But the old town is a delicious concoction of shaded squares, solid medieval houses, numerous arabesque arches and filigree façades recalling Ronda's long Moorish occupation, fine wrought-

the second oldest in Spain, after the one in Sevilla. It is generally accepted that Ronda is where bullfighting began on foot; before that it was done exclusively from the back of a horse. Few fights are held in the ring now, but there is an interesting **Museo Taurino** (952 874132, open daily 10 AM to 6 PM, €1.25, beside it, and it is a place of pilgrimage for aficionados. Two famous matadors were born in Ronda: Pedro Romero, who is credited with redefining the bullfight early last century, and Antonio Ordoñez, one of the great post-World War II matadors and Ernest Hemingway's hero. Orson Welles, another Ordoñez fan, was a frequent visitor to Ronda; there is a picture of him in the bullfight museum, as well as clothing worn by famous matadors and two stuffed bulls.

LEFT: The Moorish gate of the old town in Ronda. RIGHT: The steep approach to the town explains its strategique importance to Iberians, Christians and Moors.

Where to Stay and Eat

Ronda can be covered comfortably in a day, but its geographic location and its natural beauty encourage a stopover. As with many well-known attractions, it is at its best when the day-trip coaches have gone. The **Reina Victoria** (952 871240, Calle Jerez 25 (very expensive), is the classic old hotel where the poet Rainer Maria Rilke stayed. There is a **Parador** (952 877500 FAX 952 878188 E-MAIL ronda@parador.es, Plaza de España (expensive), built behind the façade of the original town hall and overlooking the gorge. Less expensive but perfectly adequate are the marble-halled **Polo** (952 872447 FAX 952 872449 E-MAIL jpuya@clientes.unicaja.es, Calle Mariano Soubirón 8 (inexpensive), and the **Royal** (952 871141, Calle Virgen de la Paz (moderate), which is near the bullring. The place to eat if you want to feast on the view as well as the food is **Don Miguel** (952 871090, Calle Villanueva 4, which is perched on the edge of the gorge next to the bridge that links the old and new towns (moderate). On a budget, **Fonda Carmen** (606244337 (cell), Calle Torrejones 18 (very inexpensive), is the cheapest option, but it's in a suburban setting.

LAS ALPUJARRAS

The Alpujarra mountains, situated between the Mediterranean and the Sierra Nevada, were until recently one of the remotest corners of Spain. They are nevertheless readily accessible to anyone who has a car and does not mind twisting mountain roads. The N-323 road that links Motril and the coast with Granada provides the best approach; turn east onto the C-348 which will take you through Lanjarón and into the region. This is where many of the Moors expelled from Granada in the sixteenth century took refuge and staged the last major Muslim revolt against Christian Spain.

The chain of whitewashed villages linked by capricious country roads and the simplicity of life among its friendly inhabitants, has drawn foreigners to the Alpujarras both as visitors and residents. Gerald Brenan, the British writer who wrote so well about his adopted country, lived in one of the Alpujarra villages for many years in the 1920s and 1930s. Amongst the writers, painters, "crafts" people and hippies attracted to the area have been a number of downsizing expatriates funding their escape by setting up rural hotels — and who can be very helpful in helping you share their discoveries in the country. The **Molino del Santo** (952 216151 FAX 952 167327 E-MAIL molino@logiccontrol .es, Bulevar Estación, Benaoján (moderate), in a restored flour-mill in the Parque Nacional Grazalema is one, while the **Posada del Torcal** (952 031177 FAX 952 031006 E-MAIL laposada@mercuryin .es, Carretera La Hoya-La Higuera, Villanueva de la

Concepcíon (moderate), within the Parque Nacional Torcal, is another, well worth a visit. You'll either need your own transportation or some research into sparse rural bus services to find these.

LANJARÓN

Tourism, in a modest way, has come too. Lanjarón, at the entrance to the Alpujarras and at the foot of the **Parque Nacional Sierra Nevada**, is a small and pretty spa town where one of Andalucía's most popular mineral waters originates. It has many small hotels and hostels but its flagship hotel is the **Miramar** (952 770161, Avenida Andalucía 10 (expensive).

There is also a new hotel complex of chalets at **Bubión**, built in the traditional mountain style with pine ceilings. Sharing the same valley as Bubión at an altitude of about 1,200 m (4,000 ft) are **Pampaneira** and **Capileira**, and further north is **Trevélez**, which claims to be the highest village in Europe and is known for its air-cured hams.

There is no denying that in the Alpujarras the air is certainly fresh, the water clean and the pace of life restful, but the region somehow fails to live up the rave reviews in the literature and the ecstasy of the local tourist officials. To fully appreciate it you need to put aside your car, and some time, and take to one of the many hiking trails. Or perhaps, like the lichen on the rocky hillsides, it takes time to grow on you.

OPPOSITE: The historic bullring in Ronda.
ABOVE: An Andalusian man of the soil in the Alpujarra mountains.

SIERRA NEVADA

The Sierra Nevada mountains are a surprise: for here in the hottest, sunniest region of Spain is an easily accessible mountain range of almost perpetual snow with four months of excellent skiing every year. Only 32 km (20 miles) from Granada and 80 km (50 miles) from the Costa del Sol, the Sierra Nevada has the highest peaks in Spain. **Mulhacen** is 3,478 m (11,408 ft) and **Veleta** reaches 3,392 m (11,126 ft). Worn and rounded by countless centuries of snow, ice, wind, rain and sun, both peaks can be conquered by a vigorous walk without too much effort in the summer months. At the **Solynieve** ski area the slopes are between 2,100 m (6,888 ft) and 3,470 m (11,382 ft) above sea level; the resort has 18 ski lifts and 25 marked ski runs. The **Parador Sierra Nevada** (958 480661 FAX 958 480212 (expensive) is no longer part of the state chain, and only opens in the ski season, but the mountains are popular among climbers and hikers too. There are plenty of hotels, restaurants and discotheques that cater to the *avant* and *après ski* crowds.

There is a **Parque Nacional Sierra Nevada information center** (958 340625, Acera del Darro, open daily 10:30 AM to 2:30 PM and 4:30 PM to 7 PM, which usefully (in the summer) sells hats. Access to the Sierra Nevada is easiest — and signposted from — Granada, a distance of 32 km (20 miles).

GRANADA

Part of the excitement of traveling in Spain is the approach to an unfamiliar city. Fragments of knowledge from books, articles and travelers' tales, impressions from photographs and preconceived images rising up from the subconscious coalesce as the distance diminishes. And then the scenery takes over. The approach to Granada, especially through the mountains from the coast, is an adventure in anticipation that absorbs the senses.

The best time of day to approach the town is either early morning or as the sun is setting. After a long climb you reach the inland plateau and catch sight of the snow-covered Sierra Nevada, a cool, ethereal canopy floating above the plain. Emerging from the pines, scrub oaks, wild flowers, and rocky outcrops of the hills, the road sweeps through fields of wheat and barley growing in a rich, red soil. The first glimpse of the city comes from a spot called **El Suspiro del Moro** (the Sigh of the Moor), the place where Boabdil, the vanquished king of Granada, is reputed to have turned and looked back at his beloved city for the last time and wept. The wind rippling the grain is the only sigh these days, but the sight that broke the king's heart remains. There is Granada, crowned by the towers, walls, turrets and crenellations of the Alhambra — ancient, sublime, sad Granada. Francisco de Icaza, the Spanish poet, put it well in a much-quoted but still evocative stanza:

"Dale limosna, mujer, Que no hay en la vida nada/ Como la pena de ser/Ciego en Granada."

"Give him alms, woman, For there is nothing crueler in life than to be blind in Granada."

Granada bears the imprint of the Arab conquest and civilization more emphatically than any other town in Spain, partly because the Moors were here longer than anywhere else, and partly because not much of consequence happened before they came or after they left. Unlike its sisters, Sevilla and Córdoba, it is an upland city, built on hills in the lee of mountains. Granada is 685 m (2,247 ft) above

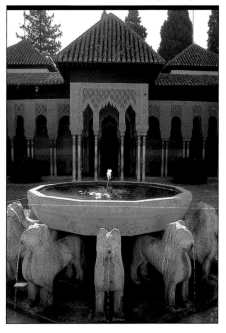

sea level — a little higher than Madrid — a city whose unique character is in good part a result of its defensive topography, its agreeable climate, and its well-watered and fertile soils.

A settlement of no particular note in Iberian, Roman and Visigothic times, Granada had to wait until the Moors arrived from Africa to see its heyday. When Córdoba, the seat of the caliphate, was in its ascendancy in the tenth century, Granada was a summer resort and leisure center. But in 1236 Córdoba fell to the Christian forces, and the defeated Moors retreated to Granada. Over the next 250 years, it became the administrative heart and cultural center of Moorish Spain.

Led by the Nasrid dynasty, which was founded by Mohammed ibn-Nasr (Mohammed I) at the time of the fall of Córdoba, the kingdom of Granada (or Karnattah as it was called in Arabic) not only survived but expanded and prospered during the thirteenth, fourteenth and early part of the fifteenth centuries, extending, at its height, to Gibraltar and Almería. The Nasrids, technically vassals of the kings of Castilla, managed this more through diplomacy and guile than by force of arms. But it worked, and in the peace and prosperity that they created they turned a small mountain resort into a jewel of a city.

The end came in the late fifteenth century, when the crusading Catholic Monarchs, Ferdinand and Isabella, set about reconquering the remaining areas under Moorish control. Fatal divisions within Granada's ruling family made the task much easier, and on a cold winter's day in 1492, Boabdil, who had usurped the throne from his father a decade earlier, surrendered the keys of the city to Ferdinand.

placency. Today, Granada's population is not much larger than it was at the zenith of the Moorish kingdom; the city has a comfortable, cheerful feel to it and lives reasonably well from internal and foreign tourism, light industry and agriculture.

GENERAL INFORMATION

The city **Tourist Information Office** (958 225980 FAX 958 223927, is at Edificio Corral del Carbón, Calle Mariana de Pineda, near the cathedral (it's open Monday to Saturday 9 AM to 7 PM, Sunday 10 AM to 2 PM). There is a **Provincial Tourist Office** (958 226688 at Plaza Miriana Pineda 10, open Monday to Friday 9:30 AM to 7 PM, Saturday

An agreement that the customs and religion of the Moorish residents should be respected did not survive the advent of the Inquisition and the arrival of Cardinal Cisneros who, according to one chronicler, found the "climate of tolerance intolerable." Persecutions and expulsions finally ended the Moorish presence. The Castilians also began putting their architectural stamp on the city in the shape of the cathedral, churches, convents, monasteries and palaces. Fortunately, most of the Alhambra, though neglected and decaying, survived the ensuing centuries. A new climate of appreciation and renovation of this unique construction came in the nineteenth century. Granada itself settled into a rather crusty and conservative frame of mind until the twentieth century when the sensibilities of Federico García Lorca, one of Spain's greatest modern poets and playwrights, and the violent passions of the Civil War shook it out of its provincial com-

10 AM to 2 PM. Tourist information is also available at the Alhambra (see below) ticket office. For transportation, contact Granada **Radio-Taxis** (958 151461. For Internet access try **Internet** (958 289269, Plaza de los Girones 3, open Monday to Saturday 9 AM to 11 PM, Sunday 4 PM to 11 PM. Medical attention is available from the **Hospital Clinico San Cecilio** (958 270200, Avenida Dr Olóriz, near the Plaza de Toros.

Busy and rewarding at any time of year, Granada does not stint itself when it comes to festivals. On January 2 every year, the Catholic Monarchs' conquest of the city is celebrated, followed later by Holy Week and, later still, by Corpus Christi. There is also a series of classical concerts in the Alhambra between April and October and a major international music and dance festival in June and July.

OPPOSITE and ABOVE: The ornate interior of the Alhambra Palace.

There is plenty to see and do in and around Granada, but the town's prime attractions are the Alhambra to the east, the cathedral and the Albaicín in the center, and Sacromonte to the north.

WHAT TO SEE AND DO

The Alhambra

"To the traveler imbued with a feeling for the historical and poetical, the Alhambra of Granada is as much an object of veneration as is the Kaaba or sacred house of Mecca to all true Moslem pilgrims. How many legends and traditions, true and fabulous, how many songs and romances, Spanish and Arabian, of love and war and chivalry are associated with this romantic pile!" So wrote Washington Irving, in his florid style, on his arrival in Granada in 1829. His tales in *The Alhambra* (1832) became a best-seller and did much to put Granada on the tourist map then and since.

Built on the top of an elongated hill that dominates the city, the Alhambra (Al Qalat Alhamra, "the Red Castle" in Arabic, from the russet colored stone that was used to build it), is a fortress, a series of palaces and gardens and, in its heyday, a small town in itself. There are a number of hotels on the hill inside and around the Alhambra (see WHERE TO STAY, below), so that you can walk up to its walls under a cool canopy of giant elms, planted by the Duke of Wellington when he wasn't fighting the French in the Peninsular War. Early morning is the best time for the freshness of the air but this isn't the only reason for arriving early. Only 7,700 admissions are allowed every day, with the time of entry to the site, and to each area, strictly controlled. The **Alhambra Ticket Office** (958 227525, Calle Real de Alhambra, winter and Sundays year-round 8:30 AM to 5 PM, summer Monday to Saturday 8:30 AM to 7 PM, does sell out, especially in the heat of high summer, and in any case you are likely to have to wait in line.

Buying a ticket in advance was always the logical solution, and this has recently become possible using a Visa or MasterCard. The **Alhambra Ticket Hotline** (902 224460 (from inside Spain) or (34) 914745920 (from abroad), while you can also book on the Internet at WEB SITE http://decompras.bbv.es. Either way, there is a commission of €0.75 on a ticket price of €6. You will then have to pick up your ticket, either at the Alhambra at least two hours before your time of entry (which is a bore), or at least 24 hours before at one of the BBV branches, of which there are 2,800 nationwide. The ticket then comes in sections for each of the areas of the Alhambra, and all of them are timed. This rather defeats any ambition you might have had of casually wandering around and soaking up the atmosphere, and sparks off the impression of being held in a holding pattern over a busy airport, or playing golf badly with a better player at your heels.

The opening hours of the Alhambra itself (rather than of the ticket office) are March to October 9 AM to 8 PM, November to February (and Sundays year-round) 8:30 AM to 6 PM. The hours are extended with floodlit visits of the Palacios Nazaries: on Tuesdays to Saturdays from March to October, (tickets from 9:45 PM to 10:15 PM, entry from 10 PM to 11:30 PM), and on Friday and Saturday nights from November to February (tickets 7:45 PM to 8:15 PM, entry 8 PM to 9:30 PM). Any adjustments to this already hideously complicated system can be tracked on the Alhambra's WEB SITE www.alhambra-patronato.es.

Once inside, start with the **Alcazaba**, the ninth-century fortress on the western end, which portrays the military power of the Moorish kingdom and affords spectacular views over the rest of what is worth seeing, namely the adjoining hill of Albaicín where the old Moorish quarter is located, Sacromonte, the home of the gypsies, to the north, and in the distance, beyond the city, the Sierra Nevada. From here you can also see El Generalife at the other end of the Alhambra, rather like looking from prow to stern on a vast, stately ocean-going liner. The highest point is the **Torre de la Vela**, the bell tower; the bell was rung to mark the times for opening and closing the sluice gates to the intricate irrigation system that fed the vega, or vale, around Granada, and to sound the alert when enemy forces were approaching — a simple and appropriate symbol of peace and war in those distant times.

The **Palacio Real**, situated at the heart of the Alhambra complex, is the main attraction and tends to be crowded no matter which time of year or day you choose. But the individual attractions are so interspersed with gardens, patios and pathways in the Moorish style that there is always room to breathe and relax before moving on to the next place. The greater part of the palace complex was built in the second half of the fourteenth century during the height of the Nasrid kingdom. Builders, architects, craftsmen and artisans from all over Muslim Andalucía had found refuge in Granada and, under the direction of a dynasty that had lost much of its political power but none of its artistic drive and sensibility, painstakingly put together this masterpiece, the last and arguably the greatest of its kind anywhere in the world.

The palace, much of which has been restored in the last hundred years or so, is divided into three functional areas. First there is the public zone where the business of government and the day-to-day dealings with the public took place. Unfortunately, Carlos V pulled down a great part of this section in the sixteenth century to build an impressive palace for himself. Perhaps he felt impelled as a Holy Roman Emperor to leave his Christian mark on this Islamic island. In another setting, his legacy would neither have seemed excessively egocentric nor out of place. But in the middle of the Alhambra it looks at best bizarre, at worst an outrage. To add insult to injury the **Palacio de Carlos V** was hardly ever used by the man who built it.

A fragment that remains is the **Mexuar** where the king listened to petitioners and held public audiences. This room and its adjacent courtyard give the visitor the first flavor of the palace, a fore-taste of carved cedar, filigreed marble, dizzying geometric patterns of blue, green, orange, brown and mauve tiles, and everywhere cool splashing, gushing, running, trickling water.

The second area consists of the state rooms where the king and his notables did their official entertaining, and most of this is still standing. The center is the **Patio de los Arrayanes** (Courtyard of the Myrtles), which has superbly carved marble arcades at each end of a rectangular pond lined by myrtle shrubs. Connecting this courtyard with the **Sala de los Embajadores** (Hall of the Ambassadors) is the curious **Sala de la Barca** (Hall of the Boat), which takes its name from its hull-shaped wooden ceiling, beautifully carved and adorned with plaster "stalactites." The Hall of the Ambassadors, where the kings of Granada received envoys from friend and foe, from Christian kings and Moorish potentates, has another marvelous view over Granada and the countryside.

The third area of the palace was where the king and his family lived, and centers on the lovely **Patio de los Leónes** (Courtyard of the Lions). Surrounded by a miniature forest of key-hole arches and arcades, a small fountain plays into a carved marble basin that in turn feeds water through the mouths of the less-than-life-sized lions supporting it. Well-pruned, rather short orange trees stands in each corner of the courtyard, casting a modest shadow and throwing in a dash of somber green to contrast with the profusion of golds, ivories and grays. Nothing is too big, excessive or overwhelming. God and king were clearly in mind as the architects planned, the builders built, and the craftsmen chiseled, but none of them ever seems to have lost sight of the fact that, in the end, this was a place for human beings to live in.

You can sit on the edge of the Patio de los Leónes in one of those traditional and stern Spanish leather chairs, and watch the smaller fountains that are built into the floor under the arcades. They throw up jets of water that catch the sunlight and toss it against the creamy filigreed marble of the ceilings and walls. The royal household lived in a series of apartments around the courtyard that included the quarters of the king's harem, baths and reception rooms. The occupants of the palace, however, were never far from a garden — or a view of one — as the **Mirador de Lindaraja**, overlooking a courtyard and garden in this inner complex, illustrates.

On leaving the palace, the Alhambra opens up into a series of gardens, arbors and pathways. The gardens of the **Partal**, with their lily-ponds, canals, flowers, high hedges of clipped cypress and fir and tiled, cobbled and brick paths, enable the visitor to make a gentle transition from the riches of the royal palace to the Alhambra's last work of art, the Generalife. Built on a hill higher than the rest of the Alhambra, the Generalife was the summer palace of the Nasrid kings. It is less than a 10-minute walk from the Partal gardens but is often dropped out of the average visitor's itinerary, though it does not deserve to be.

El Generalife (the name comes from the Arabic meaning the "garden of the architect"), is older

than the palace. It was built around the middle of the thirteenth century, and its buildings are not as distinguished, but it has superb gardens, some charming galleries and *miradors* and panoramic views. The gardens are so extensive that the head gardeners use walkie-talkies to coordinate the activities of their underlings.

Early morning is the best time to visit El Generalife, when everything is fresh and dewy. Wherever you turn there is the sound, smell and sight of water; even some of the connecting stairways in the gardens have water channels cut into their stone railings. The Generalife was the place where the Moorish monarchs, together with their families and friends, came to relax, enjoy themselves and, from time to time, indulge in illicit romance and passion. A sense of all this remains

Part of the extensive gardens that surround El Generalife.

among the flowering oleanders, roses, hibiscus, and geraniums, under the shade of ancient trees and in the music of running water.

The Cathedral

Granada's other attractions, through no fault of their own, tend to pale after a day or two of wandering around the Alhambra. But locked in the tight embrace of the old town at the foot of the Alhambra's lofty perch, the cathedral (958 222959, Gran Vía de Colón, open winter 10:30 AM to 1 PM and 3:30 PM to 6:30 PM, Sunday and holidays 3:30 PM to 6 PM, April through September 10:30 AM to 1:30 PM and 4 PM to 7 PM, Sundays 4 PM to 7 PM, €2.10, is worth visiting. Conceived by Spain's Catholic Monarchs almost as soon as Boabdil left Granada, the cathedral was not finished until the seventeenth century, when the locally born Alonso Cano added the fine main façade.

Built with Renaissance exuberance, the cathedral is barely visible from the outside, so densely packed are the surrounding streets. But inside it is rather beautiful, almost as wide as it is long, with lots of wide open spaces, white limestone pillars, and lush illuminated medieval manuscripts on display. On one wall there is a list of clerics "murdered by Marxism," recalling a much more recent and bloody fratricidal war. Ferdinand and Isabella, having achieved their life-long dream of liberating Spain from the Moors, decided to forget about Toledo and be buried in Granada. Their remains lie in the **Capilla Real** (Royal Chapel), which is an annex to the cathedral. They lie beside their beloved son, Prince John, who died when he was a student at Salamanca University, and their sad daughter, Joan the Mad, and her husband, Philip the Fair. The chapel is richly decorated but their tombs in the crypt underneath are surprisingly simple. In the sacristy adjoining the chapel, Queen Isabella's crown and scepter, her art collection, and Ferdinand's sword are on display.

The oldest Spanish part of Granada fans out from the cathedral's precincts and is both animated and picturesque. It seems to be a custom for herb sellers to pedal their wares directly outside the cathedral. Some of the herbs and potions have a modern ring but many of them don't, and the ills they are reputed to cure or prevent, such as "falling off your horse," would probably not have been out of place when the quarter was first built.

Granada, the Alhambra aside, does not make much of an impact on first acquaintance, but it grows on you. With about a quarter of a million people, it is a manageable size, enough to create a lively ambience, too few and too detached from the main commercial arteries of Andalucía to suffer the ills of large modern cities. It is therefore a good place in which to stroll, eat, drink, and take it easy.

Alhambra Palace, Granada.

The Albaicín

One of the best sections to pass time is the Albaicín, the old Arab quarter that sits on a hill next to the Alhambra. Unpretentious, friendly and clean, this over-sized village of whitewashed houses, old churches, pretty squares and remnants of Moorish fortifications, *miradors* and courtyards has a special charm. It also is the best vantage point for absorbing — and photographing — the classic view of the Alhambra, aglow in the setting sun with the snowy peaks of the Sierra Nevada in the background. For while the individual pieces of the Alhambra are all exquisite, it is the whole that is so remarkable. Be careful of your possessions here, however, as this has

recently become an increasingly fertile hunting-ground for muggers, usually feeding some sort of addiction.

Sacromonte Caves

For a change of pace there are the gypsy caves of Sacromonte, situated on another hill north of the Albaicín. Long gone are the days of spontaneous, thrilling and uncommercial flamenco among the cave-dwellers. Today, a visit may satisfy the curious who want to see it for the sake of seeing it, and who are prepared to fight off or pay off the persistent fortune-tellers and other touts. Take only the money you're prepared to spend. The caves are best in the evenings, especially on the weekends when some of them become atmospheric — if youthful — discos. Flamenco is best seen in the orderly if antiseptic atmosphere of a nightclub or at a music festival.

WHERE TO STAY

One way to circumvent, to a certain extent, the draconian opening policy of the Alhambra is to stay within its walls. There are two possibilities here: the **Parador de Granada** (958 221440 FAX 958 222264 E-MAIL granada@parador.es, Real de la Alhambra (very expensive), is set in a converted fifteenth-century convent. You have to book well ahead to get a place here, but to my taste it is a bit too thoroughly converted, and there's a lot to be said for the smaller, less expensive **Hotel América** (958 227471 FAX 958 227470 E-MAIL hamerica @moebius.es, Real de Alhambra 53 (moderate), which is tastefully furnished with antiques and with a rather younger clientele. Unsurprisingly, this is often full too.

There are plenty of good accommodation options in Granada itself. The cavernous **Alhambra Palace** (958 221468 FAX 958 226404 WEB SITE www.h-alhambrapalace.es, Calle Pena Partida 2 (moderate), is in the gardens near the Alhambra with a good view over the city and plenty of Moorish flourishes. Also near the Alhambra is the **Palacio de Santa Inez** (958222362 FAX 958 222465, Cuesta de Santa Inez 9 (moderate), which is set in a converted seventeenth-century palace and with its own garage. It almost shares a name with the **Hotel Carmen de Santa Inez** (958 226380 FAX 958 224404, Placeta Porras 7, Calle San Juan de Reyes 15 (moderate), which has oak studded doors, marble staircases and formal gardens, with valet parking to look after your car. The **Hotel Reina Christina** (958 253211 FAX 958 255728, Calle Tablas 4 (moderate), is not as intimidatingly smart as it sounds but is near the cathedral and, for the price, is good value. The **Meliá Granada** (958 227400 FAX 958 227403 E-MAIL melia.granada @meliasol.com, Calle Angel Ganivet 7 (moderate), is a centrally located and modern alternative.

Just behind the Generalife is the **Guadalupe** (958 223423, Avenida Alixares del Generalife (moderate), while those who don't want to be quite so Alhambra-focused can try the **Juan Miguel** (958 258912, Calle Acera del Darro 24 (moderate), which is old-fashioned and comfortable.

Travelers on a budget could try the **Hostal Fabiola** (958 223572, Calle Angel Gavinet 5 (inexpensive), close to the Puerta Real.

WHERE TO EAT

Granada is not a particularly gastronomic city, but you can get adequate food for reasonable prices. The visual feast offered by some restaurants that have good views of the Alhambra and city helps to compensate for any culinary deficiencies. The **Parador**, with its unique setting in the Alhambra, is a good place to have a drink and dinner. Like most Paradors the food is good, well-served and decently priced.

Carmen de San Miguel (958 226723, Calle Torres Bermejas 3 (expensive), is in an old country house five minutes' walk from the Alhambra Palace Hotel. The restaurant has a marvelous view over the city from the terrace. For international cuisine, try **Baroca** (958 265061, Calle Pedro de Alarcon 34 (expensive). The **Cunini** (958 263701, Calle Capuchina 14 (moderate) serves good fish and seafood.

Los Manueles (958 223415, Calle Zaragoza 2 (moderate), is an old tavern noted for its local dishes. The **Sevilla** (958 221223, Calle Oficios 12 (moderate), has good atmosphere; it was opened

in 1930 by Lagartijo Chico the matador. For nightlife, the supplement with the weekend paper, *Ideal*, is good, and there is a monthly what's-on guide, *Guia del Ocio*, which is available from any newsagent.

HOW TO GET THERE

Granada Airport (958 226491 takes domestic flights from Málaga, Barcelona and Madrid, but these are not that frequent, which can make problems for international arrivals. It is linked to the city center by a €2.60 shuttle bus. The **train station** (958 271272 is quite close to the center of town, but the main bus station, Carretera de Jaén, is in the suburbs. By road, Granada is 166 km (103 miles) southeast of Córdoba, 434 km (270 miles) south of Madrid, and 129 km (80 miles) northeast of Málaga.

EXCURSIONS FROM GRANADA

The town of **Guadix**, about an hour's drive northeast of Granada, is best known for its cave-dwelling gypsies. The gypsy *barrio*, or neighborhood, is in the upper part of the town, close to the ruined Moorish castle. Small streets run up and down a series of barren hills. The "houses" have whitewashed entrances and white conical chimneys poking out of the rock. Some have gardens and cars parked outside; most have television aerial antennas. This is no fly-by-night group of roaming gypsies, but a well-established community that has its mail delivered along streets that have names and lighting, and to doors, albeit cut in the rock face, that have numbers.

If you wander around the neighborhood you are almost certain to be invited into a house. Since you are a foreign tourist and your host is a gypsy entrepreneur, business is business, so you pay a negotiated fee for the visit, but it is much less commercialized than the Sacromonte caves (see previous page). The cave house I saw had the number "100" painted over the entrance and an outside privy. The surprises came inside as the lady of the household showed me round. There were eight whitewashed rooms, electricity, television, a wood-burning stove for the winter, a gas cooker in the kitchen and gas-heated running water. There were the religious and family pictures on the walls that you find in most Spanish homes, painted plates over the chimney, and rugs on the stone floors.

It was cool after the heat outside, and warm and cozy, the owner said, in winter. All very modern — with one exception. Standing in the kitchen, I heard rustling and snorting sounds that came from an adjoining room. The owner smiled and led me through. Two very fat and contented pigs raised their snouts to greet us in what had suddenly turned into a subterranean farmyard.

Northern Andalucía is not much visited by foreigners, but if you want to get a feel of the rolling countryside and ancient towns and pueblos, then a detour via **Jaén** makes sense. This is the land of the olive. Wherever you turn, legions of those strange desiccated trees, which produce such a luscious oil, march to distant horizons. Jaén sits on the side of a hill, a strategic town in the days of the Arab-Christian wars, but now something of a backwater. There is, however, the magnificent **Parador Castillo de Santa Catalina** (953 230000 FAX 953 230930 E-MAIL Jaén@parador.es, Castillo de Santa Catalina (expensive), located beside the castle at the top of the hill with superb views of Jaén and the countryside.

OPPOSITE: A pottery store in Granada. ABOVE: The Alcaicería shopping area, a silk market in Moorish times.

CÓRDOBA

Córdoba, once the first of the three grand cities of Andalucía, is now the third in importance. Built on the banks of the Guadalquivir, the city has a low profile that allows its historic landmarks to be easily seen and recognized. There is a new Córdoba, but its buildings seem to have been reined in so as not to upstage the ancient structures of the other Córdoba. The transition from the city to wheat and barley fields and country ambience is swift; Córdoba, unlike so many Spanish cities, is not confined by a straitjacket of ugly modern factories and suburbs.

The city's primacy goes back to Roman times, when it was the capital of what is now Andalucía. Its identification with learning and religion came during the Roman period. It was the birthplace of the philosophers Seneca, father and son, the poet Lucan, and, three centuries later, of Bishop Hosius, a fanatical Christian prelate who led the crusade against the Arian heresy in the fourth century AD.

There is no better way of entering Córdoba than to walk across the Roman bridge (Puente Romano) that crosses the oleander-strewn banks of the Guadalquivir and leads directly into the old town. There is no worse way than driving: car-crime here is legendary, matched only by the concern of the locals that your car should stay safe. On my last visit a total stranger asked his mother to look after the car while I went off sightseeing.

The Visigoths, in their customary undocumented way, came and went. The Moorish conquest took place in the eighth century and the city began to flourish. It rapidly became the capital of all Al-Andalus and, by the tenth century, the seat of an independent caliphate, its rulers having decided to renounce the suzerainty of Damascus. With Córdoba's political power consolidated, the city soon expanded its intellectual and artistic horizons to become the pre-eminent center of learning in Europe.

In the tenth and eleventh centuries its population rose to between half a million and a million people, it had 3,000 mosques, many libraries with vast collections of books and manuscripts, a renowned university, a bustling industrial and commercial center (Cordovan leather developed here) and 300 public baths. Like Toledo in its heyday, Córdoba was also an extremely cosmopolitan city where Muslim, Jew and Christian tolerated each other —the human synthesis produced great people and memorable works.

The savants of Córdoba were particularly notable for consolidating and translating the knowledge of the ancient world and making it accessible to contemporary and future scholars. The Moorish scientist, philosopher and doctor, Averroäs, lived in Córdoba in the eleventh century and was followed in the next by Moses Maimonides, the Jewish philosopher and physician, whose writings on the reconciliation of faith and reason greatly influenced the thinking of Thomas Aquinas.

GENERAL INFORMATION

The main **Tourist Information Office** (957 471235 FAX 957 491778, Palacio de Congresos, Calle Torrijos 10, open November to March from Monday to Saturday 9:30 AM to 6 PM, summer to 7 PM, Sundays 10 AM to 2 PM. There is also a **Municipal Tourist Office** (957 200522, Plaza Judá Levi, open Monday to Saturday 8:30 AM to 2:30 PM, which tends to be less crowded. There is an increasing number of Internet cafés springing up in Córdoba,

— one central one is **El Navegante**, Llanos de Pretoria 1, open 8 AM to midnight. For transportation, call **Tele-Taxis** (957 764100.

The interesting bits of the city are spread around amongst white-painted, narrow streets, where the beauties are kept indoors, in patios and interiors, leaving the façades resolutely blank.

WHAT TO SEE AND DO

The **Mezquita**, mosque of Córdoba's Umayyad caliphs, remains one of the great wonders and, thanks to its Christian embellishments, one of the great curiosities of Spain. It was begun by Abd ar-Rahman ad-Dakhil, the founder of the Moorish state centered on Córdoba, and construction was continued by his successors during the next two centuries. Built on a rectangular pattern, it was easy to expand by simply constructing more aisles on each side. Minarets and mihrabs (prayer recesses) were also added. Opening hours change each month: December and January 10 AM to 5:30 PM, February and November to 6 PM, March and July to 7 PM, April to June to 7:30 PM, last visit 30 minutes before, €5.40. For bookings call (957 470512.

The forest of double horseshoe-shaped arches in red-and-cream-striped stone is probably familiar to many people from photographs. But there is no substitute for wandering, perhaps a little mystified, beneath them. Cool and gloomy, the interior of the Mezquita seems like a purposeless maze yet, in its time, it was a place of spiritual and physical lightness. The trouble was that the Christian conquerors built a dividing wall between the mosque and its courtyard where there had been none, sealed up all but a single entrance and, after 300 years of thinking about it, dumped a cathedral in the middle of it.

Much of the Mezquita's original beauty is thus lost, but it is still an astonishing place. A better sense of its delicacy can be seen in the mihrab that was added in the tenth century. This is an octagonal room for prayer recessed in the wall facing Mecca. It has a lovely shell-shaped ceiling where the supporting columns reach up and interlock and whose surface is a dazzling display of mosaic tiles, the gift of a Byzantine emperor.

After taking Córdoba in 1236, the Christians built two chapels — the **Capilla Mayor** and the **Capilla Real** — in the outer walls of the Mezquita. In the early sixteenth century, the cathedral was begun — in the heart of the Mezquita. It was a bizarre idea, and it is a bizarre sight, but at least they left the rest of the mosque intact. As a religious building the cathedral is neither offensive nor particularly remarkable and it would have been fine in another setting. Curiously, Carlos V was reportedly horrified when he saw the completed building, although he had been guilty of

The Roman bridge spanning the Guadalquivir in Córdoba.

a similar architectural outrage in the Alhambra. The visual discordance is one thing — you almost stumble on the cavernous cathedral as you wend your way through the mosque — but the sounds of the Catholic liturgy, the rumble of the organ and a congregation in full voice pulsing through that vast oriental edifice is one of the strangest cultural warps Spain has to offer.

The old city behind the Mezquita has several attractions. There is the **Alcázar de los Reyes Cristianos** (957 485001, open Tuesday to Sunday 10 AM to 2 PM and 4:30 PM to 6:30 PM, €1.50, built in the fourteenth century. Its tower provides excellent views of Córdoba and its refreshing gardens owe much to the Moorish legacy.

The famous **Judería** is a jumble of cobbled streets, whitewashed houses, cool courtyards and fine mansions. The only surviving synagogue in Andalucía is here (there are only three left in the whole of Spain; the other two are in Toledo). It consists of a single high-domed room, which you enter after passing through a shaded courtyard; high up on the walls there are fragments of Hebrew script and some arabesques, but that is all. The Judería is swamped by tourist shops and by tourists themselves, but an early morning walk avoids both — the shops are not open and the tourists are having breakfast — and is the time to capture the flavor of the quiet, freshly watered streets and the scent of jasmine and orange blossom.

For those interested in bullfighting there is a fascinating museum, the **Museo Taurino** (957 485001 (open Tuesday to Sunday 10 AM to 2 PM and 5 PM to 7 PM, €3, no charge on Fridays), in the heart

of the Judería. The collection of bulls' heads and hides, matadors' clothing and equipment and some evocative art-nouveau bullfight posters concentrates on local heroes who made their names in the late nineteenth and first part of the twentieth centuries. From a later period there is a pantheon for one of the sport's greatest matadors, Manuel Rodríguez, more commonly known as Manolete, who died from a *cornada* (horn wound) in Linares in August, 1947. The skin of Islero, the bull that killed him, is stretched on the wall.

The bullfighter most closely identified with contemporary Córdoba, "El Cordobés" (Manuel Benítez), is not commemorated. It is not clear whether this is because he was born in a small

town some distance from Córdoba, or because he is not regarded as a true artist by many experts. Judging by the purist feeling, bordering on the religious, that pervades the museum — its guardians insist on an orderly progression around the exhibits and on total silence — it could be that the dashing and daring Cordoban has not yet earned a place in this particular hall of fame.

Córdoba gives the impression of being less prosperous and more religious than its Andalusian sister cities, Sevilla and Granada. While there are pockets of affluence around the Mezquita and the Judería, where many of the large hotels and best restaurants are found, there are also many areas of decay and poverty. It is a city where you still

OPPOSITE: A horse-drawn carriage in Córdoba. ABOVE, LEFT AND RIGHT: The Corpus Christi procession passing by the walls of the Mezquita in Córdoba.

see blind lottery-ticket sellers, a symbol of an older, poorer Spain, and where a homeless man can be seen making his supper — and later his bed — at the foot of the Mezquita's walls.

To catch the religious spirit, visit Córdoba during one of its many religious festivals. At **Corpus Christi**, for example, priests, monks and nuns carrying candles escort the holy sacrament through hay-covered streets. Accompanied by boys in uniform and girls in white dresses carrying bouquets of flowers, the procession makes its way to the cathedral singing hymn after hymn. The aromas of hay, wild herbs from the countryside, tallow from the candles and incense blend in the warm air and float over the heads of dense crowds

of people who have come to watch or join in the celebration. The cathedral-within-a-mosque is full on occasions like this, as it must have been in the sixteenth century when it was still being built. This is when Spain reaches back into its history and lives it without effort and without apology.

WHERE TO STAY AND EAT

Perhaps the best place too stay here is in the modern **Parador de Córdoba** (957 275900 FAX 957 280409, Avenida de la Arruzafa (expensive), a new hotel on the outskirts of Córdoba with pool, tennis courts, pretty gardens. It has views over the city, keeping a safe distance. To stay in the city itself, **El Conquistador** (957 481102, Calle Magistral González Frances 15, is modern and comfortable, conveniently situated next to the Mezquita (expensive), as is the **Maimónedes** (957 471500, Calle

Torrijos 4 (expensive). Close to the Judería, the **Meliá Córdoba** (957 298066 FAX 957 298147, Jardines de la Victoria (expensive), is functional and has a swimming pool.

Stepping down a price band, the **Hotel Los Abetos del Maestre Escuela** (957 282132 FAX 957 282175, Calle Santo Domingo km2.8 (inexpensive), is a ten-minute drive from the city center, but worth it for a colonial atmosphere amongst palm trees. Near the Mezquita is **Los Omeyas** (957 492267 FAX 957 491659, Calle Encarnación 17 (inexpensive), which, like much of Córdoba, looks plain from outside but theatrical within. On a tight budget, go for the **Fonda Agostin** (957 470872, Calle Zapateria Vieja 5 (very inexpensive).

For dining, be cautious about the restaurants around the Mezquita, as their standards have often become lowered by long reliance on tourists who rarely bother to complain. **El Caballo Rojo** (957 475375, Calle Cardenal Herrero 28 (expensive), which is touted as one of Andalucía's best restaurants, proved disappointing: undistinguished over-priced food, but the service was good. It is better to try **El Churrasco** (957 290819, Calle Romero 16 (expensive), which lived up to its reputation. "Churrasco" is a local pork dish with a peppery sauce; the restaurant specializes in Andalusian cooking and has a charming patio and a large *tapas* bar. For an atmospheric experience in a converted medieval convent, try the **Bodegas Campos** (957 497500, Los Lineros 32. For a less expensive meal, try the **Mesón San Basilio**, Calle San Basilio 19, or the **Taberna Salinas**, Calle Tundidores 3.

There are a many good, modestly priced restaurants in and around the Judería; it's always worth taking a look at the *menú del día* (daily special) before ordering à la carte in these sort of restaurants. Nightlife tends to happen away from the center, in the El Brilliante suburb a short taxi-ride to the north.

HOW TO GET THERE

Córdoba is 393 km (244 miles) south of Madrid, and 144 km (89 miles) east of Sevilla, by fast *autopista*. National roads head off south to Málaga (165 km or 103 miles) and southeast to Granada (170 km or 106 miles). The bus and train stations are combined in a spanking new building at the northern end of town, in the Plaza de las Tres Culturas, from where there are good connections throughout Andalucía and to Madrid and Barcelona.

ABOVE: The cave houses of Guadix. RIGHT: The cathedral inside the Mezquita, Córdoba.

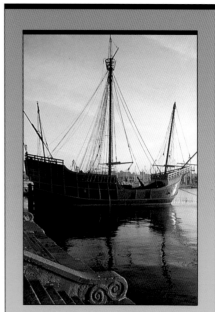

Catalunya

Nowhere is the variety of Spain displayed more vividly than in the region of Catalunya. Virtually everything is different — the landscape, the climate, the human temperament, even the language. Catalunya, a triangular wedge of mountains, valleys, plains and coastline in northeastern Spain, sits astride the main land corridor that connects the country with the rest of Europe. Catalunya is the most European of Spain's ancient kingdoms, and Barcelona, its capital, the least Spanish of its cities.

Catalunya reflects the contrasting nature of Spain through its own diversity. It has mountains (the Pyrenees), a rugged coast (Costa Brava), a gentler shoreline (Costa Daurada), pleasant valleys and productive plains, heavy and light industry, the country's largest port (Barcelona) and an industrious and creative population. The region also produces some of the best wine in Spain, including the champagne-like *cava*. First settled by the Greeks, Catalunya has always looked to the Mediterranean for its livelihood and its inspiration. The Carthaginians arrived in the third century, and Hamilcar Barca, Hannibal's father, founded Barcelona. Then came the Romans, who established a thriving province centered on the coastal city of Tarragona. Neither the Visigoths nor the Moors made much of an impression, allowing Catalunya to develop in its own distinctive way. By as early as the ninth century, the region had established a clear political identity under the Count of Barcelona, Wilfredo el Velloso (Wilfred the Hairy). Catalunya marks its formal existence from the end of the tenth century, and celebrated its first millennium in 1987.

In the twelfth century, the Catalan Count Ramón Berenguer IV married Queen Petronilla of Aragón, uniting the two states. The union brought power and prosperity to the region. Democratic institutions were created, monasteries and cathedrals built and territory conquered. At its height, the Catalunya-Aragón dominions included Sardinia, Sicily, Malta, the region of Roussillon in France, Valencia and the Balearic Islands in Spain and much of modern Greece.

This was the golden age of Catalunya, but the arrival of the Catholic Monarchs, Ferdinand and Isabella, in the last quarter of the fifteenth century set in motion an uneven but steady decline. Determined to unify Spain under their central authority, they and their successors curbed Catalunya's separatist ambitions and exacerbated internal divisions. The discovery of the New World and the trade monopoly given to Sevilla isolated Catalunya, cutting it off from the wealth that flowed in from the Americas. The long struggle between Castilla and Catalunya, Madrid and Barcelona began.

An attempt at secession in the seventeenth century undermined Catalunya's political aspirations, and they unfortunately backed the wrong side in the dynastic war of succession in the early eighteenth century. However, Catalan energy diverted itself into making the region the industrial powerhouse of Spain, strengthening its capitalists and creating a modern working class. With the declaration of the Second Republic in 1930, Catalunya received a large degree of autonomy, which it used to flirt with every imaginable political theory on the left of the spectrum, including anarchism. During the Civil War, Barcelona was the scene of great chaos — unforgettably described by George Orwell in *Homage to Catalonia* — as well as heroic resistance. The city became the last capital of the dying Republic in the final months of the war. After Franco's victory, tens of thousands of Catalans fled across the border to France and the government crushed Catalunya's freewheeling ways.

The new democratic Spain that emerged after Franco's death in 1975 endorsed a more decentralized form of government. Catalunya duly regained most of its ancient privileges, including its provincial parliament and government, and an almost unfettered use of Catalan, its own language.

A word about the Catalan language. Spoken by about six million people, every one of whom will bridle if he or she hears it called a dialect, Catalan is a Romance language derived from the Romans and much modified by the French connection from the ninth century onwards. It is closely related to Provençal and Occitan in southern France, looks like a fair mixture of French and Castilian on paper, but sounds like neither when spoken. Even the road-signs are subtly different, more like Portuguese than Spanish.

Since the death of Franco, under whose iron hand Catalan was banned, the language has flourished and is now recognized as an official tongue. It is taught in schools and used on the radio and television, and has replaced Spanish on street signs, in many official forms and in Catalonian government offices. This makes life a little difficult for the visitor, perhaps already struggling with rudimentary Spanish, but the Catalans feel that the time has come to assert their cultural heritage. To avoid further confusion while in Catalonia (Cataluña in Spanish, Catalunya in the local language), the Catalan terms for place names, streets, and so on, will be used in this book. Catalan, or a variation of it, is spoken beyond the region in and around Valencia, and in the Balearic Islands.

BARCELONA

Barcelona, the pivot and pride of Catalunya, and Spain's second-largest metropolis, has over recent years been transformed into perhaps the most visitor-friendly city in Spain. It has never been a city of half measures: it bustles, does business with

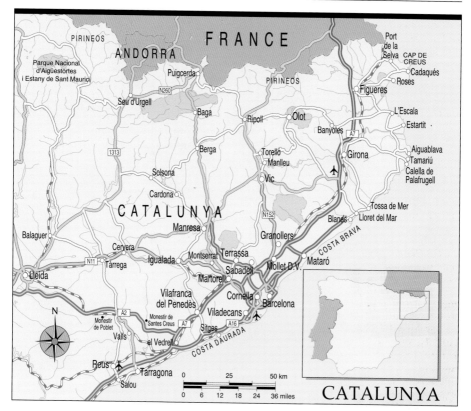

CATALUNYA

great energy, and plays as hard as it works. For years Barcelona had a rather grimy, hangdog look. But in the early 1990s it underwent a dramatic transformation — to the point where it was voted the country's leading city by a panel of distinguished Spanish architects and urban planners — and it frequently wins plaudits as a European short-break destination.

Barcelona's growth during the last hundred years or so has been nurtured by three international events: the Universal Exhibition in 1888, the International Exhibition in 1929 and, most recently, the Olympic Games in 1992. The physical changes wrought by the US$9 billion invested to host the Olympics is striking and lasting. The city's old salty face and dreary port were cleaned and transformed by the removal of old warehouses and obsolete buildings and the development of new beaches, esplanades and marinas.

The Olympic Stadium, on a hill overlooking the city, added a new dimension to sport and public entertainment, and the Olympic Village, on the coast, extended the city northward. Barcelona traditionally turned its back on the Mediterranean; now with many kilometers of seafront and a renovated port area, sea and city are finally reconciled. To round it off, Barcelona acquired a sparkling and state-of-the-art international airport and a

comprehensive network of new highways, encircling the city, which enables traffic to flow rapidly in and out. These roads are particularly helpful to the vehicle-borne traveler coming down from France or arriving at the port and wanting to get in out of Barcelona with the minimum of time and fuss.

There are plenty of reminders that Barcelona is an ancient metropolis, but it is also a city that has always been receptive to new ideas, as well as producing many of its own. From its experiments with democratic institutions in the twelfth century to libertarianism and anarcho-syndicalism in the nineteenth and twentieth centuries, Barcelona has never been a dull place. Influenced by the European Romantic movement, it experienced a cultural renaissance in the nineteenth century (the Catalan *Renaixenca*). It also nurtured painters such as Pablo Picasso, Joan Miró and Salvador Dalí, musicians like Pablo Casals, and the amazing Antonio Gaudí, the Modernist architect and designer.

It isn't all good news. There are plenty of unskilled immigrants and an indigenous underclass marginalized by the city's race to prosperity and spiraling house prices, as well as very obvious drug addicts. Petty crime is the inevitable result, so watch out for valuables and keep your car securely parked in a guarded underground parking lot.

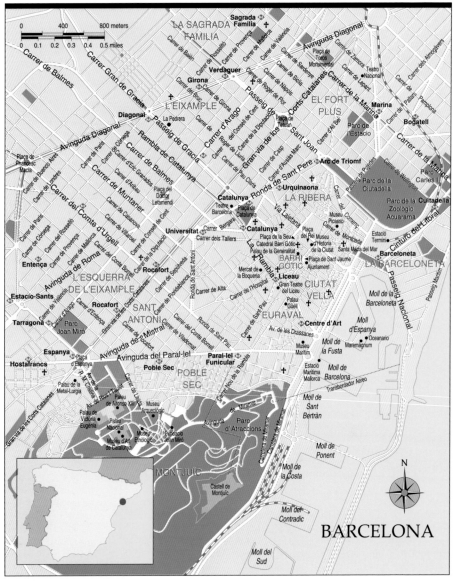

GENERAL INFORMATION

The **Central Tourist Office** (906 301282 WEB SITE www.barcelonaturisme.com, Plaça de Catalunya, open 9 AM to 9 PM, is set underground this landmark square at the northern end of the Rambla. It has a good collection of brochures and a helpful staff, but be warned: it can get very busy and you may well need to stand in line. There are also tourist offices in both the international and the domestic airports, open daily from 9 AM to 3 PM, at the Estacío-Sants (934 914431, open from 8 AM to 8 PM daily through the summer, closed in the winter after 2 PM on Saturday and Sunday. They

issue maps of public transportation (free), though the more useful city maps cost €1.25. The tourist offices also sell the Barcelona card, valid for one, two or three days (€15, €18 and €21 respectively), which gives free public transportation and discounts on most museums and some shops and restaurants. For more artistic tastes, the Articket gives access to six art centers for €15.

If all you require is information, there is an English-speaking telephone hotline (010, manned Monday to Saturday 8 AM to 10 PM.

For medical attention you can call an **ambulance** (933 002020, or contact **hospitals** at (934 546000 or 934 183400; there is a special number for **dental emergencies** (934 159922. Barcelona has a good and easy-to-use metro system, regular city buses, and plenty of taxis, summoned by calling **Radio-Taxis** (933 577755 and 933 581111. Your own car is not much help here, as traffic is heavy, parking is difficult, and casual car crime common.

For Internet access, cybercafés are springing up all the time. Two central bureaus are **Cibercafe**, Pasaje Rambla 42, open Monday to Saturday 10 AM to 8 PM, and **Cibermundo**, Carrer Bergara 3, open Monday to Friday 10 AM to 11 PM, weekends noon to 11 PM. Quite a few downtown bars also offer online terminals.

Orientation in downtown Barcelona is relatively easy. The southern border is made conclusively

the Sagrada Familia church, as you head north towards the Parc Güell.

Navigation becomes more difficult beyond the city center, as the center gives way to villages only recently unified into a single city sprawl by endless infilling, caused by spiraling property values. Narrow, winding streets, packed with traffic wending up and down steep hills, make suburban Barcelona very confusing. In these endless regions the fast blur of the city's ring road can seem very far away, and it is easy to get completely lost. This can work out well, and you'll discover a Barcelona beyond the conventional tourist area, as long as you hang onto an emergency banknote for a taxi-ride home.

obvious by the Mediterranean Sea, but at its lapping shore you'll find the newly developed Port Vell district, an upmarket if sanitized area, and its flanking city beaches. Running north from here, the Rambla is the main drag, always teeming with stalls, buskers and wandering crowds. It heads up to the Plaça de Catalunya, cutting through the narrow, teeming alleys of the Barri Gòtic on either side. Winding narrow streets, unexpected squares and a collection of well-preserved buildings dating from the thirteenth to the fifteenth centuries, erected over the remains of successive occupations dating back to the Romans, constitute the Gothic heart of the city. North of the Plaza Catalunya is the Eixample, where the city's nineteenth-century wealth expanded to build more expansive residences free of the constraints of the Barri Gòtic. Here you'll find some of Gaudí's great buildings, including

WHAT TO SEE AND DO

La Rambla

The main artery connecting the port with the more modern parts of the city is the famous Rambla, a broad tree-lined avenue with a wide central walkway full of newsstands, flower stalls, cafés, vendors selling canaries, budgerigars, rats and pigeons, performing "artistes" of varying talent, and an endless *paseo* of citizens and visitors drawn by the constantly changing human kaleidoscope.

Down in the port area, at the end of the Rambla, is the **Monument a Colom** (Columbus's Column), where you can take an elevator ride up inside the steel shaft and view the city from the top.

Going up the Rambla, away from the port, on the left hand side there is the **Barri Xines** (red light

The bustling Catalan capital.

district) and the **Palau Güell**, Carrer Nou de la Rambla 3, which has guided tours Monday to Saturday 10 AM to 1:30 PM and 4 PM to 6:30 PM, €2.40. This Gaudí extravaganza, built in 1888 for his wealthy patron, the financier Baron Eusebi Güell, was the first modern structure to receive a World Heritage designation by Unesco. Further on, you pass the old **Oriente Hotel**, the **Gran Teatre del Liceu** (Spain's most sumptuous opera house, now rebuilt after (another) disastrous fire), and the marvelously colorful and aromatic covered market, the **Mercat de la Boqueria**. On the right, going in the same direction, is the **Plaça Reial** — an arcaded square just off the Rambla that is a bit seedy but turns into an interesting stamp and coin

Plaça de la Seu, is large and spacious in the manner of Catalan Gothic architecture, with a fantastic façade. Also known as **La Seu**, it's open Monday to Friday 8 AM to 1:30 PM and 4 PM to 7:30 PM, but only from 5 PM to 7:30 PM on Saturday and Sunday €€2). It has a pretty cloister with a garden (closed on Saturday afternoons and Sunday) shaded by palm, orange and medlar trees, a fountain and a flock of white geese, said to symbolize Santa Eulàlia's virginity. It is worth going up to the top of the cathedral's bell-tower in the newly installed elevator for a panoramic view of the Gothic Quarter. There is a busy market outside the main entrance on Sundays, and the *sardana*, Catalunya's traditional folk dance, is often performed here.

market on Sundays — and a network of small, pungent streets that lead you into the Gothic quarter.

Barri Gòtic

It isn't hard to get lost in this maze of narrow streets and alleys, quiet squares and noisy bars, but the navigational landmark of the Rambla, running from the port to the Plaça de Catalunya, is so well-known that any request for directions will lead you, inevitably, back to it to find your bearings. As such, this part of the city is ideal for general, unfocussed wandering, stumbling across architectural wonders incidentally, guided only by serendipity. A lively commercial world exists amongst perfectly preserved medieval buildings, a winning combination unequalled elsewhere in the world.

There are, however, some outstanding buildings you should try to find. Begun in the late thirteenth century, the **Catedral Barri Gòtic** (933 151554,

The **Palau de la Generalitat** in the heart of the Gothic Quarter on the **Plaça de Sant Jaume** is an almost holy place for Catalan nationalists. Founded by King Jaume I in the fourteenth century, this is where Catalan parliamentary government began. The actual building dates from the fifteenth century although it has a number of more modern additions. It has been back in use since the restoration of Catalan autonomy in 1977, and is the seat of the government. It is only open to the public on Sundays between 10 AM and 2 PM. Across the square is the **Ajuntament** (City Hall), where the "Council of a Hundred" ruled Catalunya from the fourteenth century until Felipe V abolished the region's institutions in 1714. The best façade is not the nineteenth-century one facing the square but the Gothic façade that overlooks a small street at the side of the building. Inside there is a graceful Gothic gallery, a florid and much photographed late-nineteenth-century staircase and some elegant reception rooms. The oldest chamber is the atmospheric **Saló de Cent** (Hall of the Hundred), which was begun in the fourteenth century and, somewhat like the government it symbolizes, was added to and subtracted from through the ages. It has a wooden-beamed ceiling divided by two stone arches and the walls are adorned with a heavily brocaded fabric in the gold and scarlet of Catalunya.

Not far north of the Ajuntament is the **Palau de Llonctinent** (Viceroy's Palace), Plaça del Rei, built in grand style in the middle of the sixteenth century. It houses one of the world's greatest collections of medieval documents, built around the archives of the Kingdom of Aragón. Do not miss the small but exquisite **Plaça del Rei**, which captures the best of old Barcelona. The city museum, **Museu d'Historia de la Ciutat** (933 151111 WEB SITE www.bcn.es/icub, is on the Plaça (open summer 10 AM to 8 PM, closing between 2 PM and 4 PM in winter and on Sunday afternoon and all day Monday, the entrance costs a hefty €4.20). The museum houses an interesting collection of memorabilia down through the ages commemorating Barcelona's history. But perhaps more intriguing is the **Underground Museum** — the same ticket will get you in — where you can take a walk along the city's excavated Roman and Visigothic streets and see the ruins of a fourth-century Visigothic church.

Crossing the Via Laietana you enter the **Barri Santa Maria del Mar**, another medieval part of the city, which clusters around the church of the name. The history of this Catalan Gothic church is inextricably linked with Catalunya's maritime empire. A cool, uncluttered building, it is distinguished by a large central nave, soaring octagonal pillars spaced at unusually wide intervals and some lovely stained-glass windows.

Close by on the **Carrer de Montcada**, one of the city's most elegant medieval streets, is the **Museu Picasso** (933 196310 WEB SITE www.bcn.es /cub, Montcada 15-23, open Tuesday to Saturday 10 AM to 8 PM and Sundays 10 AM to 3 PM, €4.2. It is set in the **Palau Aguila**, a fifteenth-century nobleman's house. This is an appropriate setting for the great painter, who was born in Málaga but lived and worked in Barcelona from 1895 until 1904, his "Blue Period." Picasso's early artistic development is chronicled in the museum, but a number of his later paintings are on display.

The Port Vell

At the southern extent of the Rambla is the old Port Vell dockyard, redeveloped as part of the

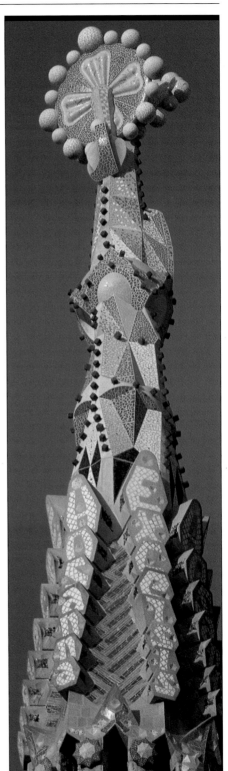

OPPOSITE: A bird's-eye view of Barcelona from Tibidabo. RIGHT: One of the spires of Gaudí's El Templo de la Sagrada Familia (The Church of the Holy Family), his monumental and unfinished church.

1992 Olympic improvements into a new complex of restaurants, bars, shops, cinemas and entertainment complexes, with a marina encompassing 410 moorings. Worth the visit alone is the **Oceanario** (93 221 7474 WEB SITE www.aquarium bcn.com, Moll d'Espanya, open daily 9:30 AM to 8 PM, €8.75, Europe's largest aquarium. There are 21 tanks holding nearly 19 million liters (five million gallons) of water that contain 8,000 fish of 300 different species. One tank, 80 m (87.5 yds) long, is pierced by a transparent perspex tunnel, through which a slow moving walkway moves you past sharks, rays and swordfish that glide overhead. Other attractions include an IMAX cinema and the Maremàgnum — a huge leisure complex filled with shops, restaurants and bars. Along the Moll de la Fusta, boats offer short rides out across the harbor, but for the most dramatic views of the city, book on to the cable-car (see below), daily, noon to 7 PM, €6 one way, which leaves from Montjuïc and crosses the harbor to the heart of the new docks and on to Barceloneta. This is more than a tourist facility: it is excellent city transportation. Even better views are had from the top of the **lift tower**, Jaume 1, which is just up the Moll de Barcelona from the Columbus Monument: the lift up costs €3.60.

Ensanche/Eixample

With industrialization, prosperity and a cultural renaissance in the nineteenth century, Barcelona broke through its medieval walls and expanded with a new section of carefully planned streets and intersections and solid bourgeois housing. This section, which is known as the Ensanche in Spanish and Eixample in Catalan (the "Broadening" or "Extension") and was the work of Ildefons Cerdà, begins when you have reached the top of the Rambla and arrive at the **Plaça de Catalunya**. The district is reminiscent of the boulevards of Paris or the Salamanca neighborhood in Madrid, but with two notable differences. Each intersection in the gridiron pattern of streets has "rounded" corners that give a greater feeling of space; and scattered through the district are a number of the colorful, convoluted creations of Gaudí and other Modernist architects.

The Eixample is where the big department stores and many hotels, restaurants and classy boutiques are located; but it also still the home of many of the city's more affluent residents.

The swankiest avenue is the **Passeig de Gràcia**, which runs from the Plaça de Catalunya up to the Avinguda Diagonal and has a number of Modernist buildings by Gaudí and his contemporaries, notably Lluís Domènech i Montaner and Josep Puig i Cadafalch. The most dramatic Gaudí building is **La Pedrera**, at the top end of the Passeig de Gràcia, which was built in 1910 and was the architect's last secular work. An amazing concoction of flowing concrete, wrought-iron balustrades, and fanciful chimneys, it represents the Modernist movement at its most flamboyant.

The Eixample's greatest Gaudí monument, however, is the **Templo de la Sagrada Familia** (Church of the Holy Family) (934 550247, Plaça Sagrada Familia, open daily 9 AM to 9 PM, €4.80, which towers over the busy, tree-lined streets and avenues of the district and is located just across the Diagonal. Unique, strange and unfinished, this modern paean to Christianity in gray reinforced concrete has to be seen to be believed. And it should be seen by anyone visiting Barcelona.

It was begun in 1882 by another architect, but Gaudí, at the age of 31, took over in 1891 and continued working on it until his death in a streetcar accident in 1926. During the next decade the façade was finished, but the outbreak of the Civil War in 1936 stopped work and nothing much was done until 1954. Gaudí left no plans, but work has resumed again using his models, although not without controversy because, as the purists who oppose any further additions point out, Gaudí usually changed his mind as he went along.

The clusters of slender honeycombed towers and spires soar to 108 m (350 ft). Visitors can take an elevator to the top of one of the towers and walk over a gently curved connecting bridge that provides a fine view of the whole building. The church is also a Gaudí museum where you can see a slide show of his other work, along with models for the building of the Sagrada Familia and how it will look when it is eventually finished. And down in the crypt, the master lies at peace under the unfinished temple that consumed almost half his life.

Sarrià

The last main section of Barcelona is known as Sarrià, which is situated beyond the Diagonal. Largely built in the nineteenth and the early twentieth centuries, on a gently sloping incline, this is an area of narrow streets, solid houses, and pretty gardens. Sarrià was originally known for its skilled craftsmen, especially master-builders, but later became a residential district. It is now part of the city and while many of the houses remain as residences, quite a few of them have been converted into offices, restaurants, art galleries and shops. The human scale of the area and its feeling of neighborhood contrast pleasantly with other more crowded sections of Barcelona, of which it is now ineluctably part.

Gaudí leaves his imprint on this district too with the **Parc Güell** that lies further up the hillside beyond the **Travesera de Dalt**. The park is a Gaudí fantasy although its original design was meant to be English, and frequently spelled "Park." The entrance is flanked by two pavilions with

La Pedrera, Gaudí's most ambitious secular building.

sweeping roofs covered in mosaics and colored tiles, a grand stairway, and a dragon heading in the direction of the **Sala Hipostila** (Hall of a Hundred Columns). The park is constructed on several levels with terrace walls supported by columns shaped like spreading palms. Nothing is predictable, nothing is dull. Even a park bench has Gaudí's hand upon it with its serpentine shape and covering of bright ceramic tile. It may not be your taste but it certainly is not boring.

Beyond the park is **Tibidabo**, Barcelona's highest hill, where a lung-full of clean air and a grand vista of the city and the Mediterranean can be had without dipping your hand into your pocket or purse. There are two other parks, much closer to

urday 10 AM to 7 PM, Sundays and holidays 10 AM to 2:30 PM, €4.81. This gallery hosts a standing collection of works by Miró, Matisse and Duchamp among many others, and exhibits visiting modern art displays of international quality, alone making a visit to the park worthwhile. Montjuïc also houses the stadium for the 1992 Olympic Games, the **Palau Nacional**, the **Palau de Victòria Eugènia** and the **Palau de Alfonso XIII**, as well as a number of museums including the **Museu Arqueològic**, the **Museu Etnòlogic** and the **Museu d'Art de Catalunya**, with its fantastic collection of medieval paintings. Oh, and there is the city's castle, the **Castell de Montjuïc**. All in all, enough for several days, but avoid Mondays as all these

the sea, that deserve a mention. The first is the **Parc de la Ciutadella**, at the north end of the port, which was the site of a fortress built by the conquering Felipe V in 1714 to keep the rebellious Catalans in order. When Barcelona was firmly under the control of its own government again in the nineteenth century, the citadel was razed and a park put in its place. It was here that the city's first international show, the Universal Exposition, was held in 1888.

Montjuïc is the hill to the south of the Port Vell, which it overlooks, and is a pleasantly green parkland containing some of the city's most important buildings. The site of the Barcelona's second global fiesta, the 1929 International Exposition, Montjuïc has an extensive park and gardens as well as the Miró museum, the **Fondació Joan Miró** (934 439470 FAX 933 298609 WEB SITE www.bcn .fjmiro.es, Parc de Montjuïc, open Tuesday to Sat-

attractions all shut. Access is easiest by the cable-car that connects Montjuïc with the Barcelona port and the new beaches at Barceloneta, but there's also a funicular that runs up from the Paral-lel metro station.

WHERE TO STAY

As one of Europe's most popular cultural and nightlife destinations, Barcelona can offer a full range of accommodation to suit all budgets.

Very Expensive

Arts (932 211660 FAX 932 211070 WEB SITE www .ritzcarlton.com, Carrer de la Marina 19–21, is one of the city's most luxurious hotels, located in one of the new skyscraper towers in the Olympic Village, now more of a fully-fledged seaside town. It is, however, a 10-minute taxi-ride from La Rambla and with 455 rooms it is too big to be too exciting. Most of the rooms do have good views though. A more central and rather less costly option is the **Claris** (934 876262 FAX 932 157970 E-MAIL claris@derbyhotels.es, Pau Claris 150, Eixample, a renovated modern luxury hotel in a nineteenth-century palace with a swimming pool and solarium on the roof. It is close to the Passeig de Gràcia and the Diagonal. **Le Meridien** (933 186200 FAX 933 017776, La Rambla 11, formerly the Ramada Renaissance, is an old hotel superbly renovated with commanding view over the Rambla. There's more atmosphere at the **Ritz** (933 185200 FAX 933 180148, Gran Vía 668, is a classic old hotel as the name suggests; it recreates *belle époque* atmosphere in style and is close to the Gothic Quarter.

Expensive

The **Avenida Palace** (933 019600 FAX 933 181234, Gran Vía 605, is centrally located and lavishly comfortable. To stay in Modernist style, try the **Hotel Duques de Bergara** (933 171063 FAX 933 173442 E-MAIL cataloni@holeles-catalonia.ex, Carrer Bergara 11, designed by Gaudí mentor Emili Sala. For a more old-fashioned atmosphere, the **Colón** (933 011404 FAX 933 172915 WEB SITE www .hotelcolon.es, Avinguda Catedral 7, has comfortable rooms and leisurely service. It is right in the heart of the Gothic quarter, opposite the cathedral. **Balmes** (934 511914 FAX 934 510049, Carrer Mallorca 216, is a good, modern hotel within walking distance of the Rambla and the Gothic Quarter, with an excellent buffet breakfast. Ideally suited to travelers who just need somewhere central to park a car and then themselves is the **Citadines Apart'Hotel** (932 701111 FAX 934 127421 E-MAIL barcelona@citadines.com, La Rambla 122, which offers an underground parking lot and super-comfortable self-catering apartments, ideally located at the northern end of La Rambla.

Moderate

The **Regina** (933 013232 FAX 933 182326 E-MAIL regina @top1.es, Carrer Bergara 2–4, is a pleasant and functional hotel just off the Rambla, while the **Wilson** (932 098911 FAX 932 008370, Avinguda Diagonal 568, is also comfortable. A step up from all these in atmosphere, but down in price, is the **Hotel Gran Vía** (933 181900 FAX 933 189997, Gran Vía Corts Catalanes 643, which is a belle époque hangover in the heart of the city.

Good for families is the **Mesón Castilla** (933 182182 E-MAIL hmesoncastilla@teleline.es, Carrer Valldonzella 5, which is in a good location and has a pretty courtyard for summer breakfasts — ideal for containing the kids. At the lower end of the moderate category is the **Hostal Opera** (933 188201, Carrer de Sant Pau 20, which is newly refurbished and quiet for its location, just behind the Liceu opera house off the Rambla.

Inexpensive

Barcelona, like Madrid, has a mass of inexpensively priced hotels, hostels and boarding houses. The Barcelona tourist authorities put out an extremely useful map, listing hotels by category on one side and showing where they are on the other. Good stand-bys include the **Hostal-Pensión El Cantón** (933 173019 FAX 933 022267 E-MAIL hostalcanton@mx4.redesb.es, Carrer Nou de Sant Francesc 40, just off the Rambla and with rooms and apartments, or the **Hostal Malda** (933 173002, Carrer del Pi 5.

WHERE TO EAT

Barcelona is second only to Madrid in its gastronomic delights, although some would say it surpasses the capital in many ways. The ingredients, from the Mediterranean and Catalunya, are superb and most restaurants do something interesting with them. Barcelona is also famous for its pastries, and it is a tradition to eat them, English-style, mid-afternoon accompanied by coffee, hot chocolate or tea. The local Penedès (especially the whites), Priorato (especially the reds) and the Cavas (Spanish champagne) are all highly drinkable, so there is no need to reach beyond the region when it comes to ordering wine.

In the expensive price-range, **Botafumeiro** (932 184230, Carrer Mayor de Gràcia 81, is a Galician establishment famous for its meat pies, *croquettes* (rissoles) and shellfish. It also has a nice oyster bar. The **Reno** (932 009129 Carrer Tuset 27, is another Sarrià restaurant that takes pains with its traditional Spanish dishes. The **Via Veneto** (932 007024, Carrer Guaduxer 10–12, is an elegant and stylish place in the Sarrià district. It serves Catalan and French food and is popular with Barcelona's fashionable crowd.

In a city made famous for its art deco heritage, this is a place where it is well worth chasing the Modernist decor for the full flavor of the city. Start, then, at the **4 Gats** (933 024140, Carrer Montsió 3 (moderate), which is the original Modernist café, where Picasso and other artists met and drank. Prices since then have gone up, but not too much, and there's a choice of Catalan and Mediterranean cuisine. Seafood is best enjoyed in sight of the sea, so try **Agua** (932 251272, Passeig Maritim de la Barceloneta 30 (moderate), on the beach. In a registered historic farmhouse, **Can Cortada** (934 272315, Avenida de L'Esatut de Catalunya (moderate), where parts of the building date back to the eleventh century but the food, specializing in Catalan cuisine, is distinctly fresher.

The **Chicoa** (934 531123, Carrer Aribau 73, is a serious Catalan restaurant specializing in fish

OPPOSITE, LEFT: Gaudí's Parc Güell. RIGHT: The unmistakable figure of Don Quixote.

dishes (*bacalao* — salt cod, is a specialty), with moderate prices, while the **Egipte** (933 173480, located on Carrer Jerusalem 3, serves good basic food in a Bohemian setting and is a favorite haunt of the theater crowd. A second **Egipte** has opened on La Rambla but the crowd is not the same. **Los Caracoles** (933 023185, Carrer Escudellers 14, offers Catalan cuisine in the Gothic Quarter; the atmosphere is good, though it can be somewhat touristic. At **Salamanca** (932 215033, Carrer Almiral Cervera 34, near the sea in the Barceloneta, you'll find good *tapas* at the bar and seafood and grills in the restaurant.

NIGHTLIFE

This city has a lively and rewarding arts scene, with classical concerts, serious theater and dynamic cabarets offering plenty of nighttime alternatives. The weekly *Guia del Ociao* has full details of what's on, and the tourist office has a free monthly guide, while further details can be collected from *Barcelona Metropolitan*, lying in piles around many hotels.

Most entertainments here, however, still revolve around alcohol, dusted with only the merest trace of food, but liberally doused in music. Madrid's animated *madrugada* (the hours between midnight and dawn) is, in Catalan, modified to *la moguda*, and Barcelona closes earlier. Catalans, unlike Castilians, always seem to remember that they have to get up and work in the morning. Apart from the usual array of *tapas* bars, cafés and cocktail lounges, the city offers the phenomenon of champagne bars, trading on the *cava* wines that are produced in Catalunya. Try **La Cava del Palau** (933 100938, Carrer Verdaguer i Callis 10, opposite the Palau de la Musica in the Gothic Quarter. More conventionally, continue with some *tapas*, sharing bar space first with office workers at **Txapela** (934 120289, Passeig de Gràcia 8-10, where the cuisine has a distinctive Basque flavor, perhaps moving on, after 8 PM, to **Tapa Tapa** (934 883369, Passeig de Gràcia 44, where you'll have 80 dishes to choose from. Take your time here, as the music bars don't wake up until late. This could be time to fit in a flamenco show, with **Cordobes** (933 175711 FAX 933 176653 WEB SITE www.tablao cordobes.com, La Rambla 35 (expensive), being one good place to see Tablao Flamenco, a free-form of the art; it has been hosting dynamic performances against a background of paella and pasta since 1970.

While the rest of Spain have *discobares*, Barcelona settles for *bars modernos* or *bars musicales*. These are most easily found around the Eixample area, and around along the Passeig del Born, by the Museu Picasso. For discos, Barcelona is expensive — though no one seems deterred — place to party, though most venues stay open until at least 5 AM,

even on weekdays. The best include **Bikini**, Carrer Deu I Mata 105, a traditional favorite just off the Diagonal, and the fashionable **Otto Zutz**, Carrer de Lincoln 15, where you have to be dressed appropriately to gain access into three designer stories of glittering youth. In any case, the disco scene changes quickly, so the doormen might have lost some of their discriminating arrogance by the time you get there. Other alternatives include **Nick Havanna** (932 156591, Carrer Rossello 208, which styles itself as "the ultmate bar"; **Satanassa** (934 510052, Carrer Aribau 27; **Trauma** (934 879447, Consell de Cent 288; **El Otro** (933 236759, Carrer Valencia 166; and, for the gay crowd, **Metro Disco** (93 323 5227, Carrer Sepulveda 185.

HOW TO GET THERE

As Spain's second city, Barcelona is well-served by air, rail, bus and road. At the **Aeropuerto de Barcelona**, international flights arrive and leave at Terminal A (934 784704, while domestic flights use Terminal B (934 780565; both are 12 km (seven miles) southwest of the city and are linked by bus and rail services. Most national and some international trains come into the **Estació Sants**, while most international and high-speed trains use the **Estació de França**, both of which link seamlessly with the metro system. The main bus terminal is the **Estació del Nord**, with international buses generally using a smaller station behind the Estació Sants.

Ferries to and from the Balearic Islands, Ibiza, Mallorca and Menorca, dock at the **Estació Marítima** at the southern end of La Rambla: contact

Trasmediterránea (932 959100 WEB SITE WWW
.trasmediterranea.es, Moll de Sant Bertràn, for
timetables and fares.

Arriving in Barcelona by car, follow signs for
the Port Vell, which will get you to the south of La
Rambla. There is a 24-hour underground parking
lot at the Plaça de Catalunya, where you can safely
leave the vehicle while you visit the main tourist
information office and get your bearings. It costs
about €15 a day to leave your car here and, in this
pedestrian-friendly city, this is money well spent.

EXCURSIONS FROM BARCELONA

From Barcelona, the traveler can follow the Mediterranean coast in either direction, north or south,
or head inland to Aragón and the Pyrenees. But
before moving on there is one place within an hour
of the city that is generally seen as an excursion
from Barcelona: the monastery of Montserrat
(52 km or 31 miles to the west).

MONTSERRAT

Rising out of a placid valley, the Sierra de Montserrat is an extraordinary geological phenomenon
that seems to defy a rational explanation. About
10 km (six miles) long by five kilometers (three miles)
wide, and over 1,200 m (3,936 ft) high, the Sierra is
a jumble of jagged peaks, solitary towers of rock
worn smooth by the elements, huge boulders, pre-
cipitous cliffs, plunging canyons and ravines, and
mysterious caves. Montserrat means "saw-toothed
mountain" in Catalan and some of the local names
given to its peaks indicate both its appearance and
its power over the minds of men. "The spellbound
giant," "the friar," "the sentinel," "death's head,"
"the camel," "the parrot" and so on.

Montserrat has always evoked wonder and
symbolism. Legend has it that Saint Peter hid an
image of the Virgin carved by Saint Luke in one
of Montserrat's caves, and in another, Parsifal
found the Holy Grail, a story that inspired Wagner
to use Montserrat as the backdrop for his opera.
The mountains seem to have had a special appeal
for German writers and poets. Schiller wrote,
"Montserrat sucks a man in from the outer to the
inner world." Goethe's view was that "nowhere
but in his own Montserrat will a man find happi-
ness and peace."

Myths and literary imagery apart, Montserrat
has had a historic role as a religious and nationalist icon for Catalans and Catalunya. Hermitages
are known to have existed on the mountains before the Moors took control in the eighth century.
Not long after the Reconquest in 880, the image
of a dark-faced Virgin was found and a chapel
built on the site. A monastery dedicated to Saint
Mary, in honor of the Virgin, was built in the eleventh century by the Benedictine monks.

The foundation prospered largely due to the
fame of the Virgin, who was affectionately called
the "La Moreneta" ("the little dark one"), as a
worker of miracles. During the Middle Ages Montserrat became a place of pilgrimage, second only
in importance to Santiago de Compostela. Its fame
spread and the famous — or later to be famous
— trekked up the mountain and paid tribute.
Ignatius Loyola was one of them, spending a lonely
vigil on his knees in front of the Virgin before dedi-
cating his life to God and founding the order of
the Jesuits.

Most of Spain's monarchs, regardless of their
views on Catalan nationalism, respected the monastic
foundation and revered the Virgin. But Napoleon's

occupying army showed no such deference.
In 1811, as a reprisal for the local Catalan guer-
rillas using the monastery as a base for operations,
the French looted and destroyed it. It was rebuilt
in the nineteenth and twentieth centuries and is
now the home of a small group of monks and the
destination of about a million visitors every year.

The monastery and basilica themselves are
almost as bleak as the mountains that surround
them. But there are striking remnants of the pre-
restored buildings, such as a Romanesque door,
and one side of the Gothic cloister. The Black Virgin
can be seen by walking up a stairway behind the
altar, and Montserrat's famous boys' choir performs twice daily. There is a great deal of commer-
cialization around the monastery — it's big tourist

OPPOSITE AND ABOVE: Los Caracoles Restaurant
in the old section of Barcelona.

business with Catalans and foreigners alike, especially in the summer — but the mountain range is spectacular.

Where to Stay and Eat

In the daytime, the food is not great, but the site is at its best after the crowds have gone in the evening. The best place to stay is the **Hotel Abat Cisneros (** 938 777701 FAX 938 777724 (moderate) which is somewhat overpriced, but convenient. There are also some much less expensive *refugios* in the mountains for basic accommodation.

How to Get There

The most impressive way to get there is by train and cable-car from Barcelona, leaving from a terminal underneath the Plaça d'Espanya, with hourly departures from 8:36 AM onwards, connecting with the cable-car to climb to the base of the monastery. Combined round-trip tickets for the train and cable-car cost €11.40, with other rates packaging together museum entry, two funicular train tickets and discounts at the site's two hotels. There are also coach tours, rather cheaper at €7:40, bookable through **Julia Tours (** 934 904000, Plaça Universitat, or through any travel agent or tourist office. If you have time, take a walk up behind the monastery; from the highest peaks have the Pyrenees, and sometimes Mallorca, can be seen. It is also a good place for hikers and, of course, climbers. Not to be missed.

NORTHEAST OF BARCELONA: THE COSTA BRAVA AND INLAND

Northeast of Barcelona is the famous Costa Brava (the "wild" or "rugged coast"), a strip of rocky indented coves and sandy beaches that runs from Blanes virtually up to the French border. The first of Spain's big coastal resorts, the Costa Brava is still developing but, unlike the Costa del Sol, the busy season is limited to the summer months, so a visit at other times of the year means less congestion.

One of Spain's first resorts was set at **Lloret del Mar**, still a busy high-rise town filled with package travelers from all over Europe, and **Tossa de Mar**, which is similar if rather prettier and less frenetic. Apart from these developments, there are many far smaller, more charming fishing villages not yet smothered by the modern obsession with suntans and sand. Lloret and Tossa apart, there is not much to distinguish one Costa Brava resort from another — the usual sun, sin, sangria and french fries — so there is only space here for a general overview.

Heading northwest up the coast, after Lloret and Tossa you'll first reach **Calella de Palafrugell**, a moderately large resort set around a fishing village and over a string of coarse-sand beaches. To stay here, try the **Hotel Batlle (** 972 615905

(inexpensive), which has 14 individually themed rooms. Light sleepers might want to avoid the Dalí room. Next is **Tamariu**, one of the most charming of all the resorts, barely developed and with a shady promenade overlooking a small, busy beach. The **Hotel Hostalillio (** 972 620228 (moderate) is set up amongst the pine trees. **Aiguablava** is more village than resort, with the modern **Aiguablava Parador (** 972 622162 (moderate) overlooking the village. Pass through the sizeable pub'n grub resort of Estartit and continue to **L'Escala**, itself a fairly developed resort, though it is possible to steer clear of it. The **Hotel Voramar (** 972 770108 (moderate) is a good three-star option. The only resort with any cultural value, though it loses out somewhat when it comes to the beach, is Cadaqués, at the northern end of the coast on the tip of Cap de Creus.

CADAQUÉS

A little isolation and a lot of celebrity status have helped to make Cadaqués different. It is difficult to reach by public transportation and in summer there is virtually no parking for cars. It has long been a center for Spanish and foreign artists, writers and less serious sojourners. Looming over Cadaqués is the persona of Salvador Dalí, who lived for many years in nearby Port Lligat and was happily surrounded by a large entourage of admirers, friends, sycophants and con men. The good news about little Cadaqués is that its natural beauty and charm survive all the hype. Its pebbly beaches, cozy bay, whitewashed houses with their red-tiled roofs, and hilly backdrop have not much changed through the years. There is, perhaps surprisingly, a choice of things to do, pleasantly tending to the artistic. The **Museu Perrot-Moore**, Carrer del Vigilant 1, is open daily 10:30 AM to 1:30 PM and 4:30 PM to 8:30 PM, €4.20, as is the **Museu d'Art Municipal**, Carrer de Narcís Monturiol, €3.60, not to mention the **Casa-Museu Salvador Dalí (** 972 251015, Port Lligat, three kilometers (two miles) to the north, €7.80, Salvador Dalí's palatial beach villa, spilling down to a private cove. Tours here are strictly by appointment, with no more than eight visitors at a time: booking is essential.

This isn't to say the artists have taken over completely. There are even a few local fishermen who still ply the coastal waters for a living and their catches often end up on your plate. The town is at its best out of season: clean, quiet and uncluttered, with just a few foreigners — artists, writers and con men — warming themselves in the winter sunshine at a beachfront café and plotting the next painting, novel, deal or coup.

There is a small **Tourist Office (** 972 258315, open Monday to Saturday July to September 10 AM to 2 PM and 4 PM to 9 PM, Sunday 10:30 AM to 1 PM, winter Monday to Saturday 10 AM to 2 PM and 4 PM to 7 PM, closed on Wednesday afternoon. If you've left finding a room until you've found the tourist office, you might well be too late, especially if there's the slightest hint of a holiday in France, when the place is often completely full. Call ahead to book rooms at either the **Hostal Marina** (972 258199 or the **Hostal Christina** (972 258127, both inexpensive, open all year, and close to the sea front with its restaurants and bars.

Cadaqués is easiest to reach by car, driving along country lanes through Roses or Port de la Selva. There are buses from Barcelona, and local ferry boats that make frequent, but often unscheduled journeys between the main resorts.

Festooned with giant eggs and loaves of bread made of plaster, the museum contains ample evidence of Dalí's painterly qualities as well as of his elliptical view of the world around him. There is a self-portrait of the artist at the age of seventeen; good pencil drawings; the famous oil painting of a loaf of bread, so realistic that you feel you can take a bite out of it; many portraits of his wife, Gala; Mae West's lips depicted as a sofa; a bathtub on the ceiling; and his custom-built Cadillac in the central well of the theater, where if you put five pesetas into a slot a light comes on inside revealing a uniformed chauffeur, Dalí and a naked Gala in the back seat festooned with ivy; there is a second's pause and then water pours over the

FIGUERES

Turning inland, the town of Figueres, the birthplace of Dalí and the site of his own personal museum, is the leading attraction from the Costa. That this is second only to the Prado in the number of visitors it receives each year is a rather sad indictment of the overwhelming success of populist art, but reflects the effective focus of this well-presented homage to the greatest of all the surrealists.

Surrealist painter, collaborator with Luis Buñuel, Spain's greatest film-maker, wry observer of life and flagrant entrepreneur, Dalí was born in the town in 1904 and died there in 1989. His museum is a fitting commentary on his life and his work: inventive, iconoclastic, wacky and above all, entertaining. The building is an old theater that was destroyed in the Civil War and restored later.

occupants inside the vehicle. The **Teatro-Museu Dalí** (972 677500, Plaça Gala-Salvador Dalí 5, is open in the winter from 10:30 AM to 5:45 PM and from July to September from 9 AM to 7:45 PM, €7.20. Its very success is what puts me off: even off-season it is heaving with slow-moving crowds, queuing for interactive mirror-pictures of often doubtful value.

Where to Stay and Eat
Well I wouldn't. The **Hostal España** (972 500869, Carrer de la Jonquera 26 (inexpensive), is about the best of the bunch for accommodation, but with the constant trail of day-trip visitors, most of the restaurants serve meals that display all the shallow flamboyance you'd expect of poster art. The

The old fishing village of Cadaqués on the Costa Brava, a haunt of Salvador Dalí and other unconventional, though not as gifted, people.

best place to eat is probably at the **Hotel Duran**, Lasauca 5, for regional dishes polished for a constant stream of one-off clients.

How to Get There

Figueres is served by bus and train from Barcelona, from which it is a little under an hour by car.

GIRONA

The central city of this northern part of Catalunya is Girona. An important Roman town, Girona suffered for its strategic position with a surfeit of sieges from the time of Charlemagne's battles with the Moors to Napoleon's invasion of Spain in the

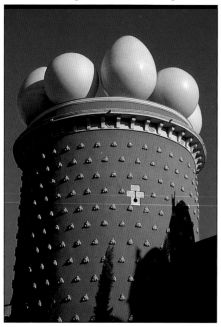

early nineteenth century. Now a modest capital of a wealthy province, Girona is notable for its cathedral and its old quarter; its beautifully preserved medieval streets are home to a chic, smart and interesting café society.

The main **Tourist Information Office** (972 211678 WEB SITE www.girona-net.com, Rambla de la Libertat 1, is open April to September from Monday to Saturday 9 AM to 8 PM and Sunday 9 AM to 2 PM, October to March from Monday to Saturday 9 AM to 5 PM and Sunday 9 AM to 2 PM. It is on the river at the south of the old town, while another office is sited in the train station. Internet access can be arranged at **Teranyina**, Carrer Bonaventura Carreras 2, a computer shop following normal Spanish office hours. Cars are not encouraged here, and it's a good idea to leave your vehicle in the underground parking lot at Plaça Catalunya, where you'll also find a taxi rank.

What to See and Do

Introduced by a massive stairway, Girona's **cathedral** (972 214426, Rambla de la Libertat (summer hours are Tuesday to Saturday 10 AM to 2 PM and 4 PM to 7 PM, Sunday 10 AM to 2 PM, winter hours vary) is a Gothic marvel. The majority was built in the fourteenth and fifteenth centuries, but parts of it are several hundred years older. Incredibly, it has no central *coro* (choir) or any supporting columns. Its huge nave, 22.5 m (73 ft) across, is the widest in all Christendom, a striking tribute to the skill and daring of Catalunya's medieval architects. Other Gothic highlights include the silver *retablo* over the main altar and the sepulcher of Bishop Bernard de Pau. The cloister and bell tower date from the earlier Romanesque cathedral, in the cathedral's museum there is a superb twelfth-century tapestry depicting the Creation, and the façade is a later baroque addition. But it is the feeling of vast vaulted space in the nave that makes the most impact — humanized by a marble sculpture of a knight over a side door, his feet resting comfortably on his dog. Just below the cathedral are the **Banys Arabs** (972 213262 (open April to September from Tuesday to Saturday 10 AM to 7 PM, Sunday 10 AM to 2 PM, in winter Tuesday to Sunday 10 AM to 2 PM, €1.20), which date back more than a thousand years to the Moorish occupation, and are the best-preserved baths (for their age) in Spain.

"Fortunately," one guidebook puts it, "the old town of Girona has been lovingly neglected." In fact, some restoration has taken place, particularly in **El Call**, the Jewish quarter. The result is an unspoiled hilly medieval town that backs on the Río Onyar, which runs through the heart of Girona. The Jewish quarter is exceptionally well-preserved and was famous in its day for mystics and cabalistic studies.

Where to Stay and Eat

Girona's most central luxury hotel is the **Ultonia** (972 203850, Gran Via de Jaume 1 No. 22 (expensive), while the **Meliá Confort Girona** (972 400500 FAX 972 243233, Barcelona 112 (expensive), offers smooth comforts in a larger hotel. On a budget, the **Pensió Viladomat** (972 203176, Ciutadans 5 (inexpensive), is a popular place that should be booked ahead.

The smartest bars and restaurants are found in on the Carrer de la Força and along the riverside Rambla de la Libertat. For moderately priced meals try the **Cal Ros** (902 201011, Carrer Cort Reial 9, and the **Rosaleda** (902 213668, Paseo de la Dehesa.

How to Get There

Girona is 100 km (62 miles) northeast of Barcelona, with the choice of two fast *autopistas* and a slow coast road up the Costa Brava to make the journey.

Its position between Barcelona and France means that **Girona railway station (** 902 240202, Plaça d'Espanya, is not just served by local trains, but also by high-speed international trains from and to Milan, Paris and Lausanne. Girona's international airport, hosting countless packaged flights for beach breaks, **Aeropuerto Girona-Costa Brava (** 972 186600 is **open** 24 hours a day in summer and during winter months between 7:30 AM to 11:30 PM.

RURAL CATALUNYA

Although the region is the most heavily industrialized in Spain, rural Catalunya is extensive, highly productive, and easily accessible. In the north there is the Catalan section of the Pyrenees where the steep-sided valleys running north to south maintain an ecology and way of life little changed by the giant transformation that has occurred elsewhere. There are meadows speckled with cows, villages clustered around sturdy Romanesque churches, streams and birch woods and marvelous mountain air.

ANDORRA

Further west there is the curiosity of Andorra, one of Europe's miniscule independent principalities. (The others are Luxembourg, Liechtenstein, Monaco, the Vatican and San Marino.) Andorra, a historical oversight, is wedged between France and Spain in the Pyrenees. It is ethnically Catalan and has two "co-princes," the President of France and the Bishop of Seu d'Urgell, who lives just across the border in Spain. A referendum in 1993 paved the way for the introduction of a constitutional democracy, but the principality's life remains tied up with selling duty-free goods to its tax-paying neighbors in France and Spain. In the winter months it is invaded by skiers, while all year round its roads are clogged with cars that arrive empty and leave with their suspension lowered by the weight of recent purchases. There is some great hiking terrain in the hills beyond the town, but most of the 468 sq km (181 sq km) of mountainous terrain is covered with scrappy hypermarkets, and few corners remain untouched.

The center of the town is a rather uninspiring line of retail outlets. Most of the restaurants, catering to the tourist trade, have menus in six languages, but although prices are low, in general, are the standards. For most people it's a place to go in, do your shopping, and get out. The **Tourist Office (** 376 820214, WEB SITE www.turisme.ad, Carrer Dr. Vilanova 1, Andorra la Vella, open Monday to Saturday 10 AM to 1 PM, 3 PM to 7 PM, Sunday 10 AM to 1 PM, will help with information about where to stay and, perhaps more usefully, bus times to plan your escape.

Andorra is is 220 km (132 miles) from Barcelona (take the N-152 north to Puigcerda, the N-260 to Seu d'Urgell, and finally the C-1313 to Andorra); and 153 km (92 miles) from Lleida on the northbound C-1313. Driving to Andorra, however, is a frustrating experience, with traffic congested and parking a constant problem and low petrol prices the only consolation. Buses from Barcelona take four and a half hours.

SOUTHWEST OF BARCELONA: THE COSTA DAURADA

To the southwest, Catalunya's "Golden Coast" curves along the Mediterranean, a 200-km (124-mile) strip of wide, sandy beaches, interlaced with pine-fringed coves, from Barcelona to the Ebro Delta. The beaches aren't great, with the notable exception of Sitges, 40 km (25 miles) from Barcelona.

SITGES

This fashionable seaside resort south of Barcelona has an Old World and slightly decadent air: perfect for a sophisticated beach-break from the city to escape the heat of a Spanish summer. The town came into its own at the turn of the century when Barcelona's literary and artistic glitterati adopted it as their summer playground. The pivot was Santiago Rusiñol, a kind of Catalan Dr. Johnson, who was a well-known writer, painter and conversationalist in his day. The Modernist architects, notably Puig i Cadafalch and Domènech i Montaner, also came and built grand seaside homes for wealthy Barcelona patrons. In modern times, Sitges has become a popular rendezvous for gays from all over Europe, changing the flavor but preserving the distinctive style of the resort. To see it at its most extreme, visit for **Carnaval** (February/March), where drag queens and outrageous costumes are de rigueur.

The old town is a collection of cool whitewashed houses and narrow streets nestling behind a picturesque baroque church, which has a curious bell tower made entirely of wrought iron. There is a fine palm-tree fringed promenade, which is the place to walk slowly, to observe, and to be observed. There are plenty of beaches, with several set aside for nudists — both straight and gay. Sitges is also known for its **Corpus Christi** festival, when the streets of the old town are carpeted with flowers, for international theater and cinema gatherings, and for a vintage-car rally that starts in Barcelona and finishes on the promenade.

General Information
The **Tourist Information Office (** 938 945004 WEB SITE www.sitgestur.com, in the Oasis shopping mall, is open from July to mid-September daily 9 AM to

The exterior of Dalí's museum in Figueres, where the artist was born and died.

9 PM and for the rest of the year Monday to Friday 9 AM to 2 PM and 4 PM to 6:30 PM, Saturday 10 AM to 1 PM. There are **taxis (** 938 941329 outside the railway station.

Where to Stay and Eat

Although there are a number of very good hotels in Sitges, they are often full in summer and closed in winter; it pays to book ahead, and for this reason here is a wider choice than might otherwise be justified. The **Hotel Terramar (** 938 940500, Paseo Marítimo 30 (expensive), provides slightly worn comforts in the upper price range, and the aptly named (if you're gay) **Hotel Romàntic (** 938 940643 WEB SITE www.hotelromatic.com, Sant Isidre 33

(moderate), is a conversion of three nineteenth-century houses and has a fine garden patio. Although it is only open in the summer, the same owners (and telephone numbers) run a more modest establishment open year-round. For location, you can't beat the **Hotel La Santa María (** 938 940999 FAX 938 947871 WEB SITE www.lasanta maria.com, Paseo de la Ribera 52 (moderate), facing the sea and with its own parking lot. For style, check into the **Hotel El Xalet (** 938 110070 FAX 938 945579, Illa de Cuba 35 (moderate), a small Modernist hotel near the railway station: booking essential. There's not much very inexpensive here, but on a budget, try the **Pensiòn Bonaire (** 938 945346, Carrer Bonaire 31 (moderate).

Restaurants here tend to be aimed squarely at the international market. Good moderately priced food, especially fish and Catalan dishes, are found at **La Masia (** 938 941076, Paseo de Vilanova 164,

and at **Mare Nostrum (** 938 943393, Paseo de la Ribera 60. For nightlife, try the pedestrian street of Carrer Marques de Montroig, where you'll find a run of disco bars pumping out competing tunes.

How to Get There

Countless trains from Barcelona arrive at the train station **(** 934 900202, where most buses also set down. Otherwise, it's a pleasant 40-km (25-mile) drive from Barcelona on the fast coast road.

TARRAGONA

Tarragona has a rather strange atmosphere — introverted, dour and preoccupied — perhaps as a result of its past preeminence and later decline. A city of immense importance during the Roman period, visible traces of an earlier Iberian grandeur remain in the huge blocks of limestone that are the foundations of the walls and ramparts of the old town. On top of those, symbolizing Tarragona's long history, are neat rectangular pieces of stone laid by the Romans, surmounted by masonry added by the English during the War of the Spanish Succession, and finally some pretty horrible twentieth-century brickwork. For maps and information, the **Tourist Information Office (** 977 245064 WEB SITE www.fut.es/~turisme, Carrer Mayor 39, is open July to September Monday to Friday 9:30 AM to 8:30 PM, Saturday 9:30 AM to 2 PM and 4 PM to 8:30 PM, Sunday 10 AM to 2 PM, winter Monday to Friday 10 AM to 2 PM and 4:30 PM to 7 PM, Saturday and Sunday 10 AM to 2 PM. There are **taxi** ranks in town or call **(** 977 221414 or 977 215656.

What to See and Do

Known in Roman times as Tarraco, the city was a great port and strategic base during the Punic Wars. Many Roman emperors spent time here, including Augustus between campaigns, and Pontius Pilate was born here. A good sense of the Roman legacy can be had by walking along the **Passeig Arqueològic**. Have a look at the **Museu Nacional Arqueològic** (open Tuesday to Saturday 10 AM to 8 PM in summer, 10 AM to 1:30 PM and 4 PM to 7 PM in the winter, €2.40), which has a good collection of mosaics. Visit the **praetorium**, which was built in the first century BC and reconstructed in the Middle Ages. Take a trip north of the town, just off the main road to Valls, to see a well-preserved **Roman aqueduct** that soars across the countryside for a distance of 123 m (400 ft). Built on a row of sturdy double arches and second only to Segovia's aqueduct in size, you can walk long the channel where Tarraco's water supply used to flow.

Tarragona also has an interesting **cathedral**, built between the twelfth and the fifteenth centuries and showing the transition from the Romanesque to the Gothic styles of architecture. Wedged into the core of the medieval town, its exterior is nothing to write home about but the interior, especially the main altar, the stained glass and a timeless cloister are all well worth seeing. Tarragona has a commanding presence overlooking the Mediterranean and has picked up recently as the center of the increasingly popular Costa Daurada. The town beach is the Platja de Miracle, but the Platja Arrabassada, a few kilometers up the coast, is better.

Where to Stay and Eat

Tarragona's grandest hotel is the **Imperial Tarraco** (977 233040 FAX 977 216566 E-MAIL imperial@tinet .fut.es, Paseo Palmeras (expensive), beautifully located overlooking the sea. Almost as smart is the **Hotel Lauria** (977 236712 FAX 977 236700, Rambla

de Santes Creus. Although not formally linked they had similar origins and trajectories of influence and decline. Both were founded in the twelfth century by Ramón Berenguer IV as Cistercian houses at the zenith of the fortunes of the Catalunya–Aragón monarchy. Both monasteries became powerful, rich and corrupt, and both were sacked in the anti-clerical upheavals of the nineteenth century. The two monasteries have been lovingly restored since and each evokes, in its own way, the vitality and creativity of the Christian monarchy and church in the Middle Ages.

These monasteries share all the elements one expects in such baronial foundations. Impressive entrances, austere chapels, vast dormitories where

Nova 20 (moderate), which is nearer to the action. On a budget, try the **Pensión Miraflor** (977 238231, Carrer General Contreras 29, (inexpensive).

Another boost to Tarragona has come from the growth of the wine industry, the best being Priorato, a delicious, smooth full-bodied red wine that can be happily drunk with — or without — anything. One of the most popular restaurants in town is the atmospheric **Can Llesques**, Carrer Natzaret 6, Plaça del Rei (inexpensive).

How to Get There

Tarragona is 100 km (65 miles) southwest of Barcelona on the A-7 freeway, served by bus and rail.

more than 100 monks bedded down in a single room, quiet cloisters shaded by cypresses and refreshed by fountains, refectories, kitchens, wine cellars and spacious gardens. Poblet, sometimes called the "Escorial" of Catalunya, contains the tombs of many of the kings of Catalunya–Aragón. Visit at least one of these monasteries if you can.

On a rather less cerebral note, **Port Aventura** (0800 966540 WEB SITE www.portaventura.es (€28.85 per day for adults), the US$500-million theme park at Salou, just 10 km (six miles) south of Tarragona, is a great place for kids — of all ages (see FAMILY FUN, page 44).

EXCURSIONS FROM TARRAGONA

There are two medieval monasteries in the Tarragona area, the **Monestir de Poblet** and the **Monestir**

OPPOSITE: The Roman aqueduct, north of Tarragona. ABOVE: The fashionable seaside town of Sitges, south of the Catalan capital.

The Levante: Valencia and Murcia

The Levante, or the "East," is strongly influenced by Catalunya, although a separate region. This is the area centered on Valencia, midway down the Mediterranean coast, and extended here to include Alicante, Murcia and Almería, fringed with coastal developments that vary from the unassuming quiet of San José to the exuberant high-rise seaview culture of Benidorm.

The Catalans drove the Moors out of the Valencia region in the thirteenth century and repopulated this fabulously fertile part of Spain with their own people. The *huerta*, or cultivated plain, around Valencia is the most densely populated agricultural land in Europe. It produces a spectacular variety of produce and crops including rice, vast groves of oranges, lemons, peaches and apricots, vegetables of every kind, and even mulberry leaves for the voracious silk worm. The local population, who are noted for their industriousness and independent spirit, speak Valenciano, a variation of Catalan, as well as Castilian. Valencia, the principal city, is the country's third largest and is a major seaport. This is not mass tourism terrain, but this can make it an even more rewarding area to discover on your own. If you should get homesick, the coastal resorts of Benidorm and Alicante will quickly bring you new friends.

VALENCIA

A prosperous, elegant and confident city, Valencia owes much to the Moors who devised the intricate and still extant irrigation system that is the mainstay of agriculture in the Levante. Water disputes are resolved every Thursday at noon — as they have been for a thousand years — at the Tribunal de las Aguas (Water Tribunal) in front of the cathedral. In other respects, however, the city is totally transformed, with a thriving nightlife and a constant succession of lavish *ferias*.

GENERAL INFORMATION

The **Tourist Information Office** (963 510417, is on the Plaza del Ayuntamiento. It opens Monday to Friday 8:30 AM to 2:15 PM and 4:15 PM to 6:15 PM, Saturday 9:15 AM to 1:15 PM. There are other offices at the Calle de la Paz 48, the Calle Poeta Querol and at the train station.

There is a range of taxi companies, including **Onda Taxi** (963 475252, **Radio-Taxi** (963 703333 and **Valencia Taxi** (963 740202.

For medical treatment, a good hospital is **La Fe** (963 862700, Avda de Campanar 21, and an **ambulance** (963 606211 will get you there.

There are several places in town offering Internet access, but one of the most central is **Ágora Internet**, Calle de la Paz, diagonally opposite the main tourist office.

FESTIVALS AND CELEBRATIONS

The most famous of the city's festivals is **Las Fallas de San José**, a pyromaniac's dream come true. This fiesta is held in the third week of March every year and celebrates the coming of spring. Rather like the Feria de Abril in Sevilla, the city is overwhelmed for a week by floats, parades, bullfights and fireworks. Neighborhoods compete with each other to produce the most impressive papier-mâché figures and tableaux. The climax comes on the last day when everything goes up in smoke and flames to the accompaniment of thunderous detonations, cascades of exploding fireworks and the sirens of speeding fire engines.

WHAT TO SEE AND DO

With so few tourists, this is one place where you don't feel ridiculous taking a horse and carriage: you're supporting a dying trade. A good way to start a tour of the city's highlights is to call a **horse and carriage** (963 824277. Alternatively, at half past the hour, starting at 10:30 AM the **Valencia Bus Turistic** (963 357261 leaves from the Plaza Reina for tours of the city's highlights in a double-decker bus. Tickets cost €80, and you can hop on and off, taking in all the major sights in a single day.

Valencia's more splendid buildings include the **Palacio de la Generalidad** (963 863461, where the region's own parliament used to meet (guided tours by arrangement on weekday mornings); the baroque **Palacio del Marqués de Dos Aguas**, Calle Poeta Querol 2, which contains Spain's **Museo Nacional de Cerámica** (963 516392 (open Tuesday to Sunday 10 AM to 2 PM and 4 PM to 8 PM, €2.40), where over 5,000 displays tell the story of local tile-making in imaginative ways, such as reproducing a stunningly beautiful all-tiled traditional Valencian kitchen that I'm still trying to replicate in the design of my home kitchen unit.

There are more ceramics at the **railway station**, which is lavishly adorned with elaborate ceramic tiles. Another of Valencia's highlights is the **Museo de Bellas Artes** (963 605793 FAX 963 609721, Calle San Pio V (open Tuesday to Saturday 10 AM to 2 PM and 4 PM to 6 PM, Sundays and holidays 10 AM to 2 PM, free), which has a wonderful collection of art housed in a stunning seventeenth-century building.

The **cathedral** (963 918127 WEB SITE www .archivalencia.org, Plaza de la Reina (Monday to Saturday 7:15 AM to 1 PM and 4:30 PM to 8:30 PM), looms atmospherically over a Gothic core. Inside there is a museum with two fantastic Goya paintings and, they claim, the original cup used at Christ's Last Supper. These make the entrance of €1.20 seem very reasonable. From the cathedral

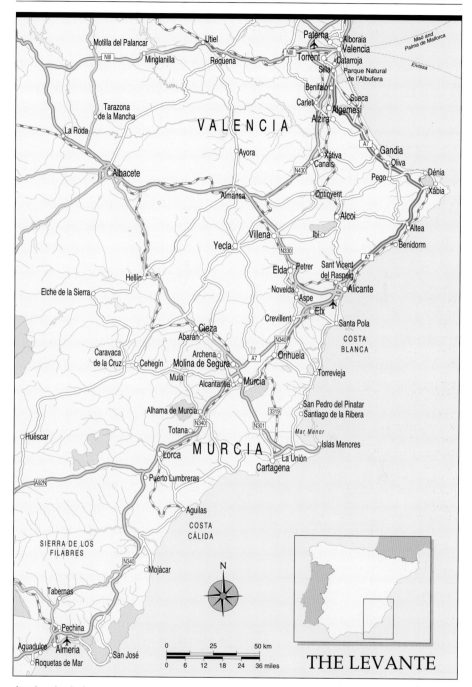

THE LEVANTE

the plaza leads down to some atmospheric alleys lined with old tiled bars, and a lovely domed **market** with stained-glass windows and a riot of colorful produce below.

But Valencia is not just rooted in the past. It also has some of the most ambitious modern architecture in Spain, still currently under construction but set to dwarf the developments even in Bilbao or Madrid. The **Cuitat de les Arts i les Ciències (** 902 100031, El Saler, is accessed by car or by buses nos. 13, 14 or 15, and is planned to include a planetarium, aquarium, IMAX cinema, theater and art gallery, the most ambitious such development ever planned in a city center.

WHERE TO STAY AND EAT

Valencia has a good range of accommodation in all price ranges. The most you can spend is at the **Meliá Valencia Palace** (963 375037 FAX 963 375522, Paseo Alameda 32 (very expensive), for smooth luxury. Alternatively the **Astoria Palace** (963 981000 FAX 963 981010, Plaza Rodrigo Botet 5 (expensive), is on the cavernous side, but central and efficient. The **Husa Dimar** (963 951030 FAX 963 951926, Gran Vía Marqués del Turia 80 (expensive), is also in the central area, as is the **Reina Victoria** (963 520487 FAX 963 522721, Calle Barcas 4 (expensive).

Ma Cuina (963 417799, Gran Vía Germanias 49, which has a varied menu reflecting what is in season. Otherwise, try **Commodoro** (963 213815, Calle Transits 3 (moderate), for local dishes; **El Condestable** (963 699250, Calle Artes Graficas 15 (moderate), for international cuisine; and, for Valencia's best known dish, *paella,* **El Plat** (963 349638, Calle Conde de Altea 41 (moderate).

After dining, Valencia's nightlife does shift around the city, and you'll need a taxi to sample most of it. There are three theaters and literally hundreds of clubs. To make your choice, get hold of a copy of a magazine called *24-7 Valencia*, available at tourist offices and many hotels and bars, and see what's on that week.

The best of the less expensive hotels is **Ad Hoc** (963 919140 FAX 963 913667, Boix 4 (inexpensive), a superbly stylish hotel whose owner is in the art business. Next to the Palacio del Marqués de Dos Aguas is the **Ingles** (963 516426 FAX 963 940251, Calle Marqués de Dos Aguas 6 (inexpensive). On a real budget, try the **Albergue Juvenil "Las Arenas"** (963 564288, Calle Eugenia Viñez 24 (very inexpensive).

When it comes to dining, Valencia, it should be noted, is the home town of *paella*, Spain's national seafood dish, though chefs from other areas mutter darkly that it is no longer the best place to sample it. A more interesting specialty is *horchato*, a slightly frozen alcoholic drink made from tiger nuts and served with a long, thin cake. Look out for it.

The most expensive restaurants include **La Hacienda** (963 731859, Calle Navarro Reverter 12, an upscale restaurant favored by businessmen, and

HOW TO GET THERE

Valencia is the major hub for eastern Spain, with *autopista* links west to Madrid, south to Alicante and north to Barcelona. Buses use the bus station (963 497222. There are also regional and long-distance trains: for information call **RENFE** (963 520202. Among the airlines that use Valencia's airport, **Manises** (961 598515, are British Airways and Iberia: the terminal is eight kilometers (five miles) west of the town center, in the heart of the region's ceramics industry.

Valencia is also the principal ferry port for the nearby Balearic Islands of Ibiza, Mallorca and Menorca; for up-to-date crossing timetables, bookings and prices contact **Trasmediterránea** (902 454645 WEB SITE www.trasmediterranea.es, or go directly at the port, Avenida Ingeniero Manuel Soto 15.

THE COSTA BLANCA

South of Valencia, the Mediterranean coast extends, in coves and beaches, stretching ever south towards the sun. These are some of the best beaches in Spain, and although parts of this coastline has been comprehensively buried under mounds of hotels, timeshares and apartments, it still provides a welcome release from the dust and heat of a Spanish summer. There's no space here to go into all the resorts and developments, but no guidebook would be complete without touching on Benidorm and Alicante, before heading off inland to Murcia.

Unbelievable, in fact, that year after year, tourists from France, Germany and Italy and, above all, the United Kingdom, should return here again after again for their annual vacations.

Benidorm does have its strengths. Highly competitive beachfront restaurants serve some of the best-value lunches in Spain, with harassed waitresses cheerily coping with a constant turnover of demanding guests. That the beach — like every inch of this booming resort — is crowded really is just a fact of life. In winter it is full of pensioners, in season stuffed with families. But no one expects a desert island here. And when the sun fades from the sky, countless bars and restaurants uncritically welcome the poor, the oppressed, and the simply

BENIDORM

Forty years ago Benidorm was a small fishing village, clustered around a church on a rocky promontory. It's nothing like that now. Traveling from rural Spain, it seems almost like New York, with towering high-rise hotels and apartment blocks crowding in on a shoreline buried in sandy bodies. Along streets advertising endless national dishes — bratwurst and fish'n chips, kebabs and burgers — T-shirted package holidayers shuffle along in endless, slow-moving crowds, tanned leathery by years of timeshare exposure to the hot summer sun.

Odd, then, that I should like Benidorm. Strange, that expatriates from all over eastern Spain head back here to meet up with friends, entertain relatives on cut-price packages, and play with children in the clear, and remarkably clean, water.

sunburned into an international mix of accents, speaking English, bringing their tastes from home. Over all this, the high-rise results of a 1960s boom are beginning to acquire a certain art-deco cool.

General Information

Benidorm centers on the Playa de Levante, the main beach that stretches for two kilometer (one and a half miles) along the Mediterranean, and the rather more sheltered waters of the Playa de Poniente to the west. Both have first aid posts and tourist information kiosks, while the main **Tourist Information Offices** (965 868189 WEB SITE WWW .benidorm.org, Avenida Martínez Alejos 16, is open Monday to Saturday 10 AM to 2 PM and 4 PM

OPPOSITE: Valencia's covered market provides a feast of color. ABOVE: The Playa de Levante-Vista is one of Alicante's most fashionable beaches, illuminated at night for strolling families on the *paseo*.

to 8 PM, until 9 PM from July through September, in what passes for the old town. Further offices are on the Avenida del Derramoor and the Avenida de Europa. To get around, call **Beni Taxi** (966 801000, Avenida de la Marina Baixa 2 or **Radio-Taxi** (965 861818.

What to See and Do

Doing and seeing is not what most people come here for. Splashing and lying around is enough for most. At the same time, it is worth looking around the old town, sandwiched between the two main beaches. There are two theme-parks ideal for young children at the **Sierra Helada** (ice-cream mountain!), Rincón de Loix at the eastern end of the Playa de Levante. **Mundomar** (965 869101 WEB SITE www.mundomar.es, is a huge themed pleasure park with regular displays of leaping dolphins, waddling penguins and an aviary. Meanwhile, **Aqualandia** (965860100 WEB SITE www.aqualandia.net, has slides, pools and wave-pools. Inland, an even larger theme park, **Terra Mítica**, dramatizes world cultures. In the evenings, the Spanish culture breaks tentatively through in the spectacular dinner-dance displays at the **Benidorm Palace** (965 851660, ignored by most of the denizens of Benidorm, who slouch from bar to bar and have a good time.

Where to Stay and Eat

Irritatingly for independent tourists, package travelers will get much lower rates at Benidorm's better-featured hotels, which are dependent on foreign tour operators and not individuals. In season it can be hard to find a room, but off-season rates plummet.

The most luxurious is the **Hotel Cimbel** (965 852100 FAX 965 860661, Avenida de Europa 1 (expensive), with two pools and good facilities. Another five-star establishment is the **Hotel Delfin** (965 853400 FAX 965 817154, Playa de Poniente la Cala (expensive), which is set in lush tropical gardens. Most establishments are less ambitious — and less expensive. The **Hotel Les Dunes Comodoro** (966 803216 FAX 966 801612 WEB SITE www.lesdunes .com, Avenida Madrid 10 (moderate), is less expensive and at the heart of the Playa de Levante, while the **Hotel La Marina** (958 53766 FAX 958 51512, Calle Gerona 21 (moderate), is set a couple of blocks back.

On a budget, the **Hotel Residencia Don José** (965 855050 FAX 965 855054, Calle Alt 2 (inexpensive), offers good value, while if your money has really run dry — or needs to last forever — try the **Hotel Residencia Asturias** (965 851456, Calle la Garita 8 (inexpensive).

Dining, here, is better known for its eggs and bacon than its regional cuisine. There are a number of perfectly good restaurants overlooking the beach on the eastern end of the Playa de Poniente.

How to Get There

Benidorm is 458 km (285 miles) southeast of Madrid and 38 km (24 miles) north of Alicante, which is the nearest airport; buses and trains take about half an hour from Alicante.

ALICANTE

Best known overseas for its busy airport, the town of Alicante has a much more illustrious heritage than you might expect. Founded by the Romans as Lucentum, the "City of Light," it spent many years under Arab control before being incorporated into the Kingdom of Valencia.

General Information

The new and palatial **Tourist Information Office** (965 200000, Explanada de Espana 23, is open Monday to Friday 10 AM to 7 PM, Saturday 10 AM to 2 PM and 3 PM to 7 PM; further branches around the town include one at the bus station. For transportation, call **Tele Taxi** (965 101611 or **Radio-Taxi** (965 252511. There is a **Healthcare Center** (965 143587, Calle Gerona 24, and for Internet access, go to **Internet@alc**, Calle Alemania 2, which is open Monday to Friday 8:30 AM to 9 PM.

What to See and Do

It is impossible to overlook Alicante's main sight, the **Castillo de Santa Bárbara** (965 263131, that towers over the old town and overlooks the sea. It has great views, and fortunately an elevator (October to March 9 AM to 6:30 PM, April to September 10 AM to 8 PM, €2.40) to get people from the beach to the top: access is from the Paseo de Gomiz behind the Playa de Postiguet. Even if you don't need vegetables, it is worth visiting the **Mercado Central** on Avenida Alfonso X el Sabio. Here, the finest produce of the land is piled high in this civic building, an art deco classic. Don't miss the **cathedral of San Nicolás** (965 212662, open Monday to Saturday 7 AM to noon and 6 PM to 8 PM, Sunday 8:30 AM to 1 PM, free. The austere Renaissance façade makes it look like the second most boring building in the country, but step inside and the aisle-less nave soars into a huge, spectacular dome, singularly graceful.

In this sunny city, the beach plays a big part in most people's lives. The main city beach is the Playa del Postiguet, just to the north of the port, which stretches for three unbroken kilometers (nearly two miles), but there are two much better beaches close by: six kilometers (four miles) to the south at Playa del Sladar, or ten kilometers (six miles) to the north at San Juan, where you find six kilometers (four miles) of sandy beach backed by bars and restaurants. These are easily reached by train.

Offshore, there are more beaches and a marine reserve at the **island of Tabarca**, reached by the

ferries (☎ 965 216396) that leave from the Explanada de España. Tabarca is the only island in the area, and although officially uninhabited was traditionally used by Berber pirates waiting to prey on passing ships. When, in 1768, King Carlos III came into ownership of 79 Genovese fishing families during the course of an African campaign, he ordered them to colonize the island. Even now most residents have Italian surnames, and there are some interesting buildings here. Visit in the low season, in August the island just gets too crowded.

Alicante is known for its nightlife, especially during its most famous festival, **Las Hogueras de San Juan** (St. John's Day Bonfires) at the end of June. This is not the most venerable of festivals, as it was invented only in 1928 as a means of encouraging tourism to the area, but papier-mâché sculptures paraded along the streets and their burning, accompanied by supporting bands playing open-air tango, salsa and rock, turn the roads into dancehalls under a sky exploding with fireworks. But this is not the only festival embraced enthusiastically here: **Holy week**, **Carnival**, as well as no end of regional celebrations are big events here. The tourist office will be able to tell you what is happening, where and when.

Where to Stay and Eat

The best places to stay are either at the newly built **Hotel Mediterranea Plaza** ☎ 965 210188 FAX 965 206750, Plaza del Ayuntamiento 6 (very expensive), or the **Hotel Gran Sol** ☎ 965 203000 FAX 965 211439 E-MAIL gransol@trypnet.com, Rambla Mendez Núñez (expensive), which is near the old town and has a certain 1970s charm. The **Hotel La Reforma** ☎ 965 928147 FAX 965923950, Calle Reyes Católicos 7

The castles that overlook Alicante testify to years of conquest by Carthaginian and Moor. Now life is more peaceful and these ancient fortifications are ideal viewpoints.

(moderate), is a clean and efficient hotel at the top of its price range. Excellent value is to be found at the **Pensión les Monges** (965 215046, Calle Monges 2 (inexpensive), while the very cheapest rooms are at the **Habitaciones La Orensana** (965 207820, Calle San Fernando 10 (inexpensive).

The best restaurants tend to be found around the Ayuntamiento, with a regional tradition of blending meat and fish with rice. And not just any rice: most good restaurants here will have their own rice chef. There is certainly one at the well-known **Restaurante Darsena** (965 207399, Marina Deportiva, Muelle de Levante 6 (expensive), in a stunning setting overlooking the yacht marina, where they claim to have 90 types of rice

Between Andalucía and the Levante lies Murcia, one of Spain's "forgotten" provinces. Much of it is arid and sparsely populated, with scenery not unlike parts of the southwest of the United States — which was why Murcia was a favorite location for Italian filmmakers during the era of "spaghetti Westerns." Murcia province is also known for its Holy Week and spring festivals, and particularly good ones can be seen in the provincial capital, Murcia, and in Lorca, which is 62 km (37 miles) southwest of the provincial capital on the N-340.

to go with the super-fresh seafood straight from the Bay of Alicante. A good mid-range restaurant is the **Nou Manolín** (965 200368, Calle Villages 3, with an excellent *tapas* bar downstairs and an even better restaurant above.

How to Get There
Alicante is 419 km (260 miles) southeast of Madrid, and 178 km (111 miles) south of Valencia, the provincial capital. As the province's second-largest city, it has good connections with Madrid and Valencia, with the **Estación de Madrid** (902 240202 and the **bus station** (965 130700 both southwest of the city center. It is also an important international hub, with charter flights and regular scheduled flights to several European cities landing daily at **Aeropuerto de El Altet** (966 919100, 12 km (seven and a half miles) south of the town center.

The Murcian coastline is not overly interesting, and perhaps the best way to get a feel of the province is to take the inland road (the N-340), which runs across it from Almería in the south to Alicante in the north, and passes through both Lorca and the capital.

MURCIA

Surrounded by mountains, Murcia is a surprisingly pleasant place, where you see very few other tourists and can get a flavor of an earlier Spain, before the invasion of foreigners on holiday.

The **Tourist Information Office** (968 366100 WEB SITE www.murcia-turismo.com, Calle San Cristóbal 6, Monday to Friday 9 AM to 2 PM and 5 PM to 7 PM, Saturday 10:30 AM to 1 PM, seems very keen to please; partly, perhaps, because tourists are such a rarity. Long may it last. Two further offices are at the Plano de San Franscisco 8 and the Calle Santa Clara. Internet access is possible at **L@Red** on Calle Antonio Puig 1, open Monday to Saturday 10:30 AM to 2 PM, 5 PM to 10 PM.

Medical treatment is available at the **Hospital José María Morales Meseguer** (986 360900; the **Cruz Roja** (968 222222 will get you there. For transportation, try **Murcia Radio-Taxis** (968 248800.

What to See and Do

It took 400 years to finally complete construction of the **cathedral** (968 216344, Plaza Hedez Amorez, which makes most horror stories about slow builders fade in comparison. The result is a mixture of styles, though the inside is predominately Gothic. The cathedral is daily from 7 AM to 1 PM and 5 PM to 8 PM, entrance is free.

Inside there is a **museum** (10 AM to 1 PM and 5 PM to 7 PM, €1.25), but both can be closed during important religious festivals. If you can't make the Holy Week procession, many of the 200-year-old carved wooden figures that are carried through the streets can be seen at the **Museo Salzillo** (968 291893, Plaza San Agustín, open Tuesday to Saturday 9:30 AM to 1 PM and 4 PM to 7 PM, Sunday 11 AM to 1 PM, closed on weekends in July and August, €2.70.

Where to Stay and Eat

Perhaps the best hotel in Murcia is the **Hotel Siete Poronas** (968 217771, Ronda de Garay 5 (very expensive), overlooking the river, but rather away from most of the attractions and the old town. More central — and much better known — is the **Hotel Rincón de Pepe** (968 212239 FAX 968 221744, Calle Apóstoles 34 (expensive), whose restaurant is almost a place of pilgrimage. Another good restaurant is attached to the **Hotel Hispano II** (968 216152 FAX 968 216859, Calle Radio Murcia 3 (moderate), while travelers on a budget should check out the friendly and central **Pensión Hispano I** (968 216152 FAX 968 216859, Calle Traperia 8.

Murcia's restaurants are at their busiest at lunchtime, when the area around the Plaza de Julián seethes with locals. For an expensive but memorable meal, the Hotel Rincón de Pepe (see above) is the best choice. The same chef oversees the **Barra del Rincón**, where you can try his delicious *tapas*, mouthful at a time, for a fraction of the cost.

How to Get There

Murcia is 405 km (252 miles) southeast of Madrid, 86 km (53 miles) southwest of Alicante and 219 km (136 miles) northeast of Almería, and is well-connected by fast roads and railways. The **bus station** (968 292211 is at the Calle Sierra de la Pila and the **train station** (968 252154 is at the Plaza de la Industria.

Murcia's airport, **San Javier**, 45 km (29 miles) to the west sees flights from Almería, Barcelona and Madrid, and Buzz, a British cut-price airline, has started a daily service from London Stansted (see GETTING THERE, page 253 in TRAVELERS' TIPS); the airport is more convenient for the beach resorts on the coast than for the city itself.

MAR MENOR

Murcia's nearest beach resort is the Mar Menor, the largest salt-water lagoon in Europe, just 72 km (45 miles) to the southeast. In Roman times this was a bay, used for fishing and making salt, but about a thousand years ago a sandbank settled on a small underwater mountain range, closing off an area of water 25 km (15.5 miles) long and 12 km (7.5 miles) wide. At its deepest, it is seven meters (23 ft) deep. Shallow and sandy-floored, this means the water warms up early in the year, staying warm until late in the season, and is ideally calm for children and for water sports.

So ideal, in fact, that although there has been a recent rush of hotel and apartment development here, this hasn't caught up with an explosion of diving, sailing and kayaking operators, and it can still be hard to find accommodation, especially on a budget. The season here lasts much longer than at resorts that depend on the relatively chilly waters of the Mediterranean sea.

In the north the leading resort is San Pedro de Pinitar. By the salt-flats, it is famous for its allegedly therapeutic mud, but has a good beach as well. The best hotel here is the **Hotel Traíña** (968 335020 E-MAIL info@hoteltraina.com, Avenida del Generalíssimo 84 (expensive), while more reasonably priced is the **Hotel Neptuno** (968 181911 FAX 968 183301 E-MAIL neptuno@accesosis.es, Avenida del Generalíssimo 6 (expensive). With scarcely a break this shades into Santiago de la Ribera, a popular resort famous for its sailing school **Luis Clavel** (968 573653. Hotels here include the **Lido** (968 570704 FAX 968 570700, Calle Conde Campillo 1 (moderate).

South and a scatter of small resorts edge the lagoon's inland coast, but most of the development has been built on the sand spit, La Manga, which means "The Sleeve," growing in a high-rise line of buildings surrounded by beaches and seawater on both sides. This is where you'll find the most luxury hotels, though strangely enough, here amongst the apartment blocks these huge monoliths just seem to drag the area down-market. For four-star luxury check into the **DobleMare** (968 563910 FAX 968 140998 E-MAIL j.munoz@husa.es, Gran Vía (expensive), or the **Sol Galúa** (968 563200 FAX 968 140630, Urbanización Dos Mares (expensive).

The baroque façade of Murcia cathedral shelters a vaulting, Gothic interior.

The easiest way to explore the Mar Menor is in a rental car. The N-301 heads south for 10 km (six miles); branch off on the C-3319 for the eastern coast, and drive 44 km (28 miles) to San Javier, or for La Mancha stay on the N-301, turning left just before Cartagena.

CARTAGENA

Either as an excursion from the city of Murcia, or as a destination in its own right, Cartagena, southeast along the N-301 from Murcia, is well worthwhile. This port was Hannibal's base on the Iberian Peninsula and was later used by the Romans. Although the suburbs are generally rundown and unwelcoming, the old city center is atmospheric and lively, encompassing art-deco buildings, ancient churches and narrow, medieval alleys.

Start by picking up a map from the **Tourist Information Office** (968 506483, Plaza Almirante Basterrech and Calle Lealtad, open daily 10:30 AM to 1:30 PM, Monday to Saturday 5 PM to 7 PM. Cartagena's naval history is taken very seriously, with a free **Museo Naval** on the Calle Menéndez Pelayo 6, open Tuesday to Sunday 10 AM to 1 PM, and a fascinating **Museo Nacional de Arqueología Marítima** (968 508415, Plaza de España, open Tuesday to Sunday 10 AM to 3 PM, also free, which has a salvaged Roman Galleon and any number of interesting artifacts pulled up from the deep. It is possible to stay here; try the **Hotel Los Habaneros** (968 505250 FAX 968 509104 WEB SITE www.forodigital.es/habaneros, Calle San Diego 60 (moderate), which has a well-respected restaurant.

Cartagena can be reached by road (44 km/ 27.5 miles) from Murcia, along the N-301, and there are regular buses and trains.

THE COSTA DE ALMERÍA

Hot and lunar inland, the semi-desert landscapes of Almería might look familiar from countless spaghetti westerns and the dune-strewn landscapes of the film *Lawrence of Arabia*. A landscape folded into mountains by the collision of Eurasian and African tectonic plates is one of the driest and hottest parts of Europe.

As a result, this is not such a great place to break down or get stuck without any water, but the coast here does get the sun earlier, and keeps it longer, than anywhere else in Europe. And the main attractions here are, indeed, on the coast, with a few small, pleasant resorts such as Mojácar, appealing mainly to English visitors, and San José, frequented mainly by Spaniards (which goes to show how much better they do their holidays). Administratively, the capital of the province, Almería, has not got a great deal of touristic interest, but is still a pleasantly untouristy place to while away a few nights.

MOJÁCAR

The leading resort on this stretch of coast has a fascinating past. In the 1960s it was a ghost town, but the local mayor sparked it into life by offering free land to anyone who would build within a year. Try that now and the developers would move in, but the policy attracted a wide mix of hippies and vaguely creative types away from all Spain's other barren, featureless bits of coast, hoping for a tourist boom. Now the descendants of these settlers have been joined by second-homers, hotels are appearing on the beachfront and the first tour operators are moving in.

The best place to stay here is in the **Parador de Mojácar** (950 478250 FAX 950 478183 E-MAIL mojácar @parador.es, Playa de Mojácar (expensive), right on the beach; with a great pool. There's better value at the **Puntazo** (951 478229 FAX 951 478285, on the seafront (inexpensive). Alternatively, one guest house that has been there since the 1960s is **Mamabel's** (/FAX 950 472448, Calle Embajadores 5 (inexpensive). This is a delightful place up in the original village, designed to perfection and with a terrace overlooking the sea. Mamabel's husband is an artist and even the furniture is hand painted; the restaurant is (inexpensively) among the best in the village.

Down on the beachfront there are various restaurants, none particularly wonderful, and bars blaring out Spanish techno music. The town is served by a slow bus that leaves Almería twice a day, but the best way to get there is with your own vehicle: take exit 520 from the N-340/E15 Almería to Alicante *autopista*. Mojácar is 15 km (10 miles) along minor roads and is signposted.

Excursions from Mojácar

Aficionados of Western movies, or those with young children, will jump at the opportunity to dive through the spaghetti-western landscapes northeast of Almería and to visit the set of *A Fistful of Dollars*, preserved and opened up to the public in a movie theme park called **Mini Hollywood** (950 365236, €13.20, daily 10 AM to 7 PM. Three times a day there's a raid on the bank. Mini Hollywood is southwest of Mojácar, past the village of Tabernas.

SAN JOSÉ

South of Mojácar, the small fishing village of San José has a less dramatic — or venal — history as a resort, and is, perhaps for this reason, much quieter. That this is my favorite resort in the area probably says more about me than it does about it. The village is set around a kilometer-long (half-mile) beach, with an active fishing harbor huddled into the northern extent. Around the town square,

The terraced fishing village of Mojácar is within easy reach of the sunny southern city of Almería.

are shops selling rubber rings, beach balls and international papers, alongside a few bars, an Internet café and a supermarket at the south.

It says a lot for this resort that the best hotel here, right in the middle of the beach and fully air-conditioned and television'd, barely creeps into the moderate price category. The **Don Ignacio (** 950 611080 FAX 950 611084, Paseo Marítimo (moderate) faces, rather strangely, sideways rather than looking out to the sea. Most of the other accommodation is in apartments, but there are a couple of quite acceptable *hostales*, including the **Hostale Bahia (** 950 380114, Calle Correos 5 (inexpensive).

There is a good choice of restaurants, perhaps best among the competing row of open-air establishments, Italian and Spanish, that line the access road to the fishing port. Unsurprisingly, fresh seafood figures on most menus, but the standards are high. And that is your nightlife.

Most visitors here will arrive in their own vehicles, taking exit 471 from the N-344/E15 Almería to Alicante road and threading their way through 25 km (15.5 miles) of minor roads. This is not a town in which you need a car, however, and San José is also served by buses from Almería, which can be a better means of access.

ALMERÍA

A thousand years ago this was the capital of the richest kingdom in all Spain. Since then piracy and plunder have ruled and ruined Almería, as raiding parties settled, besieged and conquered in the long fight for control of the Mediterranean. Its name derives from the Arabic *Al-Meriya*, meaning "spirit of the sea," and while the waters were travel routes for armies, the city itself was fortified against invasion and conquest. Turkish and North African forces, including the famous pirate, Barbarossa, were among those who based their operations here. This shows: in the impressive Alcazaba and the fortified cathedral. Unfortunately, it no longer shows in the buildings that fell to invading Moorish armies, pirate bands and troops loyal to Iberian kings.

Although there are still some alleys and old buildings around the colonnaded Plaza de la Constitución, much of the city is modern, hemmed in by barren mountains covered by long, unattractive plastic greenhouses, where techno-farming takes advantage of long hot summers to grow perfect produce for Europe's supermarkets. Tourism here, led by the long hot summer season, focuses on the beaches and barely touches the city.

General Information
The **Tourist Information Office (** 950 274355 FAX 950 274360, Calle Parque de Nicolás Salmerón, is open Monday to Friday 9 AM to 7 PM and Saturday 10 AM to 2 PM. It is ideally placed for motorists, on the main waterfront road facing the

commercial harbor. This isn't a long walk from the town center, but if you want a taxi, try **Radio-Taxis (** 950 226161 or **Tele-Taxi (** 950 251111. For Internet access try **La India (** 950 274861, Carretera de Granada 304. For medical treatment, the **Clinica Internacional Torres Bermejas SL (** 950 220324, Gran Sol 2, can cope with most emergencies.

What to See and Do
Dominating the town, the **Alcazaba (** 950 271617, open 9 AM to 8:30 PM, €1.50, free for European Union citizens, is one of the best examples of Moorish fortifications in Spain. It was built in the

tenth century, but later extended to include first a Moorish and then a Christian palace. But although at one point it was thought to rival Granada, only the walls and towers remain. The views are still terrific, looking down over the cave district and the fortified **cathedral (** 989 679003, open Monday to Friday 10 AM to 5 PM, Saturday 10 AM to 1:30 PM, Sundays at service times and only for the religiously motivated, €1:80. The cathedral was built in the sixteenth century and it is easy to imagine the fear of pirates that prompted the forbidding exterior, which makes the cool beauty of the interior even more moving.

The city beach is not greatly used. Better to travel to the east, to San José (see above). To the west the beaches of Aguadulce and Roquetas de Mar are popular, but built up. Hourly buses go off in either direction.

Where to Stay and Eat

Hotels here offer good value, with even quite good hotels in the inexpensive category, and generally there is no problem getting a room. The best hotel in town is the **Almería** (950 238011 FAX 950 270691, Avenida Reina Regente 8 (expensive), on the waterfront, with the **AM Torreluz IV**

Plaza de Carmen 7 (inexpensive), which is well located at the heart of the city. On a budget, try the **Fonda Universal** (950 235557, Puerta de Purchena 3 (inexpensive), which is central and clean. To find top-class Almerian specialties, try the **Rincón de Juan Pedro**, Plaza del Carmen (moderate), or take a stroll round the Puerta de Perchena area, where there are hundreds of *tapas* bars and restaurants.

How to Get There

Almería's newly constructed **airport** (950 213700 is eight kilometers (five miles) east of town, and gets flights from several European cities as well

(/FAX 950 23499, Plaza de las Flores 5 (expensive), in the center of town. With your own vehicle, the **Solymar** (950 234622 FAX 950 277010, Carretera de Málaga 110 (inexpensive), has superb rooms and facilities and offers quite outstanding value. The restaurant, unfortunately, is deplorable, which is why you need a car. The **Torreluz** (/FAX 950 234399 E-MAIL torreluz@torreluz.com, Plaza de las Flores (inexpensive) (not to be confused with the AM Torreluz IV), is within strolling distance of some of the city's best restaurants and bars.

The oldest hotel in Almería is the newly refurbished **Hotel la Perla** (950 238877 FAX 950 275816,

as internal flights from Madrid and Barcelona. A bus runs to the town center every half hour, to the **bus station** (950 210029, Plaza de Barcelona, and the **railway station** (950 231822 is at Al Calde Muños. There are also ferries to Morocco: call **Ferrimaroc** (950 274800 and **Trasmediterránea** (950 236155 WEB SITE www.trasmediterranea.es. Almería is 550 km (344 miles) south of Madrid, 201 km (126 miles, not all *autopista*) east of Málaga, and 292 km (182 miles) southwest of Alicante.

San José, near Almería, attracts a predominately Spanish clientele to its small but welcoming beach and active fishing harbor.

Aragón
and
Navarra

There is a fine highway that cuts across northern Spain from Catalunya through Aragón into Navarra and beyond to the Basque country and Galicia. The red clay, lush meadows, and market gardens of Catalunya give way to the chalky gray dust of Aragón, and the great upland emptiness of Spain returns: with it comes the aura of the desert and the hand of the Moor.

The highway keeps company with the Ebro, Spain's largest river. Undulating irrigated fields of wheat, barley and corn and orchards of peaches, apricots and almonds are interspersed with olive groves and copses of pine and cypress. A church tower that was once a minaret shimmers on the horizon, a punctuation mark in a vast landscape. The road continues on to Pamplona, annually animated by the lavish running of the bulls, at the heart of Navarra.

ARAGÓN

Aragón is a thick wedge of territory that starts in the Pyrenees and runs south to La Mancha; it separates the independent-minded Catalans to the east from the separatist-minded Basques in the west. Aragón is a crossroads rather than a destination for most visitors to Spain; it is also one of the least populated and poorest regions in the country. But it has a stark beauty, it resonates history, and there are a number of places definitely worth visiting.

Upper Aragón includes the highest section of the Spanish Pyrenees, where there are good opportunities for skiing, climbing and hiking. This region also has one of Spain's finest national parks (the **Parque Nacional de Ordesa**), and offers good hunting, shooting and fishing, fortified by hearty food and wine (Cariñena is the best). Further south, the Ebro flows across Aragón — bringing fertility to a land that is for the most part rocky, barren and unproductive.

Two dynastic marriages shaped Aragón's history. The first, between Queen Petronilla (daughter of Ramiro II of Aragón) and Count Ramón Berenguer, the Count of Barcelona, in 1154, gave Aragón a window on the Mediterranean and turned it into an imperial maritime power. The second, between Ferdinand II of Aragón and Isabella of Castilla in 1476, drew the kingdom into the mainstream of modern Spanish history.

After its absorbtion into the Spanish State, Aragón combined creativity and tragedy in a mirror of the national history. Francisco Goya and Luis Buñuel were born here, and during the Civil War a vast number of people died here. Aragón was one of the most bitterly contested areas and is pockmarked with battlefields. There is even a small town, **Belchite**, southeast of Zaragoza, whose ruins have been carefully preserved as a history lesson and a caution for modern Spaniards.

The attraction of Aragón is that so much of its medieval glory lives on in its churches, castles and small towns. Most notable are the Romanesque churches and monasteries in the north, many of them built along the route the pilgrims took from France to Santiago de Compostela in Galicia. There were two main crossing points in the Pyrenees, one at **Somport**, which led the pilgrims through Aragón, and the other further west at **Roncesvalles** in Navarra. The pilgrims' first stop in Aragón was the mountain town of **Jaca**. Its importance in those far off days is still reflected in the medieval buildings and most notably in the superb Romanesque cathedral built in the eleventh century and one of the oldest of its kind in Spain.

Aragón is also a showcase of Mudéjar architecture and design. Following the Christian Reconquest, the kingdom was tolerant of its Moriscos — the name given to Moors who stayed on under Christian rule — and was repaid by their skill and industry. Mudéjar work can be seen in nearly every town in central and southern Aragón, but perhaps the finest all-round display is at **Tarazona**, 85 km (53 miles) from Zaragoza. This town also has the curiosity of a traditional bullring converted into apartment houses — a boost for those in need of housing and the anti-bullfight brigade no doubt, but a blow to lovers of the sport.

ZARAGOZA

Zaragoza, the capital of Aragón, sits astride the fertile plain fed by the Ebro and can be distinguished from a great distance by the domes and spires of its cathedrals. (Like Salamanca, Zaragoza has two of them.) While much of the city is modern and industrial — it ranks as Spain's fifth largest — it has ancient roots and a rich history. The Romans were there and if you slur its Roman name, "Cesar Augusta," you will see why it is now called Zaragoza. Its strategic location at the center of Aragón on the Ebro made it as attractive to the Moors as it was to the Christians who later conquered them.

GENERAL INFORMATION

The **Tourist Information Office** (976 393537 WEB SITE www.turismozaragoza.com, Torreón de la Zuda, Glorieta de Pio XII, opens 9:30 AM to 2 PM and 4 PM to 6 PM. There are satellite *turismos* around the town, including at the bus station, the railway station and opposite the basilica (976 201200 on Plaza de Pilar. For taxis, call **Radio-Taxi Aragón** (976 383838 or **Radio-Taxi Zaragoza** (976 424242.

For medical emergencies, try the **Hospital Miguel Servet** (976 355700, Plaza Isabel la Católica 1.

The ochre of rendered walls and clay tiles sets the sunbaked tone for the small town of Somaén, above the spectacular river Jalón in Aragón.

What to See and Do

The city's cultural pleasures are dominated by the two cathedrals. The oldest, known as **La Seo (** 976 397497, Plaza del Pilar, opens Tuesday to Friday 10 AM to 1:30 PM and 5 PM to 6:30 PM, with shorter hours on weekends. Entrance is free; guided visits are held noon to 1 PM and 5 PM to 6 PM, other visits from 1 PM to 2 PM, Sunday 10 AM to 2 PM; closed Monday. It's a mixture of practically every ecclesiastical architectural style in Spain. There is plenty of Mudéjar brick and tile work, an impressive fifteenth-century alabaster *retablo*, and a tapestry museum. The second cathedral, the **Basílica de Nuestra Señora del Pilar (** 976 299564, Plaza del Pilar, open daily 6 AM to 8 PM, is newer, bigger and uglier, and is also one of the most revered in all Spain. Built with a rather cock-eyed, almost Ottoman fervor, the basilica has eleven domes and four towers that look like minarets but aren't; it commemorates the Virgin of the Pilar who is near the top of the list in the Spanish Marian hierarchy. Legend has it that in AD 40 the Virgin Mary appeared in an apparition before Saint James the Apostle (Santiago) on top of a stone pillar where the cathedral now stands. Inside you'll find the **Museo Pilarista** (9 AM to 2 PM and 4 PM to 6 PM, daily, €1.20), and from Saturday to Thursday you can go up the **Torre** (tower) for €1.20.

Other more satisfying buildings — with less fanciful origins — include the **Lonja** or merchants' exchange, built in the sixteenth century, which periodically opens to display art exhibitions, and the lavish **Aljafería Palace (** 976 289528, Avenida de Madrid, open 10 AM to 2 PM and 4:30 PM to 6:30 PM, Sundays and holidays 10 AM to 2 PM, €1.80, originally the home of the Arab rulers and later the court of the Christian kings of Aragón. Zaragoza's most important fiesta commemorates the Virgin of the Pilar in the second week in October each year, with countless concerts and performances, bullfights and dances around a main procession on the 12th. For those who like folk festivals, Aragón is renowned for its traditional songs and dances, particularly the jota, a lively dance performed by couples who leap high into the air and sing as they soar.

Where to Stay and Eat

At the top end of the market, the **Meliá Zaragoza Aragon (** 976 430100 FAX 976 440734, Avenida Cesar Augusto 13 (expensive), is a large, modern hotel in the center of city. The **N. H. Gran Hotel (** 976 221901 FAX 976 236713, Calle Joaquín Costa 5 (expensive), and the **Palafox (** 976 237700 FAX 976 234705 E-MAIL palafox@teleline.es, Calle Casa Jiménez (expensive), which has a spa and gym, are two alternatives.

For those who don't need four- or five-star luxury, the **Rey Alfonso I (** 976 394850 FAX 976 399640, Calle Coso 17 (moderate), is central, and the **Ramiro I (** 976 298200 FAX 976 398952, Calle Coso 123 (moderate), is located in the old quarter. For a modern hotel, try the **Zaragoza Royal (** 976 214600 FAX 976 220359, Calle Arzobispo Domènech 4 (moderate).

On a budget, it's hard to beat the **Hotel Las Torres (** 976 394250 FAX 976 290511, Plaza del Pilar 11 (inexpensive), overlooking the basilica.

Most of the mid-range restaurants are found around the old quarter. **Los Borrachos (** 976 275036, Paseo Sagasta 64 (expensive), serves good game, but at prices that make the locals' eyes water. The **Costa Vasca (** 976 217339, Calle Teniente Coronel Valenzuela 13 (moderate), has good Basque food and a matching wine cellar. The **La Rinconada de Lorenzo (** 976 455108, Calle La Salle 3 (inexpensive), specializes in regional dishes.

For atmosphere, try the **Bar Arranque**, Calle Jordan de Urriés 5 (inexpensive), which offers an excellent range of *tapas* and local wines, backed by traditional Spanish music. Bars and nightclubs are generally found around Calle Cantamina, with listings available in the free paper *Insomnia*, available from the tourist information offices and the livelier bars.

How to Get There

Zaragoza is 312 km (195 miles) northeast of Madrid, 309 km (193 miles) west of Barcelona and 177 km (110 miles) southeast of Pamplona. Trains arrive at the **Estación del Portillo (** 976 226598, Calle San Clemente 13. There are various bus stations: the main one is on Paseo María Agustín (** 976 229343. The **airport (** 976 349050 is to the southwest of town.

NAVARRA

Another individualistic piece of the Spanish mosaic, the region of Navarra has its head in the Pyrenees and its feet in the Ebro. An area of great physical variety, the region has a history of rugged nationalism. The Romans found it hard going and Charlemagne suffered a notable defeat at the Roncesvalles pass in the Pyrenees, where his rear guard was slaughtered by the locals. This event was immortalized in the great medieval epic poem, *La Chanson de Roland* (the Song of Roland). Roland, the commander of the Franks' rear guard, was killed in the battle. In an act of literary sabotage, Roland's chronicler turned the victorious Vascons (the Basques and Gascons who inhabited Navarra), into Moors.

Ruled from Pamplona, the Navarra region grew in strength in the Middle Ages and managed to preserve its independence until 1512 — 20 years

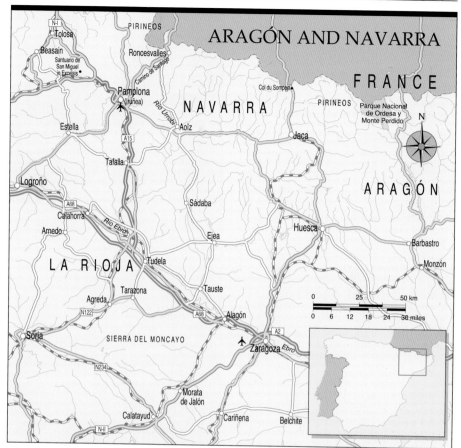

after the last Moorish kingdom in the south had succumbed to the Spanish crown. Even then it retained its identity and *fueros* (privileges) well into the nineteenth century. It supported the Carlist side in the dynastic wars of the nineteenth century and Franco during the Civil War in the twentieth. Although Navarra has a large Basque population it is not technically part of the Basque country and has resisted attempts by the Basque provinces, which lie to the west, to incorporate it.

PAMPLONA

Pamplona (Iruñea in Basque) is Navarra's capital and its cultural core. The city is believed to have been founded by the Roman general Pompey, from whom its name is derived, and passed through the hands of the Moors (twice), the Franks (Charlemagne knocked its walls down and Roland and his men paid the price), and finally the Castilians. The reason it received so much military attention is that for much of its life it was capital of the independent kingdom of Navarra: it has more to offer than you'd expect from its current status. It can also claim a role in the birth

of the Jesuits, a movement that was started by a Basque nobleman wounded in a siege of Pamplona in the early sixteenth century, later to be canonized as Saint Ignatius of Loyola.

The area also has plenty of attractions apart from Pamplona's old city, ringed as it is by a doughnut of modern high-rise suburbs. Thirty kilometers (19 miles) northwest of Pamplona, the wooded Sierra de Aralar shelters prehistoric rock art and dolmens, as well as the ancient and stunningly situated **Santuario de San Miguel** in Excelsis.

But whatever its achievements and attractions, it is as the location for Spain's most famous "running of the bulls," immortalized by Hemingway's book *The Sun Also Rises*, that Pamplona caught the imagination of the world.

GENERAL INFORMATION

Pamplona's old city is relatively compact, centered around the Plaza del Castillo. The **Tourist Information Office** (948 220741, Calle Duque de Ahumada 3, open 10 AM to 2 PM and 4 PM to 7 PM, and the **Regional Tourist Information Office** (948 206540, Calle Esclava 1, at the corner of Plaza de

San Francisco, are good sources of information the latter can do a disturbingly good job of persuading visitors to hike out into the hills. Both will help with accommodation, which can be an impossible task during the San Fermín festival.

For a taxi, call **Tele-Taxis Pamplona (** 948 232300, and for medical — or, indeed, any — emergencies **(** 112. To log on, **Internet Iruñ**, Calle Esquiroz 28, is a good Internet café.

WHAT TO SEE AND DO

Pamplona is a relaxed and civilized place, with a quaint medieval section around the tree- and café-lined Plaza del Castillo, an elegant and arcaded nineteenth-century square. The chief "sight" is the Gothic **Catedral de Santa Marta (** 948 225679, Plaza de San José, which is open Monday to Friday 10:30 AM to 6 PM, Saturdays 10:30 AM to 1 PM, Sundays and holidays 11 AM to 2 PM, mid-September to mid-July closed from 1:30 PM to 4 PM. It has what are thought by some to be the finest Gothic cloisters in Spain. James Michener, however, was less impressed, describing the cathedral as the "ugliest beautiful church in existence." There are also some fine municipal and regional government buildings and an atmospheric, and still impressive, **Citadel**, but none of these are why Pamplona has become famous and why legions of visitors are drawn to it every year. Blame it on Ernest Hemingway, if you will, but it is hard to separate Pamplona from the image of bulls charging down narrow barricaded streets as young men in white with red sashes scatter in all directions, and from days and nights of drunken carousing.

FESTIVAL OF SAN FERMÍN

That description does not do a disservice to the reality, but there is more to the Festival of San Fermín (known locally as Sanfirmines) than that. Held from July 6 to 14, the festival celebrates the city's patron saint, who was the first bishop of Pamplona and suffered a martyr's death by being dragged around the streets by a bull, or so the story goes. The irony notwithstanding, the inhabitants of Pamplona clearly love both their saint and their bulls and have no qualms risking their own lives with the descendants of the species that did in their bishop.

The running of the bulls (the *encierro* or "corralling") takes place every morning at 8 AM for six consecutive days. Originally, it was just a way of getting the bulls from their pens on the edge of the medieval quarter through the narrow streets and into the bullring for the daily *corrida.* But then it became a test of machismo and an exciting spectator event, and who better to publicize it than Papa Macho himself in one of his best novels, *The Sun Also Rises* (also known as *Fiesta*).

Pamplona showed its appreciation by erecting a statue to Hemingway: instantly recognizable with beard and roll-neck sweater, and strategically sited under the plane trees near the point where the bulls turn off the street and into the ring. There is a short affectionate inscription saying the American writer was a true friend of Pamplona.

Frankly, having seen the crowds during festival week, I am not so sure.

WHERE TO STAY AND EAT

During San Fermín, hotel prices will double, at least, and you'll also need to book well ahead.

The best-appointed hotel here is probably the centrally located **Iruñea Palace Hotel Tres Reyes (** 948 226600, Jardines de la Taconera (very expensive). VIP's and bullfighters, however, tend to stay at the **Hotel Yoldi (** 948 224800 FAX 948 212045,

Avenida de San Ignacio 11 (expensive), which has its own parking lot.

Less expensive are the **Maisonnave** (948 222600, Calle Nueva 20 (moderate), which is comfortable and close to where the bulls run, and the **N. H. Ciudad de Pamplona** (948 266011, Calle Iturrama 21 (moderate), which is near the university. Next to the bull ring is the **Orhi** (948 228500, Calle Leyre 7 (moderate), while the **Hotel Europa** (948 221800 FAX 948 229235, Calle Espoz y Mina 11 (inexpensive), in a good central location for bars and restaurants, has a particularly good restaurant.

Less expensive again are the **Hotel La Perla** (948 227706, Plaza del Castillo 1 (inexpensive), where some of the rooms have balconies overlooking the street. Hemingway, apparently, once stayed in room 217. On a real budget the **Fonda la Aragonesa** (948 223428, Calle San Nicolás 25 (inexpensive), should meet basic requirements.

For dining, the Calle San Lorenzo is the place to browse for the best alternatives. One of the best is the **Josetxo** (948 222097, Plaza Principe de Viana 1 (moderate to expensive), which specializes in local Navarrese dishes. **Las Pocholas** (948 211729, Paseo de Saraste 6 (moderate), is a charming restaurant and bar with decent food at a price the locals won't balk at: popular and rightly so. For seafood, try **El Mosquito** (948 255026, Travesia de San Alberto Magno 3 (moderate), and for an innovative take on local traditions **Hartza** (948 224568, Calle Juan de Labrit 19 (moderate), near the bullring, has imaginative cooking. For stuffed lamb and other local dishes at reasonable prices, **Alhambra** (948 255007, is on Calle Bergamin 7 (moderate).

The parade, a piece of eighteenth-century pageantry that always precedes a bullfight, in Pamplona's bullring during the feast of San Fermín in July; the bulls ran through the streets to the ring earlier in the day.

How to Get There

Pamplona is some way from Spain's major cities: it is almost exactly 400 km (250 miles) northeast of Madrid, just under 160 km (100 miles) southeast of Bilbao and 177 km (111 miles) northwest of Zaragoza.

The airport is the **Aeropuerto de Noain (** 948 168700, Carreterra Zaragoza km6.5, southwest of the center.

The **bus station** is central, on Calle Conde Oiveto, by the citadel, and the **railway station (** 948 111531, Calle San Jorge, has a central ticket office on Calle Estella 8.

EXCURSIONS FROM PAMPLONA

There are few better places than Pamplona to make an expedition into rural Spain. Navarra's northern mountain landscapes are exceptionally beautiful, and the rural hotels are well geared up for offering characterful accommodation in spectacular settings. To find out more, there is a **Central Reservations Service (** 948 206541 FAX 948 207032 E-MAIL central.reserves@cfnavarra.es, for hundreds of small and inviting bed and breakfasts.

RONCESVALLES PASS

One of the most spectacular mountain journeys here is a trip up to Roncesvalles, a pass in the Pyrenees where medieval pilgrims entered Spain from France on the long, dusty road to Santiago de Compostela, and, of course, where Roland blew his

horn despairingly for reinforcements and met his end at the hand of the local "Moors." The most attractive way — although not the shortest — is to go through Aoïz and follow the Urrobi river valley. It is rugged country relieved by fields of wheat, barley and oats ripening under the summer sun; hamlets of small stone houses, as brown as the earth itself, with geraniums on the windowsills; rows of poplar trees along the river bank, and no sound except the chatter of the birds and the babble of running water. Was it around here that Hemingway fished away a lazy afternoon and recreated it in a memorable scene in *The Sun Also Rises*?

Near the pass there is a monument to Roland, a martial figure showing him armed with a dagger

and a deadly looking mace. Underneath there is the date of the battle: 778. There is also a fine twelfth-century monastery with a beautiful, restrained church built in the French Gothic style. You can eat well and inexpensively in **La Posada**, a refectory-restaurant with massive walls, flagstone floors and heavy wooden beams inside the monastery. When I was last at the pass itself, a group of French pilgrims, carrying small crosses made of pieces of wood and twigs, were kneeling on the grass close to a flock of sheep. They placed bouquets of flowers at the foot of a statue of the Virgin and sing a hymn, as tens of thousands have done before them for more than a thousand years.

ABOVE LEFT: A street café in Pamplona. ABOVE RIGHT: The façade of Pamplona's seventeenth-century town hall. OPPOSITE: The parade of the giants during the San Fermín festival.

Camino
de
Santiago

There were two main routes that the pilgrims followed in Spain. One, known as the Asturian, went along the northern coast. Unfortunately, thanks to local brigands, this often turned pilgrims into martyrs. Even though the Asturian Route is, now, safe and delightful, far more commonly used is the Camino Francés (the "French Road"), linking the spectacular cities of Burgos and León, and leading into the green hills and valleys of Galicia to the ultimate destination of the pilgrims, Santiago de Compostela.

As Navarra gives way to Rioja, the countryside softens; expansive wheat fields the color of burnished gold await the harvester's plundering blade; vines begin to make an appearance; very old towns and a multiplicity of church towers and spires — like beacons on a rocky coast — mark the pilgrims' way. Just before Logroño, the capital of the Rioja, a sign says "Santiago de Compostela: 666 kilometers" (414 miles).

LA RIOJA

Once, Rioja did not mean much to foreigners visiting Spain. Now it is inseparable from wine, especially red wine, and rightly so. The region produces the best wine in Spain and exports it all over the world. It travels pretty well, but there is no substitute for drinking it where the grapes grow and the wine is made.

The name comes from an elision of "Río Oja," the river valley where the vines were first planted. There are three main growing areas: Rioja Alta (Upper Rioja) around Haro, a moist upland region that produces the finest wines; Rioja Baja (Lower Rioja) east of Logroño along the Ebro valley; and Rioja Alavesa, a zone north of the Ebro that borders on the Basque Country. These different areas are clearly marked on a pretty little map on the back of all Rioja wine bottles.

The soil and the climate give Rioja wines their special flavor, which is fruity and full yet light and fresh tasting. The best reds have a wonderful color and bouquet.

The wine business began in the 1880s when the railroad came to Rioja, and started to boom when the phylloxera blight decimated the French vineyards. The wine was traditionally made in oak barrels but, according to Felipe Nalda, the technical director of the *bodegas* Riojanes in Cenicero, just outside Logroño, the best wine is now made in aluminum vats. The industry is strictly controlled and the wines are, on the whole, reasonably priced. They are graded according to age: "Crianza" (literally, "maturation") means that the wine has spent at least one year in the barrel; "Reserva" indicates three years in the barrel, and "Gran Reserva" means five years spent maturing. The best of recent years are generally agreed to be 1975, 1978, 1981, 1982, 1991, 1994 and 1995.

With production now on a truly industrial scale, touring Rioja's wineries is usually only possible for groups, and the best place to ask about information on this is at the tourist office in Haro. For those expecting atmosphere, the production might well puncture some illusions.

LOGROÑO

Logroño is the administrative and commercial center of Rioja. Its modern elegance does little to endear it to tourists, but its position at the heart of Rioja, which borders the Basque Country, Navarra and Old Castilla, makes it a good base for many worthwhile excursions for those who appreciate city comforts.

General Information

The heart of the city is the Paseo de Espolón, a landscaped garden where you'll find an underground parking lot and the **Tourist Information Office** (941 291260, Calle Miguel Villanueva 10, which is open Monday to Saturday 10 am to 2 PM and 4:30 PM to 7 PM, Sunday 10 AM to 2 PM. Although there were two Internet cafés here, both have recently ceased trading, and the best way of finding a current e-mail café is to follow the signs. Taxis can be summoned from the major taxi ranks: most conveniently **Espolón** (941 224299.

There are three main hospitals, of which one is **San Millán** (941 294500. The best way to get there is by calling the **Cruz Roja** (941 222222.

Where to Stay and Eat

Perhaps because the accommodation market in Logroño is not much distorted by tourism, the rates are reasonable, with even the best hotels generally comfortably within the moderate category. The best include the **Carlton Rioja** (941 242100 FAX 941 243502, Gran Vía del Rey Juan Carlos I (or just Gran Vía) 5 (moderate), and the high-rise **Los Bracos Sol** (941 226608 FAX 941

CAMINO DE SANTIAGO

226754, Calle Breton de los Herrerors 29 (moderate), a functional hotel popular with business visitors. Rather less expensive is the perfectly acceptable **Murrieta** (941 224150, Calle Marqués de Murrieta 1 (moderate). For those on a budget the **Hostal Sebastián** (941 242800, Calle San Juan 21 (inexpensive), is reasonably priced, but make sure you get a back room.

Restaurants here are also very reasonable, with a good place to start to look being north of the Paseo del Espolón, at the start of the old town. All the following are in the moderate category. **La Merced** (941 221166, Calle Marqués de San Nicolas 109, is a former palace in the old part of town; it has a good wine cellar. **Mesón Lorenzo** (941 258140, Calle Marqués de San Nicolas 136, is another stylish restaurant in the same area. **Carabanchel** (941 223883, Calle San Agustín 2, is a reliable, long-standing establishment.

HARO

Haro, 40 km (24 miles) west of Logroño and in the heart of the wine-producing country, has a charming, if rather decaying, appeal, with its medieval buildings, faded pastel walls and casement windows, and its main square built around a graceful gazebo in the center. *Bodegas* abound in Haro, stressing the importance of wine in Rioja Alta, and there are some excellent delicatessens here — as well as a number of very good shoe shops. The town has a pleasant, prosperous atmosphere.

There is a **Tourist Information Office** (941 303366, Plaza M. Florentino Rodríguez, which is open Monday to Saturday 10 AM to 2 PM and 4:30 PM to 7:30 PM, Sunday 10 AM to 2 PM, and is the best place to arrange to visit a wine factory. The best include **Bodegas Bilbaínas**, **CVNE** and **Muga**. A more atmospheric place to sample wines is in the cavernous vaults of **Mi Bodega**, Calle Santo Tomás 13, or at any one of a number of tempting bars, selling, of course, Rioja by the glass. In the last week

in June the wines come to the main square, with plenty available for tasting among open-air concerts and processions on stilts. The culmination of the festival is on June 29, when the famous *Batalla del vino* sees everyone drenched in wine.

There is a four-star hotel here, in the moderate category: **Los Agostinos** (941 311308, Plaza San Agustín 2, stunningly set in a converted Augustine monastery. There is also at least one inexpensive one, **Higinia** (941 304344, Virgen de la Vega 31. To be right at the heart of the town though, with a balcony overlooking the central gazebo and some prime restaurants, try the **Pensión la Peña** (941 310022, Plaza de la Paz 17 (inexpensive), although there's no reserved parking and plenty of stairs.

ANGUIANO

As you move west the focus shifts from wine, and the footprint of the pilgrim becomes clear again, with a proliferation of churches, hospices, monasteries and shrines.

Using as a point of reference the old town of Nájera, which was the capital of Navarra for a period before becoming part of Castilla, there are some side trips worth taking on the road from Logroño to Burgos. A southerly loop will bring you into the Sierra de la Demanda and to the pretty mountain village of Anguiano. Here, every July 21 to 23, a strange festival takes place, where men dressed in traditional costumes climb onto stilts and dance through the streets.

SAN MILLÁN DE LA COGOLLA

San Millán de la Cogolla is a village that grew up around two famous medieval monasteries: Suso and Yuso. San Millán was a sixth-century hermit who picked this lovely spot to establish a religious community. In the tenth century, monks under Muslim rule built a monastery in the mountainside that later came to be known as the **Monasterío de**

Suso (Upper Monastery). Built in the Mozarabic style, it has arcades, key-hole arches and a finely carved tomb of San Millán. A thoughtful curator has put on display a glass-fronted case that is full of bones and a skull with excellent teeth. Another tomb contains the remains of Gonzalo de Berceo, an abbot here who was the first poet to write in Castilian. He died in the middle of the thirteenth century. The following century, the kings of Navarra built a much more elaborate Benedictine monastery down in the valley. The **Monasterío de Yuso** (Lower Monastery), sometimes known as the "El Escorial" of the Rioja, is a massive, somber and strikingly beautiful pile protected by lines of poplar trees and set against a backdrop of wheat fields

earth, grass, leaves and ripening wheat the freshest scent in the world.

To make it perfect, stay in the **Hostería del Monasterío de San Millán** (941 373277 FAX 941 373266 E-MAIL hosteria@sanmillan.com, Monasterío de Yuso (moderate, four-star). Well worth a detour. From Nájera, drive 15 km (nine miles) south to Bobadilla and then turn right and drive 12 km (seven and a half miles) to San Millán; in all, the village is 40 km (25 miles) southwest of Logroño.

SANTO DOMINGO DE LA CALZADA

Returning to the main road that leads to Burgos, the pilgrims and their latter-day followers came

and copses of trees so dark that they look almost blue in the late afternoon light.

Largely rebuilt in the sixteenth and seventeenth centuries, the monastery has a vast Renaissance church: a baroque sacristy with a painted ceiling, an alabaster floor and a Gothic cloister. There are hundreds of religious paintings, eleventh-century ivory bas-reliefs, a spectacular ivory chest, and early religious texts in Latin and Spanish.

A small group of Benedictine monks now live in the monastery where hundreds used to reside. While the human factor is less in evidence than it used to be, the rural simplicity of the countryside surrounding Suso and Yuso is remarkably intact. A flock of sheep, a couple of goats, a sheep dog and a shepherd wrapped in a blanket move slowly across a field; on the road a mule cart with a peasant and his wife pass by. And, July or not, it is raining; steady, almost Irish rain, releasing from

to Santo Domingo de la Calzada. "Saint Dominic of the Road" was an enterprising and public-spirited man who, in the eleventh century, built a comfortable stopping place for the weary pilgrims, complete with a paved road, a bridge, an inn and a hospital. He was also credited, less convincingly, with clearing whole oak woods with a magic sickle.

The hospital is now a Parador but the cathedral, built in the twelfth century, remains relatively unchanged. It is worth climbing to the top of the tower, which has eight bells and a 200-year-old clock that functions with stone weights, for a splendid view over the Ebro valley. One of the greatest curiosities in all Christendom can be seen in the cathedral. A live cock and hen are kept in an ornate cage not far from Santo Domingo's tomb. The story that had great currency, as well as great credence, in medieval Europe goes as follows. A young pilgrim rejected the advances of a local girl who, in revenge, had him unjustly accused of theft. He was summarily tried and hanged. His parents, having completed their pilgrimage — a death in the family in those days apparently did not break a serious pilgrim's stride — were astonished and delighted to find their son miraculously alive on the gibbet when they returned to the town. They rushed to inform the judge who was sitting down to dinner. Their son, he said emphatically, was as dead as the two roast fowl on the plate in front of him awaiting his attention. The words were hardly out of his mouth when the two birds leapt up and flew out of the window. Since then a live cock and a hen have been kept in the cathedral. They are killed and replaced every year, and it is supposed

The royal court of Castilla moved from León to Burgos in 1037, and the exploits of El Cid, principally as a scourge of the Moors, unrolled during the latter part of that century. ("Cid" comes from the Arabic "Sidi," meaning master or leader.) The basis of much of his reputation is contained in an epic poem, *Cantar del Mío Cid*, written about him 100 years later. In the nature of these medieval sagas, there was much exaggeration, further propagated centuries later by a Hollywood film of the Spanish hero. Nevertheless El Cid seemed to be a pretty redoubtable fellow. He is greatly revered by the people of Burgos, and his body is buried, along with that of his wife, in a marble tomb in the *coro* (choir) of the cathedral.

to bring good fortune to pluck a feather from one and wear it in your hat.

Santo Domingo de la Calzada is 40 km (25 miles) west of Logroño, off the N-120 Burgos road.

BURGOS

The cradle of the Castilian Kingdom, Burgos is an elegant, manageable city packaged in coils of narrow streets, passageways and squares around a superb Gothic cathedral. It has a fine river frontage, and the transition from countryside to the unspoiled heart of the city is pleasantly rapid. Burgos grew up as a frontier fortress against the Moors in the ninth century. It gained in importance as time went on due to its location, its thriving Merino wool trade and the exploits of its favorite son, Rodrigo Díaz de Vivar — more commonly known as El Cid.

Burgos remained the capital of Castilla for 400 years — before ceding the privilege first to Valladolid and later to Toledo. Confronted with a declining wool trade and missing out on much of the wealth of the New World — and with no new hero to keep its name on history's map — the city declined gracefully. Burgos returned to prominence during the Spanish Civil War, when Franco made it his headquarters from which to pursue his crusade against the less staunchly Nationalist parts of the country.

Nowhere in Burgos is far from the cathedral or the river, so sightseeing is both easy and pleasurable. There is good eating in town too, with a rich choice of bars, cafés and restaurants. The cathedral's lacy gray limestone towers and spires

OPPOSITE: Traditional houses in Haro, La Rioja. ABOVE: A bridge over the Río Arga in Spain's most famous wine-growing region, the Rioja.

dominate the center of the city, and it is so centrally situated that the main door is closed to deter the populace from using the building as a convenient covered walkway.

GENERAL INFORMATION

The old quarter of Burgos is to the north of the Río Arlanzón, which cuts through the center of the town. Apart from being a major attraction in itself, Burgos' cathedral is also a great navigational aid. The **Tourist Information Office (** 947 203125, Plaza de Alonso Martínez 7, open Monday to Friday 9 AM to 2 PM and 5 PM to 7 PM, weekends 10 AM to 2 PM and 5 PM to 8 PM, is a few

minutes' walk northeast from the cathedral. Taxi companies include **Abutaxi (** 947 277777 and **Radio Taxi (** 947 481010. Internet access is available at **Ciber-Café**, Calle Puebla 21, daily 4 PM to 2 PM, among others.

WHAT TO SEE AND DO

Burgos cathedral (947 204712, Plaza Rey San Fernando, open daily 9:30 AM to 1 PM and 5 PM to 9 PM (although it is closed to tourists Sunday morning and during services), €2.50, ranks with Spain's greatest Gothic creations, along with the cathedrals of León, Toledo and Sevilla. Its cornerstone was laid in 1221 but the edifice was not completed until the fifteenth century. It is a huge place but the overall sense is of light, if not lightness, and artistry.

The side chapels are as striking as the central portion by the building and there are a number of beautiful as well as bizarre things to see. The **Golden Stair** of the master carver, Gil de Siloé; the inlaid walnut choir; the **Santa Ana** chapel; the octagonal chapel of the High Constable of Castilla with its star-vaulting; and the raised **Puerta Alta de la Coronería** — the best spot to view the forest of towers and spires — all fall into the first category. Light relief is provided by the

thirteenth-century Christ-figure, made of animal skin, human hair and fingernails and dressed in a red skirt — said to be warm to the touch — in the glass-fronted **Capilla del Santo Cristo**, and the fifteenth-century clock across the nave known as the **Papamoscas** ("fly-catcher"), where a devil-like figure strikes a device that sets the clock tower bell booming on the hour.

The military architecture that characterized the early life of the city can still be seen in the old quarter. Four towers, five out of the eight original gateways and a few stretches of the thirteenth-century walls survive. The fourteenth-century **Arco de Santa María** is the most striking gate: it is embellished by impressive statues of El Cid and the Emperor Carlos V.

Down by the Río Arlanzón there is the **Paseo del Espolón**, a wide avenue reserved for pedestrians that is lined with palms, elms, chestnut trees and sculpted yews. There is a bandstand, a large open-air café and a riot of rosebushes. Through the willows that line the riverbank you can catch a glimpse of waving fields of wheat in the Castilian countryside. Somebody with skill and taste has organized the night illuminations of Burgos. For that and many other reasons, try to avoid the habit of many visitors who stop only briefly in the city. Should you decide to stay overnight, you will eat well, rest well and see a great Gothic masterpiece afloat in the night sky.

WHERE TO STAY AND EAT

Finding budget rooms here can be difficult, but there is not usually a problem higher up the scale. The greatest place to stay here is not in town, however: the **Landa Palace (** 947 206343 FAX 947 264676, Carretera N-1 km235, (very expensive) is just outside on the Madrid road. It has lovely rooms and a swimming pool; part of the hotel is a medieval tower and the furnishings include many antique pieces.

In town, the place to stay is the **Mesón del Cid (** 947 208715 FAX 947 269460, Plaza Santa María 8 (moderate), facing the cathedral, which has guest parking. All rooms are individually furnished, with no. 302 being the best. The **Almirante Bonifaz (** 947 206943 FAX 947 202919, Calle Vitoria 22–24 (moderate), is right in the center of town. The **Hotel Norte y Londres (** 947 264125 FAX 947 277375, Plaza Alonso Martínez 10 (inexpensive), is another centrally positioned hotel, with small, clean rooms; it is old-fashioned with plenty of creaking polished wood. The **España (** 947 206340 FAX 947 201330 is on Paseo de Espolón at no. 32 (inexpensive). On a budget, the **Pensión Peña (** 947 206323, Calle Puebla 18 (very inexpensive), has good, clean rooms in a central location.

Burgos has an abundance of good eating places. In the expensive range the top spot is definitely the restaurant within the **Landa Palace**. In town a good meal at a more moderate price can be had at the **Mesón del Cid** (947 205971, Plaza Santa Maróa 8, which is just opposite the cathedral in a medieval building.

Other moderately priced restaurants to try are **Los Chapiteles** (947 205998, Calle General Santocildés 7 and **Casa Ojeda** (947 209052, Calle Vitoria 5, which has a good *tapas* bar in addition to its regular restaurant service.

HOW TO GET THERE

Burgos is 238 km (149 miles) due north of Madrid, 122 km (76 miles) west of Logroño, and 182 km

SANTO DOMINGO DE SILOS

The monastery of Santo Domingo de Silos (947 390049 (open 10 AM to 1 PM and 4:30 PM to 6 PM, closed mornings on Monday, Sunday and holidays, €1.25) was founded in the tenth century and rebuilt in the eleventh after having been sacked by Al-Mansur Abu Jafar, the Moorish counterpart of El Cid. A monk called Domingo, later canonized, was responsible for the rebuilding. The church was replaced in the eighteenth century, but the twelfth-century cloister survives, a testament to the simplicity and beauty of the Romanesque style. It is a double cloister, the arcades and capi-

(114 miles) east of León. If you're walking the pilgrim's way to Santiago, you've got 515 km (322 miles) to go.

The **bus station** is at Calle Miranda 4, south of the river, while the **train station** (947 203560 is nearby at Avenida Conde Guadalhorre.

EXCURSIONS FROM BURGOS

After Burgos, the pilgrims' way leads west to León, but there is a detour to the south, to the monastery of Santo Domingo de Silos, that is worth making. Part of the pleasure is the country road, which in summer is bordered by fields of swaying grain studded with red poppies, purple lavender, pink thistles and blue cornflowers. Small farming towns, like Covarrubias, with their timbered houses, moldering castles and sleepy churches, break up the journey.

tals made of a soft yellow sandstone, with a painted wooden ceiling and pebble patterned floors. It embraces a rose garden in which there is a fountain and a single tall cypress tree.

A small community of Benedictine monks lives in the monastery, which accepts lodgers. The visitors can take part, if they wish, in the monastery's religious services, and men can stay, ridiculously cheaply, in small cell-like rooms that are austere but not uncomfortable, though one-night stands are not encouraged. Contact the Padre Hospedería (947 380768 for further details. The monks are famous for their performance of Gregorian chants, one of the reasons that outsiders are drawn to spend time in this tranquil corner of Spain.

OPPOSITE: One of the city's medieval gates, Burgos. ABOVE: The double-storied cloister at the monastery of Santo Domingo de Silos, a classic example of Romanesque style.

Conventional accommodation includes the **Hotel Tres Coronas de Silos (** 947 390047 FAX 947 390065, Plaza Mayor 6 (inexpensive), on the main square, or near the cloister entrance in the **Hotel Arco de San Juan (** 947 390074 FAX 947 390074, Pradera de San Juan 1 (inexpensive).

Santo Domingo de Silos is off the N-234 Soria road, 50 km (31 miles) southeast of Burgos.

LEÓN

León was a favorite stopping-place for the Santiago pilgrims. It was a hospitable, civilized city that offered unusually lavish accommodation, and it set them on the last leg of their journey. León's symbol is a lion: the city's origins are Roman and the name comes from the Seventh Legion. After an Arab occupation it became the Visigothic capital of Astur-León, ruling over modern Asturias to the north as well as the kingdom of León itself. León succumbed to another Moorish visitation, this time a thorough sacking, before reaching its heyday in the tenth and eleventh centuries; after which its power was eclipsed by Burgos and its former junior partner, the kingdom of Castilla.

GENERAL INFORMATION

The **Tourist Information Office (** 987 237082, Plaza de la Regla 3, is open Monday to Friday 9 AM to 2 PM and 5 PM to 7 PM, weekends 10 AM to 2 PM and 5 PM to 8 PM. Motorists will have trouble finding this as it is in the pedestrian old town: best to use one of the parking lots under the Plaza de Santo Domingo.

Radio-Taxi León (987 261415 and **Taxi Trabajo Villaquilambe (** 947 285355 can provide transportation around town, while Internet addicts can get connected at **Locutorio Telefónica**, Calle La Rua 8, Monday to Saturday 9:30 AM to 2:30 PM and 4:40 PM to 9 PM.

WHAT TO SEE AND DO

León has three major architectural attractions, the last of which you can eat, drink and sleep in. The first is the magnificent Gothic **cathedral (** 947 204712, Plaza de la Regla, open 9:30 AM to 1:30 PM and 4 PM to 7 PM, closed Sundays and holidays, generally thought to be the one of the finest in Spain. The difference between this cathedral and all the others of its kind is that it was built relatively rapidly — in less than 100 years in the twelfth and thirteenth centuries — and as a result has a completeness and a unity that the others lack. Its medieval creators also seemed to have reached the zenith of their ambition and confidence as they piled stone upon stone, exuberantly filling the walls with rich and expansive stained-glass windows.

The moment you step inside León cathedral, the idea that Spanish churches are heavy and gloomy is swept away by the countless shafts of light from all angles which illuminate the whole structure with an incandescent glow. The *coro* (choir), in the center of the nave, is open with a glass frontage so that there is a clear view from the entrance all the way to the altar. Huge rose windows at either end of the nave, the delicacy of the supporting columns, the fine vaulting and above all the dancing multicolored light splashed around the interior by the 125 stained-glass windows create an unmatched feeling of lightness and beauty. The cathedral is worth visiting at different times of day to view changes in light and mood as the sun moves on its axis. Entry to the cathedral is free, but to enter the cloisters for a guided tour, and to see the attached Diocesan Museum the fee is €3.

The second attraction is the church of **San Isidoro** (open all day) and the **Colegiata de San Isidoro** (987 229608, Avenida de Ramón y Cajal, which is open daily 10:30 AM to 1:30 PM and 4 PM to 6:30 PM, closed Sunday, €2.40. This fine Romanesque church was founded by Ferdinand I who united the kingdoms of León and Castilla in the eleventh century. Originally a reliquary for the remains of San Isidoro, the church became a pantheon for the king, who was the first to use the title "King of the Spains," and for his successors. What makes the church unique, however, are its splendidly preserved twelfth-century frescoes depicting daily life through the seasons in those far-off times. There is also a fine collection of illuminated manuscripts, altar ornaments and other religious artifacts in the church's treasury.

The last delight that León has to offer is the **Monasterío de San Marcos**, Plaza San Marcos 7,

now a Parador and a memorable place to spend a night. It was built in the twelfth century expressly to house pilgrims, free of charge, as they prepared themselves for the final stretch of the journey to Santiago de Compostela. Not a lot has changed except the addition of a plateresque façade in the early sixteenth century, and the fact that a night's lodging is no longer on the house. There is a church attached to the monastery and, with a drink in your hand, you can wander around the upper level of the cloister and view the proceedings through a glass partition. In a quiet moment it is easy to conjure up the chant of monks, the rustle of the nuns' skirts on a curving stone staircase and the smell of incense, as well as the silence of centuries.

The Monasterío de San Marcos in León, built in the twelfth century for pilgrims, is now a spectacular Parador.

WHERE TO STAY AND EAT

The best place to stay here — and perhaps in Spain — is the **Hotel de San Marcos** (987 237300 FAX 987 233458 E-MAIL leon@parador.es, Plaza San Marcos 7 (very expensive), a splendid Parador converted from a twelfth-century monastery. If you can't afford to stay here, at least make time for a drink or a meal, as it is in itself one of León's great sights. With an attractive garden and its own swimming pool, the **Conde Luna** (987 206600, Calle Independencia 7 (expensive), is the main alternative in this price bracket.

At a more moderate price, the **Paris** (987 238600 FAX 987 271572, Calle Ancha 18 (moderate), is a beautiful hotel, set in a refurbished former palace close to the city. **La Posada Regia** (987 213173 FAX 987 213031, Calle General Mola 9-11 (moderate), is a newly opened hotel in the center of town, incorporated into a building dating back to 1370, with parts of an old Roman wall still visible in the dining room. The **Quindós** (987 236200 (moderate) is on Avenida José Antonio 24.

The best budget place is **Hostal Bayón** (987 231446, Calle Alcázar de Toledo 6 (inexpensive), but its five rooms are often booked out — in which case try the **Pensión Puerta del Sol** (987 211966, Calle Puerta del Sol 1, overlooking the Plaza Mayor.

When it comes to dining, León has plenty of reasonably priced restaurants. The local specialty is garlic soup, while fresh trout and salmon feature on many menus.

Two good ones to go to are **Casa Pozo** (987 223039, on Plaza San Marcelo 15, and **Patricio** (987 241651, on Calle Condesa de Sagasta 24. However, if you haven't found an excuse to visit the Hotel de San Marcos, a fine meal can be had in its **Rey Don Sancho** restaurant.

How to Get There

León is 339 km (212 miles) northwest of Madrid and 182 km (114 miles) east of Burgos. For pilgrims, 334 km (209 miles) remain before Santiago de Compostela. The main **railway station** (987 223704, Calle Astorga, and the **bus station** (987 211000, Paseo del Ingeniero Saez de Miera, are to the east of the town center, across the Río Bernesga.

SANTIAGO DE COMPOSTELA

It is hard to imagine a cathedral city, a provincial capital and a thriving university town of over 100,000 people that owes its origins and its development solely to an improbable legend little more than a thousand years old. But that is what happened, and the result is a unique and peculiarly Spanish phenomenon blending myth, superstition, religious imperialism, nationalism and civic pride.

The story runs as follows. In AD 813 the locals were attracted to a meadow by a powerful supernatural light, turning it into a *campus stellae*, a "field of stars." Here they found the remains of Saint James the Apostle. A shrine, and later a cathedral, were built. What was he doing in a damp corner of Galicia? Well, he had apparently done some evangelical work in Spain after the death of Christ and then returned to Jerusalem, where he died a martyr's death at the hand of King Herod in AD 44.

Guided, it is said, by an angel, James's body was smuggled back to Spain in a marble boat by his followers. During the voyage, the apostle's remains performed a miracle by saving a man,

carried out to sea by a frightened horse, from drowning. Man and horse were covered with scallop shells, which were to become the symbol of the apostle, his legend, and the pilgrimage. (The fame of the emblem spread: large scallops are known as *coquilles Saint Jacques* in French and "cockle shells" feature in the anti-Popish nursery rhyme about Mary Tudor of England, "Mary, Mary Quite Contrary.")

None of this has any historical backing. More to the point, though, was the need, in ninth-century Christendom in general and in ninth-century Spain in particular, for some supernatural spine-stiffening in the bitter struggle against the Moors. Thus Saint James was depicted not only as an

OPPOSITE: A plumed functionary during the height of the pilgrimage at Santiago de Compostela.
ABOVE: The façade of the cathedral in Santiago de Compostela.

apostle, saint, and traveler, but as a fearless soldier notably adept at smiting the Muslim invader. At the battle of Clavijo in 844, for instance, not long after his remains were discovered, Saint James miraculously appeared in person on a white stallion and led the Christians to victory. He became known as Santiago Matamoros, Saint James the Moor-Slayer. This was the Christian answer to the Moor who, in turn, had his morale protected by the Prophet Mohammed's arm, kept at the time in the mosque in Córdoba.

For whatever reason, a symbol was needed to breathe courage into the Spanish soldiery, and wonder into Christian minds the length and breadth of Christian Europe. By the tenth and

eleventh centuries, it is estimated that more than half a million pilgrims a year were visiting Santiago: a tradition was born.

The myth gathered strength as time went on. Kings, popes and powerful monastic orders approved and provided patronage; Santiago became the patron saint of Spain; and the pilgrims, dressed in their flowing cloaks and wide-brimmed hats festooned with scallop shells, began to tramp the long dusty El Camino de Santiago (the Road of Saint James). In a very short time, Santiago de Compostela had joined Jerusalem and Rome as one of Christendom's holy cities, the Christian Mecca of Western Europe. And with its mellow golden granite buildings and pedestrian town center, it continues to exert a mythical appeal on a new generation of pilgrims. The whole central area has been declared a Unesco World Heritage Site, and little wonder.

GENERAL INFORMATION

The city is well accustomed to receiving visitors, even if many are stage-carrying, shell-wearing pilgrims. The center is pedestrian-only, so if arriving by car the first thing to do is to find an underground parking lot, with the most convenient being at the Plaza de Galicia, underneath one of the town's tourist information offices; or dump your wheels at your hotel. There are more than one **Tourist Information Office**, in the old streets of the city center at (981 584081, Rúa del Villar 43, opposite the cathedral on Praza do Obradoiro in the *Ayuntimiento*, and on the Praza de Galicia (981 584400. Opening hours are Monday to Friday 10 AM to 2 PM and 4 PM to 7 PM, Saturday 11 AM to 2 PM and 5 PM to 7 PM, Sunday 11 AM to 2 PM.

For taxis, call the rank at **Praza Roxa** (981 595964, and for Internet access **Ciber Novasco**, Rúa Nova 50, is open daily 10 AM to 1 PM. The **Cruz Roja** (981 586969 will take you, if required, to the **Hospital Dr Ramon Baltar** (981 540500 or to the **public hospital** (981 540000.

The best time to be here is on or around the **Festival of Saint James** on the July 25 (see below), but the town also explodes into lavish festivities through **Holy Week** and on the **Ascension**.

WHAT TO SEE AND DO

The city manages to support the weight of this great myth and reward the devotion of the millions who have made such an effort to pay homage in person. Entering from the green Galician countryside, you reach the heart of Santiago in a matter of minutes. The cathedral square, **Praza do Obradoiro**, is one of the great public spaces of Spain, a vast but finely proportioned square that gives pride of place to the cathedral itself but neither denigrates nor diminishes the other grand buildings that flank it.

Opposite the cathedral is the **Pazo de Raxoi** (Palacio de Rajoy), a stately eighteenth-century building that houses the Town Hall and the seat of the Galician Regional Government (and a tourist information office). Also opposite the cathedral stands the **Pazo de Xelmírez** (Palacio de Gelmírez) (981 572300, open Tuesday to Sunday 10 AM to 1:30 PM and 4 PM to 7:30 PM, €1.20, which was erected in the twelfth and thirteenth centuries by two archbishops. On the south side of the square stands the seventeenth-century **Colegio de San Jerónimo** while the north side is dominated by the **Hotel dos Reies Católicos** which was built by Ferdinand and Isabella for the pilgrims at the end of the fifteenth century and is now an unusual and luxurious hotel.

ABOVE: A Galician bagpiper. OPPOSITE TOP: High mass in the cathedral. BOTTOM: Galician dancers.

Today the cathedral is both a shrine and a church. Surmounted by two great towers, the façade on the square is an eighteenth-century baroque creation. The body of the cathedral, however, is Romanesque.

The best way to enter it is through the **Pórtico de la Gloria**, the work of the master medieval carver, Mateo, who managed to sculpt more than 200 figures on the doorway. At the foot of the central column there are five well-worn finger-holds where pilgrims have for centuries placed a hand while steadying themselves to lean down and bump their foreheads against the smooth stone pate of Maestro Mateo himself. The idea, it seems, is that some of his talent will rub off.

Another line of pilgrims shuffles slowly forwards to the steps behind the altar that lead up to the statue of Saint James. One by one the pilgrims file by, touching, kissing or embracing the saint's bronze garments. The south door, the **Puerta de las Platerías** is also Romanesque, and the interior of the cathedral is a treasure trove of religious paintings, statuary, carving, ancient fabrics and relics. During the height of the pilgrimage, priests hear confessions in half a dozen languages, there is a pungent smell of wax and incense and a constant movement of people.

The central core of Santiago seemed to stop developing after the baroque period, and is a delight to wander in. The prevailing stone is granite, but it is not a somber granite. There are many golden moments as the sun touches the walls of the cathedral and other buildings, with green and copper grace notes from the lichen, moss and ivy that cover so many walls, and cheerful splashes of red from the tiled roofs.

CELEBRATION OF THE LEGEND

Saint James's day is celebrated on July 25, and as the climax of the pilgrimage approaches, the city's program of entertainment picks up steam. There are concerts of folk music and dancing in the smaller squares around the cathedral, competitions for Galician bagpipers, a spectacular evening opera production in the Plaza do Obradoiro that can be watched after dinner from a balcony of the Hotel dos Reies Católicos, a greasy pole for young bloods to climb and win a prize, more "giants" and "fat-heads" and a military parade. The final event on the eve of the saint's day is a huge firework display and the symbolic burning of a Moorish façade, made of painted wood, in front of the cathedral.

A solemn mass in honor of Santiago marks the climax of the pilgrimage. In the cathedral an eager crowd moves down the aisles towards the high altar. Two jolly Spanish nuns whisper excitedly to each other as they mingle with the tourists and pilgrims. An old woman kneels in front of a statue of Saint James on horseback, sword raised and a Moor's decapitated head at his feet. (This object will later be carried around the cathedral in procession.) A priest leans out of his confessional and blinks as the crowd becomes denser and denser and the pace slows. Thousands of candles are augmented by the glare of lights for the television cameras that are now in place near the choir stalls. The organ booms forth and the *botafumeiro* begins its slow trajectory in the cross-way behind the altar. Suspended from pulleys and ropes, the *botafumeiro* is the world's largest censer or thurible. Made in 1602, it weighs 53.6 kg (118 lbs), and needs eight sturdy men to swing it.

Pulling harder and harder, the team make it move in ever-widening arcs over the heads of the congregation. As the censer cuts through the air it spews out sparks and clouds of fragrant smoke, and draws great gasps of delight mingled with fear from the people beneath it. There is a story that once when Catherine of Aragón was attending mass, the censer parted company with its moorings and crashed through a window. Otherwise, the mass, which is attended by a veritable army of lay and clerical dignitaries and is nationally televised, continues. Afterwards, the crowd streams outside into the Plaza do Obradoiro where a band is playing paso dobles in the sunshine.

WHERE TO STAY

By far the best place to stay here is in the **Hotel dos Reies Católicos** (981 582200 FAX 981 563094, Praza do Obradoiro 1 (expensive), a superb lodging (now a Parador) built by the Catholic Monarchs for the pilgrims at the end of the sixteenth century. One of the oldest hotels in the world, it shares the square with the cathedral. A comfortable hotel, though with slightly less atmosphere, is the **Araguanay** (981 595900, Alfredo Brañas 5 (expensive).

Santiago's moderately priced answer to its famous Parador is the **Hostal Hogar San Francisco** (981 572564 FAX 981 571916, Campillo del Convento

San Francisco 3 (inexpensive to moderate), an old monastery near the cathedral. Single rooms, once monk's cells, are small, but the reflective peace of this very impressive building makes this one of Spain's greatest accommodation bargains. Other, less dramatic, choices in the moderate category include **Compostela** (981 585700, General Franco 1; **Peregrino** (981 591850, Avenida de Rosalía de Castro; and **Gelmirez** (981 561100, General Franco 92.

WHERE TO EAT

The need to eat is a good excuse to gain access into either of Santiago's two most exciting period

NIGHTLIFE

Santiago by night is a lively city, perhaps thanks more to the presence of many students than the smattering of distinctively clothed pilgrims. You won't have to walk too far around the old city before finding something happening.

There are frequently displays of classical ballet at the **Teatro Principal** (981 586521, Rúa Nova 21, and traditional Galician folk music playing live most nights at the **Casa das Crechas**, Via Sacra 3. There's scope for heavy drinking too: when the Paris-Dakar race passes through, the tradition is that they start at the **Bar Paris** at one end of Rúa

hotels. Thus, for an expensive meal, head for the great vaulted dining room beneath the **Hotel dos Reies Católicos** (981 582200, Praza do Obradoiro 1, supported by hand-cut granite arches; they serve reliably excellent food and wine. Simpler and inexpensive local fare can be enjoyed in the vaulted refectory of the **Hostal Hogar San Francisco** (981 572564, Campillo del Convento San Francisco 3.

Other recommended and moderately priced restaurants in Santiago include **Don Gaiferos** (981 583894, Rúa Nova 23, with a sophisticated ambience and good range of dishes, including many Galician specialties, and the **Anexo Vilas** (981 598387, Vilagarcia 21, which is the city's oldest restaurant and serves good Galician cuisine. **Fornos** (981 565721 is located on Franco 24, and **Las Huertas** (981 561979 on Huertas 16 — it serves good Basque food.

do Franco and take a drink at each of the 48 bars to the other end, finishing at the **Bar Dakar** on Rúa de Riaña.

HOW TO GET THERE

Santiago de Compostela is 619 km (387 miles) northwest of Madrid and 334 km (209 miles) west of León. The **railway station** (981 580202, Avenida de Lugos, is conveniently close to the town center, with the **bus station** (981 587700, Anxel Casal, one and a half kilometers (about one mile) to the northeast. **Aeropeurto Internacional de Lavacolla** (981 547500 is 13 km (eight miles) east of town on the road to Lugo.

OPPOSITE: A scene from the folk festival at the climax of the pilgrimage. ABOVE: The vaulted dining room in the Hotel dos Reies Católicos, Santiago de Compostela.

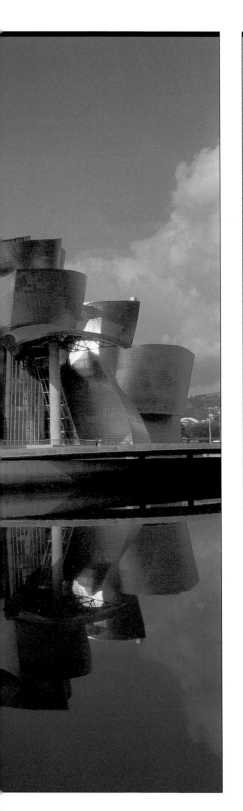

The Northern Coast

After the drama of Santiago, a journey along Spain's northern coastline is a soothing experience. It also has the merit of providing a sampling of three of the country's most distinctive areas: the Basque Country and the regions of Galicia and Asturias. It would be wise to set aside a barest minimum of three days for this trip. The distances are not great but there is a lot to see and the roads tend to be slow.

GALICIA

Galicia has been compared to Ireland and Brittany because of its isolation, its physical appearance, and its Celtic roots and temperament. Shut in by mountains in the northwest corner of Spain with Portugal to the south and the Atlantic Ocean to the north and west, Galicia was off history's beaten track. The Romans called its westernmost point Finisterre, Land's End.

It is a well-watered green land with a rocky coastline spliced by deep *rías*, or fjord-like estuaries with sandy beaches, and covered with tiny fields

and gardens separated by granite walls. Along the coast there are countless fishing villages whose reason for being remains the harvest of the sea, for which Galicia is famous, and not the tourist trade. Inland the scenery is essentially rural and timeless. Galicia has few large towns and farming is still primitive, mainly because the parcels of land are so small and scattered. Horse and ox-drawn carts, and women with baskets — and men with small haystacks — on their heads trudging along country lanes are common; cows, sheep, goats and conical hayricks adorn the patchwork meadows and old-fashioned farmyards full of chickens, ducks and geese look — and smell — like old-fashioned farmyards. Galician farms also have distinctive granaries *(horreos)* that are built on stilts to protect the grain from rats and other rodents. Like much else in Galicia, the *horreos* are made out of granite and have red-tiled roofs and usually a cross at either end. In the more remote and mountainous parts of the region, shepherds still use ancient *pallozas*, circular stone huts with conical thatched roofs that have Celtic origins.

The Celts arrived about 1,000 BC and were unchallenged until the Romans invaded some 900 years later and called the locals "Gallaeci," leaving the place a name. The Suebi, from northern Europe, came next and were followed by the Visigoths. Unlike the rest of Spain, the Moors made little impact, and thereafter Galicia was left largely to its own devices, even though it was incorporated into the Spanish state in the late fifteenth century.

The local language, Gallego, is widely spoken and is closer to Portuguese than Castilian Spanish; the region is renowned for its poetry and its folk music, notably its bagpipes (*gaita*). Galicia is also well-known for its cuisine and vies with Basque cooking for the accolade of being the best in Spain. In most of the Galician ports along the *rías* there are colorful fish auctions every morning, except Sundays and public holidays, and the quality of the region's seafood — especially its sardines, sea scallops and mussels — is exceptional. Somewhat surprisingly, given its wet, cool climate, Galicia produces good white or "green" wines (similar to Portugal's *vinhos verdes*), the best being Ribero, Albarino and Condado.

Apart from Santiago, Galicia is not noted for its cities, but some of the coastal towns are worth driving through and stopping for a brief visit. In the lower estuaries of the Galician coast (Las Rías Bajas) there is Pontevedra, a pretty place of flagstoned alleys and colonnaded squares, and the road on south to Portugal. In the north (Las Rías Altas), there is A Coruña, another port and the largest industrial city of Galicia. Inland, there is Lugo, just off the Santiago pilgrims' route but well worth a detour.

PONTEVEDRA

When, in the seventeenth century, the Lérez Delta silted up, it preserved an ancient and important port, key in Spain's discovery of the secrets of navigation and the New World. Once a busy port that was home to seafarers and explorers, including the important navigator Pedro Sarmiento, sixteenth-century author of *Voyage to the Magellan Straits*. It is claimed that one of Columbus's ships sailed from here, and even that the explorer himself was born in the town. These days the port's importance is much reduced, but no matter, it is still a charming town, perfectly preserved, with a lively atmosphere.

The **Tourist Information Office** (986 850814, Rúa Xeneral Guuiterrez Mellado 3, open Monday to Friday 9:30 AM to 2 PM and 4:30 PM to 6:30 PM, Saturday 10 AM to 12:30 PM. The town's main church is **San Francisco**, on the Praza de Ferreria, a tranquil place of rose trees and arcades, and a few small alleys lead through to the **Praza de Leña**, where the postcard photos are taken, with classic

granite columns. This is where you'll find the town's **Museo Provincial**, open Tuesday to Saturday 10 AM to 2:15 PM and 5 PM to 8:45 PM, Sunday 11 AM to 2 PM, set in two converted mansions, with some notable artworks including a room dedicated to the leading twentieth-century writer and artist Alfonso Castelao, unofficial patron saint of the Galician nationalists. Admission is free, but for some reason identification is required to enter. Continue past the fascinating two-story market building to the **Praza de España** and an imposing promenade down to the sea.

Where to Stay and Eat

The most atmospheric and luxurious place to stay here is in the **Parador de Pontevedra** (986 855800 FAX 986 852195 E-MAIL pontevedra@parador.es, Barrón 19 (expensive), set in a palace formerly occupied by the Counts of Maceda. It is right in the middle of the town, and its rooms and public areas are classically furnished in the style of the era. The next best is the **Hotel Rúas** (986 846416 (986 846411, Sarmiento 37 (inexpensive), a dignified hotel in a period building, right next to the Museo Provincial. Either of these places can be an excellent choice for a formal meal. On a budget, try the **Casa Alicia** (986 857079, Santa María 5 (inexpensive). The town is better for *tapas* than for sit-down meals: **O Melo**, opposite the Casa Alicia, has perhaps the best choice.

How to Get There

Pontevedra is linked by motorway to the main provincial capitals of Galicia. It is 23 km (14 miles) from Vigo, 55 km (34 miles) from Santiago de Compostela and 120 km (75 miles) from A Coruña. Rail and bus stations are one and a half kilometers (one mile) to the southeast of the center.

EXCURSIONS FROM PONTEVEDRA

North of Pontevedra are a number of busy resorts, including Sanxenxo and Portonovo, which rave in summer. There are lots of hotels here, but it's not especially interesting. The way south is guarded by a huge and discouraging paper factory, which can apparently be smelled 40 km (25 miles) away. Persevere: beyond are countless sheltered sandy covers of breathtaking beauty, totally unspoiled, on the way south to the small, and not especially interesting, fishing port of **Vigo**, and then on to Portugal.

A CORUÑA

The port from where the *1588* set sail to invade Britain, only to sink in the Irish Sea, A Coruña has long been at the heart of Spain's military maritime tradition. These days, however, it's just where the fish come in, into a rather attractive harbor with typical Galician houses and glassed-in balconies. Apart from the old town, which is well worth seeing, is the **Torre de Hércules** ("Tower of Hercules") on the northern tip of the peninsula — roughly a 15-minute drive from the city. Galicians proudly claim it as the only Roman lighthouse left in the world, which is half true. The lower portion of the lighthouse is indeed Roman, with the architect's name still legibly inscribed on it. But the upper functional half dates from the late eighteenth century. At least it works. The town-center beaches are perhaps the town's best feature: the **Praia do Riazor** and the **Praia do Orzán** both face north towards the Atlantic Ocean.

There is a **Tourist Information Office** (981 221822, Dársena de la Marina, open Monday to Friday 9 AM to 2:30 PM, Saturday 10:30 AM to 1 PM. There's nowhere brilliant to stay. A huge orange monstrosity on the waterfront, the **Hotel Finisterre** (981 205400 FAX 981 208462, Paseo del Parrote (expensive), has an Olympic-sized swimming pool. Rather more tasteful is the **Hostal Alboran** (981 226579 FAX 981 222562, Rúa Riego de Agua 14 (inexpensive), where some of the rooms have balconies overlooking the busy streets near the Praza María Pita. Eating, here, has got to be fish: there are a line of waterfront restaurants along the Dársena. A Coruña is 64 km (40 miles) north of Santiago de Compostela and 97 km (58 miles) northwest of Lugo on the N-VI. There are rail and bus links to all the major provincial towns.

LUGO

Set in the mountains, Lugo is a beautiful old town that is encircled by its original Roman walls.

The **Tourist Information Office** (982 231261, open Monday to Friday 9:30 AM to 2 PM and 4:30 PM to 6:30 PM, is rather hidden. Look for a small shopping mall off the Plaza España, well inside the pedestrian town center; a motorist's first priority will be to find a parking lot.

The town was built of slate and granite in the third century AD. The walls are the best-preserved Roman walls in Spain, 2.4 km (1.5 miles) in extent, 9.2 m (30 ft) high, and containing four gates and 85 towers. You can see them either by walking around the road that circles them on the outside (approximately 45 minutes), or drive around the (rather disfiguring) loop road in a few minutes. You can also walk along the top; access is at the **Puerta Nueva** and opposite the **cathedral**. The cathedral itself is a much-modified twelfth-century building with three great towers, richly decorated choir-stalls dating from the early seventeenth century, a circular eighteenth-century chapel dedicated to the **Virgen de Ojos Grandes** (Our Lady of the Big Eyes), a baroque cloister, and the rare privilege of having the Host on permanent display.

There's nowhere very good to stay here. The best hotel is the **Hotel Méndez Núñez** (982 230711 FAX 982 229738, Rúa Raina 1 (inexpensive), within the old town walls. To spend less, try the **Alba** (982 226056, Calveo Sotelo 31, of which the best recommendation is that it's inexpensive.

Lugo is 116 km (72.5 miles) east of Santiago de Compostela, 221 km (138 miles) west of León, and 506 km (316 miles) northwest of Madrid on the A6/E70. It is well-connected by rail and bus to the major towns of the province, as well as Madrid and Santander.

ASTURIAS AND CANTABRIA

Asturias is another green upland corner of Spain with few large towns and a fine Atlantic coastline. It is sometimes compared to Wales because of its appearance, its coal and mineral wealth, and the independent spirit of its people. In the same way that the heir to the British throne has traditionally been the "Prince of Wales," so, since the fourteenth century, has the heir to the Spanish throne held the title of Prince of Asturias.

Originally inhabited by a hardy Iberian tribe called the Astures, Asturias underwent Roman and Visigothic domination. The region's moment of glory came much earlier than other comparable parts of Spain. In 718, Christian forces, under a Visigothic warrior called Pelayo, defeated the Moors in a mountain valley at Covadonga, checking Muslim expansion and marking the turning of the tide from which point the *Reconquista* began. In modern times, the Asturians, particularly the miners, established a reputation for defying authority. The region has a tradition of heroic strikes and Asturians fought hard against Franco in the Civil War and paid a heavy price. Fortunately, the remarkable churches and the old city center of the capital, Oviedo, emerged unscathed, and was amongst the first of Spain's older towns to be protected from traffic as part of the national heritage.

Today Asturias is a peaceful and easy-going province that has some of the most spectacular and best preserved countryside in Spain. It is perfect hiking country, with some of Spain's finest examples of Paleolithic dolmens and cave art scattered around unspoiled, and often protected, rural areas. Like its neighbor, Galicia, Asturias is known for its hearty dishes and fresh produce. It makes delicious hams and sausages and produces a tasty blue cheese called *cabrales* which is made from ewe's milk. Its tipple, however, is not wine but apple cider *(sidra)*, a deceptively smooth concoction that disguises a strong alcoholic content.

Asturias and the neighboring region of Cantabria (to the east) share a fine coast where the

lush meadows break off abruptly and give way to clean sandy beaches and small sheltered coves. But the most dramatic gift is the Cantabrian mountain range that separates the azure Atlantic shoreline from the Castilian plateau in the south. It is here that Spain's "Alps" are found, the snow-clad summits and verdant valleys of the Picos de Europa.

East of this, the Cantabrian coast is a blend of a working countryside with holiday-making on the beaches. There is a freshness and wholesome feeling about Spain's northern coast that contrasts favorably with the crowded sun-baked *costas* of the south. But then the sun does not always shine here and there is a heavy annual rainfall that shows no respect for the beach-worshiper's schedule. The main attractions on the Cantabria coast are the city of Santander and the much-photographed Santillana del Mar.

OVIEDO

Flattened in 768 AD by the Moors, today's city of Oviedo dates back to Alfonso II, the Chaste, who moved his kingdom here, built ramparts, palaces and churches, and then moved onwards to León. Since then, Oviedo has struggled on with only limited recognition, protecting its identity with a firmly bourgeois sense of superiority over the rural society that forms the basis of its wealth.

General Information

The principal **Tourist Information Office (** 985 213385, Plaza de Alfonso II, is open Monday to

Friday 9:30 AM to 1:30 PM and 4:30 PM to 7:30 PM, Saturday 9 AM to 2 PM, and there is also a booth at Marqués de Santa Cruz 1, conveniently near a good underground parking lot. For medical attention, **ambulances (** 985 108900 will take you, probably, to the **Hospital Central de Asturias (** 985 106100. **Radio taxis** can be summoned at **(** 985 250000 and **(** 985 252500.

What to See and Do

Oviedo's three churches are the principal draw here, dating back to the early ninth century, built in a unique style developed after the Visigoth era and before the Romanesque style spread from ·France. King Alfonso II's **Cámara Santa**, a shrine built to house relics rescued from Toledo before

OPPOSITE: River-bathing in the Sierra do Alba. ABOVE LEFT: Luarca, a fishing port on Spain's "Costa Verde," Asturias. RIGHT: Picos de Europa.

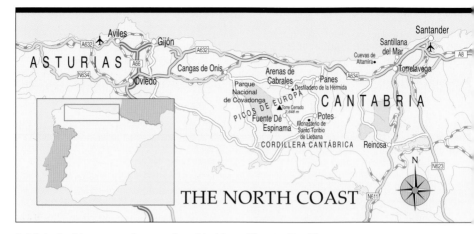

it fell to the Moors, now forms a chapel inside Oviedo's **cathedral** (985 203117, which is open Monday to Saturday 10 AM to 1 PM and 4 PM to 6 PM, €2.40. A 10-minute walk to the northeast is the church of **San Julián de los Prados** (Iglesia de Santullano) (985 282518, Calle de Gijon, which opens winters noon to 1 PM and 4 PM to 5 PM, opening earlier and later in spring and summer, closed Monday, free. It is spacious for its age (more than a thousand years old).

The highlight of Oviedo, and the third of the town's famous churches, is the **Iglesia de Santa María del Naranco** (985 295685, which is open from mid-October to April 10 AM to 1 PM and 3 PM to 5 PM, and the rest of the year from 9:30 AM to 1 PM and 3 PM to 7 PM, entrance is €1.20. Registered by Unesco in 1985, this building is three kilometers (two miles) northwest of the old town center along a clearly marked trail (Monte Naranco), on a grassy knoll with panoramic views over the city. As travel writer Jan Morris put it, it is "formidable beyond its scale," a serene and very beautiful building with open porticos and, thanks to its previous life as a hunting lodge, the signs of earlier baths and staircases. Once there, it is worth walking a few hundred meters further, to King Ramiro's private chapel, San Miguel de Lillo, probably designed by the same architect.

Where to Stay

A seventeenth-century palace is the best place to stay here, in the **Hotel de la Reconquista** (985 241100 FAX 985 241166 WEB SITE www.hoteldela reconquista.com, Gil de Jaz 16 (expensive), overlooking the Parque de San Francisco; or near the cathedral try the **Gran Hotel España** (985 220596 FAX 985 222140, Calle Jovellanos 2 (expensive, moderate on weekends). Less expensive is the **Hotel Favila** (985 253877, Calle de Uria 37 (inexpensive), while backpackers will be happiest at the **Pensión La Armonia** (985 220301, Calle Nueve de Mayo 14 (inexpensive).

How to Get There

Oviedo is 312 km (195 miles) west of Santiago de Compostela, 120 km (75 miles) north of León, and 192 km (120 miles) east of Santander. Road connections south to León and north to Aviles, Gijón and the coast are fast. The connections east are slow, if scenic, and fast roads west are currently in the process of being built. For trains, the **RENFE** (985 250202 and the **FEVE** (985 284096 stations are on Avenida de Santander, with good links east and west, and the **bus station** (985 222422 is on Plaza Prime de Rivera.

PICOS DE EUROPA: SPAIN'S "ALPS"

Running east from Oviedo and behind Santander and Bilbao there are three great mountain systems, or massifs: **Andara** in the east, **Urrieles** in the center, and **Cornion** to the west, collectively known as the **Cordillera Cantábrica**. The highest peak, **Torre Cerrado**, is 2,648 m (8,606 ft). Although for much of the year these mountains are capped in snow, they're better known as hiking country, and most mountain tourist offices open only for the summer season. It is a natural barrier that separates Spain's northern coast from the inland plains, only recently broached, thanks to huge civil engineering projects, by fast highways heading south. Use an *autopista* to traverse the mountains and it will take an hour or so through spectacular valleys and zipping through long, well-lit tunnels. Take a minor road and the same journey will take a day, winding through small villages, a rural Alpine landscape of meadows and woodlands latticed with streams and rivers.

In the heart of these ranges on the green foothills of the Cordillera Cantábrica is the Picos de Europa, protected by a newly declared national park 40 km (25 miles) in diameter. Although not the highest mountains in Spain, the Picos are perhaps the best place to see griffon vultures, kestrels and wall-creepers, amongst other birds. In the

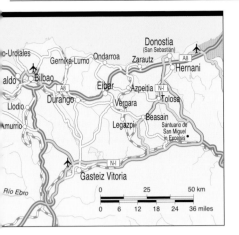

south there are still bears, with about 60 tagged specimens, but generally the only bears you'll see are on tourist-board brochures. Through the summer months, from May to October, climbing, hiking, camping, bird-watching, horseback trekking and excursions by four-wheeled-drive vehicles are on offer.

Activities and accommodation are based around the four major access towns, at Cangas de Onis, Arenas de Cabrales, Panes and, most of all, the mountain town of Potes.

POTES

Potes is one of the best places to obtain maps, supplies and information about guides, itineraries and mountain *refugios* (free, overnight shelters). The **Tourist Information Office** (942 730787, Plaza Jesús del Monasterío, is open from June to September from Monday to Saturday 9 AM to 2 PM and 4 PM to 7 PM. Unfortunately these are the very busiest months, and as long as you don't mind lower-level hikes, spring and autumn can be more enjoyable for trekking. Fortunately, many of the shops here sell good trekking maps (try **Fotos Bustamante** in the main square), and the area's hoteliers are often well informed about routes and trails.

What to See and Do
The easiest way for the casual visitor to get a feel for the Picos is to go from Potes up the **Deva** river valley to **Fuente Dé**. At the end of the road you'll find a cable car up to the summit of the mountain. The car ascends 800 m (860 ft) in a dramatic ride that takes you up over the valley floor and then intimately close to the mountainside. The views can be spectacular, but even in July there is often a cloud over the mountain, especially in early morning and late afternoon, and the car can be enveloped by dense layers of vapor well before it arrives at the snow-covered peak, which

is a good argument for staying near the cable car base station for a night or two and waiting for a break in the weather.

There is a good hike back down to Fuente Dé from the top on a clearly defined path that brings you back to the main road (N-621) at the village of **Espinama**. It is 11 km (6.8 miles) in all with about three kilometers (just under two miles) of that on the road. The walk takes you slowly out of the clouds and snow, through thin swirling mist and into bright sunlight where butterflies dance, the voice of a shepherd calling his dog rises up out of the valley below and kestrels circle overhead. Further down there are cows with bells around their necks, horses with young foals and old men in hilly pastures cutting hay with long-handled scythes. In Espinama, a village that time forgot, smoke curls from tipsy-looking chimneys, and wild flowers sprout from the flagstones.

The Picos also offer history. There is the unusually beautiful tenth-century Mozarabic church of **Santa María** in the town of **Liebana**. The drive up the **Desfiladero de la Hermida** from Potes is slow going, but the spectacular scenery and the church bring their own reward. The church is an architectural historian's delight in that it brings together the solid pre-Romanesque vaulting of the Visigoths with the horseshoe arches and graceful use of space of Islam, all in a unique mountain setting.

Then there is the **Monasterío de Santo Toribio de Liebana**, a pleasant three-kilometer (two-mile) walk from Potes. The original monastery dates from the eighth century but the present building is a later mixture of Romanesque and Gothic. The monastery's reputation is based on the fame of its eighth-century abbot, Beato de Liebana, whose *Commentaries on the Apocalypse* became popular scriptural texts all over Spain in later centuries, and on its claim to possessing the largest fragment of the cross on which Christ died.

Where to Stay
To explore the highland area around Fuente Dé, the best place to stay is the modern Parador, the **Parador de Fuente Dé** ((942) 736651 FAX 942 736654 E-MAIL fuentede@parador.es (expensive). There is also a much less expensive alternative here, which is the **Hotel Rebeco** (/FAX 942 736600, Carretera Fuente Dé (inexpensive). However, the Fuente Dé area can get crowded in the busy summer months. To plan your own walks and hikes, it is perhaps better to stay in the town of Potes itself, where the best place to stay is perhaps the **Casa Cayo** (942 730150 FAX 942 730119, Calle Cántabra 6 (inexpensive), or the more modern (and comfortable) **Picos de Europa** (942 730005 FAX 942 732060, San Roque 6 (inexpensive) on the edge of town on road to Panes, next door to the **Rubio** (942 730015 FAX 942 730405 (inexpensive).

How to Get There

Potes is most quickly reached from the coast road, the N-634 (currently being upgraded to the A-8/E-70 *autopista*), turning south onto N-621 that runs to the town. The town of Potes can also be reached from León 165 km (103 miles) to the southwest, but this will take at least four hours. **Three Palomera** ((942 880611) links Potes with Santander daily, and in the summer, three further buses every day link Potes with Fuente Dé.

SANTANDER

Santander, the capital of Cantabria, is the center of this area and functions as an important freight and ferry terminal, fishing port and tourist attraction in its own right. Overlooking a magnificent bay, Santander has a series of sweeping interlocking beaches easily accessible from the main hotels. Rather like San Sebastián, further east, Santander established a reputation as a fashionable resort where royalty and celebrities from all over Europe spent their summers. Unfortunately, most of the city was burned down in 1941, and despite a great deal of reconstruction it has never really recovered its poise. Some its earlier style is reflected in the northwest suburb of El Sardinero which escaped the conflagration. El Sardinero has two excellent beaches and its elegant boulevards, expensive shops, classy hotels and casino hark back to the belle époque and to the period between the two World Wars, and here, and on the beaches, where the majority of visitors wish to spend most of their time. Many of the accommodation offers here, however.

General Information

The main **Tourist Information Office** (942 310708 WEB SITE www.santandercuidadviva.com, Paseo Pereda, is open summer Monday to Friday 9 AM to 2 PM and 4 PM to 9 PM, winter Monday to Friday 9:30 AM to 1:30 PM and 4 PM to 7 PM, Saturday 10 AM to 1 PM. It is near the waterfront in the reconstructed center of the city and conveniently close to an underground car park. The **Cantabria Tourist Information Office** (942 216120, Plaza de Velarde, daily 9 AM to 1 PM and 4 PM to 7 PM, is at the the hub of the new city center. The rather more atmospheric suburb of El Sardinero with its two-kilometer-long (just over a mile) beach is to the north of the city center, on the other side of the wooded peninsula of La Magdálena, where there is a further tourist information office, open through the summer months, between the beach and the Plaza de Italia. For Taxis, contact **Radio Taxi Santander** (942 333333. Santander's **general hospital** (942 202520 is on Avenida Valdicilla.

What to See and Do

With a rather dull cathedral, and a municipal museum that isn't much better, it's not surprising that

Santander concentrates on its beaches and bars. Heading northeast from the city center, the Playa de la Magdalena is a very popular beach with a windsurfing school. Cross the headland (where a small zoo is housed in the gardens of the **Palacio Real**, a nineteenth-century royal palace) and you'll drop down onto the Playa del Sardinero.

Where to Stay and Eat

In the center of town the **Real** (942 272550 FAX 942 274573, Paseo Pérez Galdós 28 (very expensive), is a stylish top-class hotel near the Playa de la Magdalena with great views of the bay. In El Sardinero the **Hotel Hoyuela** (942 282628 FAX 942 280040, Avenida de los Hoteles 7 (very expensive), is the smartest option, though the nearest you'll get to the belle-époque years is in the **Hotel Sardinero** (942 271100 FAX 942 271698, Plaza de Italia 1 (expensive).

Less expensive options include, in the center, the art deco magnificence of the **Hotel Central** (942 222400 FAX 942 363829, Calle General Mola 5 (moderate), or the **Hostal Carlos III** (/FAX 942 271616, Avenida Reina Victoria 135 (moderate). In Sardinero, you'll find the **Roma** (942 272700, Avenida de los Hoteles 5 (moderate), and the **Hostal Paris** (942 272350 FAX 942 271774, Avenida de los Hoteles 6 (inexpensive). There's nothing really inexpensive here for backpackers, but the **Pensión Gómez** (942 376622, Calle Vargas 57 (inexpensive), is about as good as you'll get.

The best restaurant in town is generally accepted to be the **Canadio** (942 314149, Calle Gomez Orena 15 (expensive), which serves excellent seafood. If your budget won't stretch to it, the *tapas* at the bar are reasonably priced and excellent. The **Bodega Cigalena** (942 213062, Calle Daoiz y Velarde 19 is a good, moderately priced choice with old bottles on every wall. For seafood, head down to the waterfront, where **La Gaviota**, **Las Peñucas** and **Vivero** are lined up on Calle Marquéz de Ensanada, Perto Pesquero, serving cheap sardines and more expensive marine exotica.

How to Get There

Santander is 192 km (120 miles) west of Oviedo along a slow road, currently under improvement, 103 km (64 miles) east of Bilbao along a fast, busy highway, and 391 km (244 miles) due north of Madrid, of which 153 km (96 miles) are slow. The **railway station** is on the Plaza Estaciónes, Calle de Rodríguez, facing an underground **bus station**, with good links along the coast and inland. Santander is an important ferry terminal, with Brittany ferries from Plymouth in the United Kingdom arriving at the **Port Marítima Aucona** (942 227288, at Paseo de Pereda 13. The **Aeropuerto de Santander** (942 202100 is four kilometers (three miles) west of town towards Bilbao.

Santander's popular beaches.

EXCURSIONS FROM SANTANDER

The leading excursions from Santander are west to two places of historic and visual interest: the medieval town of **Santillana del Mar** and the prehistoric caves of **Altamira**.

Considering that Santillana del Mar has to carry the burden of being the "most beautiful village in Spain" and has been declared a national monument, it performs rather well. The time not to see it is when a dozen tourist buses descend, so the answer is an early morning or late afternoon visit or, better still, a stay overnight in the atmospheric Parador or in one of the nearby hotels. The town's

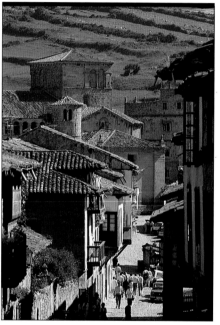

name comes from Saint Juliana, whose remains have been there since the sixth century and are in the church. "Mar" is a bit of a misnomer because the town is just over three kilometers (two miles) from the sea.

Santillana grew up as a prosperous farming community around the monastery dedicated to Saint Juliana, and attracted wealthy noblemen and clergy who built magnificent stone and timbered houses, the twelfth-century Romanesque **collegiate church** with its lovely cloister, and the seventeenth-century **Convento de Regina Coeli**. All this was accomplished in a town with only one street. Its fame spread when the eighteenth-century French satirist, Alain-René Le Sage, made it the home of his picaresque hero, Gil Blas. Local farmers still live in the town with their livestock and sell glasses of fresh milk and homemade cakes to the visitors.

The best place to stay is in the **Parador de Santillana del Mar** (942 818000 FAX 942 818391 Plaza Ramón Pelayo 11 (expensive), in the main square. Some of the building dates back to the eighth century, while most of the guest rooms are in a newly built annex. Other good and atmospheric choices include the **Posada del Organista** (942 840452 and the **Casa del Solana** (942 818106, both on the Calle Los Hornos, two beautiful restored mansions set just above the bustle of the city center, both, remarkably enough, inexpensive. On a real budget, try the **Casa Fernando** (942 818018, on the road towards Altamira (inexpensive), which is good value.

The **Cuevas de Altamira** can be reached on foot from Santillana in 20 minutes or so. At a depth of 270 m (886 ft) these caves are a veritable gallery of vividly colored paintings of the bison, horses, stags and boars hunted by Paleolithic man around 14,000 or 15,000 BC. Sealed for a millennia by a landslide, the paintings were not noticed until more than a decade after their discovery, when the nine-year-old daughter of a speleologist is reputed to have cried, "Papa, look, cows!" They are known as the "Sistine Chapel" of prehistoric art. Unfortunately, human breath was found to cause damage to the paintings, and the caves have now been closed. If you want to get in, apply in writing to the **Museo Altamira** FAX 942 840157, Santillana de Mar, Cantabria — allow three years to receive a permit. There is, however, a museum by the caves which provides a great deal of information and a well-made video of the caves; a nearby cave of stalactites and stalagmites is open to the public.

THE BASQUE COUNTRY

Finally, to the Basque Country. The official territory of the Basques covers the three provinces of Vizcaya, Guipuzcoa and Alava. But Basques also form the majority of the population in northern Navarra and in three provinces in southwestern France, and they call the phenomenon *Euskadi* ("collection of Basques"). They are without doubt the most "different" and the most separatist-minded of all Spain's regional people.

The Basques' origins and history are shrouded in the kind of mist that often envelops their beloved valleys. They are not related in any way to the Celts and come from a pre-Indo-European people. Their fearsomely complex language (Euskara) is believed to go back to the Stone Age and has no links with any European tongue. The Basques sturdily defended themselves against all comers over the centuries. The Romans conquered them but may have regretted it; the Visigoths, Moors and early Christian kingdoms made few inroads, although the Basques did adopt Christianity, embracing it with an ardor that still survives. (Saint Francis Xavier and Saint Ignatius of Loyola were Basques.)

They eventually accepted the rule of Castilla but retained their ancient *fueros* (privileges) and made it a tradition that every monarch who ascended the Spanish throne came to Guerníca, in Vizcaya, and took an oath under the Basques' sacred oak tree to uphold and protect their laws and customs.

Two critical choices in the modern period proved disastrous for the Basques. They supported the losing side in the dynastic Carlist wars of the nineteenth century and, as a result, lost their privileges. The Republican government restored their autonomy in the 1930s and, notwithstanding their strong Catholicism, the Basques remained loyal to the anti-clerical, "Red" side during the Civil War. Franco tried to break their spirit when he sent the

who seem to have chosen the non-violent option for solving their political problems.

It is not surprising that the Basques cling to their culture, which is full of folk-tales about genial giants who lived among them in the pre-Christian period and did marvelous things, and about heroes and acts of valor in a long, turbulent history that was unrecorded. Basques love singing, especially mournful folk-songs, and they love dancing. Their traditional instrument is a three-holed flute, called a *txistu*, which is played with one hand while the other keeps time on a small drum. Their dancing often ranks as a feat of athleticism, notably the Flying Dance *(Bolant Dantza)* and the Sword Dance *(La Espatadantza).*

German Condor Legion into action over Guerníca, modern warfare's first saturation aerial bombardment. The raid was timed for market day and the high-explosive and incendiary bombs virtually leveled the town and killed a third of its population. But the Basques' oak tree and their spirit survived, and Picasso painted his famous portrayal of the attack.

Franco was singularly repressive in the Basque country after the war, a situation that led to the rise of the violent, ultra-nationalist ETA movement. Spain's new democracy has since done much to address the Basques' grievances. The region has more autonomy than any other part of Spain with its own parliament, police force (wearing distinctive red Basque berets), television and radio stations operating in Basque, bilingual schools, and so on. The ETA threat remains, but the organization has lost support with the majority of Basques

The Basques are also great sportspeople, much addicted to lifting — and tossing — weights, and they invented pelota or jai alai, which is played up against two walls with a hard rubber ball hit with the hand or a basket-like racket. Basques have made their mark as Spain's gourmets (and some would add, gourmands) with the variety of their sea-food and sauces, and their love of running restaurants. Cider (*sagardua* in Basque) is the main drink, although a light, tangy white wine called *txakoli* is produced in the north and Basque-produced Riojas come from the south. There is also *pacharán*, a local distilled drink of the fire-water species.

Basques have a reputation for hard work and enterprise. Their seamen roamed the world; a

OPPOSITE: The beautiful village of Santillana del Mar.
ABOVE: The caves at Altamira have been closed, but their paintings can still be seen in faithful replica at the museum next door.

number were explorers, conquistadors and colonists. Capitalizing on their ports, timber, iron ore and other natural resources, the Basques led the Industrial Revolution in Spain. Bilbao, for example, became famous for its ship-building and is the country's sixth largest city. A disproportionate number of Basques are bankers, and Basque banks control a disproportionate amount of the country's financial business. Although the capital of the region, an international port receiving ferries from England, and newly revitalized by a flood of new investment, Bilbao is not where many visitors stay. Far more appealing are the small resort of Castro-Urdiales to the west and the rather larger resort town of Donastia-San Sebastián to the east.

BILBAO

Since the collapse of most of its major industries in the 1980s, Bilbao has staged a dramatic recovery, sparked in part by the building of the new Guggenheim Museum and a brand-new metro system. Despite being such a large city, it doesn't really feel it, comprising a scatter of independent villages still only half-coalesced into a unified whole.

General Information

The main **Tourist Information Office** (944 795760 WEB SITE www.bilbao.net, Parque d'Arenal, Monday to Friday 9 AM to 2 PM and 4 PM to 7:30 PM, Saturday 9 AM to 2 PM, Sunday 10 AM to 2 PM, has a good collection of maps and brochures. Internet access is available from **Milenium**, Avenida Lehendakari Aguirre 36; and **Antxi**, Luis Briñas 13, amongst other places. For medical treatment, call

an **ambulance** (944 100000, which may, perhaps, take you to the **Hospital de Basurto** (944 418700, Avenida de Montevideo 18.

Tele-Taxi (944 102121 and **Radio-Taxi Bilbao** (944 448888 provide taxi services, which can be the easiest option, though for any length of stay it is worth making use of the public transportation network. Although integrating the metro system with the buses is planned, it has not resulted in transferable tickets. The **metro** is flashy and efficient, with city-center tickets costing €0.80 and red-and-white buses taking you further, with tickets costing €0.72. Books of ten tickets, valid on either, costing €6, are the current answer, which can be bought from newsagents, kiosks and metro stations.

What to See and Do

The overwhelmingly beautiful cubic construction of glittering titanium that is the **Guggenheim Museum** (944 359000 WEB SITE www.guggenheim -bilbao.es, together with its unmatched collection of twentieth-century art, is Bilbao's prime attraction. Tickets are valid all day, for the fantastic collection of art that rotates between the other Guggenheim Museums of Venice and New York. There are also visiting exhibitions and a very worthwhile restaurant. All day is not too long to spend here.

There is more to see. The **Casco Viejo**, or old quarter, is where you'll find the **Teatro Arriaga**, the arcaded **Plaza Nueva** and the **Catedral de Santiago**. Apart from all these sights, this is where you'll find most of the best bars and restaurants in the city. There are beaches here as well, with perhaps the most inviting being **Sopelana** on the east bank, easily reached by metro, or **Plentzia** to the north of the city.

Where to Stay and Eat

For an urban taste of luxury, the **Hotel López de Haro** (944 235500 FAX 944 234500 WEB SITE www .hotellopezdeharo.com, Obispo Oruetea 2 (very expensive), is a good five-star option. Slightly less exorbitant is the **Hotel Igeretxe** (944 607000 FAX 944 608599, on Playa Erega, Getxo (expensive), set among the mansions of Bilbao's millionaire belt. Coming down in price, the **Hotel Neguri** (944 910501 FAX 944 911943, Avenida Algorta 14, Getxo (moderate), still offers a full range of facilities at a reasonable price. Less expensive is the **Hotel Arriaga** (944 790001, Calle Ribera 3 (moderate), near the Teatro. Poor adults are recommended to try the **Hostal Gurea** (944 163299, Bidebarrieta 14 (inexpensive), while younger backpackers should ask at the **Pensión Serantes** (944 151557, Calle Somera 14 (inexpensive).

Bilbao is an excellent place for dining, and is perfectly suited for cruising the streets and snacking on *tapas*, with the old quarter being the best place to do it. Calle Santa María and Calle Barrencale Barrena are two streets in the old town where you'll be spoiled for choice. There is plenty of live music, both classical and regional music; check local listings in *El Correo*, the local newspaper. The best venues are the **Teatro Arriaga** (944 163333 and the **Palacio Euskalduna** (944 035000.

How to Get There

Bilbao is 396 km (247 miles) north of Madrid and 103 km (64 miles) east of Santander, with both routes fast. The city is well-connected by rail, with the main **RENFE station** the **Estación de Abando** on the Plaza Circular for long-distance travel, and local services using the **Estación Axuri** on the other side of the river. For FEVE services along the coast, to Santander and beyond, the **Estación de**

The town comes in two parts: the old center, hemming in the fishing port, and the newer section, built around the Playa de Brazomar. The two towns are linked by a glorious esplanade, lined with vendors from Otavalo in Ecuador, selling a range of tourist tat with engaging enthusiasm. The **Tourist Information Office** (942 871542, Monday to Saturday 9 AM to 2 PM and 5 PM to 7 PM, is found on the waterfront of the fishing harbor, with maps, accommodation guides and ideas for exploring the surrounding countryside.

Where to Stay and Eat

The best place to stay here is the hotel **Miramar** (/FAX 942 860204, Avenida de la Playa 1 (inexpensive),

Santander is the one you need. Most buses use the **Termibús station** (944 395077, Metro San Mamés, with provincial services using the **Bizkaiabus station** on Calle Sendeja, near the main tourist office on the Parque del Arenal. The P&O services to Portsmouth in the United Kingdom leave from Santurzi, which is reached by bus and train. The **Aeropuerto de Bilbao** (944 869300 is 20 km (12.5 miles) north of town.

CASTRO-URDIALES

Tourists from the United Kingdom on the 29-hour P&O cruise service from Portsmouth are ferried east to Castro-Urdiales, but they only stay for a few hours. And although it's hard to regret their departure, they are certainly missing the best of the town, as a few days is a more reasonable time to spend in such a delightful Atlantic resort.

at the center of the Playa de Brazomar, which has excellent rooms but a less-than-glorious restaurant. The second-floor rooms have terraces facing the sea, while the first-floor rooms look over the parking area. It's not easy to see why the **Hotel Las Rocas** (942 860400 FAX 942 861382, Avenida de la Playa (moderate), charges more, although the superior restaurant certainly plays a part. On a budget, try the **Pensión La Mar** (942 870524 FAX 942 862848, Calle La Mar 27 (inexpensive), in the old town.

The simplest, cheapest, and perhaps best evening meal is racks of fresh sardines, cooked over open fires on the waterfront and washed down with inexpensive local wine. However there are

OPPOSITE: Pelota players: the game, also known as jai alai, was invented by the Basques. ABOVE: Keeping score during a pelota game in Donastia-San Sebastián.

also plenty of excellent *tapas* bars scattered around the old town, arcaded and looking over the fishing port. The restaurants in the new town tend to be less impressive, with the exception of that at the Hotel Las Rocas. Most visitors, mainly Spanish, make the trek from their new rented apartments on the beach to the old town along the esplanade, constantly busy with proudly frilled baby carriages framing much-loved children and grandchildren.

How to Get There
Castro-Urdiales is 25 km (16 miles) west of Bilbao. Frequent buses to Bilbao leave from the Café-Bar Ronda on the N-634.

DONOSTIA-SAN SEBASTIÁN

San Sebastián (Donostia in Basque) is the capital of Guipuzcoa Province and Spain's classiest seaside resort. Protected by two headlands that face each other like the claws of a crab, San Sebastián is built around a superb bay that boasts two golden beaches (**Playa de la Concha** and **Playa de Ondarreta**). To round it off there is an island (**Isla de Santa Clara**) in the middle of the bay and a river (**Río Urumea**) that flows through the city under a series of picturesque bridges. Close to the French border, San Sebastián has benefited from a French connection but it is, above all, a Basque city and proud of it.

Although ancient, San Sebastián's physiognomy and demeanor are predominantly nineteenth century, because much of the original city was destroyed in the many sackings and razings that the city had endured. Fortunately, it was the last century's upper crust that patronized the place, notably the Queen Regent, María Cristina, and the Spanish court, as well as many noble and wealthy European and South American families. The result is a city full of spacious tree-lined avenues, solid townhouses, elegant shops and a large selection of fashionable hotels. Add to that the great sweep of beach — a few paces away from the

hotels, restaurants and bars — a colorful fishing port where you can have lunch and watch someone else's dinner being landed, and a quaint old quarter (**La Parte Vieja**) where some of the best *tapas* and meals in Spain are served, and you have a gem of a place.

San Sebastián has established a reputation for being the gourmet capital of Spain. An indication is the presence of numerous gastronomic clubs where members (men only) prepare monumental meals and have a lot of fun devouring them with their pals. For the outsider, however, there is no shortage of places to eat and drink. The old quarter, usually full of students and the city's glitterati, spilling over into the cobbled streets, is the best place to begin an evening's cruise. Local Basque specialties like *chipirones en su tinta* (baby squid cooked in its ink), *idiazabel* (ewe's cheese, cured and smoked) and a variety of shellfish can be sampled in virtually every bar. Draft beer, served in small glasses called *zurritos*, is the best thing to wash all this down before moving on to the next act in San Sebastián's nightly gastronomic extravaganza.

The city broadly divides itself into the Zona Romantica, which is the old quarter of narrow streets, bars, and restaurants, and the more stretched-out pleasures of the western beaches, an area of modern buildings and quiet, soft-sand beaches, sheltered by headlands from the Atlantic waves.

General Information
The **Tourist Information Office** (943 481166, Calle Reina Regente, is open June to September Monday to Friday 8 AM to 8 PM and Sunday 10 AM to 1 PM, October to May Monday to Saturday 9 AM to 2 PM and 3:30 PM to 7 PM and Sunday 10 AM to 1 PM. There is also a **Regional Tourist Office** (943 423101, Paseo de los Fueros 1, and another at (943 426282, Calle Miramar. For transportation, try **Radio Taxi Easo** (943 450131 or **Vallina** (943 404040. In case of **medical emergency**, call (112, and an ambulance will cope with your requirements.

What to See and Do
Most of San Sebastián's greatest sights are in the Parte Vieja, huddled up against the northern bulk of the Monte Orguli peninsula. Buried into the living rock is the **Basílica de Santa María** (943 421995, at the northern end of the Calle Nagusia, which glowers atmospherically down a narrow, old-town street. The baroque façade hides a deceptively small, but beautiful, interior. More restrained is the sixteenth-century Gothic cathedral of **San Vincente**. The Basque tradition is celebrated further in the **Museo de San Telmo** (943 424970, Plaza Zuloaga, open Tuesday to Saturday 10:30 AM to 1:30 PM and 4 PM to 8 PM, Sunday 10 AM to 2 PM, free. On the harbor there is an **Aquarium** (943 440099, Paseo de Muelle 34 (open Tuesday to Sunday 10 AM

to 1:30 PM and 4 PM to 7:30 PM winter, mid-May to mid-September 10 AM to 8 PM, €6.60), and the nearby **Museo Naval** (943 430051, Paseo de Muelle 24 (open Tuesday to Saturday 10 AM to 1:30 PM and 4 PM to 7:30 PM, Sunday 10 AM to 2 PM.

Most of San Sebastián's guests, however, spend more of their time on the beaches — perhaps at **La Concha**, spreading deserted in front of the town's esplanade, or the more family-oriented Playa de Ondarreta to the east, where sheltered waters wash clear on clean sand.

Where to Stay

Hotels here don't scale the heights of luxury, but there is plenty of accommodation, at least outside the busy months of July and August. *The* place to stay is in the **María Cristina** (943 424900, Paseo República Argentina (expensive), built at the turn of the last century and luxuriously restored. **De Londres y de Inglaterra** (943 426989, Calle Zubieta 2 (expensive), overlooks La Concha Bay and is close to the beach, while the **Monte Igueldo** (943 210211, has great views of the bay from a strategic position (moderate).

Less expensive, the **Hostal Pensión Alemana** (943 462544 FAX 943 461771 E-MAIL halemana @adegi.es, Calle San Martín 53 (inexpensive), is a belle époque hotel on a budget, just one street back from the waterfront, that is worth booking well in advance — and you'll need to. More simply, the **Hotel Parma** (943 428893 FAX 943 424082, Calle General Jaruegi Gudalburuaren 11 (inexpensive), provides comfort and convenience between the Parte Vieja and the Paseo Nuevo. On a budget, the favorite hostel is the **Pensión San Lorenzo** (943 425516, Calle San Lorenzo 2 (inexpensive), which doesn't take reservations — book, and book in, early in the day.

Where to Eat

When it comes to dining, San Sebastián has a reputation for the best cuisine in Basque country and therefore, if you ask a Basque, in all of Spain. Good choices include **Arzak** (943 278465, Calle Alto de Miracruz 21 (expensive), located a few kilometers out of town, which is one of Spain's great restaurants and produces nouvelle cuisine with a Basque flourish.

Akelarre (943 212052, Paseo de Orkalada (expensive), is another top level, stylish place. For French cuisine, as well as local Basque dishes, the **Panier Fleuri** (943 424205, Paseo de Salamanca 1 (expensive), is worth a bite, and the **Casa Nicolasa** (943 421762, Calle Aldamar 4 (expensive), is highly esteemed by the city's gourmets.

Less expensive are three restaurants in the old part of the town: **Juanito Kojua** (943 420180, Calle de Puerto 14; **Patxiku Quintana** (943 426399, San Jerónimo 22, and **Kokotxa** (943 420173, Calle Campanario 11.

On the cheaper side in this gourmet city, there are many small restaurants, and countless bars, in the old town (La Parte Vieja) and the port. Try the local Basque cheese, *idiazabal,* when you are having a *zurrito,* which is a small glass of draught beer peculiar to San Sebastián.

How to Get There

San Sebastián is 101 km (63 miles) east of Bilbao, just (20 km/12.5 miles) before the French border, 82 km (50 miles) north of Pamplona and 458 km (286 miles) northeast of Madrid. Thanks to its position so near the French border, it has become something of a transportation hub, with plentiful bus and train connections (943 426430) reaching

well into France and fanning out to destinations throughout Spain. The airport, **Fuenterrabia** (943 642240, is 22 km (14 miles) northwest of town, towards France, reached by a shuttle bus running every 15 minutes.

OPPOSITE: Bilbao's main plaza, the Plaza Moyua, is symbolic of the attractive, modern city center that grew in the 1990s, in defiance of the collapse of the city's industrial base. Although now one of the most sophisticated of all Spain's cities, it still retains a friendly, village feel, with glimpses of green visible from even the most built-up areas. ABOVE: San Sebastían's harbor, with its resident fishing fleet, provides a genuine, working heart for this fishing village that has, over the last few hundred years, grown into one of the Atlantic coast's most chic and sleek coastal resorts. Fresh seafood is a key element of San Sebastián's excellent cuisine, so the local chefs keep a close eye on the fishing boats to get first sight of the day's selection.

Islas
Baleares

Spain's Mediterranean islands, which lie off the Levante coast, differ considerably from the mainland and from each other. The Balearics (Islas Baleares) have become major tourist resorts, but each of the four principal islands retains a distinctive character that is the result of geography and history.

The islands fall into two groups. Ibiza (Eivissa in the local language) and its smaller sister, Formentera, are properly called the Islas Pitiusas (from the Greek meaning "islands of pines"). Situated about 80 km (50 miles) from the Spanish coast, they are relatively low-lying — most of Formentera is as flat as a Spanish omelet — and are drier and hotter than their neighbors. Majorca (Mallorca, to the Spanish: they sometimes joke that there's a mythical island called Majorca where all the British stay) and Minorca (Menorca), some 250 km (155 miles) from the mainland, are strictly speaking the Balearic Islands and are more mountainous with a greater climatic variety.

The islands' prehistory can be traced in the caves and monuments scattered over Mallorca and Menorca. Bronze Age people left *talayots,* round watchtowers built with huge stone blocks, *navetas,* chieftains' stone tombs constructed in the form of upturned boats (which may have later served as dwellings), and the mysterious *taulas,* T-shaped monuments with one huge slab of stone balancing on top of another and found only in Menorca. The name of the Baleares is believed to have come from a Greek or Semitic word meaning skill in throwing; the ancient inhabitants of Mallorca and Menorca were apparently deadly practitioners of the slingshot.

Most of the Mediterranean's sea-faring people seem to have spent some time in the Baleares. The Phoenicians and Greeks visited and the Carthaginians turned Ibiza into a stronghold. The Romans, Vandals and Visigoths followed, and then came the Moors — who left their mark in the spectacular stonewall terracing of Mallorca's mountain hillsides, in irrigation systems that made extensive use of windmills, and in the cultivation of the olive. All of this can be seen today, including some of the actual olive trees planted by the industrious Moors almost a thousand years ago. The trees are gnarled, desiccated and enormously stout, yet they still flourish and bear fruit year after year.

In 1229, King Jaime I of Aragón and Count of Barcelona ("the Conqueror") seized the islands and drove the Moors out. As part of the growing Aragón-Catalunya dominion, the Baleares embarked upon a new age of prosperity and cultural achievement. Towns expanded, castles, churches, monasteries and convents were built and maritime trade flourished. Mallorca produced Ramón Llul, a polymath who wrote novels, poetry and, works on mathematics, mysticism and medicine

and who traveled the length and breadth of the Mediterranean. The Catalan culture and language were gradually absorbed by the inhabitants, each island developing its own dialect but none departing radically from the roots of the language.

The golden age came to an end in the early sixteenth century as the Ottoman Turks began to test their maritime strength in the western end of the Mediterranean, and as Spain became obsessed with the New World and neglected its Mediterranean interests. The Baleares became a happy hunting ground for foreign navies and corsairs. Watchtowers on rocky promontories and walls around cities, villages and manor houses, many of which still exist, were a product of this period.

In the eighteenth century, Menorca fell under British rule, giving the island a distinctive flavor. Father Junipero Serra, who went on to found many famous Californian missions, was born in Mallorca. Foreign travelers made the islands better known in the nineteenth century by recording their experiences and sometimes deciding to settle for good. George Sand and Frederic Chopin spent a rather miserable winter in Mallorca, where he composed some lovely music and she wrote an acerbic travel book, after which they left. Archduke Louis Salvador, a scion of the Austrian Habsburgs, fell in love with Mallorca and with one of its peasant girls and stayed.

In the twentieth century, more foreigners settled, attracted by the islands' natural beauty, tolerant and friendly population, low cost of living and proximity to the rest of Europe. Robert Graves, the British poet and writer, came to Mallorca in 1929 with the American poet Laura Riding after publishing *Good-bye to All That*, his moving account of life and death in the trenches during World War I. Other British, American, French, Italian and German writers, painters and poets followed Graves' example.

The Civil War did not last long on the islands, though some old scores were bloodily settled. Life went on fairly serenely until the late 1950s when the hippies discovered Ibiza and millions of more conventional visitors found that the Baleares was a fine spot to indulge in some *sol, vino* and *playa* at very modest cost. Tourism expanded to what is now almost a year-round business and brought prosperity. The islands also became the home of retired expatriates, many of them on the retreat from the ebbing British empire. The Baleares were — and still are — attractive to the sailing and boating fraternity, drawn by the indented coastlines and the numerous harbors and marinas. Spaniards from the mainland are now visiting in increasing numbers and the Spanish royal family vacations in Mallorca every summer.

The seaview from the terrace of La Hacienda Na Xamena hotel, Ibiza.

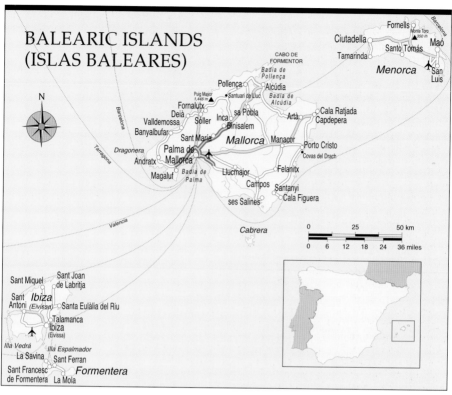

BALEARIC ISLANDS
(ISLAS BALEARES)

N

Barcelona

Tarragona

Dragonera

Valencia

Barcelona

CABO DE
FORMENTOR

Badia de
Pollença

Pollença
Alcúdia
Badia de
Alcúdia

Puig Mayor
1,445 m ▲ • Santuari de Lluc
Fornalutx
Deià
Valldemossa
Sóller
Inca
sa Pobla
Banyalbufar
Binisalem
Artà
Cala Ratjada
Capdepera

Sant Maria
Mallorca
Manacor
Porto Cristo
Covas del Drach

Palma de
Mallorca

Andratx
Magaluf
Badia de
Palma
Llucmajor
Felanitx

Campos
Santanyi
Cala Figuera

ses Salines

Cabrera

Fornells
Monte Toro
▲ 350 m
Ciutadella
Santo Tomás
Maó
Tamarinda
Menorca
San
Luis

Barcelona

0		25		50 km
0	6	12	18	24	36 miles

Sant Miquel
Sant Joan
de Labritja

Sant
Antoni (Eivissa)
Ibiza
Santa Eulàlia del Riu

Talamanca
Ibiza
(Eivissa)

Illa Vedrá
Illa Espalmador
La Savina
Sant Ferran

Sant Francesc
de Formentera
La Mola
Formentera

MALLORCA

The largest island, with over half a million people, Mallorca is blessed with a varied topography that offers rugged mountains, sandy beaches, rocky bays or *calas* and flat fertile plains. There are three distinct areas: the mountainous northwest range with its spectacular coastline; a lower range of hills in the southeast, and a broad central plain that runs between the bays of Alcúdia and Pollença in the north and Palma's bay in the south. Mallorca has some satellite islands, mostly uninhabited like Dragonera to the west or naval stations such as Cabrera in the south. The island is a manageable size, about 90 km (56 miles) long and approximately 70 km wide (43 miles), which means you can see much of it in a short visit yet avoid the crowds if that is your choice.

PALMA DE MALLORCA

Palma de Mallorca, the capital of the Baleares, is an old city that has managed not to ruin itself as industry, mass tourism and the vulgar temptations accompanying sudden wealth have descended upon it. Since it is protected from the north winds by the mountains and faces south, Palma has a milder climate than other parts of the island, a fact that draws visitors throughout the year.

Built on a lovely wide bay, Palma's architectural treasures are best first seen from the sea, and arriving on one of the overnight ferries from Alicante, Valencia or Barcelona provides a perfect method. The ships usually sail in just after dawn when everything is fresh and glowing. On a hill above the city stands Castell de Bellver, palm trees and flowering oleander and hibiscus delineate the sweep of the bay, the old quarter looks peaceful as the sun warms the yellowing walls and red roofs, and on the right Palma's great Gothic cathedral sits, the monarch of all it surveys.

General Information

There are two main sources of tourist information here, the **Regional Tourist Information Office** (971 712216, Plaça de la Reina 2, off the Passeig Born, open Monday to Saturday 9 AM to 2:30 PM and 3 PM to 8 PM, Sunday 9 AM to 1:30 PM, and the **Municipal Tourist Information Office** (971 724090, Carrer Sant Domingo 11, open Monday to Friday 9 AM to 8:30 PM, Saturday 9 AM to 1:30 PM. Both readily hand out maps and travel information. Taxi companies include **Radio Taxi** (971 307000. For Internet access, two central cybercafés are **Cyber Central**, Soledad 4, and **L@Red**, Jaume 3, both open from 11 AM to late. For medical emergencies go to the **Hospital General** (971 728484, Plaça Hospital 3.

What to See and Do

The central boulevard of the city is the **Paseo Borne**, a broad avenue lined with plane trees, with a wide central walkway, similar to La Rambla in Barcelona. It runs at right angles to the sea and is a good spot to take one's bearings for an exploration of the older parts of Palma. The **cathedral** (971 723130, Plaça Almoina, 10 AM to 3 PM, closed Sundays, €2, is on the right hand side of the Paseo Borne as you walk into the city from the sea. It was begun in the thirteenth century, shortly after the Reconquest, but not finished until the sixteenth century. It has a huge airy nave and some particularly fine stained glass windows. A curious touch is Gaudí's signature in this otherwise strictly Gothic presence. He was commissioned to do some restoration work in the sculptural details of the royal chapel, the canopies over the high altar, and one of the pulpits.

Next to the cathedral is the **Palau de l'Almudaina** (971 727145, Carrer Palau Reial, which was built in the thirteenth century on the site of a Moorish fortress. This palace is another classic Gothic building but its protective cypress trees and the well-watered gardens that surround it recall its Moorish heritage. Behind the cathedral and Almudaina are a collection of churches, squares and mansions that are well worth exploring. The **Banys Arabs (Arab Baths)** (971 721549, Serra 7, daily 9 AM to 8 PM, €1, the only Moorish remnant in Palma, are in this district. There are also the Gothic churches of **Sant Francesc** (971 712695, Monday to Saturday 9:30 AM to 1:30 PM and 3 PM to 6 PM, Sundays and holidays 9 AM to 1 PM, €0.50, and **Santa Eulàlia** (971 714625, Monday to Saturday 7 AM to 1 PM and 5:30 PM to 8:45 PM, Sunday and holidays 8 AM to 1 PM, €0.50, both in squares named after them, which are fine examples of the period. Sant Francesc has a quiet cloister and the tomb of Ramón Llul, Mallorca's illustrious medieval scholar.

There are several fine examples of Majorcan domestic architecture here too, in the houses of noblemen and wealthy merchants, built between the sixteenth and eighteenth centuries with spacious patios, stone staircases and galleries.

On the other side of the Paseo Borne, closer to the port, is **Sa Llotja** (La Lonja, in Castilian) (971 711705, Passeig Sagrera, an elegant fifteenth-century Gothic building with a crenellated tower at each corner, where Palma's medieval merchants did their business; next door is the galleried **Consolat de Mar**, built in the seventeenth century. Continuing round the bay in a westerly direction there are many hotels, the suburb of **Terreno** (which was fashionable in the earlier part of the last century and has become the center of Palma's nightlife) and, above it all, **Castell de Bellver** (971 730657, Carrer Camilo José Cela, open daily 8 AM to 8 PM, Sundays and holidays 10 AM to 7 PM, €1.25, built in the thirteenth century. There is a small museum and marvelous views from the tower.

Palma is a great yachting center — sail and motor — and there are several sailing clubs with extensive facilities. There are also colorful markets, good seafood restaurants down by the port, and plenty of *tapas* bars in the cool narrow streets behind Sa Llotja. There is a large bullring but the fights are usually disappointing. Conventional wisdom faults on one hand the spectators, who are largely tourists and therefore neither knowledgeable nor critical enough to keep the matadors on their toes, and on the other seasick bulls which have had to endure a sea-crossing from the mainland. The best beaches are east of the city, in the direction of the airport, notably **Ca'n Pastilla** and **El Arenal**.

outside the city, with golf course and a sweeping view of Palma's bay. The **Meliá Victoria** (971 732542 FAX 971 450824, Avinguda Joan Miró 21, and **Sol Bellver** (971 736744 FAX 971 731451, Paseo Marítimo, are two hotels on the sea-front overlooking the port, both expensive. The **San Lorenzo** (971 728200 FAX 971 711901 E-MAIL san lorenzo@fehm.es, Carrer Sant Llorenç 14, and **Ca Sa Galesa** (971 715400, Carrer Miramar 8, both in the moderate price category, small and charming luxury hotels in converted noblemen's houses in old Palma. San Lorenzo has six rooms and Ca Sa Galesa has eleven.

Less expensive, the **Saratoga** (971 727240 FAX 971 727312, Passeig Mallorca 6 (moderate), is

The main roads fan out from Palma to all parts of the island. There are few highways on Mallorca so drive with special care, especially on the mountain roads. In addition to moving around by car and bus, there are two quaint railroads. One goes to **Inca** (971 752245, in the center of the island, and the other takes you through a mountain tunnel that seems to go on forever to **Sóller** (971 752028, in the northwest not far from the sea. Both trains leave from the tiny station on the Calle Eusebio Estata on the junction with Plaça Espanya on the north side of Palma. With departures almost every hour and negligible fares, this is a great way to see the rural parts of the island.

Where to Stay

Son Vida (971 790000 FAX 971 790017, Urbanización Son Vida (very expensive), is Palma's top hotel. It is in an old castle set in palatial grounds just

close to the main shopping center and has a rooftop pool and many rooms with balconies overlooking the street. The **Sol Jaime III** (971 725943 FAX 971 725946, Passeig Mallorca 14 (expensive), is only a few doors along the street from the Saratoga and also has balconies but is slightly more expensive. The **Hotel Born** (971 712942 FAX 971 712618, Carrer Sant Jaume 3 (moderate), is centrally located in a recently renovated seventeenth-century mansion.

Gran Hotel Bonanza Playa (971 401112 FAX 971 405615, Paseo Illetas 21 (moderate), located on the coast just outside Palma, is a good, unpretentious hotel with decent food.

On a budget, the **Hostal Residencia Pons** (971 722658, Carrer VI 8 (inexpensive), is set around a pleasant, plant-filled courtyard.

The port of Sóller, Mallorca.

Where to Eat

Restaurants in Mallorca, especially outside the tourist areas, tend to offer good value and excellent cuisine, with international cuisine and Catalan menus co-existing.

The following restaurants are listed in descending order of price — from the more expensive down to the moderate.

Koldo Royo (971 457021, Avinguda Gabriel Roca 3, is run by one of Spain's top chefs, who serves Basque-inspired cuisine with an imaginative use of local produce. The **Porto Pi** (971 400087, Avinguda Joan Miró 174, is the place to go for first-class cooking in an Old World setting, and the **Caballito de Mar** (971 721074, Passeig Sagrera 5, in the port area, serves excellent fish and seafood. The **Ca'n Nofre** (971 462359, Carrer Manacor 27, is a good choice for sampling Majorcan dishes.

Two relatively inexpensive places worth mentioning are **La Cantina**, a fish restaurant in the Club Nautico section of the port and, on the other side of the Paseo Marítimo, near the Lonja, **La Bóveda**, a charismatic *tapas* bar and small restaurant that specializes in *serrano* ham and local dishes.

For those whose idea of a night out stretches to dawn and above, Mallorca's clubs, while not in the same league as Ibiza, are pretty wild. Find them at Magaluf, six kilometers (four miles) west of Palma, a resort fairly bursting with bars through the summer. The biggest club here is **BCM**, boasting 10,000 watts of sound and well-known visiting disc jockeys.

How to Get There

Many visitors arrive in Mallorca on international flights, touching down in the **Son San Joan** (971 809000, nine kilometers (five and a half miles) south of Palma, where there is a full range of ATM cash machines, as well as a tourist information kiosk. Many others arrive by boat, with **Balearia** (971 314005 crossing to Ibiza and Formentera; **Pitiusa de Transportes** (971 191068 and **Umafisa** (971 310711 sailing to Alicante, Ibiza and Barcelona; and **Trasmediterránea** (902 454645 WEB SITE www .trasmediterranea.es, Muelle de Paraires, which runs to all the above destinations as well as Valencia, with high-speed ferries in the summer.

EXCURSIONS FROM PALMA

There are a number of interesting excursions from Palma, with no need to follow a rigid pattern as distances between places are relatively short. Perhaps the best way to cover the ground is to follow the island's natural features. Let's start at **Andraitx** in the southwest tip of Mallorca heading for the northwest mountain range. A new highway runs down to **Palma Nova** and then the old road continues, linking up a series of small villages that have become tourist and residential

resorts. Andraitx is a typical unpretentious Majorcan farming town built, like so many towns on the island, away from the coast to avoid the attentions of pirates and other unwelcome visitors. Most of these towns, however, developed small fishing ports, and Andraitx has a heavily developed one set in a perfect bay. The road then heads north and so starts the journey along one of the most glorious and unspoiled coasts in the Mediterranean. If you do nothing else in Mallorca, take this drive.

After **Banyalbufar** make a short diversion to **Valldemossa**, a pretty inland town, famous (or infamous, depending on your reading of history) for being the place that George Sand and Chopin chose to stay in the bitter winter of 1838-39. They

lived in the **Cartuja** (the Carthusian Monastery), which had been built 500 years earlier. Chopin managed to finish his *Preludes,* although ill with tuberculosis. The free-thinking, free-loving Sand took her revenge on what she deemed to be a primitive island, populated by boorish peasants and compounded by atrocious weather, by letting it all hang out in a slim volume entitled *A Winter in Majorca.* It provoked an uproar among the locals. A Palma newspaper denounced her as "the most immoral of writers and the most obscene of women." (The book is available in several languages in many bookstores around the island.)

But, in the words of the PR industry, there is no such thing as bad publicity. Valldemossa is full of sightseers all year round, and whether or not you are intrigued by the famous lovers, the Cartuja and its gardens repay the small effort of breaking the journey.

The monastery, which overlooks a lush valley of olive groves, orchards and gardens, was built as a palace and then given to the Carthusian monks at the end of the fourteenth century. In 1835, during one of Spain's anti-clerical phases, it was expropriated and opened up to outsiders. Apart from Chopin and Sand, Nicaragua's national poet Rubén Darío, Argentine writer Jorge Luis Borges and the Spanish writer Miguel de Unamuno also stayed there. The monastery has a vast library, an eighteenth-century pharmacy and some frescoes in the church painted by Goya's father-in-law. The gardens around the monastery are a delight. Valldemossa can also be reached on a more direct road from Palma that runs through almond groves, winds its way up to Valldemossa and links up with the coast road.

Returning to the coast, the next stop is **Son Marroig**, one of the homes of Archduke Louis Salvador (1847–1915), which is now a rather chaotic but charming museum displaying his house and his interests. During the summer classical music concerts are held there and the views from the house and its gardens are among the best along the coast. Turning inland and down a long hill is the village of **Deià**, where Robert Graves lived for nearly 50 years. He, like several other foreigners who adopted Deià, is buried in the tiny cemetery adjoining the village church that sits high on a hill overlooking the valley.

Sóller, further north, is a market town in the center of a fertile vale. Its plane trees and central square give it a French flavor, the result perhaps of well-established trading ties with France. The port, though encircled by hotels and modern apartment buildings, retains much of its original character and is connected to the town by a slow-moving, open-sided tram. After Sóller the road climbs out of the valley, bypassing **Fornalutx** — another picturesque mountain village much favored by expatriates — through tunnels and along the lee of the **Puig Mayor**, Mallorca's highest peak at 1,445 m (4,740 ft), past **La Calobra**, a tiny village with a sandy bay at the foot of a gorge, and the **Santuari de Lluc** (museum and restaurant); to **Pollença** and its port, and finally to the **Cabo de Formentor** (Formentor Cape) at the northernmost tip of the island.

A good way to see the central plain and the hillier eastern part of Mallorca is to take the road from Palma to Alcúdia. This passes through almond groves, olive orchards and wheat fields and links a series of small country towns that vary from the bleak to the picturesque but usually have some local product to offer the passerby. **Santa María** has handmade fabrics and antiques, **Binisalem** is the wine-making center of Mallorca, and **Inca** produces leather goods as well being known for its sucking pig. At the northern end lies **Alcúdia**, a town of Roman origins (there is a ruined amphitheater east of it) that has good fourteenth-century walls, and its small port. You might, at this point, want to break your journey: a good place to stay is in the **Hotel Es Convent** (971 548716 FAX 971549803, Progrés 6, Alcúdia (expensive). For more accommodation options, call into the **Tourist Information Office** (971 892615, Carretera d'Artà 68, Monday to Saturday from 9 AM to 7 PM.

Turning east along the bay of Alcúdia brings the traveler to **Artà** and its caves. Further south on the coast, just beyond **Porto Cristo**, there are more caves, the **Covas del Drach** (Dragon's Caves) and underground lakes that can be toured by boat to the music of a floating chamber ensemble.

Manacor, the second largest town on the island but still pretty small, is where most of Mallorca's cultured pearls come from, and pottery is the specialty of **Felanitx**. There are some attractive seaside resorts and small bays with sandy beaches strung out along the eastern coast, from **Cala Ratjada** in the north to **Cala Figuera** in the south. And in the center there is **Petra**, where Father Junipero Serra, the missionary who made such an impact on California, was born.

MENORCA

Menorca (Minorca to the English) is poorer and less visually impressive than Mallorca, and not as hip or trendy as Ibiza. It has been described as the plain Jane of the Baleares and is often the island travelers choose to skip. Therein lies its charm. Menorca does not offer sophisticated nightlife, courtyard orchestras, flamenco or bullfights. Instead, there are sandy coves and an azure sea — often without another human being in sight — Bronze Age monuments clearly visible from the main roads, two architectural urban gems (Maó and Ciutadella), enough history to satisfy an

OPPOSITE: The dramatic northwestern coastline of Mallorca. ABOVE: The same coast near the village of **Deià**.

historian, and festivals in unspoiled market towns where you might well be the only foreigner present.

Menorca has not, of course, escaped mass tourism, but the invasion came later than on the other islands. The tourist armies, led by the British and followed by the Germans, have confined themselves to specific parts of the coast and usually stay in small hotels, apartment complexes and villas. There are no large hotels in Menorca, not even in the two main towns, and this has helped to separate tourism from the island's natural rhythm and lifestyle.

The island's profile consists of a low plateau with some broken hills and one high peak (Monte Toro) roughly in the center. It has countless coves, bays and inlets, making it specially attractive to sailors and windsurfers. Inland, Menorca is still rural, its small fields separated by dry stone walls interspersed by contorted outcrops of rock. V.S. Pritchett, the English writer and critic, described the island as having "the toughened look of a Mediterranean Cornwall."

While the stony fields, the prehistoric artifacts and the peasant farming conjure up Celtic lands farther north, the Mediterranean character of Menorca is all pervasive. You see it on the hilltops in the brilliantly whitewashed farmhouses with their ivy green shutters (in a passion for whitewash some Menorcans whiten their tiled roofs as well), you smell it in the scent of pine and thyme, you hear it in the howl of the *tramontana* wind that sweeps across the island from north to south, permanently bending the wild olive trees in that direction so that no one is ever at a loss over where the points of the compass lie.

So much of the land is covered with barren rock, wild olive trees, pines and a succulent called *mata*, whose red berries the partridges love, that agriculture appears a foolhardy pursuit. Yet it remains a major industry, and Menorca is a significant producer of dairy produce, notably a fine cheese with a golden rind and a robust flavor that you can buy directly from cooperatives around the island.

The Mediterranean marrow in Menorca's ancient bones is nowhere more evident than in its history. Believed to have been inhabited since the early Bronze Age (2000 BC), its population was probably larger in 1000 BC than it is today. This was the great age of the *talayots*, the best preserved being El Tudons, which can be seen and easily reached from the Maó–Ciutadella road. There are also many distinctive T-shaped *taulas* and some spectacular prehistoric caves on the south coast at Cala Covas, where modern man, in the shape of several hippie families, has taken up residence in his troglodyte ancestors' dwellings.

Menorca may have become a backwater but it was a prize plum throughout most of its history. Phoenicians, Greeks, Carthaginians, Romans, Vandals, Byzantines, Moors, Spaniards, the British and the French all pounced on the island at one time or another. Menorca's history can best be seen in its two contrasting principal towns. Maó, the current capital, wears the imprint of the eighteenth-century British occupation clearly in its terraced houses, steep cobbled streets, sash windows and Georgian doors with heavy brass knockers.

Ciutadella, the former capital and still the religious center, is a lovely town with old faded pastel palaces, generous squares, narrow curving streets, and a cozy port nestled at the foot of towering battlements.

FESTIVALS

Menorca has several lively festivals throughout the summer months. Ciutadella celebrates the feast of **San Juan** on June 23 and 24 with horsemen dressed in medieval costume and with some vigorous jousting; Maó goes to town on September 8; and in between, the smaller places have their own events. One of the main features of most of these celebrations is a challenge for the young bloods who try to distract the horses by pushing them round in circles. The riders' task is to remain calm and, above all, in control of their steeds.

MAÓ (MAHÓN)

Maó, also known as Mahón, is where most visitors arrive on Menorca, whether traveling by air or sea. The **Tourist Information Office (** 971 363790, Plaça Esplanada, Monday to Friday 8 AM to 3 PM and 5 PM to 7 PM, Saturday 9 AM to 2 PM, is a good place to start, with its free maps and comprehensive supply of leaflets about every aspect of the island. It is also next to the main taxi rank; alternatively call **Radio Taxis (** 971 367111. For an **ambulance**, call **(** 112, with the main hospital the **Verge del Toro (** 971 157700, on Barcelona.

The town is best explored on foot: the old center, beautifully set above the port, contains four small squares. The Plaça d'Espanya, the Plaça Carme (with a range of shops set in the cloisters of a Carmelite church), the Plaça Conquesta and the Plaça Constitució, where Maó's main church, Santa María, is found. To find out more about Menorca's ancient past, go through the cloisters of San Francesc to the **Museu de Menorca (** 971 350655, Dr. Guardia, Plaça Monestir, open Tuesday to Saturday 10 AM to 2 PM and 5 PM to 8 PM, Sunday 10 AM to 2 PM, free, where the largest collection of prehistoric artifacts are displayed.

If all this has made you tired, there are free pick-me-ups available at the **Zoriguer Gin Distillery**, near the port, Monday to Friday 8:30 AM to 7 PM, Saturday 9 AM to 1 PM, where guided tours are topped off with tasting sessions of the island's distinctive and much sought-after gin.

Where to Stay and Eat

What accommodation there is in Menorca is usually either block-booked by tour operators or, in the winter, closed. Don't leave finding a hotel until too late.

Hotel Port Mahón (971 362600, Avinguda Fort de L'eau, Maó (expensive to very expensive), is probably the island's best address, with 74 luxurious rooms. The **Hotel del Almirante (** 971 362700 FAX 971 362704, Carretera de Villacarlos (moderate), once home to Admiral Collingwood, Nelson's second-in-command at Trafalgar, is in Ex Castell to the south of Maó; the atmospheric older rooms are furnished with antiques while there are other, newer rooms set around a courtyard. The hotel is closed from November to April. The **Hostal Sheila (** 971 364855, Santa Cecilia 41 (inexpensive), is a smart, 11-bedroom hotel in a large terraced house, and on a budget the **Hotel La Silsa (** 971 366492, Santa Caterina 4 (inexpensive), is a good one-star. If all else fails there are plenty of hotels, mostly large, in Cala Galdana. Try the large 250-room hotel of the same name, **Cala Galdana (** 971 374209.

When it comes to dining, Menorca's claim to fame is that it invented mayonnaise (*Mahónesa*). **Pilar** restaurant **(** 971 366817, Forn 61, Maó (moderate), is one of the few family-run restaurants to specialize in Menorcan cuisine, and enjoys an excellent reputation. Reservation advisable. The **Jágaro (** 971 362390, Moll de Llevant 335 (expensive), is elegant and sophisticated, with a large dining hall and terrace, while the nearby **Gregal (** 971 366606, Moll de Llevant 306 (moderate), is known for its seafood. For an inexpensive meal, or just a few *tapas*, try **El Viejo Alencén**, Moll de Llevant 75-77, with an ancient interior, waterfront terrace, and excellent selection.

How to Get There

Most visitors arrive here by air, flying in to the **Aeropuerto (** 971 369015, five kilometers (three miles) to the west of Maó, which has its own Tourist Information Office **(** 971 157115 and a few car-rental companies. A taxi into town will cost about €8. Island buses leave and arrive at the Avinguda Quadrago, while local buses for the southeast coast stop outside the tourist office. Ferries from Barcelona and Palma moor beneath the town center outside the offices of **Trasmedditeránea (** 971 366050 WEB SITE www.trasmediterranea.es.

CIUTADELLA

The Romans liked it. The Moors chose it as their Menorcan port. Even the Catalans made it their base during the *Reconquista*, calling it Ciutadella, a name that has, with the locals at least, stuck. Even thought the Turks sacked Ciutadella in the sixteenth century, it was rebuilt over the seventeenth century and grew fat and wealthy over the next 200 years. When the British took over in the eighteen century they found the port too narrow for their ships and moved the capital to Maó, but their neglect was Ciutadella's blessing. Neglected and overlooked, it retains an aristocratic, almost Italianate air and an intensely private sense of place. Its narrow, cobbled streets thread past baroque churches and Gothic buildings in one of the Mediterranean's most atmospheric waterfront towns.

The **Tourist Information Office (** 971 382693, Plaça de la Catedral 5, May to October Monday to Friday 9 AM to 1:30 PM and 6 PM to 8 PM, Saturday 9 AM to 1 PM, is opposite the cathedral in the center of town. There is a taxi rank in the Plaça de Pins, or call **Auto Taxi (** 971 384179. Internet access here is ahead of Maó, with **Acceso Directo (** 971 484062, Plaça Esplanada 37. For **emergency services** call **(** 122.

Ciutadella's attractions are close together in the town center: the **Castell de Sant Nicolau (** 971 484155; the **Museu Municipal de Ciutadella (** 971 380297, 10 AM to 2 PM in winter and not much more in summer, free; and the **Museu Diocesà de Menorca (** 971 385136, Carrer de Seminari 7, €2.40, open 10:30 AM to 1:30 PM and 6 PM to 9 PM. Rather than any specific sight, however, it is the pleasure of strolling around this perfectly preserved microcosm of a distant age that is the main pleasure here.

Where to Stay and Eat

There isn't that much choice of hotels at the top of the market here, though the **Hotel Residencia Patricia (** 971 385511 Camí Nicolau 90 (expensive), is a business traveler's favorite — try to get one of the upper rooms, with views over the sea from their balconies. The **Hotel Alfonso III (** 971 380150 FAX 971 481529, Camí de Maó 53 (inexpensive), is a simple but well-run hotel; avoid the front rooms, over the busy road. On a budget, try the **Hotel Oasis (** 971 382197, Carrer San Isidre 33 (inexpensive), a more-than-adequate one-star.

For dining, **Cas Ferrer (** 971 480784, Carrer Portal de sa Font 16, is one of the island's finest restaurants (expensive). While most restaurants close for the winter, this one lights up log fires. For seafood, try **Casa Manolo (** 971 380003, Carrer Marinaq 117, which is one of the best of many restaurants lining the hotel harbor.

How to Get There

Menorca is not as well connected to the mainland — or, for that matter, to Mallorca and Ibiza — as its sister islands, and the best way to approach it is by air from Palma which is a 20-minute flight. There is also an infrequent car ferry service between Palma and Maó. But once there, it is easy to get around, though you do need to rent a car, which can be done inexpensively at the airport. The island is only 48 km (30 miles) long and 16 km

(10 miles) wide and has a serviceable main road linking Maó in the east with Ciutadella in the west. The other roads are not as good but in three days you can cover much of the island.

Without an airport to call its own, the poor little town of Ciutadella is best reached either with your own car or an island bus, which stops at the main square, the Plaça d'es Born. Hydrofoils from Alcúdia, Mallorca, also dock here.

IBIZA (EIVISSA)

Party capital of the Mediterranean, Ibiza (Eivissa) lies southwest of Mallorca, closer to the mainland, and is both warmer and drier than its more northerly sisters. First made popular by hippies in the 1960s, It soon turned into the Mediterranean's dance capital. A few years ago, Ibiza's popularity with British clubbers and ravers looked like it was bringing its demise: conventional wisdom dictated that nowhere could stay so cool for long. As so often before, Ibiza has confounded its critics, and continues to be a magnet for Europe's youth as a hot summer clubbing destination. The world's best DJs descend on Ibiza every year, while the tolerant locals look on, gently amused by the wildest excesses of their guests. There's nothing they haven't seen before, and, under the warmth of the summer sun, if they can be shocked, none of their guests seem to have worked out how to outrage.

Like Menorca, Ibiza is hilly but not mountainous and is generously endowed with long sandy beaches and rocky bays, all of which are easily accessible by bus, car, moped or small boat. The island is only 41 km (25 miles) long and 20 km (12 miles) wide.

The first impression of Ibiza brings Greece to mind. The whitewashed houses that climb the hillside around the port, the unpretentious, unadorned churches and the quality of the light — purer and more luminous than in Mallorca and Menorca — are particularly striking. But then the embattled history of Spain makes itself felt in the great walls that were built to defend Ibiza town from pirates in the sixteenth century and in the severe countenance of the cathedral that presides over it.

The town was founded by the Carthaginians in the seventh century BC, and the island prospered under their rule. The Phoenicians, Greeks, Romans and Moors followed each other and evidence of all these occupations can be seen in the Museu Arqueològic, which is opposite the cathedral, and in the necropolis of Puig des Molins (Windmill Hill) at the foot of the hill on Vía Romana. The museum has an impressive collection of Punic art and pottery including a terracotta bust of the Carthaginian goddess Tanit. The necropolis has hundreds of tombs cut into the rock and many artifacts from the Carthaginian and later periods.

GENERAL INFORMATION

Ibiza's **Tourist Information Office** (971 301562, Antoni Riquer 2, is open from 10 AM to midnight daily. Ibiza **Radio Taxis** can be reached at (971 307000. Internet Access is available at **Chill**, Vía Púnica 49, Ibiza, Monday to Saturday 10 AM to midnight, Sunday 5 PM to midnight. For medical attention, the **Hospital Can Misses** (971 397000 is near the airport.

THE OLD TOWN

For those up in the day, the best way to see **d'Alt Villa**, or old town, now recognized by Unesco as a World Heritage Site, is to enter through the sixteenth-century gateway, the **Portal de Tablas**, and wind your way up the steep streets, past many fine mansions as well as more cramped quarters,

until you reach the **cathedral** (971 312773 (open June to September, Tuesday to Friday 10 AM to 2 PM and 5 PM to 8 PM, October to May 10 AM to 2 PM, free) and the **Museu Arqueològic** (971 301231 (open in summer from Tuesday to Saturday 10 AM to 2 PM and 5 PM to 8 PM, Sunday 10 AM to 2 PM, in winter Tuesday to Saturday 10 AM to 1 PM and 4 PM to 6 PM, Sunday 10 AM to 2 PM, €1.80. From that point there are unparalleled views over the busy harbor and out to sea.

The views can help you with the island's main daytime obsession: to plan which beach to choose for a long day's tanning and swimming. The crowded town beaches are Figueretes and Platja d'en Bossa, with Talamanca being quieter. Short, inexpensive ferries leaving from the Avinguda Santa Eulàlia provide easy access. To the south of Ibiza town the coast is taken up with salt flats, but buses reach **Ses Salines** and the gay beach of **Es Cavallet**.

AROUND THE ISLAND

The rest of the island offers little of historic interest. The main towns, **Sant Antoni** and **Santa Eulàlia del Riu**, grew rapidly to cope with the booming tourist trade. But there are a number of small villages and hamlets that have character and give the visitor a sense of what the real Ibiza was like before the latest invaders hit the beaches. **Sant Miquel** and **Sant Joan de Labritja**, at the north end of the island, are good examples; there are also a number of small churches, built on unusually simple lines and immaculately white-washed, which enliven the landscape.

Ibiza, traditionally poorer than either Mallorca or Menorca, has passed through different phases of the tourist phenomenon. It began as a place for

The inviting swimming pool La Hacienda Na Xamena hotel, Ibiza.

writers and painters, and then the hippies discovered it. Later, the beautiful people came, many staying and opening boutiques, bars, restaurants, hotels and antique shops. And throughout there was the steady throb of jet engines as the package tourists poured in.

All these elements are present today, and during the seven-month season (May through October) it is sometimes hard to find a local inhabitant. You can still occasionally see old peasants in traditional dress, but the suspicion is that they, like almost everyone else, have a commercial motive in mind. What draws people to Ibiza is the marvelous turquoise sea, the evening parade down in Ibiza port, followed by a wild nightlife, and that dazzling sun, which seems to bestow an especially dark tan, as if the skin's pigment has been permanently changed.

WHERE TO STAY AND EAT

La Hacienda (071 334500, on Na Xamena, Afores, Sant Miquel, is the island's most expensive and most beautiful hotel (very expensive). Set high up in the mountains overlooking the sea, it has panoramic views and full facilities. Like many hotels here, it closes in winter. **La Torre del Canónigo (** 971 303884 FAX 971 307843, Calle Mayor 8, Dalt Vila, is a hugely luxurious apartment hotel next to the cathedral (very expensive). The **Royal Plaza (** 971 310000, Pere Frances 27-29, has much the same facilities but not the same charm (expensive). Central for the clubs **Ocean Drive (** 971 661738 FAX 971 312228 WEB SITE www.oceandrive.de, Port d'Eivissa (expensive), is an art-deco palace 15 minutes walk from Ibiza center overlooking the harbor — in the winter prices tumble.

For movie fans, **El Palacio (** 971 301478 FAX 971 391581, Calle de la Conquista 2, set in a thousand-year-old palace, is stuffed with film memorabilia and with rooms dedicated to various stars, and furnished in style (expensive).

Less expensive options include **Hotel Residencia Montesol (** 971 310161, Passeig de Vara de Rey 2, which is very central and charmingly old-fashioned (inexpensive), and the more modern **Hostal Residencia Parque (** 971 301358, Caieta Soler (inexpensive). On a really tight budget, the **Hostal Bimbi (** 971 305396 FAX 971 305396, Carrer Ramón Munaner 55, Figueres, is a good bet, near to the beach and center (inexpensive).

A number of restaurants here cater to the fuller wallet. **La Marina (** 971 310172, Carrer Barcelona 7, on the waterfront, is known for its seafood, while the elegant **La Brasa (** 971 301202, Carrer Pere Sala 3 has a great terrace. **Sa Capella (** 971 340057, Puig den Basora, Sant Antoni, is set in a deconsecrated church and is noted for its good food, its folk dance show and its unusual ambience.

More moderate are the **C'an Alfredo (** 971 311274, Passeig de Vara de Rey, and the fashionable and somewhat glamorous second-floor **Los Passajeros**, Carrer Vicent Soler.

NIGHTLIFE

It is at night that Ibiza comes into its own. The clubs are vast and bristle with the latest gimmickry, flood with dry ice and, occasionally, foam, and are guaranteed to stay open until dawn and beyond. The season runs from May to September, and the opening and closing parties are the most spectacular of all.

The clubs are found in Ibiza town or Sant Antoni, or along the road in between. For a warm-up drink the **Rock Bar** in the heart of Ibiza is where you'll spot the most celebrities, with the **Jockey Club** good for an alfresco dance. When it comes to clubs, **Amnesia**, half way between Ibiza and Sant Antoni, is a long-standing favorite, only slightly tarnished by the roof and walls forced on it by local — and not-so local — complaints about the noise. **El Paradis** is another favorite, famous for flooding its dance-floor twice a week for a "Fiesta del Agua," and with a hydraulic roof to let in the morning sun. One of the only clubs to stay open through the winter is **Pacha**, opposite the Marina, with Britain's "Ministry of Sound" resident in summer. In Sant Rafel, **Privilege** is famous for its bad-behavior Mondays, and with a capacity of 10,000 is one of the island's biggest venues.

HOW TO GET THERE

The island can be reached by a 30-minute flight from Palma, or, more commonly, on an international charter, with the **airport (** 971 302200 six kilometers (four miles) southwest of Ibiza town. There are two ferry terminals, with ferries from the mainland and Mallorca (**Trasmediteránea (** 971 315050 WEB SITE www.trasmediterranea.es and **Baleària (** 971 314005) arriving at the Passeig des Moll, and local boats to Formentera and smaller coastal towns (**Transmapi (** 971 310711 and **Umafisa (** 971 314513 among others), docking at Avinguda Santa Eulàlia: from Palma, a car ferry takes about four hours.

FORMENTERA

Formentera, seven kilometers (four miles) from Ibiza, is easily accessible by boat and makes a pleasant diversion from the tempo of life on the larger island. Known as the "wheat island" to the Romans, Formentera is the least developed of the Baleares and is still largely rural in character, with an economy based on producing wheat, almonds, figs and grapes. Its lakes and salt flats attract many birds, including flamingos; it has a

Bronze Age megalithic monument near Sant Ferran and five fortified watchtowers that were built in the eighteenth century.

GENERAL INFORMATION

The **Tourist Information Office (** 971 322057, Monday to Friday 10 AM to 2 PM and 5 PM to 7 PM, Saturday 10 AM to 2 PM, is by the ferry terminal at La Savina, where you'll also find bicycles for rent for about €5 per day. Taxi companies include **Taxis La Savina (** 971 328016, and the **medical emergency number** is **(** 061. Communications are dealt with by the post office in Sant Ferran, open 9 AM to 2 PM and 5 PM to 8 PM, which has **Internet** access.

which is especially useful for finding villas or apartments: the **Central de Reservar Formentera (** 971 323224 WEB SITE www.formeterareservations .com. Open all year is the well situated 40-bed-roomed **Hostal Bellavista (** 971 322255, Passeig de la Marina, La Savina, on the harborfront. It comes with a waterslide (moderate). Alternatively, try the **Hostal La Savina (**/FAX 971 322279, La Savina (inexpensive).

For dining, **Es Molí de Sal (** 971 136773, at Ses Illetes, was an old salt mill and is now a fashionable restaurant (expensive), while the moderately priced **Restaurante Le Cyrano** on the Paseo Marítimo at Playa de Pujols is a French-owned restaurant with good food.

WHAT TO SEE AND DO

The best way to move around is by moped or bicycle, both of which can be rented at the port of **La Savina**. The "capital" of the island is **Sant Francesc** (population 800) which has an eighteenth-century church. There are a number of beaches, the best being **Es Pujols**, a long stretch of fine sand in the north. On the far side is **La Mola**, the highest point of Formentera, which offers a lighthouse, some high cliffs and a great panoramic view over land and sea.

WHERE TO STAY AND EAT

It is recommended to book your accommodation here early: most visitors day-trip here and rooms are scarce. There is a central reservations office next to the Tourist Information Office

HOW TO GET THERE

Formentera is usually reached from Ibiza by ferry, (€15 round trip), taking about an hour, depending on currents, or rather faster by hydrofoil (€23). Check on the return times, as tickets are not transferable between operators.

A popular beach in Ibiza.

Travelers'
Tips

GETTING THERE

BY AIR

From the United States, **Iberia Airlines** TOLL-FREE IN THE US 800 772 4642 WEB SITE www.iberia.com, is the national carrier and has regular flights to Spain (non-stop to Madrid and Barcelona and connecting to any of Spain's smaller airports). **American Airlines** TOLL-FREE IN THE US 800 433 7300 WEB SITE www.americanair.com flies from Chicago and Miami to Madrid, **Continental** TOLL-FREE IN THE US 800 231 0856 WEB SITE www .flycontinental.com flies from Newark to Madrid, **Delta** TOLL-FREE IN THE US 800 241 4141 WEB SITE www.delta-air.com flies from New York to Madrid and Barcelona, and **United** TOLL-FREE IN THE US (800) 538-2929 WEB SITE www.ual.com flies from Washington to Madrid. There are currently no direct flights from Canada, but routings through London or one of the European hubs are easy to arrange.

From the United Kingdom, **Iberia Airlines** ((0990) 341341 WEB SITE www.iberia.com operates direct flights to those cities plus Alicante, Bilbao, Palma de Mallorca, Santiago de Compostela, Sevilla and Valencia, while **British Airways** ((0345) 222111 WEB SITE www.british-airways.com has regular flights to a number of Spanish cities as well as a daily run to Gibraltar, from where it is possible to cross over into Spain. A less expensive way is to take a charter: holiday companies run low-frill flights into the popular airports of the Costas, including Alicante, Málaga and Almería, with the disadvantage that there is rarely any flexibility in departure times (except they almost always fly late), nor any opportunity to change your dates.

Even cheaper, currently, are the new crop of low-cost airlines operating out of London's minor airports, Stansted and Luton, which currently consist of **Easyjet** ((0870) 600-0000 WEB SITE www.easyjet.com, which flies from London Luton to Barcelona and Palma; **Buzz** ((0870) 240-7070 WEB SITE www.buzzaway.com, which flies from London Stansted to Jerez and Murcia; **Go** ((0845) 605-4321 WEB SITE www.go-fly.com, which flies from London Stansted to Barcelona, Palma, Ibiza, Alicante, Bilbao, Madrid, Málaga and the Canaries; and **Ryanair** ((0870) 156-9569 WEB SITE www .ryanair.com, whose routes from London Stansted include flights to Perpignan (near Barcelona) and to Biarritz (near Donostia-San Sebastián). Bear in mind that car rental is more expensive in France than in Spain.

Iberia flies direct to most other European capitals, with **Air France**, **Lufthansa**, **KLM** and **Sabena** amongst the national carriers that now have reciprocal rights.

From Australasia, flights via Asia are cheaper and quicker than those traveling via the United States. On a budget, the lowest fares will be via the United Kingdom, linking with one of the low-cost airlines, but the slightest delay can mean non-refundable flights are missed. Best, usually, to take a round-the-world ticket, or look for deal with Japan Airlines into Madrid, Olympic Airways via Athens, or Thai, Air France and Lauda Air, all of whom connect with Iberia.

BY SEA

The sea connections between Britain and Spain are from Plymouth to Santander with **Brittany Ferries** ((0870) 901-1500 WEB SITE www.brittanyferries.com (24 hours), or from Portsmouth to Bilbao with **P&O** ((0870) 242-4999 WEB SITE www.poef.com / portsmouth (29 hours), both modern and efficient car ferries with two weekly sailings. Fares on these crossings vary with season and the length of your visit: allow €760 to €1,200 for a vehicle and four passengers, including accommodation on board but not the (relatively expensive) food. Allow a lot more (probably) if you're planning on a visit to the onboard casino. Tickets can be cheaper bought through a special Internet ticket agent such as **Ferrysavers** WEB SITE www.ferrysavers.com, which can usually shave 20 percent or more off the price. If you are traveling from North Africa, most ferries make land in Algeciras after short and uncomplicated crossings.

BY TRAIN

There are a number of rail routes that link Spain with the European mainland. The way to San Sebastián is through the French frontier town of Hendaye at the western extremity of the Pyrenees. A more central route goes through Toulouse and Pau and enters Spain at Somport-Canfranc in Aragón, while Barcelona is linked to Perpignan, and beyond, by rail. From the United Kingdom, it takes about 24 hours by train to reach Barcelona from London using Eurostar to Paris (rail/ship channel crossings are less expensive), changing to travel on to Port Bou at the eastern end of the Pyrenees. For further information, contact **Rail Europe** ((0870) 584 8848 WEB SITE www.raileurope .co.uk, 179 Piccadilly, London W1V, or Victoria Station, London SW1.

If traveling by train, it is well worth looking into buying an **Interrail** ticket WEB SITE www.inter-rail.co.uk, which can be purchased from Rail Europe. This is not always quite the bargain it appears as many of the faster trains are liable to surcharge, but will spare travelers too close an experience of the many ramifications of Spanish rail charges.

Valle de los Caídos ("Valley of the Fallen"). Franco's Civil War monument and tomb.

OVERLAND

The bus routes to Spain from England cross the channel on the shortest available crossing and then broadly follow the main driving routes. For tickets and details call **Eurolines** ((0870) 580 8080 WEB SITE www.gobycoach.com, National Express, 164 Buckingham Palace Road, London SW1. Direct routes include London to Barcelona (25 hours), Alicante (39 hours), Madrid (27 hours), Pamplona (23 hours) and Santiago (32 hours).

There are a number of alternative routes if you travel by car, but the bus times above give some idea of how long they will take. Bear in mind that

BORDER TOWNS

Many visitors to Spain drive there, the vast majority coming through France. Apart from the natural inclination to get across any border as fast as possible and into the heart of the destination country, there is not much along Spain's frontiers to delay the motor-borne traveler. In the northeast, **Girona** is the first town of any consequence, and the temptation to press on to the Costa Brava or Barcelona usually proves overwhelming. In the Pyrenees, there are no towns of any size close to the border, but on the Atlantic end there is the elegant city of **San Sebastián**, which easily justifies spending a night or more.

international buses rarely stop, whereas you, as a motorist, almost certainly will stop — and often. The most direct route from London is via Calais and Paris, then toward Bordeaux to enter Spain along the Atlantic Coast, or toward Perpignan to enter Catalunya at La Jonquera and head down to the Mediterranean coast. For Spain's Atlantic seaboard the best way is via Hendaye. There are also a number of lovely scenic mountain roads through the Pyrenees. Roncesvalles and Somport are the old pilgrim entry points and the Puigcerda entry point leads to Andorra. Unless you have plenty of time and patience and you'll be traveling mainly on toll roads, and you'll need to bear in mind these add up. Allow about €55 at least to get across France and nearly as much to get across Spain. An international driving license and car insurance are needed to enter Spain with your own vehicle.

ARRIVING AND LEAVING

American, Canadian, Australian and New Zealand citizens do not need visas for stays of up to three months, though they do require a passport, valid for at least six months from date of entry. Citizens of European Union countries can travel freely in Spain on their national identity cards. British travelers, in the absence of an identity-card system, need their passports to travel. Visa formalities, however, do change, and it is best to check for the latest situation at the nearest Spanish embassy or consulate. Customs formalities at all entry points are usually pretty relaxed — Spain has adopted the "green" door for people with nothing to declare and the "red" one for those with goods to declare.

The good news: Spain does not impose a departure tax.

EMBASSIES AND CONSULATES

SPANISH REPRESENTATION ABROAD

Australia Embassy ((02) 6273 3555, 15 Arkana Street, Yarralumla, ACT 2600; Consulate ((02) 9261 2433, 24th Floor, St. Martin Tower, 3131 Market Street, Sydney NSW 2000. The Australian Embassy also serves New Zealand.
Canada ((613) 747-2252, 74 Stanley Avenue, Ottawa, Ontario K1M 1P4; ((514) 935 5235, 1 Westmount Square, 1456 Avenue Wood, Montreal, Quebec H3Z 2P9.

Canada (914 314300, Núñez de Balboa 35, Madrid.
Ireland (913 190200, Paseo de la Castellana 46, Madrid.
New Zealand (915 230226, Plaza Lealtad 2, Madrid.
United States (915 774000, Calle Serrano 75, Madrid. Consular office for passports is around the corner at Paseo de Castellana 52.
United Kingdom (913 190200, Fernando el Santo 16, Madrid.

TOURIST INFORMATION

Even when Spain had a reputation for a top-heavy bureaucracy and Latin inefficiency, its tourism

Ireland ((01) 2691640, 17a Merlyn Park, Ballsbridge, Dublin 4.
United Kingdom ((020) 7589 8989, 20 Dracott Place, London SW3 2RZ.
United States Embassy ((202) 728-2330, 2375 Pennsylvania Avenue NW, Washington DC 20009; Consulate ((212) 355-4090, East 58th Street, New York, New York 10155; Consulate ((323) 938-0158, 5055 Wilshire Boulevard 960, Los Angeles, California 90036.

FOREIGN REPRESENTATION IN SPAIN

Many countries have consular representatives in Spain's major cities and resort areas. Here, however, are just those in Madrid, the main representation for diplomatic and other matters.
Australia (914 419300, Paeseo de la Castellana 143, Madrid.

operation was both professional and effective. There are Spanish National Tourist Offices in a number of countries, and they are invariably staffed by high-grade officials. They speak the necessary languages and offer a wide range of brochures, booklets, travel information and maps — all free. The material, glossy and well-produced, will weigh your luggage down a bit but it's worth the effort. Less heavy information is also available on the Internet, with the official site comprehensive and welcoming: log on to WEB SITE www.tourspain.co.uk. Some addresses include the following. Australians and New Zealanders should address the Australian Embassy for information.
Canada Tourist Office of Spain ((416) 961-3131 FAX (416) 961-1992 E-MAIL toronto@tourspain.es

OPPOSITE: The façade of the Gothic cathedral in Barcelona. ABOVE: El Escorial, King Felipe II's magnificent monastery and palace.

WEB SITE www.tourspain.toronto.on.ca, 2 Bloor Street West, 34th Floor, Toronto, Ontario M4W 3E2. **France** Office Espagnol du Tourisme ((01) 45038257 E-MAIL paris@tourspain.es WEB SITE www .espagne.infotourisme.com, 43 Rue Decamps, 75784 Paris.

Germany Spanisches Fremdenverkehrsamt ((030) 8826036 FAX (030) 8826661 E-MAIL berlin@tourspain.es, Kurfürstendamm 180, 10707 Berlin.

Italy Ufficio Spagnolo del Tursimo ((02) 7200-4617 FAX (02) 7200-4318 E-MAIL milan@tourspain.es WEB SITE www.turismospagnola.it, Via Broletto 30, Milano 20121; ((06) 6783106 FAX (06) 6798772 E-MAIL roma@tourspain.es, Via del Mortaro 19, Interno 5, Roma 00187.

Portugal Delegaçao Oficial do Tourismo Espagnol ((021) 354-1992 FAX (021) 354-0332 E-MAIL lisboa@tourspain.es, Avenida Sidonio Pais 28, 3 Dto, 1050-215 Lisboa.

United Kingdom Spanish Tourist Office ((020) 7486 8077 FAX (020) 7486 8034 E-MAIL londres @tourspain.es WEB SITE www.tourspain.co.uk, 22-23 Manchester Square, London W1M 5AP.

United States Tourist Office of Spain Chicago ((312) 642-1992 FAX (312) 642-9817 E-MAIL chicago @tourspain.es, Water Tower Place, Suite 915 East, 845 North Michigan Avenue, Chicago, Illinois 60611; Los Angeles ((213) 658-7188 FAX (213) 658-1061 E-MAIL losangeles@tourspain.es, 8383 Wilshire Boulevard, Suite 960, Beverly Hills, California 90211; New York ((212) 265-8822 FAX (212) 265-8864 E-MAIL nuevayork@tourspain.es WEB SITE www.okspain.org, 666 Fifth Avenue, 35th Floor, New York, New York 10103. Miami ((305)

358-1992 FAX (305) 358-8223 E-MAIL miami @tourspain.es, 1212 Brickwell Avenue, Miami, Florida 33131.

Within Spain itself there are also plentiful tourist information offices, whose contact details and opening hours are listed in their appropriate place in the touring chapters, although popular tourist destinations will, in season, sprout temporary kiosks in well-frequented areas to give travelers further help. These offices are useful with all aspects of traveling in the country, have stacks of printed information, and can and will help with all levels of accommodation queries. They are, in short, highly recommended. They are especially useful to find out what fiestas and other cultural events are going on in the town and the surrounding area. The offices are usually open Mondays to Fridays, 10 AM to 1 PM and 4 PM to 7 PM, and Saturday mornings, and usually closed on Sundays and public holidays — where possible, their opening hours are listed in the appropriate place in the touring chapters.

GETTING AROUND

Spain has a comprehensive transportation network to cater to all budgets. There are plenty of airports and a good network of scheduled domestic flights. Roads are good and the *autopistas*, at least, are not crowded, while most major towns have railway stations and good links with Madrid, the central hub, at the very least. Public transportation comes into its own for visiting Spain's cities, as most historic centers are off-limits to vehicles.

INTERNAL FLIGHTS AND FERRIES

Internal flights are operated by Iberia and Aviaco, are frequent between most cities and are well run though relatively expensive. There is an "air bridge," or "shuttle," between Madrid and Barcelona that goes each way hourly through the day. Some flights to popular resorts — Málaga, Palma de Mallorca and Ibiza, for example — can become heavily booked in the summer months, so make reservations as far ahead as possible. The same principle applies to the car ferries that ply between the coastal ports of Barcelona, Valencia and Alicante and the Balearic Islands. The company that operates these ferries (Trasmediterránea WEB SITE www.trasmediterranea.es) has offices in Madrid and in the main Mediterranean ports.

TRAINS

Spanish trains tend to be slow, but are a good way of getting around, mixing with the locals and seeing the countryside change with a drink in your

ABOVE: Alhambra gardens, Granada. RIGHT: Parade in front of El Rocío church, Andalucía.

hand and your feet up. **RENFE** is the Spanish rail company, presiding over a network of Gothic complexity. *Cercanias* are local trains, *regionales* are slowish services between major cities, and *largo recorrido* are long-distance trains, of varying speeds and effectiveness. As they get faster (under a bewildering ranking system of *diurno*, *intercity*, *talgo*, *talgo P*, *talgo 200*, and *trenhotel*) they get more expensive, and need to be reserved ahead, much as you would for an international flight. The pride of the Spanish fleet is the superfast **AVE**, running fast from Madrid to Sevilla, and **Euromed** from Madrid to Alicante.

Unfortunately, the train system is not easy to use. The different services produce different brochures, there are a range of discounts applicable to the old, the young, the unwell or even the simply cunning, and 20-percent discounts (on round-trip journeys only) are given on so-called **días azules** ("blue days"). Increasingly, outlying train services are being replaced by something called a rail bus, indistinguishable from a normal bus, which leaves from the bus station but is run by the rail company. **Travel passes** include *Tarjeta Explorerail* for the under 26, *Spanish EuroDomino Pass*, which offers three, five or ten days travel per month, and *Flexipass*, which, available in first- and second-class options, allows travel for a certain number of days over a two-month period. North Americans can take advantage of Rail 'n' Drive passes, which combine some days rail travel with some days car rental. The various limitations and surcharges levied on these passes can be Byzantine in their complexity, and to do them justice this book would be bigger and heavier. For more information on rail passes the following addresses might be useful. In the United Kingdom contact **Rail Europe** ((0870) 584-8848 WEB SITE www.raileurope.co.uk, 179 Piccadilly, London W1V, and in the United States contact **Rail Europe** TOLL-FREE (800) 438-7245 WEB SITE www.raileurope.com, 226 Westchester Avenue, White Plains, New York 10604, and in Australia call **Spanish Tourism Promotions** ((03) 9650-7377 or **Rail Plus** ((03) 9642-8644 E-MAIL info@railplus.com.au, or in New Zealand call ((09) 3032484.

Car rental, however, is inexpensive in Spain (see below). Often it is easiest to use a travel agent sporting the RENFE logo, or use their 24-hour **Telephone Reservation Service** (902 240202, which works nationwide, or visit their WEB SITE www.renfe.es.

In a category of its own is **Al Andalus**, the luxury sightseeing train that takes its pampered occupants at a leisurely pace through the main cities of Andalucía. You join the train in Madrid or Sevilla for a week's tour, sleeping on the train and having most of your meals in smart restaurants

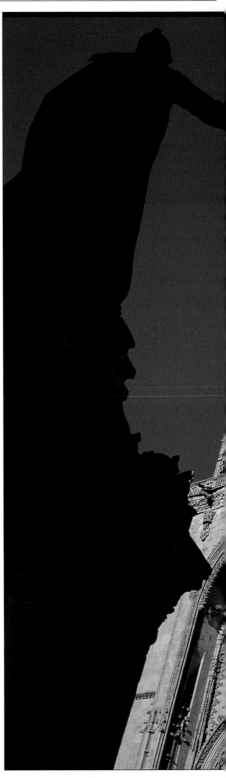

The Catedral Nueva in Salamanca.

and hotels en route. The Al Andalus is designed for that special occasion and is priced accordingly. Contact Al Andalus Expreso (915 701621 FAX 915 717482 WEB SITE www.alandalusexpreso.com, Iberrail SA, Calle Capitan Haya 55, 28020 Madrid. There are also two inexpensive independent train routes: one runs along the Cantabrian coast (**FEVE**) and the other does a circuit of the main cities in Andalucía.

CAR RENTAL

It is easy and relatively cheap to rent cars in Spain, with only two real problems. The first is car crime. This is common in throughout Spain, certainly in cities, and especially in the south, with Sevilla and Córdoba particularly bad. You will quickly see that Spanish motorists don't tend to leave *anything* visible in their cars when they park — even radios are often removed. For laden tourists on a grand tour of Spain this isn't always easy, and if you're living in a scatter of maps, cameras and guidebooks it won't be too long before a window gets broken and storing your luggage will cease to be your problem.

Fortunately, the Spanish have had to react with a good supply of guarded underground parking lots in their major city centers, where in any case vehicular access is restricted. These are often open 24 hours, and will keep your property relatively safe. The only drawback is the cost, which can easily be €16 per day in more popular destinations. Hotels with secure parking also often charge a premium for looking after your car — money well spent in my opinion.

The second problem lies with Spanish drivers. It won't be long before you start to understand why they have the worst per-capita accident rate in Europe. They combine excessive speed with moments of complete dither, and it takes great care to avoid getting driven into. On freeways (*autopista*), often with only two lanes, you'll get slow cars, trucks and campers bumbling along in the slow lane, while Audis and Mercedes will power along in the fast lane at speeds up to 200 km/h (125 mph), their drivers chattering away on their cell phones. When they find a car passing in heavy traffic at a more reasonable speed, they eschew early warning headlight flashes, as is the norm in neighboring France, opting instead to emotionally, if not physically, push the slower car off the road by braking at the last minute and continuing to drive inches away from its rear fender. Add erratic indication, fairly narrow lanes and poor lane discipline, and the dire Spanish road statistics are explained.

Bear in mind also that when driving, you need to be carrying your passport and driving license. Otherwise you'll be in big trouble. It's also very advisable to get legal insurance. Without this your car will be impounded — and you might be as well — following an accident, until it is decided who was to blame. As a foreigner, it will likely be you — the Spanish seem to labor under the hopelessly unrealistic illusion that, as a people, they drive well, even though this is demonstrably untrue.

Speed limits are 120 km/h (75 mph) on the freeways (*autopistas*) (though you'd never believe it), 100 km/h (62 mph) on other roads, and 60 km/h (37 mph) in built-up areas. Seat belts are compulsory. Take extra care on the two- or three-lane national highways (*carreteras nacionales*), prefixed by the letter N, where the heavy trucks belt along and sometimes pass when they shouldn't; relatively common speed traps along the way (instant fines) enliven your journey. Also remember that traffic coming from the right has priority on traffic circles (roundabouts). Gasoline and tolls (on the fancy new highways) are expensive, but diesel is significantly cheaper. If you choose a small car, preferably diesel, stay on the older roads, where there are no tolls, and avoid speeding through villages (at least while the police are out with radar guns); you can cut your costs and see more of the country in the process.

The large international car-rental companies — **Hertz** (901 101001, **Europcar** (901 102020 and **Avis** (901 135790 — have branches in most of the major cities and at the major airports, and there are a number of good Spanish rental companies, notably **Atesa** (902 100101 WEB SITE www.atesa.es and **Marsans** (902 306090 WEB SITE www.marsans.es. If you are coming from Australasia the United Kingdom, or North America, make the reservation before leaving; there are often better rates offered on bookings made prior to arrival.

URBAN TRANSPORTATION

Spanish buses are clean and functional, and cover the ground well in the major cities. Madrid, Barcelona and now Bilbao have good subway systems with excellent directions and maps. Fares are very reasonable, especially if you buy a book of 10 tickets at a time. The subways are less complicated to use than the buses and are the most efficient way of getting around Madrid and Barcelona, though in Bilbao you'll probably end up using both. Taxis are plentiful in most cities and relatively inexpensive, and although their drivers do not believe in dawdling, they usually drive well. They are also polite and do not expect large tips (5 to 10 percent of the fare is normal.)

ACCOMMODATION

It is always a good idea to reserve your accommodation well in advance when planning a trip to Spain, especially in the summer and during the popular festival seasons. A good travel agent can do it all for you without any difficulty, the local tourist offices can help, and the contact details in this book will let you get in touch directly, though bear in mind there might not be much English spoken at less-expensive establishments. The Paradors have their own central reservation system (see below). If, however, you do not want to structure your travel too precisely, you can usually find a comfortable and affordable bed wherever you go in Spain, especially out of season and away from the heavily traveled tourist tracks.

All Spanish hotels are graded and regulated by the government. **Hotels (H)** are rated by stars: one to five in ascending quality. A one-star hotel

is generally reasonably priced, costs over €465 per couple, per night. The seven percent *IVA* sales tax is charged on hotel rooms, which can come as a surprise at checkout.

The rates can vary from the figures given, as prices often triple over local fiestas, and often plummet off-season or if, for some reason, there are too many spare beds. Do not be afraid to bargain with smaller, less expensive hotels — or even obviously empty big ones — as the room rates are rarely set in stone. If, for any reason, you fall out with your hotel, ask to see the complaints book, the *libro de reclamaciones*. By law, every hotel must have one of these, but they will go to great lengths to ensure there is never an entry.

will not necessarily be inexpensive, and usually falls within the "moderate" price range. *Hotel Residencias* **(HR)** have similar ratings but do not have restaurants. *Hostales* **(Hs)** and *Pensiones* **(P)** are more modest lodgings and are rated by one to three stars. Then come *fondas* **(F)**, or inns, and *casas de huespedes* **(CH)**, similar to one-star *hostales*. The grade of each establishment is identified outside the building on a pale blue plaque.

In this guide the prices given are per couple per night, usually for bed-and-breakfast accommodation. *Very inexpensive* is up to €11.6, a rate which is increasingly rare in Spain and only commonly found in remote areas — even then you might be in a campsite. *Inexpensive* is under €58, *moderate* is between €59 and €116; *expensive* is between €117 and €232 and *very expensive* between €232 and €465. *Extremely expensive,* something of a rarity in Spain, where accommodation

Hotels usually ask for your passport on registering and return it the next day. If it is not waiting for you at the reception desk, don't forget to ask for it. It is not amusing to find yourself at your next destination, reaching for the precious document, and having to slog back to retrieve it.

PARADORS AND ESTANCIAS

In 1926, the Marquis of Vega-Inclán, Spain's Royal Tourist Commissioner, came up with the idea of establishing a chain of state-run inns based on the tradition of the *parador* (literally, "stopping-place"), the upscale inns of the past where the better kind of traveler lodged for the night while his servants and horses went to the local *posada* or coaching inn. The first Parador was opened in

The interior of the Hotel de San Marcos, León. This sixteenth-century convent is now a Parador.

1928 in the Sierra de Gredos mountains, and since then 85 more have opened their doors.

The marquis's concept was not just a way for the state to cash in on the tourism business, but to take Spain's surplus antique housing stock — castles, palaces, monasteries, convents and so on — and put it to good use. It was a brilliant and innovative idea, and there is still nothing quite like the Paradors anywhere else in the world.

The chain includes thirteen medieval castles, nine Gothic and baroque palaces and six monasteries and convents.

The most spectacular are the **Hotel dos Reies Católicos** in Santiago de Compostela, built as a hostel for the pilgrims by Ferdinand and Isabella

in 1499 ("the world's oldest hotel," according to the brochure); the **Hotel de San Marcos** in León, a stunning sixteenth-century convent; the **Parador de Granada** in the Alhambra, another convent, founded by the Catholic Monarchs after the capture of Granada, with splendid views of the Alhambra; and the **Parador de Benavente**, a twelfth-century castle on a hill where the court of the King of León often met.

Not all Paradors are as attractive, or as old. Many are modern buildings, functionally designed with touches of tradition such as antique furniture and rugs and old paintings. Some of these compensate by being located in such a position that guests can see something interesting from their bedroom windows or balconies. The modern Paradors of **Toledo** and **Salamanca** are good examples, each having superb views over its parent city.

Paradors are no longer inexpensive, most falling into the three- or four-star hotel category, but they invariably have good food and service and are worth stopping at for a meal or a drink if the cash flow does not permit an overnight stay. There are also discounts for the over-sixties, for stays of two nights, and for five-night vouchers, that allow you to stay at the Parador — or Paradors — of your choice.

Further information and reservations can be made at the **reservations center** (915 166666 FAX 915 166657 E-MAIL info@parador.es WEB SITE www.parador.es, Requena 3, 28013 Madrid. The Paradors are generally located in town and near principle attractions, so are ideal for those traveling on public transportation or on tours.

There is a slightly less expensive alternative for travelers who want to discover a more rural side of Spain but still like to stay in character accommodation. The **Estancias de España** (913 454141 FAX 913 455174 WEB SITE www.estancias.com E-MAIL info@estancias com, Menéndez Pidal 31, 28036 Madrid, is a portfolio of upmarket hotels scattered around the country. To get really rural, the government tourist offices will be able to help with information about accommodation, often absurdly inexpensive, available off the beaten track.

Alternatively, just use this guidebook, as some thought has gone into choosing the best hotels in the various price categories. I hope you agree.

VILLA RENTALS

Families, especially, will appreciate self-catering villas, a hugely popular way to take some of the stress — and expense — out of hotel accommodation. Although there are agencies in the United States offering holiday lets, the competitive market in the United Kingdom means that prices are lower booked through British companies. They're lower still booked locally, direct with the owner, but for first-time rentals it's best to book through an established agency, which should be able to help if things go wrong.

Leading agencies include the upmarket **International Chapters** ((020) 7722 0722 WEB SITE www.villa-rentals.com. Less exclusive are Citalia's **The Real Spain** ((020) 8686 3638 WEB SITE www.citalia.co.uk; **Magic of Spain** ((0990) 462442 WEB SITE www.magictravelgroup.co.uk; **Individual Travellers Spain** ((0870) 078 0187 WEB SITE www.indiv-travellers.com; and **Open Holidays** ((01903) 215215 WEB SITE www.openholidays.co.uk.

For the mass market the offerings are more likely to be apartments in resorts, but if this is what you want try **First Choice Villas** ((0870) 750 0001 or, if you're determined not to stray too far

ABOVE: The Monasterío of Yuso, La Rioja. RIGHT: A water mill on the Guadalquivir, near Córdoba.

from the beach, try **JMC Beach Villas** ((0870) 558 5858 WEB SITE www.jmc.com. They will, at least, be inexpensive.

EATING OUT

Eating out in Spain is often a rare pleasure. It offers a range of eating opportunities, with grazing on *tapas* an easy way to keep hunger at bay, and set menus bringing even quite upmarket restaurants in reach of modest budgets.

The only problem might be for those used to eating at certain times, as these almost certainly won't coincide with the Spanish routine. Spaniards tend to have lunch at about 2 PM, and very rarely dine before 9 PM, often leaving their evening meal as late as midnight. Travelers determined to stick to their home routine will find that many of the best restaurants, catering for a native market, will not be animated, or sometime even open, when they want to eat.

Best to adapt to local conditions and join the locals as they cruise from bar to bar, using *tapas* to keep drunkenness — and hunger — at bay, before settling down for the main event.

When it comes to eating, there are is whole range of different establishments that offer different gastronomic experiences at different budgets. Least expensive are *commodores*, becoming a rarity, which are usually family-run restaurants serving set meals for a very reasonably price. They are rarely signposted, but you might catch sight of one at lunchtime, when they serve their most substantial meals, attached to a bar or an inexpensive hotel. *Cafeterías*, rated by the local council from one to three cups, tend to limit themselves to a few self-service options or serve a *plato combinado*, which is an inexpensive plateful of food, often in quite alarming combinations depending on what they have available. *Restaurantes* and *marisquerías* (which serve only seafood) are graded from one to five forks, and vary in price accordingly. Tipping is regarded as usual, but 10 percent of the bill is perfectly adequate.

Where restaurants have been noted in the text, the price bands have been set at the cost of the *menú de diá*, which will usually be three courses including wine. *Inexpensive* costs less than €18, *moderate* from €18 to €49, while the *expensive* category, fairly rare in value-conscious Spain, covers those places that charge more than €50.

TIPPING

Most hotels and restaurants include a five-percent service charge on their bills, on top of the value-added tax, or sales tax, known as *IVA* in Spain, which is seven and a-half percent. It is customary, however, to add a tip of between five and ten percent depending on the service you received

and on the size of the bill. Taxi-drivers usually get a tip of five percent of the fare, while in bars some small change is adequate. Watch Spaniards closely; they nearly always tip, but modestly.

BASICS

Electric current is 220–225 volts and plugs are the round, two-pronged variety. Many modern hotels have special 110–125-volt circuits in the bathrooms for electrical appliances.

Addresses are written with the number after the street name, though further complications can arise with street-names being changed when they are named after the now-discredited fascist generals of the Franco regime, and also with the creeping use of Catalan, Galician and Basque on maps.

Spanish **time** is one hour ahead of Greenwich Mean Time, with daylight savings clocking in when the clocks go back in the last week of March and forward in the last week of September. Spanish time is six hours ahead of United States Eastern Standard Time, and nine hours ahead of Pacific Standard Time.

Weights and measures use the metric system, using kilometers and meters for distance, and liters for fuel and liquids.

CURRENCY

Spain is one of the European countries that signed up to convert their currency to the Euro in the first two months of 2002. Thus the peseta, which used to be used in the thousands to pay even quite small amounts, is doomed. And it is the Euro (€) that will prevail, partially from January 1, 2002, and completely two short months later after the end of February. It remains to be seen how the Spanish people will cope with the change, or even how the currency itself will cope. At the time of publication, US$1 bought €1.108.

Travelers' checks still appeal to a significant proportion of travelers, and are accepted at *cambios* found in all tourist areas, and banks, as, of course, is cash. Banks are particularly slow and commission, of course, is invariably charged. Credit and debit cards, most widely Visa but also MasterCard, are far more useful, with your pin number, as ATM machines are widely available and often functioning all day and all night. Credit cards are also accepted in most restaurants, travel agents and shops, and are also especially useful for car or motorcycle hire, where a deposit is required.

COMMUNICATIONS AND MEDIA

Post Offices (*Correos*) are plentiful but usually only open six days a week, from 9 AM to 2 PM. Although you can also buy stamps in shops that sell tobacco (*tabacleras* or *estancos*), they sometimes run out. Mailboxes are painted yellow, though there are not many around and it is usually easier to mail your letters and postcards from your hotel, which often sells stamps too.

The Spanish **telephone system** has been modernized and works well, though it remains to be seen how they will survive the introduction of the euro, and what changes will be seen in the phone booths themselves which, in the days of the peseta, were clunky and difficult to use. Local calls are timed, so plenty of coins were needed in reserve. Phone cards are the most likely solution to the conversion to the euro, which will be a significant improvement.

Britain and the United States are also available. They can cost double of what they would back home.

There are an increasing number of **English-language publications** produced in Spain, including a monthly called *In Spain* containing general information about hotels, restaurants and so on. *Guidepost* is a weekly aimed at the American community and *Lookout is* another monthly produced on the Costa del Sol but full of general articles and useful information for anyone visiting or living in Spain. Few of these are independent of their advertisers, however, so take their features with a pinch of salt. There is a good English-language bookshop in Madrid called **Booksellers (** (91) 442-7959, Calle José Abascal 48, Madrid.

There are no public telephones in post offices, but there are central telephone offices called *Telefonicas* where you can place international calls. Avoid making international calls from hotels — there is invariably a huge surcharge.

The **Internet** has made a huge impact in Spain over recent years, with Internet cafés now found in most major towns and even some quite minor ones. Charges are in the region of €3 per hour, and they are often open late, up to midnight or later.

The best national **newspapers** are *El País* and *El Mundo*, which generally include regional "what's on" supplements in their weekend editions. British newspapers, printed in Madrid, are widely available in cities and tourist areas, as are copies of the *International Herald Tribune*, as well as newspapers, magazines, periodicals and books, in half a dozen different languages. *Time, Newsweek, The Economist*, and most of the glossy magazines that you find in

On the **radio**, the BBC's World Service programs can be picked up throughout Spain and around the clock on the 19 m, 25 m and 49 m wave bands. Voice of America also broadcasts in Spain, although it can be hard to tune in to in more remote areas. In popular tourist areas, such as the Costa del Sol and Mallorca, there are English-language radio stations playing music and broadcasting local news. Pan-European **television** programs are reaching Spain with films, sports events and news in several different languages. CNN and other satellite programs are available in the better hotels, but apart from these regions television is exclusively in Spanish, with television soaps through the daytime and plenty of sport, especially football, in the evenings.

Barcelona's Chicoa Restaurant — a popular Catalan restaurant renowned for its seafood specialities, and particularly for its *bacalao*, or salt cod.

ETIQUETTE

The Spanish are pretty relaxed in most areas of etiquette. Although they generally take their appearance very seriously, there are few places that enforce any particular dress code, especially in the summer months. The Ritz Hotel in Madrid seems to be the only exception, where an iron-fisted dress code is in operation at all hours of the day and night. The manager of the best hotel in San Sebastián, a five-star gem, tried to institute a dress code of jacket and tie for dinner when he first came to the hotel. "After one night I gave up," he told me ruefully. "They just came along in open-necked shirts and casual slacks and ignored my little rule."

One area to be a bit careful is on the beach. On beaches popular with foreigners, topless bathing has become routine, but in rural areas sensibilities are less relaxed, and it is better — and wiser — not to give offence.

HEALTH

The health service in Spain is good and effective, with private and publicly funded hospitals available in every town and major cities.

Citizens of European Union member countries are theoretically covered by reciprocal health arrangements, provided they can produce an EIII form and a health card from home. North Americans and Australasians should ensure they have adequate health insurance in place.

Most Spanish hotels, even some of the smaller ones, have a "house doctor," whose services can be obtained through the hotel staff. Pharmacies (farmacias), indicated by a green cross on a white background, work on a rotation system so that there is at least one open 24 hours a day.

Tap water is safe to drink in almost all of Spain, but sometimes is unpleasantly chlorinated. Bottled water (sin gaz, still, and con gaz, fizzy) is widely available.

TOILETS

Spain is not a place where public toilets flourish outside of train and bus stations and airports. However, every bar, café and restaurant has them and Spaniards use them as if they were public property, whether they are buying a drink or not. The phrase is: "Dónde estan los servicios, por favor?"

SECURITY

Car crime (see above) is the most common threat to tourists. However it is not the only one. Thanks to a significant drug problem, muggings are on the increase, especially in the cities, with Barcelona currently a hot spot. Violent crimes tend to happen more at night: avoid deserted roads, dead-end alleys and unlit stairs and, if necessary, take taxis. During the day, pickpocketing and bag-snatching, often Italian-style by the pillion passenger of a speeding motorcycle, are more usual dangers. Watch out for people loitering close, and always be suspicious of people who stop you in the street and claim to have found dirt (dog-pooh, or sometimes shampoo) on your clothes, and offer to help clean them off. They, or an accomplice, will have just placed it there — this is so common a pickpocketing ploy you're safe to discount the distant possibility you've met a good Samaritan.

Spain used to be known for its macho men, but women traveling alone have far less trouble now than in years go by. Be a bit careful — and respectful — in rural areas where the local population may still exist in unrelenting poverty. In city centers large, sociable groups provide easy protective cover for people on their own, and gigolos hanging around tourist areas are no worse than their counterparts elsewhere.

GAY AND LESBIAN TRAVELERS

Ibiza is probably the gay and lesbian hub of Spain, but substantial gay scenes can be found in Cádiz, Madrid and Barcelona (especially at the nearby resort of Sitges). The age of consent is 18.

DISABLED TRAVELERS

Although Spain does require new buildings to offer disabled access, it is making slow progress towards opening up its greatest treasures. They have a task, of course: old city centers are steep and cobbled, and hilly fortified villages, by definition, need plenty of steps. But I could only watch in awe as disabled travelers managed to get around a network of rickety ramps supposed to open up the Alhambra Palace, and share their frustration as they were turned away from some of its greatest sights.

There are associations that can help. In the United Kingdom, **Holiday Care** (01293 774535 WEB SITE www.holidaycare.org.uk, Second Floor, Imperial Building, Victoria Road, Horley, Surrey RH6 9HW, provides information on travel, and in Brussels **Mobility International** ((+322) 201-5711 FAX (+322) 201-5763 WEB SITE www.mobility-international.org, Boulevard de Baudouin 18, Brussels B1000, provides information, guides and exchange programs for European travelers. In North America, **Wheels Up!** ((888) 389 4335 WEB SITE www.wheelsup.com, Box 5197, Plant City, Florida, provides discounted airfare and tours, as well as a free newsletter and website.

Leather goods on sale in Córdoba.

WHEN TO GO

The best times to visit Spain are in the spring (mid-March to June) and the fall (mid-September to November). Summer is fine if you want to spend a lot of time on the beach but be ready for consistently hot days and warm nights. The exception is the northern coast, which has cooler weather and some rainfall during the summer months. Spain's central plateau, the *meseta*, has a typical continental climate. The Mediterranean coastline and the Balearic Islands have hot, dry summers but milder winters with a considerable amount of rain. The saving grace of the Spanish weather

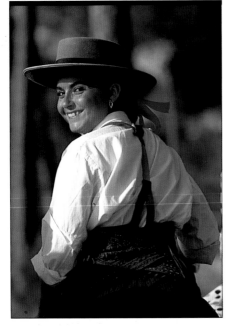

is that, on the whole, humidity is low, with the exception of the northwest where constant moisture produces the lush greens and mists of Ireland or Wales. While winters can be cold in central Spain, there are many sunny days. If beaches and sunbathing are not your thing, this is a good time to visit the cities and monuments of Castilla and other areas of the Spanish heartland.

PUBLIC HOLIDAYS

Spain's public holidays are:
New Year's Day
January 6, the Epiphany
Holy Thursday and Good Friday
May 1, Labor Day
Corpus Christi (late May or early June)
July 25, the Feast of Santiago (Saint James)
August 15, the Feast of the Assumption

November 1, All Saints' Day
December 6, Constitution Day
Christmas Day.

As you can see, the Spaniards are generous to themselves when it comes to holidays. But keep an eye open for even more, since many regions and municipalities take additional days off to celebrate a local event or saint.

WHAT TO TAKE

The general rule of taking half the luggage and twice the money is as true for travel in Spain as it is anywhere else. Warm clothes, of course, are needed in winter and for traveling in the mountains, but most of the things you need can easily be bought in Spain. There's not much you can't find in a good branch of El Corte Inglés.

PHOTOGRAPHY

Buy and develop your film at home if you can, and keep it out of the sun as much as possible. There is no shortage of film in Spain but it tends to be expensive. Batteries and other electrical accessories are plentiful and cost much the same as they do in the rest of Europe and in the United States. There are several cathedrals and museums that don't allow photography, as the flash damages sensitive pigments, but in any case most amateurs can never hope to match the quality of the postcards available, inexpensively, right outside, so in many ways these regulations just save you film. Here, as anywhere, taking photographs of people requires sensitive handling: although Spain hasn't yet caught up with American requirements for such things as model release forms, clearly some people will not want their image captured and taken away and should be given the opportunity to object. Usually they will be more than happy to oblige.

SPANISH: A SAMPLER

As has already been mentioned, Castilian Spanish is not the only lingua franca in Spain. Catalan, Galician and Basque are also widely spoken. Almost all Spanish citizens will, however, speak and understand Spanish even if they don't always want to.

It is fortunate, then, that Spanish is one of the easier languages for English speakers to learn, as well as one of the most useful. Any knowledge of a Latin-based Romance language (French, Italian or Portuguese) will help. Pronunciation is phonetic and regular and the rules are simple. The most difficult aspects are the verbs, the different accents encountered in many parts of the country, and the speed with which most Spaniards talk. (Andalucía is notorious for its tricky accent where, as in many Latin American countries, consonants disappear and unfamiliar words and phrases intrude.) It is worth remembering that the Spanish of Spain is usually known as Castellano or Castilian, and that Catalá or Catalan is spoken in Catalunya, Valencia and the Balearic Islands, Euskera or Basque in the Basque Country, and Gallego or Galician in Galicia.

Perhaps the most difficult aspect for new students is the pronunciation, which is not quite what English-speakers expect. The rules are simple, however, and generally consistent. **A** usually follows the sound of the "a" as in rather. **E** is spoken as in bet. **I** sounds like the "i" in nice, **O** is simlar to the "o" in pot, and **U** sounds like the "u" in rule. Of the consonants, **G** is gutteral with a touch of "h," while the Spanish **H** is always silent. **J** sounds rather like "y," while **LL** sounds exactly like "y." **N** is similar to its English namesake, while **Ñ** sounds like the English "ny." **QU** sounds like a hard English "k" while **V** sounds more like "b." **R**'s are rolled, and double Rs are rolled a lot. Most problematic are the ubiquitous **D**'s, which are pronounced, tongue between teeth, as "th."

A FEW USEFUL WORDS AND EXPRESSIONS

a little   *poco*
a lot   *mucho*
all   *todo*
before   *antes*
big   *grande*
bill/check   *cuenta*
cheap   *barato*
closed   *cerrado*
cold   *frío*
Do you speak English?   *¿Habla usted inglés?*
down   *abajo*
excuse me   *perdón/disculpe*
expensive   *caro*
fast   *rápido*
good afternoon   *buenas tardes*
good morning   *buenas días*
good night   *buenas noches*
goodbye   *adiós*
hello/hi   *olá*
hot   *caliente*
How are you?   *¿Cómo está usted?*
How much is that?   *¿Cuánto es?*
How much?   *¿Cuánto?*
I am hungry   *tengo hambre*
I am sorry   *lo siento*
I am thirsty   *tengo sed*
I am tired   *estoy cansado*
I don't understand   *no comprendo/entiendo*
it doesn't matter   *no importa*
it's all right   *está bien*
later   *después*
left   *izquierda*
madam   *señora*
menu   *carta*
miss   *señorita*
month   *mes*

never   *nunca*
no   *no*
nothing   *nada*
now   *ahora*
OK   *vale*
open   *abierto*
please   *por favor*
right   *derecha*
sales (in shops)   *rebajas*
see you later   *hasta luego*
sir   *señor*
slow   *despacio*
small   *pequeño*
speak slowly please   *hable despacio por favor*
straight ahead   *todo derecho*
thank you   *gracias*
today   *hoy*
toilets   *servicios/aseos*
tomorrow morning   *mañana por la mañana*
tomorrow   *mañana*
up   *arriba*
wait a moment, please   *espere un momento, por favor*
waiter   *camarero*
week   *semana*
What is that?   *¿qué es eso?*
What is your name?   *¿cómo se llama usted?*
what   *qué*
when   *cuándo*
where   *dónde*
who   *quién*
why   *por qué*
year   *año*
yes   *sí*
yesterday   *ayer*
you're welcome   *de nada*
Buen víaje.

RECOMMENDED WEB SITES

The following sites are interesting in their own right, and provide good links onwards to other sites relevant to Spain and the Spanish.

Dónde http://donde.uji.es
This search engine for Spanish-language sites is especially useful if you can read the language.

El País Digital www.elpais.es
This online version of one of Spain's leading papers is essential reading to take the pulse of the country before your visit.

El Vino www.elvino.com
This hymn to the liquid nectar that will ease your passage around Spain expounds on good years, great grapes, and does so with loads of enthusiasm.

A horse-borne pilgrim strutting her stuff at the El Rocío pilgrimage, Andalucía.

Hotel Search www.hotelsearch.com
For accommodation options, this site offers a nationwide but not comprehensive database.

Museums in Spain www.icom.org/vlmp/spain.htlm
This site covers Spain's museums and art galleries.

OK Spain www.okspain.org
A cheerful guide to Spain, OK Spain provides loads of information and offers to answer questions.

Soccer Spain www.cannylink.com/soccerspain.htm
Spain's national obsession has its very own English-language website. Perfect for lovers of the

sport or the brainwashed victims of an international media conspiracy.

RECOMMENDED READING

The literature of Spain technically starts with Seneca and the Romans. These, however, are now a little abstruse, and most readers start a bit later, with *Don Quixote*, of which the Penguin Classic edition, translated by JM Coehn, is the best. The British filmmaker Terry Gilliam famously signed up the rights to film this story without ever having read this, the first of the world's novels, saying "everyone knows what it's about." In fact, it would probably be more accurate to say that no one knows, as the enigmatic tale of a lone aristocrat, tilting at windmills, has about as many interpretations as it has had readers.

The early days of El Cid are portrayed in "The Poem of the Cid," first published in about AD 1140, translated by R. Hamilton and Janet Perry (Penguin), while the Moorish era in general is best analyzed by Titus Berkhardt in *Moorish Culture in Spain* (Allen and Unwin, 1972), which is a good general work on the Muslim influence on Andalucía. As a general, sprawling but certainly effective summary of a nation's history, James A. Michener's *Iberia* does the epic job it intends.

Poignant, particularly in view of his later death at the hands of nationalists, are the plays of Frederico Garcia Lorca, whose *Three Tragedies & Five Plays: Comedies and Tragedicomedies*, first published in 1940, are now published by Penguin, though many find a more considered approach in Gerald Brenan's *Spanish Labyrinth* (Cambridge, 1943) which analyzes the circumstances leading up to the Civil War, and is brought up to date by Thomas Hugh's *The Spanish Civil War* (Penguin, 1961), which is still the best general history of the conflict.

For a first-hand account of these cataclysmic times, it is hard to beat George Orwell's *Homage to Catalonia* (1952). The writer actually fought in the Civil War on the Aragón front, and his first-hand accounts, recalled with Orwellian clarity and the emotion of actual experience, bring the era to life.

From here, overseas romantics hold pride of place on most reading lists. Ernest Hemingway's seminal works include *The Sun Also Rises* (1926) (sometimes called *Fiesta*), a stirring account of Pamplona, bullfighters, fishing and frustrated love, as well as *Death in the Afternoon* (1932), Papa's classic on the art of tauromachy.

Then the British took over. Laurie Lee's *As I walked Out One Midsummer's Morning* (1932), *A Moment of War* (1954) and *A Rose for Winter* (1952) (all published by Penguin), tell the story of a Spain met through the eyes of a young wanderer, with notebook and violin, just before the Civil War, during it and then two decades later. All are fantastic reads. Then move over to Jan Morris, whose book *Spain* (1964), marvelously written in 1960s Romantic style, was flawed by inaccuracies and some sweeping generalizations.

In the face of such concerted international attention, the indigenous literates hit back. Perhaps the most important is Juan Goytisolo, whose *The Young Assasins* (1959), *The Island* (1961), *Island of Women* (1962), *Juan the Landless* (1955) and *Quarantine* (1964), explore the Basque identity, mainly from self-imposed exile in Morocco and Paris. For a dry and sophisticated take on modern Spain, try *Murder in the Central Committee* and *Galindez* (1992), racy thrillers written by Manuel Vasquez Montalban, a columnist on the influential *La País* newspaper. Another thriller writer, disturbing the incense-scented world of the southern cities with tales of bankers and bodies, is Arturo Péres Reverte, whose book *The Seville Communion* (1990) is published by the Harville Press.

To read further than these authors, it helps to read Spanish. But suffice it to say that, with the huge Hispanic market worldwide, Spanish literature is breaking away from centuries of repression to finally find a voice of its own.

ABOVE: A wine bar in Sevilla. RIGHT: Burgos's massive Gothic cathedral in the heart of the city.

Travelers' Tips

Quick Reference A–Z Guide
to Places and Topics of Interest

Photo credits

All photos in this book are by Nik Wheeler except those listed below:

Tor Eigeland: pages 4, 5, 6 *right*, 7 *left*, 10–15, 18–19, 22–23, 27, 28, 32, 33, 34, 36, 40, 43, 44, 46, 56, 57 *top and bottom*, 58–59, 60, 62–66, 70, 125, 130–131, 172 *right*, 206–207, 222–223, 233, 236.

Nicolas Fauqué: 45, 78–79, 83, 84, 86, 92 *left*, 168, 256, 171.

Spanish Tourism: Pages 182-183, 187–195.